ARMED MADHOUSE

Praise for Greg Palast and *Armed Madhouse*

"*Armed Madhouse* is great fun. Palast, detective style, provides . . . pieces of the secret puzzle."   —*The New Yorker*

"No one has investigated the Bush clan like Greg Palast—and lived to write about it."   —*Baltimore Chronicle*

"The last true investigative reporter in America. [*Armed Madhouse*] shows how [the war in Iraq] was all planned from the beginning. . . . *The story is like a spy thriller.*"   —Robert F. Kennedy Jr., Air America

"Greg Palast is a heroic figure—perhaps the last honest journalist. . . . If there's a thorny issue involving corruption, graft, or fraud, from the World Bank to the Bush Family, chances are investigative reporter Greg Palast knows the real story."   —*Index Magazine*

"One of the best tomes on politics written in modern days."
    —Howard Zinn, author of *A People's History of the United States*

"At once scary, infuriating, fascinating, and frustrating, this book covers almost all the controversial political territory of the new century. Palast is a refreshing, fearless witness to the American political landscape."
    —*Publishers Weekly*

"*Book of the Year*: Greg Palast's *Armed Madhouse,* his long-awaited follow-up to *The Best Democracy Money Can Buy,* is just as incendiary an affair as its predecessor, and his virtuosic dismantling of the saurian global-market apologist Thomas Friedman had me cheering on my feet."
    —*New Statesman*

"Greg Palast is Jack Kerouac meets Seymour Hersh. That's quite a combination. The guy is insightful, entertaining, and does his homework."   —Buzzflash.com

ALSO BY GREG PALAST

The Best Democracy Money Can Buy:

The Truth About Corporate Cons, Globalization, and High-Finance Fraudsters

(Plume, 2004)

Democracy and Regulation:

How the Public Can Govern Essential Services

(with Jerrold Oppenheim and Theo MacGregor)

(United Nations-ILO-Pluto Press, 2003)

FILM

Bush Family Fortunes

(British Broadcasting Corporation Program, 2003)

SPOKEN WORD CD

Weapon of Mass Instruction

(Alternative Tentacles, 2003)

GREG PALAST

ARMED MADHOUSE

From Baghdad to New Orleans—Sordid Secrets &

Strange Tales of a White House Gone Wild

A PLUME BOOK

PLUME
Published by Penguin Group
Penguin Group (USA) Inc., 375 Hudson Street, New York, New York 10014, U.S.A. • Penguin
Group (Canada), 90 Eglinton Avenue East, Suite 700, Toronto, Ontario, Canada M4P 2Y3 (a divi-
sion of Pearson Penguin Canada Inc.) • Penguin Books Ltd., 80 Strand, London WC2R 0RL, En-
gland • Penguin Ireland, 25 St. Stephen's Green, Dublin 2, Ireland (a division of Penguin Books
Ltd.) • Penguin Group (Australia), 250 Camberwell Road, Camberwell, Victoria 3124, Australia
(a division of Pearson Australia Group Pty. Ltd.) • Penguin Books India Pvt. Ltd., 11 Community
Centre, Panchsheel Park, New Delhi – 110 017, India • Penguin Group (NZ), 67 Apollo Drive,
Mairangi Bay, Auckland 1311, New Zealand (a division of Pearson New Zealand Ltd.) • Penguin
Books (South Africa) (Pty.) Ltd., 24 Sturdee Avenue, Rosebank, Johannesburg 2196, South Africa

Penguin Books Ltd., Registered Offices: 80 Strand, London WC2R 0RL, England

Published by Plume, a member of Penguin Group (USA) Inc. Previously published in a Dutton
edition.

First Plume Printing, May 2007
10 9 8 7 6 5 4 3 2

Copyright © Greg Palast, 2006, 2007
All rights reserved

Portions of this book have appeared in some form in *Harper's* magazine, the *Guardian* and *Observer*
newspapers, *The Nation*, *In These Times*, *Lobster*, TomPaine.com, Alternet.org and *Old Trout*.

℗ REGISTERED TRADEMARK—MARCA REGISTRADA

The Library of Congress has catalogued the Dutton edition as follows:
Palast, Greg.
    Armed madhouse : who's afraid of Osama Wolf? the best legal whorehouse in Texas, the scheme
to steal election '08, no child's behind left, and other investigative stings / Greg Palast.
    p. cm.
    ISBN 0-525-94968-2 (hc.)
    ISBN 978-0-452-28831-7 (pbk.)
    1. United States—Politics and government—2001– . 2. United States—Foreign relations—
2001– . 3. United States—Economic policy—2001– . 4. Political corruption—United States.
5. Presidents—United States—Election—2000. 6. Presidents—United States—Election—2004.
7. Presidents—United States—Election—2008. 8. Iraq War, 2003– . 9. War on Terrorism,
2001– . 10. Petroleum industry and trade—Political aspects—United States. I. Title.
    E902.P36 2006
    973.931—dc22   2006007726

Printed in the United States of America
Original hardcover design by Carla Bolte

To Gil and Gladys Palast. The originals.

Do not destroy oil wells.
—President George W. Bush

Who's zoomin' who?
—Aretha Franklin

At the age of 25 most people were finished. A whole god-damned nation of assholes driving automobiles, eating, having babies, doing everything in the worst way possible, like voting for the presidential candidate who reminded them most of themselves.

—Charles Bukowski

CONTENTS

CHAPTER 1

THE FEAR

Who's Afraid of Osama Wolf? 9

Including Marines in a tube, learning to speak Terrorist, Bush's Khan job, National Security Document 199-I and Osama's Mission Accomplished. What are you afraid of? Our Fear Salesman-in-Chief has something for everyone.

CHAPTER 2

THE FLOW

Trillion Dollar Babies 51

A five-and-a-half-part tale including Nose-Twist's Hidden Hand, Kissinger's man in the dream palace, the No-Brainer vs. The Witches' Brew, the Other Downing Street memo, the Houston Insurgency, Amy's alligator boots, Mr. 5%, a call to Riyadh, Wolfowitz Dämmerung and "especially the oil."

ARMED MADHOUSE

★ ★
★ ★
★ ★

THE BEGINNING

"Like the Cowardly Dog He Was"

President Jeb Bush declared his reelection victory early, in August, before the machines were fully programmed, but the results were nevertheless assured. President Jeb accepted a call from "Hillary Kerry Gore"—the virtual candidate, put up as quadrennial opponent, designed to lose—who always made the same moving concession speech, "American democracy has triumphed again," written for her by Karl Rove. The official voting won't take place until November.

"Our nation," Vice-President Kate Harris assures us, "is safer and more prosperous than at any time in our history."

But there are dissenters from this happy new America—shivering in their basements: Michaelites with their icons of St. Moore. The film-director/holy man was martyred when, through a rapid expansion caused by self-righteousness and fried food, he simply exploded onstage at the 2011 Cannes Film Festival, a fitting end given his final film, *I Hate the Bushes So Much I Could Explode!*

There are few complaints, certainly none expressed openly after the Health Insurance Riots of 2009 when the last licensed union members were "removed" to Guantánamo. "Orange Suit City" is now America's eighth largest metropolis, "safer and more prosperous than ever."

Still, every morning, the Rio Grande chokes with swarms of obese, illiterate Texans wading across to their 70-cents-an-hour jobs in the maquiladoras of Juárez.

Now, more than ever, America is the Lord's land. Wal-Mart super-mega stores have metastasized into monumental "Retail Cathedrals" where true believers in cheap and disposable appliances come to pray and pay.

And we are well entertained. We have 11,000 TV channels, with every program chosen personally by Rupert Murdoch's brain, now wired up in a pickle jar on the desk of Fox network president Roger Ailes. Tonight, Bill Clinton launches his fourth autobiography—with even more whoppers than the last three: "I was born in a log cabin mobile home"—"I did not sleep with that woman Hillary!"

The sovereign government of Iraq is still holed up, as it had been for the past decade, in the U.S. embassy in Baghdad. This week, Iraq's President du Jour declared his own reelection victory. "Iraq is safer and more prosperous today than at any time in Iraqi history," he said as mortar rounds whumped into the compound.

And back in the USA, after curfew, one can hear the screams and cries of the tots in the workhouses, locked behind the menacing signs, NO CHILD'S BEHIND LEFT.

Democracy flourishes. Yesterday, President bin Laden of Eurasia also reelected himself and received a congratulatory phone call from President Bush. "How long can we keep this up?" whispered Osama. Our President replied, "Just as long as the boobs and rednecks and berserkers and believers stay whipped up and angry . . . forever and ever, pardner."

Nameless barbarians will assassinate the President tomorrow. Or will appear to. It's all in the plan, where made-for-TV dramas and news are switched as needed to titillate the numbed public. "President Bush died like the cowardly dog he was," the "terrorists" will say . . . and another Bush will replace him vowing to fight the unseen enemy in a war without end nor hope of an end.

If my report from the future gives you the creeps, the present ain't a joyride either. The day before I wrote this, Carlos Arredondo, forty-four, of Hollywood, Florida, attacked a military van first with a sledgehammer and then set it and himself on fire. For twenty minutes he had repeatedly pleaded for the three harbingers of death to leave his home after they had delivered the news that his son was dead in Iraq. A total of 26% of his body was burned as the three Marines, the casualty assistance team, looked on. Neighbors said Arrendondo went crazy. I don't think so. I think he went sane.

What's insane is a regime that grants no asylum from militarized greed, whose sole saving grace is its incompetence: If they knew what they were doing, it would be worse. Arredondo put into action the wisdom of my late teacher, Allen Ginsberg: *The soul,* he wrote, *should not die ungodly in an armed madhouse.*

Loo Reading

Before I took up journalism just a few years ago, I worked for a living. I was an investigator, a "forensic economist." Like the forensic pathologists on TV, I sliced into cadavers for evidence of fraud, racketeering and conspiracy; but in my case I cut into the bodies of companies; Exxon and Enron were two of them.[1] My idea had been to apply those old-style gumshoe techniques to reporting. The results can be viewed by most of the planet on my broadcasts for BBC Television's *Newsnight.* In the USA, these investigative reports have appeared on Channel Nothing, thereby maintaining America's news virginity inviolate.

I like to read in the loo, so this book, like my last, can be read in short spurts, in any order. To that end, I've eliminated the consistency and continuity that I despise in other books. Nevertheless, be aware of the chronological arc. We move from September 11, 2001 (The Fear), to fear's foreign outing in the oil fields of Iraq (The Flow), to the widening global economic conflict (The Network), to the concomitant need to manipulate the elections of 2004 and 2008 (The Con), concluding with the drowning of New Orleans, the Gettysburg of The Class War.

---

[1] I remember facing off against one deviously brilliant corporate trickster, John Perkins, who recently came out of the cold with his *Confessions of an Economic Hit Man.*

Chapter One. In most wars, strategic intelligence is the key. For the Bush Administration, the key is strategic stupidity. As the FBI told us when we found their confidential bin Laden files, there are certain things the public "ought not to know." Chapter One, **The Fear**, tells you a bit of what you are not supposed to know, from the pre-—September 11 investigations of terrorists spiked by the FBI, to the writings of Osama bin Laden, to health insurance in America. In other words, it's the chapter with the most laughs.

Chapter Two. Then it's war. Conspiracy theorists believe George Bush, long before the invasion of Iraq, had a plan to control its oil. That's wrong. He had *two* plans and my investigative team obtained both. The conflict between these two plans is what has kept our soldiers pinned down on the Tigris. The war is about the oil, for certain—not to get it for our SUVs, but to *prevent* us from getting it. The war is not about bringing down Saddam but about lifting up OPEC. In **The Flow**, we discover that the real insurgents come from Houston.

Chapter Three. Class war goes global. Three decades ago, I co-authored a book, *The World as a Company Town*, on a new phenomenon, "globalization." Hardly anyone noticed, except for a malevolent, dwarfish gnome who had seized control of the economics department of the University of Chicago. Milton Friedman, rather than recoil at my warnings, thought a future world of multinational mega-corporations kicking down national boundaries and dictating their terms to hapless, helpless democracies would be *really cool*. Today, Friedman has grown a foot taller, glued on a lopsided moustache, and under the name "Thomas," this newly morphed Friedman writes hosannas to the brave new free-trade horror show, most recently in a book, *The World Is Flat*. Chapter Three answers Milton Thomas Friedman by way of the movie *The Network*.

Chapter Four. In November 2000, for the London *Observer* newspaper, I revealed that, five months before the presidential election, Florida's Governor Jeb Bush and his Secretary of State Katherine Harris had ordered the purge of 57,000 citizens from Florida's voter rolls, supposedly convicts barred from voting. Most were Black, almost all innocent of any crime except VWB, Voting While Black. The faux-felon purge gave Jeb's brother George Bush the presidency. Now, there's no sense stealing the White House if you have to give it back four years later. To prevent the voters from interfering with the outcome, something extraordinary occurred in the 2004 presidential election: three and a half million ballots were cast but never counted. And guess whose votes didn't count? Chapter Four, **The Con**, is the story of confidential Republican party "caging lists" that made their way to BBC, of empty ballot boxes in New Mexico and George Bush's plurality among the undead. It doesn't give away anything to tell you: Kerry won. More important is how the 2008 race will begin with a one-million-vote head start for the Republican candidate for president before a single ballot is officially cast.

Chapter Five. Sometimes, the ranks of the loser class must be thinned. Most of those drowned in the New Orleans flood of 2005 lived near the shorter levees along Lake Pontchartrain. The lower your income, the lower your sea barriers . . . and the lower your trade barriers. Chapter Five, **The Class War**, is about the death of General Motors, the rise of China and what that means for your Social Security and social insecurity. The president is solving the problem. Unfortunately, he's the President of Venezuela.

New Afterword: Busted. After *Armed Madhouse* hit the streets in 2006, I thought the story was complete. But, later in the year, in tracking down some hoary new info in New Orleans, my film crew was charged by the Department of Homeland Security with violating anti-terror laws. Beyond the fun tale of how our terror-busters ended up capturing me instead of Osama, I've added here un-fun revelation of exactly how the White House let New Orleans down.

Then, the 2006 midterm elections, despite the election of a Democratic majority to Congress, exposed how the GOP has already locked up the race for 2008 with imaginative new ballot-box shenanigans. Because I don't want to end on an angry note, this new chapter explains now only how they'll steal your vote but how you can steal it back.

Everyone wants to write an immortal book, one that transcends time. This isn't it. Hopefully. Everything you will read here—about stolen elections, stolen countries, stolen dignity and lives—will, knock wood, be forgotten in the new American Elysium, the Eden of Democracy that awaits us in the future. More likely, the book will be confiscated under Patriot Act VII.

Here's what you will get between the covers: news not allowed on your nightly tube, old-fashioned gumshoe investigative reports for BBC Television's *Newsnight*, where my stories are exiled to safety in London, and a few reports expanded from those journalistic safehouses, *Harper's* magazine, Britain's *Guardian* papers, and several seditious Web sites.

Think of these chapters as a way to count backward from ten: At the end, you can snap your fingers and wake up; the spell is broken, the hypnotic narcosis of America's Fox-ified news is gone.

Before you enter these pages, I should warn you: I am not a nice man. Ask Alan Colmes, Fox's house Liberal. He once said to me, "Greg, you have no respect for the office of the President." No, I don't. Not one iota. But I'm not prejudiced: It's not just Oval Office residents who make me gag, it's holders of offices in state capitols, in corporate towers and in a few churches too.

You want something heartwarming, Alan? Buy a puppy. But if you want just the facts, ma'am—facts rarely cuddly or cute—here's your book.

The Trickle Down Theory ©Winston Smith 1997

CHAPTER 1

THE FEAR

Who's Afraid of Osama Wolf?

Including Marines in a tube, learning to speak Terrorist, Bush's Khan job, National Security Document 199-I and Osama's Mission Accomplished. What are you afraid of? Our Fear Salesman-in-Chief has something for everyone.

So, Osama Walks into This Bar, See?

. . . and Bush says, "Whad'l'ya have, pardner?" and Osama says . . .

But wait a minute. I'd better shut my mouth. The sign here in the airport says, "Security is no joking matter."

But if security's no joking matter, why does this guy dressed in a high-school marching band outfit tell me to take off my shoes? All I can say is, *Thank God the "shoe bomber" didn't carry Semtex in his underpants.*

I'm a bit nervous. It's an "YELLOW ALERT" day. That's a "lowered threat" notice. According to the press office of the Department of Homeland Security, lowered threat Yellow means that there will be no special inspections of passengers or cargo today. Isn't it nice of Mr. Bush to alert Osama when half our security forces are given the day off?

Hmm. I asked an Israeli security expert why his nation doesn't use these pretty color codes.

He asked me if, when I woke up, I checked the day's terror color.

"I can't say I ever have. I mean, who would?"

He smiled. "The terrorists."

America is the only nation on the planet that kindly informs bombers, hijackers and berserkers the days on which they won't be monitored. *You've got to get up pretty early in the morning to get a jump on George Bush's team.*

There are three possible explanations for the Administration's publishing a good-day-for-bombing color guidebook.

1. God is on Osama's side.
2. George is on Osama's side.
3. It's about the oil.

A gold star if you picked #3.

Osama's Mission Accomplished

On Thursday, May 1, 2003, President Bush landed on the deck of the aircraft carrier *Abraham Lincoln*. Forgetting to undo the parachute clips around his gonads, our President walked bowlegged on the ship's deck in a green jumpsuit looking astonishingly like Ham, first chimp in space. The scene was so exciting that the media failed to notice that the War on Terror had ended on the previous Tuesday.

On that day, Secretary of Defense Donald Rumsfeld quietly acknowledged that he was withdrawing America's armed forces from Saudi Arabia.

I'm always surprised at the debate over "What drives Osama? What does Al-Qaeda want?" There should be no confusion: Al-Qaeda states its mission, like most enterprises, on its Web site. Osama had it written out in English, in capital letters, so it wouldn't be difficult to get the point.

DECLARATION OF WAR AGAINST THE AMERICANS
OCCUPYING THE LAND OF THE TWO HOLY

PLACES—EXPEL THE INFIDELS FROM THE ARAB
PENINSULA

The "two holy places" are Mecca and Medina, and their "land" is
Saudi Arabia. That's what Osama wanted: U.S. troops out of Saudi
Arabia.

Bin Laden issued his demand on August 23, 1996; and on April 29,
2003, the Tuesday before the President was chauffeured by fighter jet
onto the deck of the *Abe Lincoln,* Mr. Bush gave bin Laden exactly
what he wanted: U.S. troops sent packing from the Land of the Holy
Places.

That's astonishing. Until George W. Bush, the United States of
America has never, *ever*, removed all our military bases from a foreign
land no matter how much locals bitched or moaned. We even keep
troops in Okinawa over the island's strong objections, and World
War II ended *sixty years ago*.

Am I accusing George Bush Jr. of being the first President of the
United States to cravenly accede to the demands of terrorists? No,
Reagan got there first, in 1984, when he gave in to Hezbollah's de-
mand and ordered our Marines to retreat from Lebanon.

No matter, President Bush was correct in announcing, "Mission
Accomplished." However, it was not America's mission that was accomplished. It was Osama's.

What Does Osama Want?

So what is his mission? What *does* Osama want? Why kick the U.S.
out of Saudi Arabia?

When, in March 2003, George Bush told the people of Iraq, *"Do not
destroy oil wells,"* his words were heartfelt but hardly original. In bin
Laden's 1996 Declaration of War, he warned all good Muslims against:

> Destruction of the oil industries. . . . I would like here to
> alert my brothers, to protect this oil wealth and not to in-
> clude it in the battle.

Bin Laden listed other beefs in his Declaration of War. There are some who have the notion that bin Laden, though inexcusably violent, is somehow giving voice to the oppressed. Those who fancy bin Laden as the defender of the wretched of the earth have neither read his writings nor followed his actions. The poor get no column inches in his "Declaration." Creating a Palestinian state? It's not mentioned in his fabulously long screed. Rather, the billionaire scion and former heir to the bin Laden Construction fortune launches into an angry diatribe about, of all things, Saudi Arabia's failure to pay past due invoices owed to:

> great merchants and contractors [waiting for] hundreds and thousands of millions of riyals owed to them by the government.

The House of Saud, it seems, was late in paying bin Laden Construction (which had a huge contract to rebuild Mecca).

Bin Laden is no fool; he knew why the Saudi government became a deadbeat bill payer. He was writing in 1996 when the price of oil was flat on the floor, near $10 a barrel, an all-time low; and Osama cried:

> People wonder, are we the largest oil exporting country?

So much oil, so little cash to show for it.

What drove Osama's declaration of war? The poverty in Islamic nations? Not a mention. Lack of freedom? Forget it. Bin Laden's *causus bellum* for war on America:

> The presence of the U.S.A. Crusader military forces on land, sea and air in the states of the Islamic Gulf is the greatest danger *threatening the largest oil reserve in the world.*

Threatening Islamic oil reserves. Osama even launches a sophisticated tirade against the suppression of oil production by U.S. operators in the Gulf. This wealthy engineer knows the petroleum biz, that's for sure.

If you want to know what motivates Osama, follow his path. Long before Al-Qaeda destroyed the World Trade Center, Osama, after removing, with U.S. help, the Soviets from Afghanistan, set up operations in Sudan, where oil men expected to find the next big gusher. Osama's next target was not The Great Satan America but The Little Satan: Iran. In Osama's view, Iranians are Shia "dogs and lackies" who hold, infuriatingly, OPEC's third largest oil reserves. Osama was especially affronted by Iran's rising influence in Afghanistan at the time, thereby blocking his ability to link up with fundamentalist militants in Uzbekistan and Tajikistan who were fundamentally coveting control of the Caspian nations' oil wealth. Osama expressed his displeasure with Iran's incursion on his turf by ordering the slaughter of the entire Iranian diplomatic mission to Afghanistan. After eliminating his Shia Iranian competitors in Afghanistan, Osama financed the Wahabi-influenced Taliban. Notably, Osama had no objection to the Taliban signing pipeline deals with U.S. oil firms.

In other words, if you follow Osama's movements and read what the man says, you realize he has been less coy than Bush about his true program: Get the oil. The steps are: First, remove the Soviets from the Caspian oil fields and pipeline routes; second, remove the man he called an evil "socialist," Saddam Hussein, from the second largest OPEC reserve; third, keep the Shia "dogs" who control the third largest reserve from expanding their influence outside Persia; fourth, remove U.S. troops from the Land of the Holy Places (and largest oil reserve), Saudi Arabia; then fifth and last, overthrow the House of Saud and re-create a new Caliphate stretching from Sudan to Kazakhstan, every province an oil state, a Petroleum Kingdom of God, presumably under His blessed servant and contractor Osama.

And so, to protect those reserves—if his foolish "brothers" don't burn the oil wells—he's declared his own Operation Islamic Liberation. O.I.L.

What motivates Osama? Same thing as George and Dick. It's all about the oil.

Terror in Tiny Town

The astonishing thing about bin Laden's Caliphate atop the "world's largest oil reserves," Land of the Holy Places, is that it includes my tiny town of Southold, New York. At the least, the town is, apparently, on top of Al-Qaeda's roster of targets.

Southold, if you look at a map, is situated at the ass end of nowhere. We are known hereabouts for our Strawberry Festival and fire truck parade. According to the census, this tiny place is made up almost entirely of inbred farmers, real estate speculators and volunteer firemen.

At one end of town is the "Brand Names Outlet Mall" and the waterslide park. At the other end, there's a ferryboat that takes those who feel lucky to the Mashantucket–Pequot tribe's casino in Connecticut. And in between, there's Main Street, where we hold the Strawberry Festival.[2]

In July 2005, Mayor Josh, with powers granted to him by the Department of Homeland Security, declared a "national security emergency." (Mayor Josh Horton is called by his first name because he was elected at the precocious age of 26—based, it seems, on his stellar qualifications: He wears shoes.) In light of the clear and present threat of attack, Mayor Josh ordered everyone taking the ferryboat to the Indian casino to park in the dirt lot across from Jenny's Country Store and not along Route 25.

It was just after the London bombings and Mayor Josh (his official title is "supervisor") insisted this was truly a matter of preparing for terrorist attack, though a farmer on the Town Board said he suspected it was less about Al-Qaeda and more about zoning. Mayor Josh had been trying all year, unsuccessfully, to change the zoning on the dirt

---

[2]The festival is a quaint and annoying white-folks' ritual, an opportunity for backstabbing, petty infighting and all-American small-mindedness. But that's another story altogether.

lot next to the ferryboat launch from "farming" to "parking" to boost the town's take from the inebriated gambling tourists. To scare off both Al-Qaeda and parking violators, Josh has posted, care of the federal treasury, an SUV at the ferry dock armed with two .50-caliber machine guns. I kid you not.

The ferry to the Indian casino is our officially designated town CAVIP—"Critical Asset and Vulnerability Infrastructure Point." All over America, vulnerable towns and villages with critical assets were picking their CAVIPs. (If you don't pick a terrorism Vulnerability Point, your burg can't get its slice of Homeland Security loot from the federal government.)

In Southold, every ferryboat passenger is now asked for their home phone number, though if they are suicide bombers, they most likely will not, after they strike, answer the phone. No matter.

In 2005, the U.S. Department of Homeland Security assigned three guardsmen, armed and armored, to the Critical Asset and Vulnerability Infrastructure Point because the town police are a little shorthanded since the village disbanded its minuscule police force after a grand jury called in the cops to explain allegations of sexual acrobatics on the police chief's desk and missing baggies of pot.

Some townfolk are ready to sacrifice all to take a stand against Osama's hordes, even if that means rezoning. Our local Pennysaver printed a letter from John Wronowski saying, "National security and safety [must be] at the forefront of our efforts . . . since September 11, 2001." Of course, Mr. Wronowski owns the ferryboat and parking lot.

The local paper interviewed a passenger who bravely travels to visit his in-laws twice a week. He said, with patriotic grit, "I am not afraid."

But *I* am. What if there's a sleeper cell in Southold? All they have to do is review the Homeland Security Web site for the town's Vulnerability Point and they'll know, "Hit the waterslide, Ahmed! The casino ferry's being watched!"

And there's more here that scares me. There's a jug out at the Lickity Splitz Ice Cream Parlor on Route 25 for the Cennar family. It seems that one of the Cennar kids has been diagnosed with a terrible disease. Undoubtedly, the doctor bills are killing the family, could bankrupt them—and the community jug is out, as it was for Kimberly Haeg. The 7-Eleven and Bob's Hardware have this up on thumbtacks near the cash registers:

> Hometown Fundraiser to benefit Kimberly Haeg. This 18 year old Southold High School Student was tragically injured in an auto accident. Her medical bills are staggering and she is need of financial assistance from our great community.

There's always a jug out for someone who's ill or severely crippled and whose bank account is getting wiped away.

I spoke with Kimberly's mom, Lorraine. Her family's two health insurance plans were supposed to cover the care of her daughter, who is now a quadriplegic. She can breathe only with help of a machine. According to Lorraine, her first insurer cut off full care after forty days; the second one, New York Empire Blue Cross, said Kimberly no longer needed full-time nursing help. Despite her insurer's laudable faith in miracle cures, Kimberly's need to breathe remained after the forty days.

And I thought: *This is a national security threat.* With the lumberyard shut and the nearby plastics plants gone to China, Al-Qaeda could quite easily gain a couple of recruits in our town: All bin Laden has to do is offer them decent health insurance.

The Khan Job and the "Back-Off" Directive

On November 9, 2001, BBC Television Centre in London received a call from a phone booth just outside Washington. The call to our *Newsnight* team was part of a complex prearranged dance coordinated with the National Security News Service, a conduit for unhappy spooks at the CIA and FBI to unburden themselves of disturbing information and documents. The top-level U.S. intelligence agent on

AN OPPORTUNITY FOR AL-QAEDA?

Hometown
Fundraiser

To benefit
Kimberly Haeg

This 18 year old Southold High School Student was tragically injured in an auto accident. Her medical bills are staggering and she is need of financial assistance from our great community.

This is how you can help!
Show you care and attend the fundraiser!!!

Fri. Nov. 26,2004
6-10 P.M.
Horsd'oeuvres & Music
Adults $40.00 / Students $20.00

Soundview Restaurant
Route 48, Greenport, NY 11944
Info/tickets (631)▬▬▬▬▬
Tickets available at Southold Pharmacy and Southold Curves

(Source: Haeg family)

the line had much to be unhappy and disturbed about: a "back-off" directive.

This call to BBC came two months after the attack on the Pentagon and World Trade Towers. His fellow agents, he said, were now released to hunt bad guys. That was good news. The bad news was that, *before* September 11, in those weeks just after George W. Bush took office, CIA and Defense Intelligence Agency (DIA) personnel were told to "back off" certain targets of investigations begun by Bill Clinton. He said,

> There were particular investigations that were effectively killed.

Which particular investigations? The agent was willing to risk his job to get this story out, but we had to press repeatedly for specifics on the directive to "back off." The order, he said reluctantly, spiked at least one fateful operation. As he talked, I wrote in my notebook, "Killed off Conn. Labs investigation." Connecticut Laboratories? I was clueless until my producer Meirion Jones, a weapons expert, gave me that "you idiot" look and said, "Khan Labs! Pakistan. The bomb."

Dr. A. Q. Khan is known as the "Father" of Pakistan's atomic bomb. He's not, however, the ideal parent. To raise the cash for Pakistan's program (and to pocket a tidy sum for himself), Khan sold off copies of his baby, his bomb, to Libya and North Korea—blueprints, material and all the fixings to blow this planet to Kingdom Come.

From another source inside the lab itself, we learned that Dr. Khan was persuading Pakistan to test his bomb—on India.

Why would Team Bush pull back our agents from nabbing Libya's bomb connection? The answer in two words: Saudi Arabia. The agent on the line said, "There were always constraints on investigating the Saudis."

Khan is Pakistani, not Saudi, but, nevertheless, the investigation led back to Saudi Arabia. There was no way that the Dr. Strangelove of Pakistan could have found the billions to cook up his nukes within the budget of his poor nation. We eventually discovered that agents knew the Saudis, who had secretly funded Saddam's nuclear weapons ambitions in the eighties, apparently moved their bomb-for-Islam money from Iraq to Dr. Khan's lab in Pakistan after Saddam invaded Kuwait in 1990.

But, said the insider, our agents had to let a hot trail grow cold because he and others, "were told to back off the Saudis." If you can't follow the money, you can't investigate. The weapons hunt was spiked.

BBC got the call about Dr. Khan's bomb in November 2001 and reported it that night on the tube and in the London *Guardian*. Over two years later, on February 11, 2004, President Bush, at an emergency press briefing, expressed his shock—*shock!*—at having learned that Dr. A. Q. Khan of Pakistan was running a flea market in fissionable material. This indicated a major Bush policy shift since my last book and report. In 2001, regarding the Khan bomb, the administration dismissed our story as imaginary. With his 2004 press conference, the President shifted from obfuscation to prevarication, denial to mendacity.

Our report on Dr. Khan's nuclear bazaar was confirmed in 2004, not by U.S. intelligence, but by one of Khan's customers, Muammar Gaddafi, the mischievous tyrant of Libya. It was Gaddafi's last little bit of fun with Mr. Bush and Britain's Prime Minister, Tony Blair. The U.S. and Britain had agreed to end their trade embargo on Libya in return for Gaddafi's shutting down his bomb program and, not incidentally, Gaddafi's giving an exclusive oil drilling agreement to British Petroleum.

So with Libya giving up Dr. Khan's bomb, it appears we have a happy ending for the safety of the planet. Unfortunately, while Homeland Security, our Armed Forces and Mayor Josh were staking out the Indian casino ferry landing in Southold, New York, Khan had given the secret of the bomb, hardware included, to Kim Jong Il of North Korea, a despot in a leisure suit a little less stable than Charles Manson.

The U.S. government missed discovering Dr. Khan's radioactive fire sale because our agents were hard at work ignoring the Saudi money trail. If the agencies had not been told to "back off" the Saudis and Dr. Khan, would the U.S. have uncovered the nuclear shipments in time to stop them? We can't possibly know, but, to paraphrase Yogi Berra, it's amazing what you don't see when you're told not to look.

"Hijacking for Idiots"?

But fear not. While Team Bush were averting their gaze from Dr. Khan, the new Department of Homeland Security and the FBI were busy staking out Marian the Librarian.

Libraries have always given up records when crimes are committed and subpoenas served. Killers can't hide in the stacks. But, after 9/11, the feds began trolling library borrowing records *without* subpoenas. Just browsing. When legal nitpickers questioned the constitutionality of this KGB-style snooping, Congress rushed in to extend the Patriot Act to permit the FBI to hunt library records without showing any reason or cause.

Congress took this bold step in July 2005, two days after the bombings in London. Exactly which suicide bomber or sleeper cell has been exposed by this powerful new intelligence weapon we have not been told. Did Osama fail to return his copy of *Harry Potter*? Or

WARNING
Under **Section 215** of the federal
USA PATRIOT Act
(Public Law 107-56)

records of **books** and other materials **you borrow** from this library **may be obtained by federal agents.**

This law also **prohibits** librarians from **informing you** if federal agents have obtained **records** about you.

Questions about this policy should be directed to the **Attorney General's** Office, Department of Justice, Washington, DC 20530.

POSTED PER RESOLUTION APPROVED AT THE TOWN MEETING
OF BRIDGEWATER, MA, NOVEMBER 8, 2004

(Source: Citizens for an Informed Community, Bridgewater, MA. William D. Haff, designer.)

Hijacking for Idiots? Or, *Blown Away: The Very Short Autobiography of a Suicide Bomber?*

What we have here is the Great Con: to get us to pull each other's hair over the sanctity of library card privacy. While Mr. Khan is out peddling nukes, we are dragged into a nitwit debate over "the balance between security and civil liberties"—with the defenders of America against terrorists sneering at the sissies from the ACLU.

Civil libertarians are all shook up that the FBI is going through our summer reading list. My concern is deeper. What I want to know is, who at the FBI is poring over my choice of novels? How much do we pay this guy, and why isn't he reviewing Swiss, Pakistani and Saudi bank transfer records instead?

You Speakie Terrorist?

Once we had the Mattituck Library staked out and could read over the shoulders of suspicious characters, our terror-huntin' boys soon realized that the literature and Web sites of the dangerously disaffected are not all in the King's English.

It so happened that one of our researchers' friends, Selda Arman, a Muslim with patriotic notions and a fluency in Turkish, offered her translation services to our government. In response, Selda received a call from our nation's protectors, which we've transcribed directly from her answering machine:

> Hi. This message is for Selda. My name is Joe McCollum and I'm with the Department of Defense, calling you regarding a language analyst position available. I see that you speak Terrorist . . . uh, uh . . . Turkish! . . .

Selda's response was, "Fucking assholes!" a Turkish phrase difficult to translate. Selda did *not* apply for the job.

She asked us not to use her real name, but I've included McCollum's true name as a public service—in case you are seeking work and speak fluent Terrorist.

What You Ought Not to Know: The 199-I Document

Once our G-men obtained translators and library cards, they were ready to take on the big national security threats.

On May 28, 2004, the FBI and the "Joint Terrorism Task Force" surrounded the offices of a soccer league and kids' club in suburban Falls Church, Virginia. Fifty Task Force paramilitaries in heavy armor hit the office suite like a bad scene from *The Untouchables*—and netted several soccer balls, baseball gloves and file cabinets filled with the goods on soccer moms and day campers. The commandos then sealed off the World Assembly of Muslim Youth (WAMY) sports and education office.

"SUSPECTED TERRORIST ORGANIZATION"?

FBI National Security Document 199-I "SECRET"

You may feel safer now that those World Cup posters are securely in federal custody.

But I don't. Because I had in my hand a dozen-page fax marked, "199-I—WF" and "SECRET." This was another piece of disturbing news unloaded and passed to our BBC team by some unhappy FBI agents who "accidentally" dropped the file on a desk at the National Security News Service.

The code "199-I" means "national security matter" in FBI-speak. It was about the soccer club, WAMY, which agents deemed "a suspected terrorist organization."

What made the document special—and earned the anger of the two agents who "lost" it for us—is that it indicates that the "suspected terrorist" activities were *not* investigated until September 13, 2001, despite a desire by agents to investigate these characters years earlier when the file was first opened on them and then "closed."

Was there good reason to have looked into this group, or was this another goofball assault on the civil liberties of Muslims?

The truth is, WAMY had more than soccer moms on its roster. According to the court record, the crew convicted of the first attack on New York's World Trade towers in 1993 kept literature handed out by WAMY at their homes. At BBC we obtained some from the bombers' lair. WAMY won U.S. tax-exempt status by stating its purpose as "fostering understanding and tolerance of all cultures." Here's a sample:

> *The Jews are enemies of the faithful, God and the angels.*
> *Teach our children to love taking revenge on the Jews and the*
> *oppressors.*

And they provide several examples on what specifically to teach the children.

> *In 1989, Abdel-Hadi Nemim carried-out his own heroic oper-*
> *ation while on Bus # 405 of Tel Aviv-Jerusalem line; he*
> *charged at the bus driver chanting "Allah Akbar," twirled the*
> *steering wheel towards the cliff and causing the bus to take a*

big fall. As a result of his courageous act, 14 Israelis were killed and 27 were injured.

The literature supplied by WAMY is ecumenical in its venom. There is the claim that Shia Islam was created by a Jew to lead Muslims into evil. Amazingly, WAMY "educational" literature was handed out at a New York prison, even though tensions existed between Sunni and Shia inmates that would lead to the alleged beating of four Shia inmates at another New York penal facility. At BBC we got a hold of a talk at one of WAMY's kiddy camps in Florida in which the speaker praised the seizing of Russian Orthodox hostages. Not everyone gets a bad rap from WAMY. One film sold by WAMY praises that "compassionate young man, Osama bin Laden."

But, hey, it's a free country and everyone's entitled to their opinion. But it's more than talk at issue. According to Dutch intelligence services we contacted, and officials of the Indian, Pakistani and Bosnian governments, WAMY is in the business of indoctrinating jihadis, recruiting them, and in some cases, transporting them to trouble spots on the globe—or spots where the jihadis would like to make trouble. WAMY denies ever being involved with or arming jihadis. It said it carefully restricted itself to sending and receiving "volunteers" to and from Bosnia.

So the question is not why was WAMY investigated, but why *wasn't* it investigated until September 13, 2001?

Or, more precisely, *who* was exempt from investigation? For the answer, look to page 2 of the 199-I document. WAMY isn't some little kids' club. It operates in 55 countries; its budgets run into the high millions, cash that comes directly from the Saudi Arabian royals who control the network from Riyadh. The Saudi supreme dictator (they call him "King" Abdullah, but let's remember that Saudi kings are simply dictators in robes) praised WAMY, saying, "There is no extremism in the defending of the faith." That's *his* opinion. WAMY's U.S. founder? "ABL" in the 199-I document, Abdullah bin Laden, nephew of Osama. Investigators were looking for Abdullah as well as another relative, Omar bin Laden (or "Binladden" in the alternative translation of the Arabic name). But by September 13, when the restrictions on agents were removed, the bin Ladens were gone.

The WAMY offices in Falls Church, Virginia, are down the road from the home of the hijackers that hit the Pentagon. I am not surprised that WAMY's offices were raided, but I *am* surprised that it took over *two years*. By that time, the Eliot Ness–style raid could collect only empty file cabinets and T-shirts. Why so long? And why, after sitting on their hands for two years, did the FBI suddenly strike at bin Ladens' operation?

The answer is in Saudi Arabia. The FBI raid occurred just days after religious extremists blew up an oil workers' compound in Riyadh. The snakes had bitten their master's hand and the Saudis were in a vengeful mood. There you have it. Messing with the oil sheiks gets the Bush Administration's attention. Falling towers in New York, however, are only good for Republican politician photo ops.

Yes, Bill Clinton was also a bit too tender toward the oil men of Arabia. The WAMY investigation was first shuttered in 1996 under his laid-back watch. But, in 2000, after the bombings of U.S. embassies in Africa, Clinton, we learned, sent two secret high-level delegations to Riyadh, one headed by Clinton's national security Advisor, Sandy Berger, to suggest to the Saudi royal family that they crack down on "charitable donations" from their kingdom to the guys who blew up our embassies and first tried to take down the Trade Center in 1993.

Ronald Reagan's "counterterrorism ambassador" Robert Oakley, advisor to the Bush Jr. transition team, said, "The only major criticism I have [of Clinton] is the obsession with Osama. . . ." When the failed oil man from Texas took over the White House in January 2001, the U.S. government "obsession" with Osama ended—until September 11.

In November 2001, when we were about to televise the 199-I memo, the BBC sought out the FBI's comment, assuming we'd get the usual, "It's baloney, a fake, you misunderstand, it ain't true." But we didn't get the usual response. Rather, FBI headquarters in Washington told us:

> There are lots of things the intelligence community knows
> and other people ought not to know.

"Ought not to know"?

What else ought we not know, Mr. President? And when are we supposed to forget it?

The Frankenstein Factory

There is one big problem with theories that George Bush knew about the September 11 attack in advance. At BBC, my producer insists that one has to have solid evidence before accusing Bush of knowing *anything at all*.

So, who did it? Here is what we have on videotape:

> We calculated in advance the number of casualties from
> the enemy, who would be killed based on the position of
> the tower. We calculated that the floors that would be hit
> would be three or four floors. I was the most optimistic of
> them all. (. . . Inaudible . . .) due to my experience in this
> field, I was thinking that the fire from the gas in the plane
> would melt the iron structure of the building and collapse
> the area where the plane hit and all the floors above it only.
> This is all that we had hoped for.

The speaker is a grinning, chuckling, "optimistic" structural engineer, Osama bin Laden, recorded on film on December 13, 2001, in Afghanistan. Some would suggest it wasn't really Osama—maybe it was Karl Rove in a turban stretched to six feet six. Sorry, it really is bin Laden. The point is that there is more than one flavor of evil on this sad planet. George Bush can't account for it all, even with the help of Darth Cheney. An addiction to helping millionaires help themselves, carelessness about the deaths of thousands and a penchant for

The identity of the real terrorists is in your face, in your hands, with you every single day.

The new U.S. $20 dollar bill contains details of the World Trade Centre and Pentagon attacks!

see for yourself...

1> FOLD A NEW $20 BILL THIS WAY

2> CONTINUE TO FOLD THIS WAY.

Compare your fold to this picture.

3> FOLD THE RIGHT SIDE UNDER, exactly as you folded the left side. You'll immediately see the Pentagon ablaze!

4> NOW FLIP IT OVER AND SEE OTHER SIDE
The Twin Towers of the World Trade Center are hit and smoking.

What are the odds that a simple geometric folding of the $20 bill would accidentally contain a representation of both terror attacks?

Need more proof?
You can even fold the $20 to say OSAMA!

Need even more proof?
9+11 = 20
With just 2 more folds your $20 bill turns into a airplane!

Connect the Dots

One of my readers, Mr. "Silver Lion" (no first name), cracked the case for us.

mendacity does not mean George and Dick planned the September 11 attack.

No way around it, Osama made The Plan. But who made Osama?

Jeddah, Saudi Arabia, 1987

In 1987, attorney Michael Springmann, a State Department officer in Jeddah, reviewed visa applications to the U.S. from "engineers" claiming they were going to an auto parts trade show. Springmann asked the engineers what city the show was in. They "couldn't remember." Visas denied. Then, over Springmann's objections, the U.S. embassy gave the "engineers" their visas to enter the USA.

From 1987 through 1989, as Reagan autumn turned to Bush winter, more visas were issued to Pakistanis and others suspiciously shuttling through Saudi Arabia.

Other consular officers didn't like what was going on. One, John Moller, quit over it:

> I was against the issuance of nonimmigrant visas except within the regulations. . . . I was unable to get anyone to relent on the matter and, rather than endure the situation further, elected to take my retirement.

Yet another U.S. consulate official, Lonnie Washington, privately wondered why his questions, sent in plaintive reports to Washington, were purged from the files, unprecedented for missives classified "Secret."

Still another State Department official, in the Office of the Inspector General, Marvin Groeneweg, wondered why the CIA was "playing fast and loose" with visa applications.

Moller, Washington and Groeneweg had no idea what the heck was going on; Springmann suspected just some small-time embassy bribery scheme. But that didn't explain the high-level disappearance of documents nor the CIA's involvement. Back in Washington, Springmann uncovered the mystery.

It was, said Springmann, "An effort to bring recruits, rounded up by

Osama bin Laden, to the United States for terrorist training." To blow up the Pentagon? Heavens, no. These were part of the Reagan-Bush jihad against the Soviet Empire's seizure of the Afghan oil pipeline route.

The film WAMY showed of the "compassionate young man, Osama bin Laden," was part of this campaign. Recruitment for Afghanistan was smiled on, recruitment of jihadis for Bosnia winked at—so WAMY and other Saudi-linked charities must have been stunned when, in 2005, the Terrorism Task Force struck. After all, the Saudis were guests invited by the President's father.

Paris, France, 1996

May 1996. The scene is now the *très* posh Hotel Royal Monceau in Paris. Saudi billionaires—including an investment "angel" who saved George W. Bush's oil ventures—and the kingdom's intelligence chief, Prince Turki al-Faisal, meet in private. According to our sources, they are joined by a financial bagman for Islamic charities whose money finds its way to Al-Qaeda.

Keep in mind, these Saudis don't like Osama—he wants their heads, their yachts and their oil. But a hefty payment to charities that will send jihadis to educate Central Asians in their fundamentalist faith will keep Osama busy in the 'Stans (Uzbekistan, Kazakhstan, etc.) and away from mischief in the Gulf.

A well-known arms dealer, not a Muslim, but a profiteer in mayhem of any sort, attended. It is from the arms dealer's partner I first received an attendance list. Another source within French intelligence obtained notes from the meeting and confirmed the attendees. It looked like protection money—Osama is more John Gotti than Ayatollah Khomeini—to keep Osama from blowing up the Saudis' yachts. But there's a problem with giving cash to freewheeling "charities." Sometimes they misuse their allowance. As the lawyers for the families of the victims of 9/11 claim, with donors not looking closely, the money for "education" could end up buying flying lessons for people who don't intend to land the plane.

French intelligence was concerned. U.S. agencies, apparently, were not. The money trail went cold.

Washington, DC, USA, 2005

In July 2005, the airport security system at Dulles International set off alarms when Sarah Zapolsky's eleven-month-old baby tried to board a plane to Phoenix. The suspect child was on the Terrorism Watch List. Two months later, the original funder and strategist for the Taliban slipped into the same capital airport, grabbed a limo to his elegant new home and prepared for his meeting at the White House. Prince Turki, the man reportedly at the Hotel Monceau meeting, former chief of Saudi Arabia's feared intelligence apparatus, presented his credentials as Ambassador to Condoleezza Rice and received his two-cheek kiss from President George W. Bush.

Did our President know that he had offered his cheek to the co-funder, with Osama, of the Taliban? Robert Ebel, formerly the CIA's top expert on oil, compiled a series of excellent briefing papers on Central Asian oil, including this note:

> In the 1980s, Arab volunteers, financed by Saudi money . . . founded Wahabi schools . . . waged a campaign against Afghanistan's indigenous Islam . . . and destroyed Sufi sacred sites (*zyarats*). The Taliban are the final and most formidable product of this long-term strategy. . . . They are part of the post-1992 U.S. strategy to maintain a high level of influence in the energy belt from the Caspian Sea to the Persian Gulf. . . .
>
> The question of whether the United States actively supported the Taliban or, as one U.S. ex-official put it, merely "winked" as Pakistan and Saudi Arabia did the actual work, is controversial and difficult to resolve.[3]

---

[3]Ebel and Menon, *Energy and Conflict in Central Asia and the Caucasus,* National Bureau of Asian Research (Rowman & Littlefield, 2000).

Whether the USA supported or winked at the Taliban is not the point. America's policy was bent to this purpose: stopping the Iranians from supplanting the Saudi's control over OPEC. Seizing OPEC was the real, if unannounced, dream of the Ayatollah Khomeini and the Shia mullah-crats in Iran when they attacked Iraq in September 1980. They hoped for a Shia uprising to overthrow Saddam that would join their state with Iran. That failed and Iran then looked to the Shia minority to its north, in Afghanistan.

Had Iran controlled the Afghan corridor to the Caspian, this combine of Shia states could have created an oil colossus rivaling the Saudis', thereby making Iran "swing" producer and controller of OPEC. The United States, the Saudis—and bin Laden—could not let that happen. Here was something the USA, Saudi Arabia and Al-Qaeda could all agree on: No "Shia dogs" (the Iranians, in Qaeda terminology) were going to control a new oil caliphate from Kazakhstan to the Tigris.

To prevent this scenario, everyone did their share. America aided Pakistan, whose Interior Minister (i.e., head of the secret police, the ISI) said, "I'll see to it that Iran is neutralized in Afghanistan" by arming the Taliban. The Saudis, under the direction of their Intel chief al-Turki, funded the Taliban for the same purpose. Bin Laden did his share. Besides murdering every Iranian in their Afghan embassy, he created the Taliban's only effective fighting unit, Arab Battalion 055. To block the Iranians, the U.S. winked, blinked and nodded at the blood-bathed birthing of the Taliban terror state, demanding solely the arrest of Osama himself.

In 1995, Unocal Petroleum's deal with the Taliban to run a natural gas pipe to Pakistan through Afghanistan was not significant as an energy source. It was, however, significant as a Saudi/CIA stick in Iran's eye.

At the time, a few U.S. congressmen grew a bit uncomfortable about cuddling up with Al-Qaeda's sponsors. One, Benjamin Gilman, Republican of New York, Chairman of the House International Relations Committee, demanded confidential documents he was certain would detail Prince Turki's engineering, with U.S. and Saudi approval, the Taliban's seizure of power in Afghanistan. On May 21, 1999, Gilman wrote to the Clinton State Department:

> Terrorism, opium production and massive human rights violations underscore the urgency of my request.

But once Gilman's man Bush took control of the files in 2001, the terrorism, opium and human rights violations were not so urgent. And even if Gilman got the files now, what would he do? It's not the kind of thing you'd bring up to the Prince over barbecue at the Crawford Ranch. We mustn't discomfit the Saudis over their contributions to Terror-R-Us—especially if America itself is stinking with "winking."

The problem with creating Frankensteins, whether an Osama or a Taliban, is that these creatures often rise and turn on their creators.

For example, another creepy critter to crawl out of the Reagan-Bush anti-Iran Frankenstein factory is identified in this State Department memo, marked "SECRET":

> In his 90-minute meeting with Rumsfeld, Saddam Hussein showed obvious pleasure with President's [Reagan's] letter and Rumsfeld's visit. . . . Rumsfeld told Saddam U.S. . . . had successfully closed off U.S.-controlled exports by third countries to Iran. In response to Rumsfeld's interests in seeing Iraq increase oil exports . . .

Unfortunately, Reagan's words that pleasured Saddam remain classified.

The Reagan-Bush Frankenstein Factory is still producing new models. Pervez Musharraf, personal protector of the atomic bomb salesman, Dr. Khan, can be seen in photos arm in arm with our president as if they are going together to the senior prom. Given our experiences with Saddam and Osama, our monsters tend to get out of control after about eleven years. Therefore, we can expect, in the year

"Obvious Pleasure" Saddam and Rumsfeld meeting

Above is a photo of the actual secret memo of Donald Rumsfeld's visit with Saddam Hussein in 1983. My question is, what indicated to Rumsfeld that Saddam "showed obvious pleasure with President's [Reagan's] letter"? Hand-clapping? A visible tent in Saddam's pants? Coca-Cola or blood spurting out his nose? The Secretary of Defense's office did not return our calls.

2013, President Jeb Bush will have to order the 82nd Airborne into Pakistan to remove Musharraf, the Killer of Karachi.

George and Tony Get Their Al-Qaeda Fix

We take off our shoes at the airport in Pittsburgh, we have robot chips planted in our driver's licenses, we have our cousin Larry in Falluja.

But there seems to be one thing missing in the War on Terror: the terrorists.

Where *are* they? Are they *at all*?

What about the July 2005 bombings in London? The cruel, evil jerks who blew up the London Tube, despite appropriating Al-Qaeda's name for their Web site and T-shirts, had about as much to do with Al-Qaeda as a Beatles tribute band has to do with the Fab Four. It was a horror—but no September 11. American-bred monster Timmy McVeigh slaughtered a lot more people in Oklahoma City with his cow-poop bomb.

I'm not belittling the heartbreaking hideousness of the London bombings, but let's get the facts straight. If Al-Qaeda is the Panzer Division of terrorism, these London bombers were terrorism's Cub Scouts: A handful of poor young Muslim schmucks whipped into a frenzy by mewling mullahs, like the cleric in North London who enjoyed the comfortable middle-class dullness of England during the week while on weekends preaching "a 9/11, day after day after day." But there has been no 9/11 day after day.

And that's no little matter. *Because George Bush and Tony Blair are Al-Qaeda junkies.* They've sold us on everything from fingerprinting five-year-olds to invading Baghdad to tolerating plummeting paychecks in the USA all on the slick line that we are under attack by a - well-trained, well-armed, well-funded hidden army called Al-Qaeda.

And that is why, after these four teenage fools in London blew themselves up, Blair's foreign secretary dramatically dashed out to tell us that the explosions had the "hallmarks of Al-Qaeda." Our Commander-in-Chief, looking as commanding as possible (no reading of kiddie stories this time), could not have been more satisfied. "Hallmarks of Al-Qaeda"? Horrible? Yes. "War"? Bullshit.

Our "War President," as he arrogantly calls himself, is having a little problem with his War on Terror. The enemy's gone AWOL. Except when *we* go *looking* for trouble, as in invading Mesopotamia. Otherwise, trouble pretty much stopped looking for *us*. Admit it, we're pretty darn safe.

America is *not* under attack. There is no WAR on terror because, except for one day five years ago, there has been no terror attack. This isn't Lebanon or Israel or Chechnya. We don't go to a pizza parlor wondering if we'll get our keisters blown off before the last slice. This is *not*

Iraq, with the daily bombing in the Kasbah as Shias, Sunnis, Turkmen and Kurds settle matters of religion and petroleum with Semtex.

Even September 11. Forgive me for pointing this out, but it was, in the end, the deed of a bunch of wingnuts with box-cutters hankering for a hot time with virgins in the next life who got "lucky" and killed a horrendous number of my former coworkers at the World Trade Center.

Where are the terrorists? We've got a boatload of sorry-ass losers in orange suits in Guantánamo we captured five years ago who are supposed to tell us Osama bin Laden's address. Even if they had it, Osama's probably moved. And, since he was dying of kidney problems, he's a goner.

Where is Osama? He's last year's model. Even if he survives, he's no longer a player. That's because first, George Bush gave him what he wanted, U.S. troops out of the Land of the Two Holy Places, Saudi Arabia. Second, bin Laden's ultimate goal is a bust. Terror, at least big-time global terror, is, like the war in Iraq, all about the oil. Bin Laden was an artifact of $10-a-barrel crude. As he made clear in his Declaration of War, the failings of the Saudi royals were in allowing the West to bring down the price of the great oil reserves under Islamic sands.

Ironically, Osama's obtaining his goal, raising oil prices, is his undoing. With oil up, Osama's war platform crumbles beneath him. It's amazing how much political-emotional-religious angst among Saudi Arabians is cured by $50-a-barrel crude. The Saudi royals no longer fear Osama nor need to fund him; Pakistan's dictator has control of Afghanistan without need of the Taliban; the Caspian's oil is safely "privatized"; the Libyans have signed with BP; working-class Iranians are voting against mullahs who promise jihad instead of a piece of the oil pie; and overwhelmingly, Muslims would rather not spend their weekends blowing up their neighbors.

Yes, Bush can say there have been no terror attacks since September 2001 because of the wonderful way he and Sheriff Dick have protected us. But, that's like the guy in my old neighborhood on the

Lower East Side who said his dog, a Rhodesian ridgeback, is trained to scare away lions. I asked him, "How do you know they scare away lions?" He pointed down Second Avenue and said, "See any lions?"

Neither America nor Britain are at war. This is not the Blitz. If anyone thinks I'm belittling the killings in New York, in London, or in Madrid, you've got me wrong. These are true *crimes*. The problem is that Bush's declaring a War on Terror, mirroring Osama's own Declaration of War, draws us into the *totalen Krieg* (Total War) mentality in which all perfidy is excused, from our President's coddling Pakistan's bomb merchant to our Congress's repealing your right to know the poisons created at your neighborhood chemical plant. A whole list of corporate gimmes sought by lobbyists before September 11 are now marketed to Congress as protection from Al-Qaeda. To cover this extreme greedismo, we've been sold a new Red Scare, and that is certain to bring us the new McCarthyism. Get ready.

Are there still killer fanatics in Pakistan screaming, "Death to America! Death to the Jews!"? Yes, always have been. Always will be. But they don't constitute an organized armed force ready to call up their thousands from sleeper cells in Cincinnati.

Despite this, I'm telling you now: We will be hit again. Bush has made that horribly certain by poking hornets' nests worldwide and offering punishment to the planet instead of prosperity. And despite the machine guns at the Indian casino parking lot in Southold, America is prepared neither to prevent nor to respond to attacks by small groups of committed fanatics. Homeland Security's loot is spent on cyber toys, color schemes, kicking in the doors of the local library, or, as I discovered, manipulating elections in Latin America. Against the crimes of religious fanatics or skinhead berserkers, foreign or domestic, we are less prepared than under the Clinton Administration. The entire USA PATRIOT act was written, let's not forget, *before* the September 11 attack. It was aimed at slicing a hole in civil liberties and filling the pockets of connected hucksters and database magnates while budgets for simple police work, the guts of real protection, bleed away.

And who will get us next? Don't assume they'll be clutching Korans. Another Hurricane Katrina and America won't need to look abroad for insurgents. Until September 11, 2001, the deadliest terror attack in American history was carried out by an all-American Gulf War veteran. It is worth remembering that Bill Clinton pretty much ended that threat with solid police work (treating terror as a crime, not a war) and a truly powerful weapon: a series of lawsuits that cost the skinhead Right its assets. Note that Clinton quashed the terror (Oklahoma was not the lone incident) without invading Idaho or invalidating the Constitution.

Outside the war zones we create, organized terror's power is diminishing, and for Bush and Blair, that is a political problem. That's why the attack by the loony London teenagers in 2005 was such a boon to the Al-Qaeda addicts in the White House and Downing Street: They needed a new terror fix. Even if it wasn't the real Al-Qaeda, it was enough for Bush and Blair to mainline into the body politic a big, fat dose of fear.

Once they had the world media all jumped up on a new fear high, Bush and Blair could resume their sales pitch for their two-barrel cure: less liberty, more weaponry.

Our leaders are counting on cowardice in the hearts of the heartland. In 2004, the Republicans' unstated reelection campaign slogan was, *"They are coming to get us."* Americans, scared for their lives, soiled their underpants and waddled to the polls crying, "Georgie, save us!"

From his bunker, Mr. Cheney has created a government that is little more than a Wal-Mart of Fear: midnight snatchings of citizens for uncharged crimes, wars to hunt for imaginary weapons aimed at Los Angeles, DNA data banks of kids and grandmas, even the Chicken Little sky-is-falling Social Security spook-show.

In 1933, Franklin Roosevelt calmed a nation when he said, "We have nothing to fear but fear itself."

Today, George Bush says, "We have nothing to *sell* but fear itself."

Double Cheese with Fear

Fear sells better than sex. But who's buying?

The mothers of this country who are wrestling with threats!

Oh, my! What threats? If you thought it's just Osama, you're taking big chances, because more danger is just outside your door, ringing the bell.

It's the pizza delivery guy. Aren't you afraid yet? Did you know that 25% of pizza delivery drivers have been in jail within four months of starting the job bringing you your pie? From Sing-Sing to your doorstep! One in four!

Who said so? Derek Smith said so. He said (I can't make this up):

> What pizza do you like? At what price? *Are you willing to take the risk* associated with dealing with a company that doesn't screen their drivers?

Who *is* this guy? Derek Smith is the founder of a company called ChoicePoint, prime contractor for the Department of Homeland Security. He's the man standing between your family and Al-Qaeda's mushroom-and-pepperoni sleeper cells. You should know something about this Smith, because he knows an awful lot about you.

Last time I checked, Smith and ChoicePoint had piled up over 16 billion files on every living and dying U.S. citizen, and they've put it up for sale, bit by bit.[4] The company pulled in over a billion dollars in revenues in 2005, only eleven years after Smith founded it.

ChoicePoint, the largest personal profile database company in America, is the leader in the Fear Industry. The problem for CEO Smith and the firm he founded in 1994 is that, at first, the public wasn't buying . . . until September 11, 2001, when ChoicePoint's new business plan fell from the sky.

"The War on Terror hasn't been decided yet, but a few winners are emerging," wrote *Forbes* a few months after the attack. "High up on the list of businesses that will benefit . . . ChoicePoint, Inc."

They didn't have to wait. ChoicePoint's Bode Technologies division picked up a $12 million contract to identify by DNA testing pieces of corpses found in the Staten Island garbage dump holding the Twin Towers.

Al-Qaeda's attack set up an explosion of demand for Smith's top product. His top product is *you.* Your Prozac prescription, Satan's church donations, Victoria's Secret bill payments, driver's license, voting record, you name it. And George Bush is buying. ChoicePoint is operating a private FBI or, more accurately, a private KGB, because they keep files on you that the law doesn't allow the FBI to hold.

The law in question is the U.S. Constitution, which says the government can't spy on you unless you're suspected of a crime—but ChoicePoint can, and that's where the game begins. Under the USA PATRIOT act, Congress has outsourced the snooping. The Act allows the Feds to ask ChoicePoint for data the government itself cannot legally obtain. The spooks at the new Total Information Office (now "Terrorism" Information Office since Congress changed the name and removed the logo, the All-Seeing Eyeball—no kidding) couldn't wait. In one classified document that came our way, a Total Info honcho exhorted agencies to come up with "far-out, funky" uses of the Choice-Point info they aren't supposed to have. Groovy, man.

---

[4]ChoicePoint has written me to say, "No data files or 'dossiers' exist at ChoicePoint." Darn strange for a data company.

And what does the family Bush do with ChoicePoint's funky information? In Florida, it was ChoicePoint's DBT unit that came up with the list of 94,000 "felons" to purge from Florida voter rolls before the 2000 election. At least 91,000 were innocent legal voters, and the vast majority of these were guilty of nothing more than being Black, Democrats or both. (See Chapter 4.)

And now, ChoicePoint wants your blood. Why? Because "Choice-Point Cares." That's the name of its program to reunite those kiddies on milk cartons with their loved ones. And they'll need your DNA to do it.

That's the point of the ghost stories of pizza men coming to snatch your milk-carton baby, to convince "the mothers of this country facing threats" to raise no objections to the data goldminers digging into your bank accounts, medical records and bloodstream. And now, with Osama out there, Americans can't wait to rush into the protective arms of our computerized Big Brother.

But come on, if ChoicePoint gets the bad guys for us, who cares? However, ChoicePoint, unlike the Canadian Mounties, is not likely to get their man. The Illinois State Police, for example, tested Choice-Point's DNA-matching evidence used in more than a thousand rape cases. The police scientists say ChoicePoint got it wrong 25% of the time. In some cases, it appears, ChoicePoint produced test "results" on evidence that didn't exist.

As you see, ChoicePoint cares, but ChoicePoint also lies. In November 2000, when our *Observer*-BBC Television team discovered the false tagging of Black voters in Florida, I expected their PR men to give me the usual song and dance to slither out of the tough questions. But Choice-Point's spokesmen simply made it up, telling me they'd checked the names against Social Security numbers. I got the scrub sheets, and they hadn't checked in 95% of cases. They did, however, list each voter's race.

The company flat-out denied to one reporter that they give DNA to the feds, but when one of my investigators called, posing as a student interested in a career in "data management," the firm boasted it is the biggest supplier of DNA *information* to the FBI. "And that scares the hell out of me," said a ChoicePoint executive (who has since bailed out of the company) on condition of anonymity. ChoicePoint says it only keeps DNA records on bad guys. However, said the insider, "Derek said his hope [is] to build a database of DNA samples from every person in the United States . . . linked to all the other information held by CP," from medical records to voting records.

So what? Because, the executive told me, they get it wrong. Way wrong, says the World Privacy Forum's Pam Dixon, who sampled ChoicePoint's credit-reporting wares and found 90% of the records contained errors. At least they've improved from Florida days.

Bad information spread about you can ruin you. But so can good information in the wrong hands. In 2005, ChoicePoint mistakenly sold 145,000 credit card records to a band of identity thieves. That little slip earned them, in 2006, a $15 million fine from the Federal Trade Commission, the highest in FTC history.

Your data wasn't protected, but the company's inside track is well bullet-proofed. Its retainers include Vin Weber, former congressman and a cofounder of Project for a New American Century (PNAC) with Richard Armitage, who served on the board of ChoicePoint's Florida unit. (Armitage, after the vote-purging work was done, was appointed a Deputy Secretary of State.) The remainder of the ChoicePoint Board of Directors looks like a Bush fundraising gala, including Home Depot founder Bernie Marcus and his partner Ken Langone, Treasurer of Rudy Giuliani's aborted Senate campaign against Hillary Clinton.

Billionaire Langone is perfect for ChoicePoint, a man who knows how to make good use of data: He was charged with insider trading by the Securities Exchange Commission in 2004. Admittedly, the chief of the New York Stock Exchange, Richard Grasso, likened the accusations against Langone of a massive fraud to "a traffic ticket." The stock market regulator Grasso might have been a wee bit influenced by Langone's secretly approving Grasso's taking more than $100 million in extra pay from the Exchange. Apparently, the Attorney General of New York thought so and, in a civil complaint, has charged Grasso and Langone with conspiracy, charges both are fighting. But let's not single out one Board member. ChoicePoint CEO Smith is, in 2006, himself

Freedom of Information?

Why does ChoicePoint get a no-bid contract from the Bush Administration? Here's the answer we received in response to a "Freedom of Information" request. At least they've crossed out the "secret" stamp. (Source: EPIC)

under investigation for insider trading. Smith failed to notify victims of the credit card number theft until after he had unloaded some of his own ChoicePoint stock. The Securities and Exchange Commission raised some questions about the suspiciously brilliant timing of Smith's sales. The company has said the sales were entirely proper.

But I digress. Or maybe not. Because it's all about the exchange of information—who knows what and who knows whom. Every war needs intelligence. It's not the War on Terror these guys are fighting, it's the Class War. Information is a weapon and our betters are arming themselves. The Bush Administration has reversed the flow common to democracy: Instead of information about the government going to We The People, it is now information about We The People going to government, or better, contractors beholden to board directors, not voters.

This Class Info-War is global. And ChoicePoint is on the front lines. Working with an extraordinary group of disaffected intelligence experts from the Electronic Privacy Information Center in Washington, we got our hands on a copy of a $67 million agreement between Homeland Security and ChoicePoint. The agreement was so confidential it was not even given a contract number. It was a no-bid deal, of course. But if it gets the Qaeda network, who's going to moan about a little secrecy.

But take a look at this document marked, on page 44, "FEDERAL BUREAU OF INVESTIGATION—SECRET." It is about the FBI's contract with ChoicePoint to obtain government records on every citizen in half a dozen countries. The September 11 hijackers came from Saudi Arabia, the Gulf emirates and Pakistan. But the FBI has, oddly, chosen Mexico, Argentina, Brazil, Honduras and Venezuela. Is there an exploding enchilada conspiracy sneaking over the border? Or is it something else that put these nation's citizenry on the terror watch list? Notably, each nation had an anti-Bush president running for re-election or an anti-Bush candidate in the lead for the presidency. Hmm. When I was in Venezuela in 2004, I noted that Súmate, a group seeking the recall of Bush's bête noire, President Hugo Chávez, had at each registration booth a laptop computer with the voter rolls. The anti-Chávez group could challenge improper (i.e. pro-Chávez) voters. Was this Florida-goes-Latin? No one could say where Súmate got the lists or if these were the ones lifted by ChoicePoint. We do know that Súmate received cash payments from the Bush Administration.

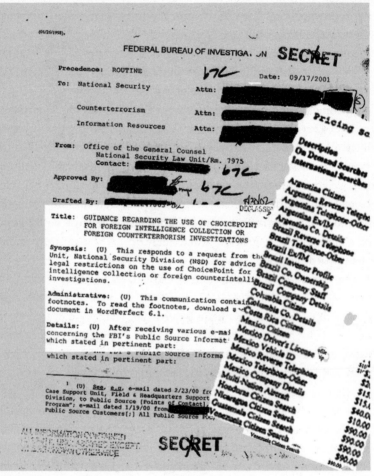

Hunting for Hijackers . . . in Venezuela?

Every September 11 hijacker came from the Arabian Peninsula or Pakistan. Yet, from a source with a copy not blacked out, we learned the hunt was limited to Venezuela, Mexico and other Latin nations with presidential elections favoring anti-Bush candidates.

The interesting thing about ChoicePoint's obtaining these citizen files from Venezuela, Mexico and Argentina is that according to press reports and officials I spoke with, in those countries this is *a crime.* ChoicePoint blames any misconduct on its operatives. Nevertheless, Mexico contractors were busted; arrests were avoided in Argentina when ChoicePoint promised to erase its copies of the list. But what about Bush's copy?

Creating a master file on you—from your DNA to your party registration (what do you think new voter IDs are *really* about?)—makes us safer, right? As ChoicePoint CEO Smith tells us, the September 11 hijackers checked in under their real names. Had his data system for the new Transportation Safety Administration been in place on that day, the bad guys, all on ChoicePoint lists, would have set off warning blinks when they checked in, like the alarm that nabbed Mrs. Zapolsky's baby. There is, however, a minor flaw in his system: Osama and friends no longer book flights under their own names—even though this has cost them thousands of frequent flier miles.

Marines in a Tube

We know the cure for The Fear is "less liberty, more weaponry." ChoicePoint will help dispose of our liberties cheap, but how can we *defend* ourselves?

General Dynamics, Northrop Grumman and Lockheed Martin have just what we need to stick in our nation's holster: the Virginia-class submarine.

The Virginia-class U-boat was originally designed to hunt Soviet subs. The problem with the 1996 design is that the Soviet Union went out of business seven years earlier. Never mind. That didn't stop our triumvirate of corporate warriors. They've redesigned the Virginia-class for the War on Terror.

Given that our enemies today are mostly guys carrying box cutters and stuffing TNT in their shoes, I was curious as to how these sub-o-saurs would be helpful in post-cold-war theaters of battle. Our BBC team called Northrop Grumman and asked. Their PR man explained that the firm is, "reconfiguring it for the new type of war—the new military situation."

We called during the invasion of Afghanistan. Afghanistan is *land-locked*.

No matter. Iraq was on the horizon and, if you look at the map, there is an itty-bitty piece of beachfront near Basra. The weapons maker explained, you could use the ship "to land commandoes" on the beaches to seek out hiding places of terrorists. I remembered that the Israelis, who have a smaller budget than ours, land commandoes in canvas *canoes*. But I didn't want to quibble with Lockheed over price. Still, one thing about the scheme to use the Virginia-class to land commandoes concerned me: It's a big boat, about the size of an underwater aircraft carrier. Exactly how would one sneak up on the beach with this thing?

The defense expert snorted at our lack of knowledge of the weaponry. For an extra $400 million per vessel, they had been "refitted." The torpedoes have been retooled to fit nine sailors each so they can be *shot onto the beach*.

I can't make this up. In one design, four marines lie down sideways, five marines are launched in headfirst. "Specifically configured to put Navy Seals into torpedoes, [a] 'lock-in/lock-out' trunk," we were told.

I was curious about the submarine's three-headed corporate team deal among what used to be fierce competitors for Navy work. They may be competitors, but, notes a Navy spokesman, they "do not 'compete' in the traditional sense." Indeed they don't. In fact, they don't com-

Note: This image is taken directly from the US Defense Department web site. No kidding.

pete at all. Rather than bid against each other, which might reduce the cost, they settle on a single price. What used to be called a "price-fixing conspiracy" is now called a "consortium," after the word "consort," which referred to the king's concubine. A kind of weaponry OPEC.

The consorting companies were willing to part with one of these sub-surface sailor injectors for a billion and a half dollars. Our President, knowing a bargain when he sees one, ordered thirty-six. Later, as U.S. troops in Iraq demanded such retrograde material as armor for their Humvees, the President cut back his sub order. The consortium obliged by agreeing to make fewer boats—for *two* and a half billion each.

The result of all this consorting is that General Dynamics' profit is, for the first time in its history, exceeding a billion dollars a year. Lockheed Martin is doing even better, scoring a record $2.5 billion in profit for 2006, beating out Northrop Grumman's $1.5 billion. I know that with weaponry profits bouncing off the clouds, you're concerned that the firms will have a huge tax bill. Not to worry. In 2004, just before the election, the Bush Administration slipped a special provision into tax legislation to cut the tax on war profits to an effective 7% compared to the 21% paid by most U.S. manufacturers.

Despite the consortium's commitment to corporate socialism, Lockheed Martin has become top dog among corporate arms dealers. It became the number one recipient of funds from the U.S. Treasury among all U.S. companies on the wings of the F-22A, a fighter designed to defeat the Soviet Union's MiG 29 UBM. The MiG 29 was never built. And the Soviet Union doesn't exist—proof of the extraordinary effectiveness of the F-22A. We've got 83 of them. Bush has ordered 96 more at $130 million per airplane. That's double the old price, but the new price comes with a new name, the F-22A *Raptor*. Is that cool or what?

Who makes these Humvee-armor-vs.-Raptor-and-subs decisions now that Paul Wolfowitz is no longer our Deputy Defense Secretary? The answer: his replacement, Gordon England, former Executive Vice President of *both* General Dynamics and a Lockheed unit. Now *that's* a consortium.

Lockheed's not Halliburton. Vice President Cheney gets nothing from Lockheed's success, unless his wife shares. Lockheed still pays the pension of their former board member, Lynne Cheney, Mr. Cheney's wife. Another war industry consortium.

But as long as a single terrorist is out there, or even if there isn't, Lockheed's work is not done. In 2005, after London subways were attacked by teenagers with exploding backpacks, Lockheed parlayed its expertise in counter-terrorism on the sea and in the air into a big contract to protect the New York City subways from attack.

The firm could not explain to us how they are going to launch those Marines into the "A" train.

Lockheed and General Dynamics cannot win the War on Terror on their own. They needed The Crusader.

The Crusader is a "self-propelled howitzer," a kind of tank. But it has a problem. First, of course, is that a weapon called "Crusader" to be used against yet another Muslim nation has a serious PR problem.

The second problem with this self-propelled howitzer is that it can't propel itself. It's so beastly heavy and corpulent that it needs a bulldozer in front of it to clear a path and dig a resting place for it.

The Crusader has fearsome high-tech plating that can fend off armor-piercing shells. Unfortunately, the same can't be said for the bulldozer in front of it. Even our toy-dazzled military knew this would pose some difficulties for our all-volunteer army.

So Congress canceled the $450 million contract for assembling them. Instead, they are paying the contractor $450 million *not* to assemble them. In budget speak, this is called, "winding down."

Now, some of us "wind down" by having a glass of wine and vegging out in front of the tube. We usually don't get half a billion to lay down our tools. But the downward winding contractor in this case is "United Defense," funded by the Carlyle Group, James Baker III, Senior Counsel. Does anyone believe Carlyle's fees to both Bush Senior and Junior had nothing to do with the lucrative kiss good-bye to their overweight howitzer?

And that's how Lockheed, General Dynamics and James Baker III are winning the War on Terror.

The Joke's on Us

Fear is the sales pitch for many products: the new zoning for the Indian casino ferry parking lot to war on the Euphrates to billion-dollar underwater sailor injectors. Better than toothpaste that makes your teeth whiter than white, this stuff will make us safer than safe. It's political junk food, the cheap filling in the flashy tube. Real security for life's dangers—from a national health insurance program to ending oil sheiks' funding of bomb-loving "charities"—would take a slice of the profits of the owning classes, the Lockheeds, the ChoicePoints and the tiny-town big shot who owns the ferry company. The War on Terror has become class war by other means.

Oh, hey, you never got the punch line.

So Osama walks into this bar, see, and George Bush says, "Whad'l'ya have, pardner?" and Osama says, "Well, George, what are you serving today?" and Bush says, "Fear," and Osama says, "Fear for everybody!" and George pours it on for the crowd. Then the presidential bartender says, "Hey, who's buying?" Osama points a thumb at the crowd sucking down their brew. "*They* are," he says—and the two of them share a quiet laugh.

Oil War ©Winston Smith 2002

CHAPTER 2

THE FLOW

Trillion Dollar Babies

The secret plans for Operation Iraqi Liberation that turned a
three-day military fling into Vietnam on the Tigris

*A five-and-a-half-part tale including Nose-Twist's Hidden Hand,
Kissinger's man in the dream palace, the No-Brainer vs. The Witches'
Brew, the other Downing Street memos, the Houston Insurgency, Amy's
alligator boots, Mr. 5%, a call to Riyadh, Wolfowitz Dämmerung and "especially the oil."*

There are kooks and cranks and conspiracy nuts out there who think
George Bush, from the moment he took office, had some kind of *secret plan* to invade Iraq and grab control of its oil. They're wrong.

There were *two* plans. I've got them both. One is 323 pages long,
the other 101 pages. How I got them, I can explain later.[5]

[5]See next page.

There are two Chalabis in this story, two Aljiburys and two confidential plans. To guide you through this Washington-Baghdad hall of mirrors, I've designed this handy timeline.

Conspiracy nuts think George Bush, from the moment he took office, had a secret plan to control Iraq's oil. They're wrong. Bush had two plans. Here they are: one crafted by neoconservatives at the Pentagon, another fashioned by the State Department and Big Oil. This is the history of the secret cold war between these two power elites, which drives the hot war on the Tigris.

July 5, 1990

James Baker III, Secretary of State to George Bush, Sr., sends Saddam a diplomatic message that the United States would wink at his invasion of Kuwait: "We have no opinion on . . . your border disagreement with Kuwait. . . . The issue is not associated with America."

February 2001: Plan A

Within a month of Bush Jr.'s first inaugural, the National Security Council and State Department convene a confab in Walnut Creek, California, to plan the invasion of Iraq. The group auditions replacement for Saddam.

Host Falah Aljibury, a top U.S. oil industry advisor on Iraq, says one plan was for "an invasion that acted like a coup . . . shut down for two or three days . . . then everything is . . . as is." "As is," especially in the oil ministry, which would retain the government oil monopoly.

December 2000–March 2001

James Baker III Institute and the Council on Foreign Relations, sponsored by Saudi Arabia, to map global energy plan. The bug in the soup: Saddam Hussein, who's jerking the oil markets, "posing a difficult situation for the U.S. . . . requiring an immediate policy review—military, energy, eco-

WAR OVER OIL IN IRAQ

nomic, diplomatic." In March, Baker-CFR group member Ken Lay and other industry chiefs meet secretly with Vice President Dick Cheney. They review this map of Iraq's oil fields.

October 2001–Feb 2003: Plan B

Emboldened by the September 11 attacks and ease of conquering Afghanistan, neo-conservatives draft their counter-plan: a yearlong occupation to re-

make Iraq into a free market miracle. The 101-page secret program becomes a Christmas tree for insider lobbyists, including Grover Norquist, who help load it with corporate goodies: copyright protection for Microsoft and Sony, and the CPP ("Comprehensive Privatization Program") to sell off "all" state assets, "especially the oil."

September 2002

The purpose of "privatizing" Iraq's oil in Plan B, "The Economy Plan," is laid out by Ari Cohen of the Heritage Foundation for neo-cons at the Pentagon: Destroy OPEC and the Saudis. Oil privatization is the key, "a nobrainer": abolish Iraq's state oil monopoly, sell their fields, ramp up production beyond the OPEC quota, destroy OPEC, crush oil prices, and bring Saudi Arabia to its knees. Plan B promoters: neo-cons Donald Rumsfeld, Paul Wolfowitz, Richard Perle, and Harold Rhode, boosters and members of the Project for a New American Century.

January 2003

State Department denies its "Future of Iraq" group discusses oil. But Bush team sends Robert Ebel, former CIA and industry oil specialist, to London to meet secretly with "Future of Iraq" leader Fadhil Chalabi to discuss post-invasion oil setup. Fadhil, like his fellow tribesman Ahmad Chalabi, wannabe potentate of Iraq, joins forces with neo-cons in plan to sell off Iraq's oil fields, break up and sell its state oil company, increase production, quit OPEC. CIA industry man Ebel tells Chalabi his numbers are "ridiculous."

March 17, 2003

President Bush broadcasts this message to Iraqi people: "Do not destroy oil wells." So begins what White House spokesman Ari Fleischer terms, "Operation Iraqi Liberation"—OIL—swiftly changed to OIF: Operation Iraqi Freedom.

March 27, 2003

Deputy Secretary of Defense Wolfowitz testifies Iraq will be free—not "free" as in democratic, but "free" as in this-won't-cost-us-a-penny. "There's a lot of money to pay for this that doesn't have to be U.S. taxpayer money," he tells Congress, contrary to the secret analysis he receives from the CIA and Department of Energy. Was it perjury?

April 21, 2003

Three-star general Jay Garner, appointed occupation chief by President Bush, is personally fired by Defense Secretary Rumsfeld. Garner had demanded swift elections and refused to sell off Iraq's oil fields; resisting the neo-con's 101-page "Plan B" cost him his job.

May 2003–June 2004

"Jerry" Bremer, Managing Director of Kissinger Associates, replaces Garner, cancels elections, and appoints a new government under the control of neo-con favorite, convicted bank swindler Ahmad Chalabi. The neo-con junta fires pro–State Department, pro-OPEC oil ministers and implements Plan B, from selling off Iraq's banks to changing copyright laws. The result: 60 percent unemployment and an "insurgency" fueled by poverty, occupation, and rumors of oil privatization.

September–October 2003

U.S. oil industry chiefs block oil field sell-off. Phil Carroll of Houston, ex-CEO of Shell Oil USA, arrives in May to take charge of Iraq's oil ministry;

tells Bremer, privately, there would be "no privatization of Iraqi oil . . . end of statement." Leaving in September, he passes control to Houston buddy Bob McKee, Chairman of a Halliburton Company and former SVP of Conoco Oil. McKee orders a bullet in the head to oil privatization: a write-up of Plan A re-establishing a state oil monopoly.

November 2003–January 2004

Amy Jaffe of the James Baker III Institute, along with oil industry experts, secretly writes up details of original "Plan A." The 323-page Options for Iraqi Oil for the State Department contains only one option: a state oil company that would "enhance [Iraq's] relationship with OPEC." Privatization and OPEC-busting are out. The neo-cons are kept in the dark about the new policy guide.

May 2004–March 2005

Dick Cheney sides with Big Oil over the neo-cons. May 20: Ahmad Chalabi sought for arrest on espionage charges; his "governing council" is shuttered, replaced with "sovereign" government headed by Baathist blessed by State Department. Pentagon favorite Bremer is booted for John Negroponte, Big Oil's friend at the State Department. Wolfowitz is removed from the

Pentagon. The Council on Foreign Relations rejoices, "The realists have defeated fantasists!" Pro-OPEC Baathists fired by Bremer and Chalabi now return to run oil ministry and establish a state oil monopoly. OPEC is saved. Oil prices bust over $50 a barrel and reserves of top five oil companies increase in value by over $2 trillion.

February 2005 and Beyond

The wheel turns again. Negroponte replaced as U.S. viceroy for Iraq by neo-con PNAC favorite Zalmay Kalilzad. Chalabi returns to power with Shi'ites, names himself temporary oil minister, fires Big Oil's favorites—but does not dare privatize oil fields or bust OPEC. Crude rises to over $60 a barrel.

PART 1

PLAN A: IN AND OUT IN THREE DAYS

Walnut Creek, February 2001

In February 2001, just three weeks after Bush and Cheney took power, Plan A was launched at a confidential gathering in Walnut Creek, California. The official justification for invading Iraq, the September 11 attack, was still seven months in the future. But let's not quibble about chronology.

Iraq Plan A was short and sweet: in and out in three days. "It was an invasion disguised as a coup," an insider—the planning group's host—told me, one of four who, when our team's knowledge of events was evident, conceded details of the program.

The "disguised coup" was simplicity itself, kind of a Marine-supported Bay of Pigs. Once the tanks crashed through the palace gate in Baghdad, they would parachute in a Ba'athist general cashiered by Saddam, a war hero—some Iraqi Eisenhower who'd beaten the Iranians in 1988—which one didn't matter. The idea was to hand the new strongman Saddam's moustache and his military-political enforcement machine—the secret group was already contacting Saddam's generals to switch allegiance. Then, according to their playbook, there would be snap elections, say within 90 days, to put a democratic halo on our chosen generalissimo.

Who launched this "disguised invasion" scheme? This will come as unhappy news to fans of Colin Powell. After the war turned ugly, the *Washington Post*'s Bob Woodward, fed with strategic leaks, told us the Secretary of State secretly opposed the invasion. That was Powell's self-serving fairy tale. Powell didn't oppose the *invasion*, he opposed *occupation*.

At the direction of Powell's State Department, Pam Quanrud, then with the National Security Counsel and now with the U.S. embassy in Moscow, organized the Walnut Creek session at the home of State's point man, Falah Aljibury. Aljibury was Ronald Reagan's and Bush Sr.'s back-channel to Saddam when Saddam was *our* Butcher of Baghdad. (In 1988, Saddam gassed Iranians on the al-Fao Peninsula, a chemical attack Reagan's intelligence apparatus made possible by providing satellite maps to Saddam.) After Saddam went renegade in 1990 and attempted to shoplift Kuwait's oil, Iraqi-born Aljibury followed the Bush family in their twist from Saddam backers to Saddam bashers. American oilmen pay Aljibury well for his intelligence on Iraq's industry. Hess Energy Trading, Bank of America and the oil-speculating arm of Goldman Sachs are all his clients.

The Three-Day Plan made some real tracks at first. Aljibury and his team even interviewed Ba'athists for the part of puppet president. Think of it as a kind of beauty contest for wannabe dictators. This "primary" was conducted under Saddam's nose with advice from top men in Iraq itself. One candidate that State and the CIA fancied was General Nizar Khazraji, Saddam's exiled army chief, then under house arrest in Denmark for war crimes. (Two days before the U.S. invasion, he disappeared from Copenhagen. Like Elvis, Khazraji has been sighted in Qatar, Kuwait, dead in Najaf and alive again in Kurdistan.)

Crucially, the quickie coup-cum-invasion had friends where it counted. "The petroleum industry, the chemical industry, the banking industry," Aljibury told me. "They'd hoped that Iraq would go for a revolution like other revolutions that have occurred in the past and government was shut down for two or three days"—just like the last one that brought Saddam to power in 1979. The U.S. oil, chemical and banking guys liked that one too, at the time.

The idea was that no matter which strongman the Bush team designated, they would "Bring him in right away and say that Iraq is being liberated—and everybody stay in office . . . *everything as is*." And by "everything" he meant, first and foremost, the key thing, the oil ministry and state oil company. While the Walnut Creek committee was busy-busy with many topics, Aljibury said, "It quickly became an oil group."

Why would Aljibury agree to speak with me? Once he knew we'd gotten word of the plan, he wanted to defend it. More than anything, he wanted us to know that the oilmen's plan would not have left us with what we have today: a tribal, shattered, blown-to-hell Iraq.

War Drums Across the Potomac

Alas, the three-day wham-bam-thank-you-ma'am revolution was not to be.

Aljibury and his NSC–State Department crew had expected neither the ferocity nor tactical brilliance of their enemy in Iraq: the Pentagon.

Iraq today, busted and bloody, is the detritus-strewn battlefield of a war between two political armies arrayed across opposite banks of the Potomac. On one side, the occupation-phobic Arabist realists at Foggy Bottom; on the other, bivouacked at the Pentagon, Defense Secretary Donald Rumsfeld, his deputy Paul Wolfowitz and former Iran-Contra convict Elliott Abrams, Special Advisor to the President, all three signers of that manifesto for benevolent empire, "Project for a New American Century" (PNAC), the neo-conservative Weltanschauung.

Unlike the wussies at State, these were real warriors, unafraid of moving toy tanks around the Pentagon War Room. Bush Security Advisor Michael Ledeen, one of the desktop Napoleons, encouraged his fellow neo-cons with this rallying cry,

> Wage a total war . . . and our children will sing great songs
> about us years from now.

It was inspiring but not original. "*Wollt ihr den totalen Krieg?*" *Do you want total war?* Joseph Goebbels asked his Nazi Party faithful in February 1943. Two years later, the total warriors of 1943 would be crushed. But in November 2001, after the easy conquest of Afghanistan, total war looked like a cakewalk, and the neo-conservatives exploited the patriotic, triumphal mood to draft their "Plan B" for Iraq.

Plan B: "Especially the Oil"

It was nothing like State's three-day quickie. The neo-cons' 101-page confidential document goes boldly where no invasion plan had gone before: the complete rewrite of the conquered state's "policies, laws and regulations." Here's a sample:

- Pages 8 & 21: A big income tax cut for Iraq's wealthiest and complete elimination of taxes on business revenues.
- Pages 35 & 73: The quick sale of Iraq's banks, bridges and water companies to foreign operators.
- Page 45: The application for Iraq to join the World Trade Organization, kindly ghostwritten by U.S. government contractors.
- Page 28: A "market-friendly" customs law—a kind of super-NAFTA—aiming for a complete wipeout of tariffs that had protected Iraq's industry from cheap foreign imports.
- Page 44: New copyright laws protecting foreign (i.e., American) software, music and drug companies

An odd list to attach to an invasion plan. It was more like a corporate takeover, except with Abrams tanks instead of junk bonds. There wasn't a whole lot of thinking going on about strengthening the borders against insurgents, disarming private armies or securing Baghdad from looters; and not a thing about elections or "democracy." Instead, there was much about securing a "market-friendly regulatory environment" and "strengthening property rights-related legislation, corporate and contract law."

The draft that came my way, in February 2003, just as our tanks were about to cross Iraq's border, has a pleasant title: "Moving the Iraqi Economy from Recovery to Sustainable Growth."

What would get "moved"? Selling off banks and bridges was just the beginning. The would-be conquistadors left nothing to chance—or to the Iraqis. At page 74, the plan's authors required Iraq to "privatize" (i.e., sell off) "*all* state-owned companies." In Iraq, that's just about everything worth having.

And it would all be open to foreign ownership. That would be convenient for Anglo-American bidders. Post-invasion, Iraqis with their just-about-worthless Saddam dinars would have nothing to bid with anyway.

All this—from the big asset sell-off to the World Trade application—would have to take longer than the State Department's three-days-slam-bam invasion plan. According to Annex D of the plan, the schedule, economic conquest would take 270 to 360 days. Logically, that would require 270 to 360 days of American boots on the ground, a year of full-scale occupation before Iraq could be given back to the Iraqis.

And certainly, this full year of occupation would be needed for the big prize targeted on page 73:

> . . . privatization, asset sales, concessions, leases and management contracts, especially those in the oil and supporting industries.

Especially the oil: complete and total sell-off of Iraq's oil assets from the pipes to the pumps to the crude in the ground.

The Plan makes it clear to me that, even if we didn't go into Iraq for the oil, we sure as hell weren't leaving without it.

Nose-Twist's Hidden Hand

The document gave off a strange odor. The weird details gave it away. *I smelled Grover Norquist.*

Norquist is the *capo di tutti capi* of lobbyists of the rich and the Right. In Washington, every Wednesday, Norquist, former lobbyist for Bill Gates and for American Express, hosts a powwow of big business political operatives, conservative media moguls, the National Rifle

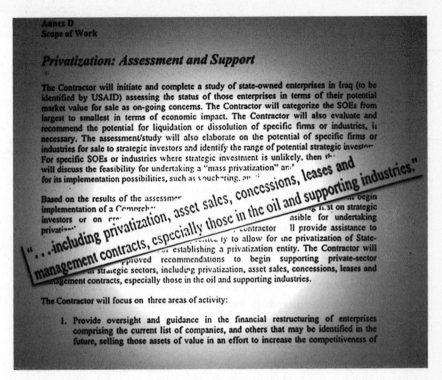

Plan B: Neo-Con's Oil Field Sell-Off

Neo-Cons planned to create a Chile on the Tigris, a free-market miracle including "privatization," i.e., the sell-off of all state-owned enterprises, "especially those in the oil and supporting industries." This is a confidential draft copy from February 2001.

Association and right-wing muscle groups. Officially, he fronts Americans for Tax Reform, a kind of trade union for billionaires (he won't name them) whose cause is a regressive "flat-tax" scheme to cap income taxes on the super-rich.

Karl Rove calls him, with admiration, "The Impresario." You could call him "Satan's lobbyist," but that would be wrong. After all, his Wednesday group includes the Lord's designated representatives, Pat Robertson's Christian Coalition. Indeed, the devout Norquist channeled nearly a million dollars from his tax group to the Alabama Christian Coalition to fight the devil's tool, legalized gambling. He didn't tell them he got the cash from an Indian tribe running a casino in Mississippi that didn't want competition in next-door Alabama. But then, the "Christians" didn't ask.

Who drafted the extraordinary "Economy Plan"? The Defense Department flat-out denied involvement, but after a week of calls, our research team (working for BBC TV London, *Rolling Stone,* and *Harper's* magazine, New York) reached a diplomat in Kazakhstan, a State Department man, who confirmed that the Pentagon had barged in on the drafting. If the Pentagon was in on it, that meant neo-cons were involved. And if neo-cons were toying with another nation's assets, Norquist was certain to be circling nearby, salivating for a taste of the asset action. I'd picked up that several likely lobbyists were hanging their balls on this Christmas tree, but the "reform" of Iraq's taxes—from soak the rich to fleece the poor—carried the unmistakable fingerprints of Norquist's soft little hands.

Acting on this scant info, I took a chance and dropped by the super-lobbyist's Washington office tower on L Street. Norquist greeted me under a huge wall-spanning photo of his idol, Richard Nixon, with the disturbing slogan, "Nixon—*NOW MORE THAN EVER.*"

With his pudgy red freckled face under a Dennis-the-Menace hairdo, Norquist looked like an oversized toddler. His rivals call him Gopher Nose-Twist, but they're just jealous of Norquist's ability to auction off access to the White House.

As Nixon's eyes followed us to his desk, Grover saw the 101-page Iraq plan in my hand and beamed. His baby! Rather than attempt to cover his involvement, he nearly autographed it. He couldn't wait, now that I was in on the secret, to boast how he'd waltzed with ease through the Pentagon, the Treasury and the State Department, busy for months before the invasion, planning Iraq's economy for the Iraqis.

In Iraq, the neo-con plan would create a private enterprise utopia in Mesopotamia. The model, said Norquist, was Chile under General Augusto Pinochet.

> Chile's low-tax free-trade property-rights model led to its
> growth . . . even though at the time it was not fully demo-
> cratic.

Not fully democratic is one way of putting it. Pinochet, a South
American Saddam Hussein, created his free-market "miracle" in 1973
after he murdered Chile's elected president and executed 3,000 dissenters. The Chile model is indeed instructive on what was in store
for Iraq. Pinochet's cronies plundered the government's assets and
drove the nation into a deep depression. But Norquist found the free-
market "deregulation" that the dictator ordered very much to his lik-
ing. Iraq, he decided, could do with a little of the Pinochet treatment.

In all fairness to the rottweiler of the radical right, the hidden plan
had an unwitting public proponent stationed within the influential
liberal *chatterati*. The *New York Times* columnist Thomas Friedman
also pumped for democracy à la Pinochet in Iraq. "Economic reform"
first, vote later, he wrote in his column. For Friedman, "economic reform" translates to privatization, asset sales and free market rigma-
role. Now that we've seized Baghdad, U.S. occupiers . . .

> . . . should not focus on holding national elections—the
> hardware of democracy. Elections should come last. In-
> stead, it must start with the software.

Software? "Free press, free speech," Friedman begins promisingly,
but, first and foremost, "*economic reform*"; which Friedman defines as
lots of deregulation and privatization.

While star columnist Friedman was motivated by his dilettante's
exuberance for economics lessons half learned, Norquist's well-heeled
backers and corporate allies would have had different motives: Undoubtedly, they would have expected something *tangible* from their investments in Washington politicians. And they got it. Through the
Economy Plan, Iraq became Pig Heaven with something for everybody
in corporate America. This was undoubtedly history's first military assault plan appended to a program for toughening the target nation's

copyright laws. This change in "intellectual property" rules suggested by Norquist means that nevermore would Iraqi Ba'athists threaten America with bootleg dubs of Britney Spears' ". . . Baby One More Time."

Wolfowitz's Gusher

Whether it's Wal-Mart or war, Americans just can't pass up a bargain. As tanks rolled toward Baghdad, Paul Wolfowitz offered America the Bargain of the Century: *a free Iraq*—not "free" in the sense of "freedom and democracy" but free in the sense of *this won't cost us a penny.*

On March 27, 2003, the Deputy Secretary of Defense testified:

> There's a lot of money to pay for this that doesn't have to be U.S. taxpayer money.

And where would these billions and billions come from?

> It starts with the assets of the Iraqi people. We're dealing with a country that can really finance its own reconstruction and relatively soon.

We could bomb them and then the wrecked nation would pay to rebuild itself—free of charge to the USA!

Now, wait a minute. The President's own Chief Economist, Larry Lindsey, had said a war in Iraq could cost $100 billion. The Bush Administration corrected Lindsey's error: He was fired.

Lindsey, apparently, didn't figure in the Black Gold. Wolfowitz, by contrast, gushed before Congress:

> The oil revenues of that country could bring between *$50 and $100 billion* over the next two or three years.

This was no small matter. The vulpine Deputy Secretary was the Bush team's salesman-in-chief for the war. For Europeans, the question of invading Iraq was a joust over whether Saddam did or did not have evil germs and nukes. U.S. Congressional debate fixed on the weightier issue, "What's this little war going to cost us?" There was no way the Senate would vote to authorize an adventure with a price tag of $100 billion.

That's when Wolfowitz made oil spring forth from the desert.

Wolfowitz said it and the sheep-o-witz press published it. The sale was made and Congress voted for Wolfowitz's invasion on the cheap.

The *Wall Street Journal* editorial page went further: The invasion would be *cheaper* than free. With the colossal oil strike Wolfowitz promised we'd find in Iraq, it stood to reason that the price of oil would *fall worldwide*. The invasion would not only be free to the U.S. taxpayer, gasoline would flow like discounted milk and honey into our SUVs. But I had some questions. Between Lindsey's calculations in September 2002, and Wolfowitz's testimony in March 2003, who discovered this massive oil windfall? Who said that Iraq could pump that much oil?

"*Nobody* ever said that," Aljibury told me, speaking of his hidden group of oil experts working with the State Department. Well, what *did* the experts tell Wolfowitz?

Looking back, it's easy to say Wolfowitz was wrong: stunningly, breathtakingly, eye-poppingly wrong. The bill for Bush's big adventure in Iraq has taken over a quarter trillion dollars from the U.S. taxpayer. Wrong is one thing. Anyone can make a mistake. But if Wolfowitz was told one thing in his ear but something else came out of his mouth, that could be perjury.

We wanted to find out what Wolfowitz had been told—the Administration's real working numbers for Iraq's potential oil production. These would have come from Guy Caruso, head of the Energy Information Administration. Caruso, a source informed us, was stunned to hear Wolfowitz's oil-gusher claims. The informer, a Saudi intelligence operative I reached by phone in Riyadh, said, "Guy Caruso, he was like '*what are they getting this from?*'"

But Caruso, who'd come to the Energy Information Administration job from the CIA, knew how to keep a secret. Caruso's little secret—that Iraq could not produce what Wolfowitz promised—was significant. Just as significant, the *Saudis*, not the U.S. Congress, knew about it. "Leading up to the war," the Riyadh source told me, "I was just giving the Saudi view on this. I was [saying], '*You gotta be joking, right?*'"

Some joke. In March 2004, I flew to Washington to ask Caruso himself about what Wolfowitz knew and when he knew it. It was Caruso's job to project those Iraq figures for the Pentagon. At his Energy Department office suite, an affable, sharp and very guarded Caruso led me through an enchanting forest of technical details—"West Texas Intermediate," "7-11 buy-back," "bandwidth"—which, when I did the arithmetic, got us less than halfway to Wolfowitz's magic $50 billion. Did Caruso give the Deputy Defense Secretary this bad news? Knowing where I was heading, he passed the buck to "my numbers man, Bob Ebel," who had performed the calculations and carried them, in confidence, to the Defense Department, Wolfowitz's warriors.

That grabbed my attention: Robert Ebel doesn't work for the government. I found Ebel at the Washington Center for Strategic and International Studies, one of those think tanks where our betters choose our wars for us. It's an ecumenical house of power worship. Its fellows include National Security Advisor Richard Allen, former Secretary of State Madeleine Albright, Nixon's chief-of-staff and Reagan-era Secretary of State Alexander Haig, and a "Henry Kissinger chair" for them to sit in funded by corporate donors. Ebel is no hands-off think-tank egghead. For eleven years, Ebel was the CIA's brain on oil. Other posts of influence followed, including fourteen years with international energy giant ENSERCH Corp.

With Caruso's unofficial approval, Ebel agreed to speak with me. He said he'd been quietly dispatched in 2002 and 2003 to London and elsewhere by the Pentagon to meet with Saddam's former Minister of oil and his "Future of Iraq Group." How odd. In September 2002, the State Department insisted to *The Washington Post* that the

U.S.-sponsored Future of Iraq Group "does not have oil on its list of issues."

State Department pronouncements notwithstanding, Ebel last met with Saddam's former oil minister Fadhil Chalabi before Wolfowitz testified. Fadhil Chalabi (not to be confused with *Ahmad* Chalabi), in frustrating exile in London, had big plans for Iraq's oil. You could read Chalabi's thoughts in a report on the target nation's petroleum industry. He sold copies for $52,000 each, with lunch and a seminar thrown in. Given Chalabi's influence over the Pentagon's team of handpicked rulers-to-be, it was an offer oil companies could not refuse.

Ebel didn't need a copy. He had clearance and access to the CIA reports showing Saddam's fields in a crippled state. Repairs and new equipment for a big new drilling push, Ebel knew, could eat up $40 billion, more than Iraq could sell in years. The get-together was less than pleasant. Ebel told Fadhil and his chums flat out that their projections of pumping three to three and a half million barrels a day out of a post-invasion Iraq were "ridiculous."

Fadhil Chalabi didn't want to hear that. There was more at stake in the big numbers than flim flamming a docile Congress. Joining Fadhil in the meeting with Ebel in London was Ibrahim Bahr al-Ulum, son of a top Iraqi sheik. He was quiet and subservient, and nodded, grinned and agreed when Fadhil spoke. The sheik's son had plans to sell off Iraq's oil fields as soon as the 82nd Airborne had them in hand. The sell-off was worth billions of dollars—maybe a *trillion* to Iraq. The wannabe rulers' trillion-dollar oil field sell-off hung precariously from Wolfowitz's phantasmagorical projections of the amount that could be pumped.

Which takes us back to our original question: Was it madly wrong or was he trying to mislead Congress? If Fadhil Chalabi's oil projections were "ridiculous," what would Ebel call Wolfowitz's testimony promising up to $100 billion in oil profits to pay for reconstruction? After our formal television interview for BBC was over, I asked Ebel, *What about the Wolfowitz numbers?*

Ebel smiled. "It was just part of the sales pitch, wasn't it?"

The sales pitch. War for sale—cheap!

You could say that one man's sales pitch is another man's perjury. If Wolfowitz had knowingly concealed the Caruso team's findings while testifying under oath, the question of perjury arises. In fact, another Bush neo-con poobah, Elliott Abrams, was convicted in 1991 of lying under oath to Congress over selling arms to Iran. But no need to worry yourself with these weighty questions. Wolfowitz can't be guilty of perjury. Since Abrams' conviction, Wolfowitz and other Bush boys *do not testify to Congress under oath.*

He did not raise his hand and swear to "tell the whole truth, so help me, God," he's off the hook. How the Lord will judge Wolfowitz's testimony, we cannot say.

PART 2

CHICAGO TAKES BAGHDAD

On March 17, 2003, President George Bush gave Saddam and his sons 48 hours to get out of Baghdad—or we were coming in to *take* him out. Like a scene from *High Noon*: forty-eight hours to get out of Dodge.

This was war. Then our President turned to the camera and said, "I'd like to speak to the Iraqi people."

They speak Arabic, but never mind, I was intrigued. I'd thought our Commander-in-Chief would say something like, "Dear people of Iraq, our kids are coming in to liberate you . . . so don't shoot them." But instead of telling Iraqis not to kill our troops, the President warned the people of Iraq:

<blockquote>Do not destroy oil wells.</blockquote>

Do not destroy oil wells.

Meanwhile, Tony Blair assured Britain's Parliament, "Our actions have nothing to do with oil or any of the other conspiracy theories put forward."

Ari Fleischer, "Operation Iraqi Liberation"

And so began what White House press spokesman Ari Fleischer called:

> Operation
> Iraqi
> Liberation

O.I.L.

Everybody loves a joke, but this was a bit too droll even for Karl Rove's spinmeisters, who barked out the new brand name for the war: *OIF! OIF!* Operation Iraqi *Freedom!*[6]

The General Toppled

But before Iraq and its oil could be liberated, there was the strongman in Baghdad to remove. On April 7, 2003, U.S. tanks broke through

---

[6]For those who dismiss the White House announcement of "O.I.L." as urban myth, check the BBC's White House archive via www.gregpalast.com/detail.cfm?artid=419&row=2

the walls of Saddam's palace and two days later pulled down his statue. That was good TV, but not Rumsfeld's real target. It wasn't until two weeks later, on April 21, that the Defense Secretary succeeded in pulling down General Jay Garner.

Only four months earlier, in January 2003, Bush appointed Garner as viceroy of soon-to-be-occupied Iraq. Garner was certainly the man for the job, known and liked among Iraqis and beloved among the Kurds for whom he acted as protector from Saddam's revenge in the year following the first Gulf War. In 1991, in just a few months, he'd turned Northern Iraq into an economically strong, relatively peaceful sovereign state. But there were questions about his record: He'd gotten along well with the old guard around Colin Powell *and* he was a registered Democrat.

The general didn't waste time in provoking the neo-con planmeisters. Just days after Bush's "do not destroy oil wells" speech, in Kuwait City, Garner, fresh off the plane from the USA, promised Iraqis they would have free and fair elections as soon as Saddam was toppled, preferably within 90 days. That was a problem. Garner's 90-days-to-democracy pledge ran into that hard object, the neo-con's Economy Plan's "Annex D." Disposing of a nation's oil industry, let alone redrafting trade and tax laws, couldn't be done in 90 days. There was no way to shorten the Norquist/neo-con schedule to transform Iraq into a Chile on the Tigris. Democracy was a problem. Even if Iraqis allowed the Pentagon to rewrite the nation's tax laws, it was utterly inconceivable that any popularly elected government would let America flog off the nation's crown jewels: its oil.

An insider working on the game plan for Iraq's oil put it coldly:

> They have Wolfowitz coming out saying it's going to be a democratic country . . . but we're going to do something that 99% of the people of Iraq wouldn't vote for.

Elections would have to wait. As Norquist explained when I asked him about "Annex D":

> The right to trade, property rights, these are not to be determined by some democratic election.

The lesson of General Pinochet's Chile was that asset sales and free markets must, Norquist said, "predate" elections.

I assumed Garner was unaware of the Pentagon plan's timetable when he made his 90-days-to-elections commitment. Not so. When we met in his Washington office a year after the invasion, Garner told me he chose to *ignore* it. He said he had other things on his mind as he crossed the Kuwaiti border. "You prevent epidemics, you start the food distribution program to prevent famine, you try to get the electricity going again."

Seizing ownership of the oil was not on Garner's must-do list, nor was Washington's rewrite of the tax laws and trade rules, and the rest of the elaborate free-market makeover scheme. In his mind, such radical legislation required a legitimate government. "My preference," the general said in his understated manner, "was to put the Iraqis in charge as soon as we can and do it in some form of elections."

Garner didn't just fall off a watermelon truck: He knew elections would mean the compost heap for the neo-con program. But he couldn't care less. "I don't think they need to go by the U.S. plan. I think that what we need to do is set an Iraqi government that represents the freely elected will of the people." He added, "It's their country . . . their oil."

Apparently, the Secretary of Defense disagreed. On April 21, the very night Garner arrived in Baghdad from Kuwait, the general received a call from Washington. It was Donald Rumsfeld. In so many words, Rummy told Garner, don't unpack, you're fired.

I should note that Garner tried to explain to me that he wasn't "fired," just "replaced." Maybe "fired" is the wrong word. Garner was not merely sacked, he was savaged with terms like "incompetent" and "hapless" by whispering sources from within the President's inner circle. The White House needed to do more than remove Garner, they needed to discredit him and his talk of Iraq for Iraqis.

"BUSH CALLS ON MIDDLE EAST TO OPEN ARMS TO DEMOC-RACY," ran the headline in *The San Francisco Chronicle* . . . but not until the oil fields change ownership.

Garner, until he agreed to appear for my British TV audience, hadn't spoken out about the problems he caused himself by confusing Bush's call for democracy with holding elections. Throughout our talk, he remained gracious toward the President and Rumsfeld; first, because the guy has class, and second, because, as Douglas MacArthur said, old soldiers never die; nowadays, they become executives of defense contractors. Garner is CEO of SYColeman, subsidiary of L-3 Communications, the hot rising defense and spyware firm. George Bush's wars (in Iraq and on terror) have juiced L-3's bottom line big time, with sales up 167% in the first four years of war.

Let's not confuse Garner with Thomas Jefferson. Like the gang at the State and Defense Departments, he had his own ideas and uses for Iraq. The military man dreamed of turning Iraq into another Philippines, the U.S. colony so useful a century ago when coal was king. He explained:

> The Philippines was in essence a coaling station for the Navy. And it allowed the U.S. navy to maintain a presence in the Pacific. It's a bad analogy, but I think we should look right now at Iraq as our coaling station in the Middle East . . . and it gives us a strategic advantage there and we ought to just accept that.

"But the privatizations," he added, "that's just one fight you don't want to take on right now."

Kissinger's Man in the Dream Palace

But that's just the fight the neo-cons wanted, and in Rumsfeld's replacement for Garner, they had just the man for the fight. Unlike Garner, Paul Bremer III had no experience on the ground in Iraq, no training to fight a guerrilla insurgency, and no background in nation-building. But he had one unbeatable credential that Garner lacked: Bremer had served as Managing Director of Kissinger and Associates.

Thirty years ago, in greenlighting the assassination of Chile's elected president, Henry Kissinger said, "The issues are too important to be left for the voters." It was a lesson in *Realpolitik* Garner missed, but it was not lost on Kissinger's protégé Bremer.

In his rush to democracy, Garner had planned what he called a "big tent" meeting of Iraq's tribal leaders to plan national elections. Garner knew these characters well and figured he had only those 90 days to keep the Sunni, Shia and Kurdish factions under the tent from slitting each other's throats. The general planned to seal a deal before a slighted group would launch an "insurgency."

Bremer knew better. In April 2003, pausing only to install himself in Saddam's old palace—and adding an extra ring of barbed wire—"Jerry" Bremer cancelled Garner's "big tent" meeting. Instead, Bremer appointed the entire government himself.

National elections, Bremer pronounced, would have to wait until 2005. The delay, incidentally, would be long enough to lock in the laws, regulations and irreversible sales of assets in accordance with the Economy Plan's timeline.

After just a month in the palace, in June 2003, Bremer ordered a halt to all municipal elections including the crucial vote about to take place for mayor of the city of Najaf. The front-runner in Najaf, moderate Asad Sultan Abu Gilal, warned, "If they don't give us freedom, what will we do? We have patience, but not for long."

Back in Washington, Garner fretted that holding off elections to promote neo-con schemes would come to no good. This was not ideological: The general's a tough old dog trained as a historian, well read in the grim story of Britain's decades-past occupation of Iraq. You don't have to give Iraq to the Iraqis but, then, as the British learned, you'd better expect them to shoot at you. Garner told me, "I'm a believer that you don't want to end the day with more enemies than you started with."

But then, what's a War President without a war? And what's a war without enemies, lots of them?

And he got them. Immediately after Najaf was denied the ballot, Garner's grim warning became reality when Najaf's patience did, as predicted, run out. Local Shias formed the "Mahdi Army" and voted with bullets. Religious leaders calmed this first insurgency, but George Bush preferred to taunt the locals. "Bring 'em on," he said.

And Iraqis responded to his call. It blew in Najaf again, when, in March 2004, a local paper, printed by the big-time sheik Moqtada al-Sadr, criticized Bremer, the sensitive CPA chief shut down its printing presses. The sheik's militia responded to this journalism faux pas by killing 21 U.S. soldiers and seizing control of the holy city for five months.

The War President had the war he wanted—just in time for the re-election battle back home.

Round-up at the Not-OK Corral

What happened to that group of Ba'athist generals and collaborators Pam Quanrud's State Department group had successfully nurtured under Saddam's nose? The Ba'athist officers had done their duty, keeping almost all of Iraq's army from resisting the U.S. invasion. When the cooperative Iraqis arrived for their reward, the Pentagon's crew had them arrested. "U.S. forces imprisoned all those we named as political leaders," said a bitter Aljibury. That raises the question: Was their crime supporting Saddam's regime or supporting the U.S. State Department team over the Pentagon?

Aljibury's main concern was that busting State Department collaborators and Ba'athist big shots was a gift to the insurgency, which thereby gained experienced military commanders, mostly Sunnis, who then had no choice but to fight the U.S.-installed regime or face arrest, ruin and maybe death.

And Bremer would make sure the insurgency would not lack for weapons or personnel. Bremer's Order Number One, "De-

Ba'athification," disbanded the army, throwing nearly half a million armed men out of work, leaving the Shia and Kurdish militias as the only local military forces.

The Pentagon neo-cons wanted total war and they were going to make sure they got it.

New World Orders 12, 37, 39 and 40

But before the blowback blew in Iraq, on September 19, 2003, Bremer, having transformed his post from occupation administrator to Pasha Omnipotent, signed orders 12, 37, 39, 40 and a blizzard of others that imposed the terms and conditions laid out in the neo-con Economy Plan.

While we often hear of the tragedy of war, or the horror of war, Bremer began each proclamation by citing, "my authority under the *usages* of war." "Usages"? It is worth a closer look at these new world orders to find out what makes war so useful.

Consider Order Number 37, "Tax Strategy for 2003." Here is Grover Norquist's dream come true, a flat tax on corporate and individual income capped at 15%. The U.S. Congress rejected a similar Norquist plan for America, but in Iraq, with an electorate of one— Jerry Bremer—the public's will was not an issue.

Most important was that Bremer's Order 37 would apply "for 2004 *and all subsequent years.*" A future government elected by Iraqis could not undo what the occupiers had commanded, not even their own nation's tax rates. The tax order, like every order, was designed so that future puppet governments would remain tangled in Bremer's strings long after his official departure.

Order Number 40, "the Bank Law," sold off Iraqi banks to three foreign financiers. This implements pages 30 to 42 of the Economy Plan. Notably, Bremer chose to announce his fiat, not in Iraq, but in Dubai, at a meeting of multinational bankers.

Bremer lauded the "extra element of competition" that would result from his piecing off Iraqi banks; but competition was ruled out of the lucrative bidding itself. The fire sale was limited to Bremer's handpicked lucky few: Hong Kong Shanghai Banking Corporation, National Bank of Kuwait and Standard Chartered Bank of London, the junior partners of JP Morgan Chase of New York. Everybody got a piece of the Iraqi bank pie—except the Iraqis.

Simultaneous to parceling out Iraq's banks, Bremer eliminated the prohibition on their charging high—"usurious"—interest rates, a sensitive issue in a Muslim nation. "This means," said Bremer, without a hint of humor, "Iraqis can enjoy modern banking and earn market rates of interest on their money."

Unfortunately, there are not many Iraqis with money to put into their new modern banks, especially after Bremer signed Order 12, "Trade Liberalization Policy." Here the free-market fanatics' dream came true, turning Iraq into the world's first large economy with no tariff protection whatsoever. No nation on the planet, except occupied Iraq, operates without tariffs (taxes on imports) or quotas (limits on imports). Free-market America wouldn't do this nor free-market Britain nor free-market Chile—for a good reason. A nation without protection is subject to "dumping" of surplus subsidized products, which would completely demolish local producers.

And that's exactly what happened in Iraq. Iraqi industry, having gone without new equipment for a decade due to sanctions, crawling back to life after the invasion, was shattered by Order 12. From candy kitchens to washing machine makers, Iraqi businesses went bankrupt.

The U.S. "shock and awe" bombing campaign left manufacturing intact, but the bombardment of foreign goods without control flattened industry. This is free trade with a bullet, and it was devastating. Kevin Danaher runs Global Exchange, a not-for-profit group trying to help Iraqis rebuild. He told me, "They were *just wiped out*. Iraqis can't compete against cheap Chinese junk dumped into Baghdad." The result, a year after "liberation," was a shocking, awful unemployment rate of 60%.

And they were hungry.

General Garner had a solution to starvation: Buy up Iraq's own harvest. This would feed the people and, just as important, keep Iraq's farmers in business and planting. But Bremer had a better idea. In Order 12, he stripped tariff protection for the nation's growers and eliminated taxes on foreign-grown food.

This was not a method for feeding the hungry; it was, rather, shock-and-awe economic therapy prescribed by the Pentagon's fanatical free-marketeers in their Economy Plan. Iraq did not need a flood of cheap imported grain. Before the wars, Iraq fed itself and was a big exporter of vegetables and fruit. Saddam-era sanctions prevented repair of irrigation pumps; cattle herds died from lack of vaccines. Instead of giving local farmers and ranchers help to repair the nation's feeding machinery per Garner's plan, Bremer crushed them with Order 12.

Not everyone felt the pain of this reckless rush to a free market. Cargill of Minneapolis, the world's largest grain merchant, flooded Iraq with hundreds of thousands of tons of wheat from both its U.S. and Australian units.

The invitation to tax-free dumping of Cargill grains into Iraq was organized by the occupation's agriculture chief, Dan Amstutz, himself an import from the USA. He was well qualified, a kind of Grover Norquist of wheat, as CEO of the North American Grain Association. Just prior to George Bush taking office, Amstutz chaired a company founded by . . . Cargill.

In May 2004, in the final days before Bremer escaped out Baghdad's back door, he took time from the burgeoning insurrection to sign a score of new orders, including numbers 81, "Patents," and 83, "Copyrights." Here, Grover Norquist's hard work once again paid off. Fifty years of royalties would now be conferred on music recordings and twenty years on Windows code.

Not all of Iraq's laws were "de-Saddamized." The dictator's prohibition on public-sector labor union activity remains with a vengeance. In December 2003, Bremer's troops *arrested the entire board* of the Iraqi Workers Federation of Trade Unions, then released them, though not until U.S. soldiers painted the union's building marquee black.

I called Falah Aljibury for his take on what was happening in his home country under the Bremer regime. Even if it was not his or Powell's "disguised coup," this new political-economic order was Aljibury's long-dreamed-of "liberation" come to life. He was the last person I expected to say, a year after the invasion, "The people are worse off today than they were before we went in." Oilman, Reagan man, maybe, but first and foremost, he is scion of the Aljibury tribe, the largest in a nation of tribes; and his million-strong "family" was reporting to him daily. They weren't sending congratulations.

> You could say that Saddam was killing them, murdering them. He was awful, he was terrible, but at least the people were living. People don't have livelihood today. You've got 15 million people without food. Does anybody care? Does anybody think if you are hungry and your children "hungry you don't care if you die? And all they tell you is "Saddam is gone." Well, thank you very much—the second day you need to eat.

Missing: A Billion and a Half in Oil

But Bremer's Governing Council feasted.

Instead of installing one of the State Department's four-star strongmen in Baghdad, Bremer chose the Pentagon's pet Iraqis for his Governing Council ("GC") that stitched together Kurdish warlords, scary sheiks and sticky-fingered ex-pats under the control of Ahmad Chalabi, a convicted bank swindler sought by Jordanian authorities. Despised but not feared, Bremer's GC could not hold power without a huge American guard.

In no time, the Oil for Food program, which had been, under the former regime, a tightly controlled conduit for kickbacks to Saddam's buddies, became, under U.S. rule, a loosely controlled conduit for *huge* kickbacks. With a nod and wink from the UN and, let's not forget, U.S. brokers who bought the stuff, Saddam skimmed $1.7 billion off the $65 billion program. This was amateur stuff, a rake-off, re-ported *The Wall Street Journal,* of only about fifty cents a barrel.

Under the new regime, "Corruption is rampant—more than ever," worse than under Saddam, one oilman complained to me, on condi-tion, as you can imagine, of anonymity. The kickbacks kicked up into higher percentages.

> It's, *"you wanna get a contract you gotta get the people who participate in it,"* so it's you know, it's direct pay-offs to Government officials, by commercial operators, who de-mand it in order to give people access to anything, whether it's oil or information.

Oil simply disappeared. During its one year in power, Bremer's Civilian Provisional Authority says Iraq's Governing Council sold $10 billion of petroleum—or maybe they sold $11.5 billion, depending on which set of reports you check. Wonder how to lose track of a bil-lion and half dollars in oil? Answer: Iraq's oil was *unmetered.*

Investigators with George Soros's Iraq Revenue Watch and Christ-ian Aid of Britain did their best to find the Iraqis' oil money, but the CPA, once it closed shop, sealed their books, which, along with the oil, disappeared.

Who pocketed the loot? Don't ask Mr. Bremer. Before he slipped out of Baghdad, he had a little trouble with CPA bookkeeping himself. We all lose an expense receipt or two on occasion, but the CPA's petty cash drawer was fatter than most. They kept $200 million *in bricks of U.S. currency* in a room in Saddam's palace and another $400 million tucked away here and there. Agents could check out these cash bricks, like library books. Unlike a library, they didn't have to return them as long as they brought receipts. One agent took $23 million in a tub of cash and returned with $6 million in receipts. Another took $25 mil-lion and returned, it appears, with nothing at all. In all, 363 *tons* of U.S. currency were shipped to Iraq. Where did the cash go?

Let's get realistic. A little grease around the edges is the norm for war. But we're not talking edges here. According to U.S. government inspectors, of the $8.8 billion spent by the Bremer "interim government," $8 billion is not properly accounted for. Ninety-six million dollars from Bremer's cash piggy bank is gone with the wind. Bremer didn't take it, but he just can't say for sure where it went. Inspectors examined 198 contracts at random and found that 148 showed no evidence that that the money paid for anything, neither work nor goods. Another test of $327 million in contracts showed payment figures off by $228 million.

Where did the money go? The Bremer-Bush regime's policy is, "Don't ask, don't tell." The interim government stonewalled international auditors. However, contract employees, nauseated by the hogs at the trough, brought claims under U.S. law, which bars war profiteering. But the CPA had a perfect defense: This isn't U.S. taxpayer money. The missing cash and the billions handed out without receipts by Bremer's crew were taken from *Iraq's* own accounts at the U.S. Federal Reserve. This was cash left over from the Oil for Food program and its successor, the "Development Fund for Iraq," made up of donations and profits from Iraq's own oil sales.

What about Iraqi law? Forget it. The money was given to the "Civilian Provisional Authority"—which isn't a U.S. agency and it's not an Iraqi agency. And now it doesn't exist. Not only are the billions gone, but so is the Authority itself. The perfect getaway car—one that simply disappears.

Not just bricks of dollars took flight. The Pentagon plan called for replacing the Iraqi money which had Saddam's smirking face on it with new "dinars." Nineteen billion in the new dinar notes (about U.S. $1.3 million) were found, mysteriously, on board a plane in Lebanon sent from Iraq by the Interior Minister of the Bremer "government."

Chicago Boys to Baghdad

Where did they find these guys?

I asked insiders how Ahmad Chalabi, a fugitive from Jordanian jailers, who hadn't set foot in Baghdad since he was a child, could have floated to the top of the neo-con list to replace Saddam.

His career as leader of Iraq was not born in Baghdad but in Chicago, where he and his two schoolmates, Paul Wolfowitz and Richard Perle, spent their sober, unyouthful days. This was the sixties. While the rest of us at the University of Chicago grew long hair and wore peace symbols, these guys had briefcases and discussed the "manly art of war" and "graduated deterrence" bombing with strange Professors Leo Strauss and Albert Wohlstetter. In other rooms, the "Chicago Boys" took lessons from Milton Friedman and his acolytes. (I joined them, surreptitiously working for the electrical and steel-workers unions, trying to figure out what the Chicago Boys were up to.) There the Chicago Boys planned for General Pinochet, the free-market-and-interim-dictatorship model that would eventually mutate into the neo-con "Economy Plan" for Iraq.

Chalabi's unwild college days with future gods of the neo-con pantheon gave him access and protection, but his power, I'm told, came from a lesser-known neo-con light: Harold Rhode.

When Bush came to power, the Arabic-speaking Rhode was strategically placed at the Pentagon's "Office of Net Assessment," one of those oddly named fulcrum points of hidden power. We now know (see "The *Other* Downing Street Memo," below) that, in 2002, the British Defense ministry told the Prime Minister Tony Blair that the Pentagon had "fixed . . . facts and intelligence" on Iraq to match George Bush's sales pitch for war. The Office of Net Assessment was one of the repair shops accused of smoothing and repainting views not conforming to the neo-con stratagem or Bush's bias. When I interviewed Bob Ebel, the former CIA oil expert, he suggested, when the cameras were off, that Net Assessment was the dream factory that produced the fantasy oil gushers for Wolfowitz.

By control of information flow, Net Assessment could allay any qualms about the people of Iraq's love of the neo-cons' anointed man, Chalabi. (However, once Chalabi took power in Baghdad, a large U.S. occupation force would be needed to ensure Iraqis' affection for him.)

Rhode is "one of those Arab-haters, Muslim-haters, *everything* haters," hissed a well-placed Saudi Arabian out to discredit him.

Rhode is no such thing. In practice, Rhode is an *OPEC*-hater. But, of course, to a Saudi, OPEC, the Organization of the Petroleum Exporting Countries, the oil monopoly, *is* everything.

Rhode, said the Saudi, saw Iraq as the weak fissure in the OPEC edifice. The right tool—Ahmad Chalabi—properly placed in the crack, could break OPEC apart. Chalabi was right for the task, a rare "Iraqi" ready to call for his nation's quitting the OPEC cartel.

And the tool was cheap as these things go, the rental already paid. The CIA and Defense Intelligence Agency, beginning in 1992, had been giving Chalabi's group, the "Iraqi National Congress," monthly stipends of typically $335,000 per month. The "Iraqi National Congress" was neither in Iraq nor a Congress, but with CIA pay stub in hand, Chicago ties, and the neo-con plan in his pocket, Chalabi made himself a government in exile. The convict, still on the run from Jordanian police, opened Iraq for business even before he arrived there. In late 2002, Ahmad Chalabi met privately with executives from three big U.S. oil companies. With his fellow tribesman, Fadhil Chalabi (in London), Ahmad Chalabi was hot to sell off Iraq's oil fields—in accordance with page 73 of the neo-con Economy Plan. We only know of the secret meeting because British Petroleum screamed bloody murder over being left out of Chalabi's sale-a-thon.

The aim of the neo-con Chicago Boys was for Chalabi to get Iraq out of OPEC, or at least bust its quotas. But before he could be used to destroy OPEC, Chalabi, who hadn't lived in Iraq for four decades, had to get back in—and quickly, before the State Department put others in power. On April 6, 2003, two weeks after U.S. motorized cavalry sped through southern Iraq, when enemy fire would not ruin the photo-op, Chalabi landed at Nasariyah at the head of a "liberation" force of 700 Iraqi exiles. They had secretly trained for the mission in Hungary. Saddam, whose intelligence agents had likely infiltrated the group, would have known they were coming. Nevertheless, I'm told, the invasion force realized its goal: The State Department, kept in the dark about the Pentagon's airlift of Chalabi's army, was taken completely by surprise.

A BRIEF HISTORY OF GULF WARS
ONE THROUGH SIX

The *Other* Downing Street Memo

In the "Downing Street Memo," top-secret meeting minutes (secret no more), Britain's Prime Minister was told in July 2002, eight months before the invasion, that "the facts and intelligence were being fixed" for President Bush to justify his plan to attack Iraq.

It would also be useful to review *other* memos to the Prime Minister at No. 10 Downing Street written by military diplomats on the ground. One wrote:

> The people of England have been led in Iraq into a trap from which it will be hard to escape with dignity and honour. They have been tricked into it by a steady withholding of information. The Baghdad communiqués are belated, insincere, incomplete. Things have been far worse than we have been told, our administration more bloody and inefficient than the public knows. It is a disgrace to our record, and may soon be too inflamed for any ordinary cure. We are today not far from a disaster.

The Prime Minister did not ignore the missive. He responded, after Fallujah was retaken:

> You do not need to bother too much about the long term future in Iraq. Your immediate task is to get a friendly Government set up in Baghdad.

The diplomat, in this case, was T. E. Lawrence—"Lawrence of Arabia"—and the Prime Minister, Winston Churchill (words actually written years later, after Fallujah was captured in 1941).

A hyperventilated tour of history is in order here.

In 1920, the Kurds were gassed. But you can't blame Saddam for this one. It was Churchill, who'd suggested a scientific study:

> I am strongly in favor of using poisoned gas against unciv-
> ilized tribes to spread a lively terror . . . against recalcitrant
> Arabs as an experiment.

The Royal Air Force thought Churchill squeamish—the politician wanted to paralyze Iraqis, not kill them. The RAF ran their own experiment, initiating what may be history's first-ever mass aerial assault, killing 9,000 Iraqis with 97 tons of bombs, a kill-to-munitions ratio not matched until Gulf War 5 ("Desert Storm") in 1991, when U.S. and British high-level carpet bombing of lines of refugees from Basra killed thousands of Shias. (An odd favor for Saddam who thought there were too many Shias anyway.) Of course, in 1920, Churchill had a right to be angry at the ungrateful Middle Eastern nation: He'd just invented Iraq the year before in a deal with the French.

That happy event occurred in 1919, when, as Air and War Minister, Churchill argued the next world war would be fought with airplanes. That would require air bases and airplane fuel. So Iraq was born, as the "coaling station" for the new Royal Air Force—General Garner's scheme was not an original—sewn together from three large potential oil fields at Kirkuk-Mosul, at Baghdad and at Basra. Two years later, in 1921, the British crowned a Saudi Arabian, Faisal I, as King of Iraq, a place he'd never seen. (At least, when the Americans repeated British precedent, the Pentagon chose a leader, Mr. Chalabi, who had at least *visited* Iraq's Kurdish zone seven years earlier.)

Pundits today say Churchill's design showed his ignorance of the centripetal ethnic conflicts inherent in this amalgam. Far from it. A maker of history but also a student of it, Churchill would have realized this arrangement suited war's needs well. A hopeless and hapless mix of Kurds (Kirkuk), Shias (Basra) and Sunnis (Baghdad) could be counted on to cut each other's throats before they would join together to challenge their colonial authority.

Lawrence of Arabia warned the Brits that they would reap the whirlwind by promising Iraqis freedom then holding them as an oil colony—but he died too young to see his jeremiads come true. That would happen in 1941, when Rashid Ali, a nasty little man with a moustache, seized power to become dictator, hoping to win his place in the hearts of Muslims worldwide by supporting the Palestinian cause. But the Palestinian cause also became Hitler's cause and the Palestinian leader, the Mufti of Jerusalem, taking sanctuary in Baghdad, was soon wooing Iraqi strongman Ali toward a deal to supply oil to the Nazi's New World Order then arriving by Panzer division through southern Russia.

Churchill countered by ordering a landing at Basra. (In 2003, the U.S. military assigned the Brits to take Basra once again, further proof that Americans have a sense neither of history nor of irony.) The Brits of '41 crushed the Iraqi army within weeks at Fallujah, then took Baghdad with just a couple of tanks, and set up a Governing Council. Hitler's Russian assault ran out of gas, literally.

As to Churchill's "ignorance" in 1919 in further dividing Kurdish lands among several ad hoc states, that is an unlikely charge against an accomplished historian. He knew the Kurds well. It was a Kurd, Salah al-Din Yusuf ibn Ayyub ("Saladin"), who defeated the Crusaders (including "Ivanhoe") at Jerusalem in 1187. The lesson is nearly a thousand years old, but Brits never forgot that an armed and independent Kurdish state is a dangerous state.[7] It is true that the Kurds are among the world's sad peoples who remain stateless in a land in which they are a homogeneous majority. But it should be noted that the Kurds created Kurdistan by driving away or murdering others within a sword's length. Much is said about the Turkish massacre of a million and a half Armenians in 1915, the twentieth century's first of many genocides. In fact, while it was the Ottoman Turkish military that directed the killings, the Turks merely had to arm the Kurds, who merrily completed the job of slaughtering Armenians and taking their homes. It's a fine tradition of ethnic cleansing

---

[7]In 2005, all appears forgiven. Iraq's new President, Jalal Talabani, the Kurdish warlord/lawyer, assented to a no-bid no-cost deal for analyzing extraction from the Qaiyarah field in Kurdistan to *Ivanhoe Energy*.

the Kurds continue today in a free Iraq, ridding Kirkuk of its Turkmen minority.

The Kurds' mass murder of Armenians would not have disturbed Churchill per se, but he could not ignore the fact the Kurds committed the atrocities at the command of Britain's enemy (the Ottomans). In the gentleman's great game of empire, this could not go unanswered. One can imagine Winston, border-cutting scalpel in hand, inspired by his fourth brandy, placing the blade at the heart of Kurdistan and thinking, *Your turn.*

Gulf War Six

It seems the British attitude toward Iraq is, *it's a nice place to conquer, but not a place you'd want to occupy.* For America, the invasion of 2003 was Gulf War Two. For the United Kingdom, this was Gulf War *Six.* And we're not counting the itsy-bitsy interventions or proxy wars—nor the Crusades, though Muslims would *certainly* count them. For Britain, this is a history gone and forgotten; for Americans, a history not learned in the first place.

1916–18   Gulf War 1: War of Independence from Ottoman Empire instigated by "Lawrence of Arabia."

1920   Gulf War 2: War of Independence from British Empire. Crushed when UK bombs Kurds and Arabs.

1941   Gulf War 3: Reconquest of Iraq by British Empire. British invasion overthrows Iraqi/Palestinian allies of Hitler.

1956   Gulf War 4: Suez "Crisis." Canal retaken.

1991   Gulf War 5: Desert Storm.

2003   Gulf War 6: Operation Iraqi Liberation.

____?   Gulf War 7:_____

PART 3

THE WAR FOR OPEC: THE NO-BRAINERS VERSUS THE WITCHES BREW

"Was the invasion about the oil?" Bob Ebel asked himself, anticipating my question. "No," he answered himself, "it was about getting rid of Saddam Hussein."

Then why did the Pentagon fly him to London?

"The morning *after*, it's about oil."

But *what* about the oil?

Here's what I found. It's not the oil itself—the United States could have doubled our take from Iraq simply by lifting sanctions. It's all about George Bush's seat on OPEC. That is the real, if never discussed, booty of this war.

But what George Bush should *do* with his OPEC perch is what requires the occupation to drag on, not the provincial tussle between Shias and Sunnis, but the gladiatorial fight to the death between neocons and the Big Oil establishment.

This was The Prize: Through the new captive state of Iraq, the power to control or destroy OPEC, the Organization of Petroleum Exporting Countries, the elite club that sets oil's price.

And it all began with Ari Cohen.

The Godfather of Plan B

"It's a no-brainer," Cohen told me of his grand design to divide and sell Iraq's entire oil industry. Cohen operates from the Heritage Foundation, the madrassa of neo-con fundamentalism in Washington, DC. For the neo-cons, this was The Big One. Long before the State Department dreamed of the three-day coup, long before George Bush "won" Florida in 2000, Cohen and his neo-comrades at the Heritage Foundation and American Enterprise Institute had big plans for the Middle East. Their true target was *not* Saddam. He was just a troublesome *nudnik* whose replacement would provide the hunting blind to shoot at bigger game: the Saudi Arabians. Getting at the Saudis required tearing apart OPEC. And tearing apart OPEC was completely dependent on the privatization of Iraq's oil reserves, the second-largest in OPEC after the Saudis.

A year before the invasion, Cohen laid out his scheme for an OPEC-free world in a report for Kim Holmes, the Heritage chief, who took it inside the Bush Administration when Holmes became an Assistant Secretary of State. It included the neo-cons' call for a "massive . . . privatization of State-owned enterprises, especially the restructuring and privatization of the oil sector." There it is: "especially the oil"— Cohen's words which would be sucked in, virtually unedited, in the Economy Plan which Defense would attempt to shove down General Garner's throat.

Details of Cohen's talks with Bush insiders remain confidential, but Ari considers his theories too brilliant to keep under wraps. He explained the no-brainer to me in baby steps.

1. OPEC's power comes from imposing production limits ("quotas") on its member states, limiting supply and raising prices.
2. Iraq's quota is well below what it can produce. Iraq kept a limit on output through its 100% government-owned oil monopoly ("SOMO," the State Oil Marketing Organization).
3. If you sell off Iraq's oil fields in itty-bitty pieces, dozens of operators will maximize their production from each field, jumping up Iraq's output to 6 million barrels a day, way above the OPEC quota.
4. The additional two million barrels of oil a day from Iraq will flood the market, OPEC will dissolve into mass cheating and break apart. With every nation pumping to the max, the price of oil will fall over a cliff, and . . .
5. . . . Saudi Arabia, financially and politically, will fall to its knees.

And there were additional bonuses to privatizing oil fields in Iraq, Cohen told me. Taking away oil revenues from the Shia clerics who will certainly take over Iraq will deny them "the cash cow for the project of forced Islamization." There was more. With OPEC smashed, the former Soviet states, including Russia, completely dependent on oil income, will be at America's mercy.

But, on the way to Iraq's new government implementing Cohen's no-brainer, something went wrong. Bremer had marched through Iraq's economy like Sherman marching through Georgia, issuing his 100 orders while Iraqis bowed and cowed. Yet, one part of the neo-con Economy Plan seemed forgotten: Page 73, the no-brainer, the privatization, the total sell-off of Iraq's oil fields.

So what happened, Ari? Who undermined your plan? I spoke to Cohen in his small, dim office at Heritage. For a man with a plan to shake the economic planet, his station seemed a bit diminished. In a dark Russian accent, Cohen hissed the names of the saboteurs.

> *Arab economists* hired by the State Department who are supporting the *witches' brew* of the Saudi royal family and the Soviet *ostblock*.

("Ostblock" is the Cold War name for the Soviet sphere of influence. Neither the *Ostblock* nor the Soviet Union still exist—except, in Cohen's mind, in the machinations of Russia's President Vladimir Putin.)

Ari, exactly *which* Arab economists were in on the conspiracy?

You know who they are, he answered.

And I did. One Saudi in the shadows had to be Nawaf Obaid. However, to label Obaid simply "an economist" would be, as our President says, to "misunderestimate" him.

If your prejudices lead you to expect Saudi princelings to sound like they just fell off a camel, Obaid would take you by surprise. The urbane, savvy graduate of Harvard and MIT jets between homes in Riyadh and London, has a seat at Bob Ebel's elite think tank in Washington and his post with the Saudi National Security Assessment Project. He's less a power in his own right than the semaphore holder who signals what the landlords of our oil supply are thinking. "He works for Saudi intelligence," said a very close associate of his who gave me Obaid's cell phone number in Saudi Arabia.

Obaid agreed that Ari Cohen and the neo-cons' bust-OPEC scheme was a no-brainer. It came, he said, from the other end of their thinking system.

> From the Saudi perspective we're, like, they're just crazy talking out of their asses again.

The Saudi was unimpressed with Ari's five steps to an end to Saudi Arabia's authority.

> The neo-cons [say] "you smash OPEC you smash Saudi Arabia's power," and yeah, they're going to use Iraq to do it. Yeah, we were baffled, you know, *Ramp up production! Break all the quota!*" . . . This is crazy.

Interestingly, Obaid knew in detail about the initial 2001 State Department plan for a three-day "disguised coup" and the meetings convened in Walnut Creek. He could recite details of the ins and outs of State's fight against the neo-cons' OPEC-smashing scheme and, as well, the inside story of Chalabi's surprise "invasion" at Nasiriyah.

I asked the Saudi, What's so crazy about smashing OPEC? Why was he so confident the neo-cons were talking through their blowholes?

Obaid explained the oil facts of life. In the short term, Iraq's fields were trashed even before saboteurs torched them. The CIA and the Pentagon knew it no matter what Wolfowitz said to bobble-headed Congressmen. In the long run, however, many years from now, Iraq, with 114 billion barrels of proven reserves, might be able to crank up above its OPEC quota.

But that won't happen. The globe is littered with the economic skeletons of nations that flagrantly busted their OPEC quotas. There's the skeleton of Venezuela. In 1973, Venezuela broke the first Arab oil boycott. But in 1997, when Venezuela again ramped up production, punishment was swift. Saudi Arabia, which can live without big oil revenues for up to a year, opened its spigots and drowned the market. The price of oil dropped to $8 a barrel and Venezuela went bankrupt. Its government fell. The current President of that nation, Hugo Chávez, is now a very good member of OPEC, indeed its most fanatic adherent to the quota system.

The Soviet Union was also given a price-cut whupping. In the 1980s, the Saudis dropped the price of oil to punish Russia for its wild expansion of oil-pumping capacity and for the Soviets' invading Muslim Afghanistan. This choking loss of oil income had a lot more to do with the Soviet Union's collapse than Ronald Reagan's crooked smile.

Saudi Arabia has kept its economic knife sharp for Iraq if, under neo-con influence, Iraq were to exceed its OPEC quota. The war-stoked jump in oil prices put $120 billion in Saudi Arabia's treasury in just one year (2004), triple its normal take. This gives the kingdom the cash to hold its breath economically should it need to drop the price of oil for a year to bring Iraq, or any quota-busting nation, to its knees.

Besides, said Obaid, why should President Bush allow troublemakers at the Pentagon to use Iraq to attack the House of Saud when the Saudi royals were so supportive of Mr. Bush's goals?

The Saudis just want to be helpful. In December 2002, for example, Obaid wrote publicly to assure the Bush administration that, while Saudi Arabia could not officially support a U.S. invasion of another Muslim country (Iraq), the Saudis would pump enough oil to hold down prices once U.S. tanks rolled.

But that was just cheese for the trap. Admittedly, in early 2003, just before the invasion, the Saudis, for the first time in memory, pumped flat out, providing nearly 12 million barrels a day. But once American forces were irreversibly committed and Iraq's pipelines in flames, the price of oil rose and the Saudis kicked it higher by withholding more than a million barrels a day from the market. The one-year 121% post-invasion jump in the price of crude, from under $30 a barrel to over $60, sucked that $120 billion windfall to the Saudis from SUV drivers and factory owners in the West. The OECD, which measures these things, estimates the U.S. economy lost 1.2% of GDP, costing the USA just over one million jobs. The harm to Africa and Asia was many times higher.

You'd think our President, as consumer-in-chief of the infidel world, would say something to Crown Prince (now King) Abdullah about the worldwide economic devastation caused by high oil prices when the Saudi monarch visited Mr. Bush at the Crawford ranch in April 2005. The newspapers show they held hands, they scooted around in our President's golf cart (Mr. Bush seems to have an aversion to horses) and the Prince left with a smile—then kicked up the price of crude another two dollars.

Maybe Mr. Bush has his own reasons to be grateful to the prince. I wasn't in the golf cart but I know this: The only other time in the past decade the Saudis have produced flat out to bring down the price of oil was just before the 2004 U.S. presidential election.

OPEC, Big Oil and the Trillion-Dollar War Bonus

But neither our President's affection for Abdullah, Saudi threats, nor the "witches' brew" of Saudi economists and Russia-lovers at the State Department could have stopped Cohen's "privatization" plan, i.e., the sale of Iraq's oil fields, if the U.S. petroleum industry wanted those spoils of war. However, the *last* thing the oil companies wanted was ownership of Iraq's reserves, especially if it would lead, as the neo-cons hoped, to the destruction of OPEC.

It has been a very good war for Big Oil—courtesy of OPEC price hikes. The five oil giants saw profits rise from $34 billion in 2002 to $81 billion in 2004, year two of Iraq's "transition to democracy." But this tsunami of black ink was nothing compared to the wave of $120 billion in profits to come in 2006: $15.6 billion for Conoco, $17.1 billion for Chevron and the Mother of All Earnings, Exxon's $39.5 billion.

For these record-busting earnings, the industry could thank General

Tommy Franks and the troops in Baghdad, the insurgents and their oil-supply-cutting explosives. But, most of all, they had to thank OPEC and the Saudis for keeping the lid on supply even as the planet screamed in pain for crude.

And the industry was not going to let neo-con think tank fantasists kill the OPEC goose that laid the golden earnings. When OPEC raises the price of crude, Big Oil makes out big time. The oil majors are not simply passive resellers of OPEC production. In OPEC nations, they have "profit sharing agreements" (PSAs) that give the companies a direct slice of the higher price charged. More important, the industry has its own reserves whose value is attached, like a suckerfish, to OPEC's price targets. Here's a statistic you won't see on Army recruitment posters: The rise in the price of oil after the first three years of the war boosted the value of the reserves of ExxonMobil Oil alone by just over $666 billion. The devil is in the details.

Smaller Chevron Oil, where Condoleezza Rice had served as a

Increase in value of reserves since the onset of war in Iraq.

director, gained a quarter trillion dollars in value. Chevron named a tanker after Rice, but given the firm's change in fortunes once she became National Security Advisor and then Secretary of State, they should rename the *whole fleet* in her honor. Altogether, I calculate that the top five oil operators saw their reserves rise in value by over $2.363 trillion. There is, however, a threat on the horizon: If the neocons get their way in Iraq and use it to smash OPEC, the treasure ships will sink fast.

The Houston Insurgency

On May 1, 2003, our President landed on the deck of the aircraft carrier *Lincoln* and announced "mission accomplished." But that very week, the Insurgency was about to launch its counterattack. For the powers that be, this was the *real* insurgency, not the sore-headed Sunnis with their homemade Humvee busters, troublesome yet manageable, but the angry oilmen of Texas rising up against the occupation of the White House by the East Coast neo-con clique.

As the Heritage Foundation crowd and the Wolfowitz gang were to learn, the Oil Establishment can be toyed with, but never disarmed. In the first week of May, a formidable weapon was loaded aboard a jet in Houston and, after a stop in Washington, transferred to the hold of a C-17 cargo airship for the long haul to Baghdad: Philip Carroll, former CEO of Shell Oil USA, who was deployed immediately. Wheeled off the airship by his military escort, Carroll met new occupation chief Bremer, who was, at that moment, in accordance with the neo-con blueprint, in a frenzy selling off every Iraqi government asset not bolted down (and many that were).

Carroll is an oil executive cast for an Oliver Stone film. Six foot plus and ramrod straight, with a full head of white hair and a soft Texas drawl that is gracious, ruthless, commanding and final. If there were any questions about his authority, it should be noted that besides heading Shell Oil, he'd also been CEO of Fluor Corporation, the biggest contractor in Iraq after Bechtel and Halliburton.

The double-CEO laid down the law to Bremer. Carroll told me: Neo-con plan be damned, *"I was very clear that there was to be no privatization of Iraqi oil resources or facilities while I was involved. End of statement."* Furthermore, Carroll would permit no "De-Ba'athification" purge in "his" ministry—oil.

The diminutive Bremer did not have the political testosterone to reply that, on paper, it was *Bremer's* ministry and as chieftain of the Provisional Authority, Bremer, not Carroll, was in charge. But Bremer understood that in the Great Game, a well-placed pawn, even one who used to play Kissinger's game, does not overrule a knight of the oil industry. Carroll's orders stood.

His veto of Bremer's "De-Ba'athification" diktat at the oil ministry was an industry demand. In particular, Carroll energized a political-protection force field around Thamir Ghadbhan, oil minister, and Mohammad al-Jiburi, head of the State Oil Marketing Organization, SOMO. They both had unparalleled experience drilling and selling Iraq's oil, albeit for Saddam, and in those posts had made good friends with all the right Texans. Furthermore, they'd been anointed to take charge of Iraq's oil operations by the State Department's "Walnut Creek" invasion-planning crew as far back as 2001. True, they had been Ba'athists, but they knew how to move crude. Shell Oil and the rest of the industry were comfortable with these technicians who could serve democrats or dictators alike with cold efficiency. Bremer and the neo-cons would not be allowed to mess with the order determined by the industry.

I heard about Carroll's ultimatums to Bremer from Carroll himself. I flew to meet the super-executive in March 2005 at his private office, a simple suite that topped a dull building looking out on the mindless Houston skyline. (I suppose God's punishment for men with too much oil is that they have to live in Texas.) Carroll chatted propped against a tastefully modest desk decorated with one unshowy photo of the Shell chief with Prime Minister Margaret Thatcher.

What about privatization, Ari Cohen's "no-brainer"—couldn't that ultimately bring down OPEC? He said:

I would agree with that statement, that privatization is a no-brainer. It would only be thought about by someone with no brain.

What about the neo-con think-tankers with their plan to use Iraq to bust OPEC?

I guess if you're in a think tank you have to think sometimes, not always clearly.

You could get to like this guy.

But I thought it worth noting to him that oil companies are, after all, capitalist enterprises. Don't they have an affinity for private ownership over government?

"Many neo-conservatives have certain ideological beliefs about markets and democracy and this, that and the other. International oil companies," he explained coolly, "without exception, *don't have a theology, they don't have a doctrine.*"

There's a certain attractiveness to amoral avarice: In war zones, the greedy are the peacemakers.

After six months in Baghdad, Carroll, his main task done—defending the ministry's Ba'athists from neo-cons, repairing the pipes and cutting the heart out of "privatization"—returned to America. Staying would have meant the loss of the lucrative corporate board seats he'd taken leave of. First things first.

Bremer, it seems, couldn't wait to wave good-bye. The CPA chieftain may have saluted Carroll to his face, but as soon as Carroll turned his back, Bremer stuck in the knife. As Carroll's exit jet pulled up its wheels, Bremer allowed Ahmad Chalabi to demote Carroll's man Ghadbhan and to fire al-Jiburi. Al-Jiburi went into exile in Westchester, New York.

(Bremer must have grinned. But his turn would come. Within months, Bremer himself would be fired and his favored Iraqi, Chalabi, ordered arrested. But let's not get ahead of the story.)

Carroll had turned over his oil ministry babysitting job to a Houston buddy, Rob McKee, who'd been with ConocoPhillips Petroleum. Conoco gave him an unforgettable good-bye kiss: McKee picked up a $26 million paycheck in his departing year. That wasn't, it seems, quite enough for McKee. Unlike Carroll, he wasn't going to jeopardize his corporate ties over silly conflict-of-interest concerns: All through his tenure in Baghdad as shadow minister of Iraq's oil, McKee maintained his post as Chairman of Enventure, a subsidiary of Halliburton Corporation.

Ahab of Arabia

But while the cats were away, Chalabi could play. As Carroll departed and before McKee landed, Chalabi turned the oil ministry over to Ibrahim Bahr al-Ulum, a small-time petroleum engineer trained in New Mexico. A puzzled *Wall Street Journal* headlined, "Iraq Council Taps Obscure Engineer As Oil Minister." Obscure to the *Journal* maybe, but not to those on the inside of the game. A "nothing" in the industry, Falah Aljibury told me, but Bahr al-Ulum's daddy was a big "something": Muhammed Bahr al-Ulum, one of the rotating presidents of the Governing Council and a Shia cleric with powers not to be messed with. Even more important, the younger Bahr al-Ulum, you may recall, was the quiet one sitting at Fadhil Chalabi's knee in the pre-war London meeting with Bush emissary Bob Ebel, the ex-CIA man.

Let's return to those prewar London meetings and Fadhil Chalabi. To rate a long-distance journey by Bush emissary Ebel, Fadhil Chalabi had to be someone special. He was in many ways more important than his fellow tribesman and ally, Ahmad Chalabi, the "Chicago" boy. Fadhil Chalabi was not only Saddam's former oil minister but, more important, former Secretary General of OPEC. Yet, while perched at this, the top job at the oil industry's peak, the Iraqi seethed. Fadhil Chalabi was sick with jealousy over Saudi Arabia. "OPEC is Saudi Arabia" is a phrase I've heard from a dozen oilmen. The Saudis alone set each nation's oil production quota by brute authority of Saudi Arabia's cash reserves. The Saudis had, since OPEC's birth, assigned Iraq, despite its massive oil deposits, a humiliatingly small quota exactly equal to that of the despised Shia of Iran. Supposedly, this Iran-Iraq equality would prevent war between the two nations. It didn't. But the low quota did keep Iraq from full access to its petro-wealth and the political power that comes with it.

Fadhil Chalabi left OPEC dreaming and scheming of an Iraq producing not just six million barrels a day (the neo-con hope) but *twelve* million barrels a day, exactly one million more than Saudi Arabia's eleven. That would restore Iraq to its rightful place at the very top of the world of oil, dictating to the Saudis.

Possessed by this vision, Fadhil Chalabi is to OPEC as Captain Ahab was to Moby Dick: he would conquer it or kill it. And he certainly knew where to begin: by privatizing the oil fields of Iraq, then opening the spigots wide. And for that, he had U.S. troops, neo-con patronage and now, his protégé, the "nothing," Ibrahim al-Ulum, ready to carry it out.

Swinging between the political arms of the two Chalabis, with a push from his father, the younger al-Ulum swung into place as oil minister, positioned to carry out, knowingly or not, the grandiose dreams of his mentor Fadhil Chalabi as well as the best-laid plans of Harold Rhode and the neo-conservatives. For a "nothing," al-Ulum was doing pretty well for himself.

But immediately, there was trouble. The Americanized al-Ulum loved to talk to the western press. He began gabbing about his grand plans from the neo-con playbook. "Iraqi oil needs privatization," he said. But, he added, that raised some "cultural" issues for Iraqis.

That was an understatement, to say the least. When word of al-Ulum's plan to sell off the nation's patrimony hit the street, all hell broke loose, literally. Falah Aljibury told me:

> We saw an increase in the bombing of oil facilities and pipelines on the premise that privatization is coming. In-

surgents and those who want to destabilize Iraq have used this, saying, *"Look, you're losing your country, you're losing all your resources to a bunch of wealthy people; a bunch of billionaires want to take you over and make your life miserable, and the means to live for your children are going to be taken away from you."*

(The godfather of privatization, Ari Cohen, suspected Iraqis might get a bit testy when his theories were implemented. Prudently, for in-country work, he told me in his Russian grammar, "I left other people to get their ass to get shot off.")

The Conoco/Halliburton executive McKee arrived in Baghdad from Houston in October 2003 to find pipelines on fire, explosions every day. Under al-Ulum's amateur supervision, sabotage and corruption vied for supremacy, though they often combined: In the Northern zone, tribes that lost bids for Bremer's pipeline security contracts showed their displeasure by blowing up the pipes.

Enough was enough. Oil privatization needed a bullet to the head and, the month he arrived, McKee ordered the hit.

McKee's Bullet: The Secret Return of Plan A

Given that Ahmad Chalabi's neo-con influenced crew of grasping privatizers had run amok in Iraq's oil ministry, it was time for the adults in the game to put the State Department and oil industry plan, a state-run oil company, into writing. McKee ordered up a detailed blueprint to hand the ministry that would lay out for Iraq exactly what should be done with Iraq's oil.

The industry drafting party would take place in Houston in November and December 2003. No Iraqis would be invited. Oil would remain a state enterprise whose output would dance to the tune of Saudi OPEC quotas.

Proving this new document existed, getting a copy of it and the

Tribes of Iraq, Tribes of America

Six of the main Iraqi characters in this story share but three names: Ahmad and Fadhil Chalabi, wealthy exiled leaders of the invasion and their allies, the al-Ulums, and the oil industry spear-carriers, Mohammad al-Jiburi and Falah Aljibury (same name in Arabic, spelled differently in English).

Don't let the melding of names confuse you. In fact, the common names are a key to understanding the tribal roots of Iraqi politics (and Iraqi gunfire). While you've heard much about religious differences among Iraqis (Sunni, Shia and Kurd), that's *nothing* compared to tribal affiliation.

In Iraq, tribal rivalries are as deep as tribal rivalries in Washington—the Neo-con Nation, for example, versus the Big Oil tribesmen. To keep the players clear, here is a chart of tribal affiliations and their creeds:

ALJIBURY / AL-JIBURI CLAN	CHALABI / AL-ULUM CLAN
State Dept. Clan	Defense Dept.–Pentagon Clan
The "Witches' Brew"	The "No-Brainers"
Big Oil	Neo-cons
State-owned oil	Privatized oil
Drill less oil	Drill more oil
OPEC supporters	OPEC smashers
323-page "Oil Options" plan A	101-page "Economy Plan" B
3-day "disguised coup"	Long-term occupation
"Everything as is"	Total makeover
Council on Foreign Relations	Heritage Foundation
James A. Baker III Institute	Project New American Century
Backed by Dick Cheney	Backed by Dick Cheney

story behind it became a close-to-pathological obsession for our investigations team in New York and London.[8]

Under the Freedom of Information Act, you'd think Americans would have a right to the economic schemes that our generals carried into war. But since regime change in Washington in 2001, documentation has been neither free nor informative. The State Department, the Treasury Department and the Defense Department took us on a six-month journey through national security Kafka-land. At first they stone-cold denied the Iraq Oil Plan ever existed.

We couldn't track McKee, so we turned to Ed Morse. Morse is little known to the public, but he's one of the men to whom Washington looks for the winks and nods that indicate the wishes and wisdom of Big Oil. When he's not tidying up policy for the Bush team, Morse, executive advisor to Hess Energy Trading, is raising money for Democrats. He was fielding as many as six phone calls a day from the administration for guidance on Iraq. The calls began more than a year before the invasion. Morse held the formidable title of Chairman of the Council on Foreign Relations–James A. Baker III Institute Joint Committee on Petroleum Security.

Morse sneers at "the obsession of neo-conservative writers on ways to undermine OPEC." It may be a cute idea to smash the Arab oil cartel, he said, but Iraqis know that if they start pumping six million barrels a day, two million above their OPEC quota, they will "crash the oil market" and bring down their own economy.

And McKee of Conoco Oil knew it too. Installed in one of Saddam's former palaces, McKee never lost sight of his Houston roots; and he was not going to let neo-con ideologues bring down the international petroleum industry. "Rob was very promotive of putting in place a really strong national oil company," Morse told me. McKee's industry was fed up with the damage to the petroleum

---

[8]Special thanks to investigator Leni von Eckardt, her best selection of British accents and her preference for documentation over sleep.

flow caused by the neo-cons playing get-the-Saudis in Iraq's oil patch. Privatization was out of the question. Morse would say no more.[9]

Our big break came when I reached Amy Jaffe, first in Amsterdam, then at her lair at James A. Baker's think tank in Houston. I dropped Ed Morse's name and others, and Amy convinced herself I had authority to know about McKee's request for a blueprint for Iraq's oil, its secret drafters, contents and directives to the occupied nation—and I saw no reason to disabuse her of this misimpression. Besides, if America has a government of the people and by the people, then I, presumably one of the people, should have a copy of the Oil Plan if Jim Baker gets one.[10] Governments don't keep secrets to protect the public, but to deceive the public.

I asked Amy what her draft was called: I wanted to know if it was the same as mine. In fact, I didn't have the title, nor the document, and I didn't know if it even existed. Politely, Amy gave it away: *Options for a Sustainable Iraqi Oil Industry*.

Once we were able to confront the State Department with the exact title and authorship, coupled with a threat of legal action, the official keepers of the Bush administration's secrets relented. On July 1, 2004, State finally handed over *Options for a Sustainable Iraqi Oil Industry*.

On the cover, the plans carry the byline of a consultant contractor, BearingPoint. The substantive designers of the strategy had modestly removed their names. The Washington, DC, consulting firm's logo stayed on the cover, but it was crafted in Houston, under the tutelage of oil industry experts—including, we discovered, Donald Hertz-

[9]Why would Morse tell me these things? He says he *didn't*—and his lawyers threatened to sue *Harper's* magazine over my oil wars dispatches. He never spoke to me, he said, and if he did, I misquoted him. Did I speak with Morse? Let's just say I've transcribed accurately from my undisclosed recorder. Have a nice day, Ed ☺.

[10]In all fairness, I should note Amy says I've misrepresented her words—and I'm certain I have not. And just to make sure, I kept my recorder on. I hadn't mentioned that to her, and the law says I don't have to. If that seems a bit rude, I apologize.

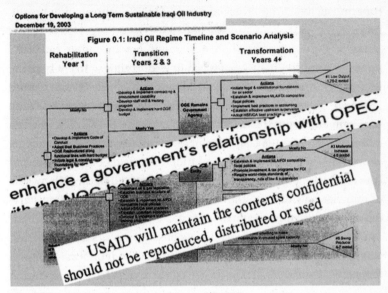

Options for Developing a Long Term Sustainable Iraqi Oil Industry
December 19, 2003

Figure 0.1: Iraqi Oil Regime Timeline and Scenario Analysis

Big Oil's Plan for Enhancing OPEC

This confidential plan, written for State Department consultants by a group from the James Baker Institute that included oil company executives, promotes a state-owned oil company for Iraq to "enhance [Iraq's] government's relationship with OPEC."

mark, an advisor to the Indonesia state oil company, and Garfield Miller of Aegis Energy, advisors to Solomon Smith Barney, all hosted by Jaffe at the James A. Baker III Institute.

"Contents Confidential": Big Oil's Plan on Paper

The 323-page multi-volume *Options for Oil* document begins with the expected dungeons-and-dragons warning:

> The report is submitted on the understanding that [the State Department] will maintain the contents confidential.

The Iraqis will have a choice of seven options for their oil—all of them the same: seven flavors of state-owned oil companies. Not one

"option" included the Pentagon's page 73 OPEC-threatening privatization.

OPEC-busting privatization was simply not an option; but that's
not to say that the Iraqis would be allowed to choose freely from the
options given. Iraqis were warned away from the Saudi Arabia
"Aramco" model. Aramco used to be known as the "Arab-American
Oil Company" until the House of Saud expropriated the U.S. share in
1980. Today, notes the *Options* paper with disapproval, no infidels are
allowed to own any part of the production fields on holy property
(the oil fields). Big Oil will not let that be repeated in the unholy land
of Iraq. Such an attempt, the oil consultants warn, will result in starving Iraq of investment capital.

Instead of the Saudi model, the *Options* crew touts the happy outcome in the "Stans," the old Soviet Central Asian republics, as a good
model for Iraq.

> *Countries with less attractive geology and governance, such
> as Azerbaijan, have been able to partially overcome their risk
> profile and attract billions of dollars of investment by offer-
> ing a contractual balance of commercial interests with the
> risk contract.*

Translation: Azerbaijan's looney tunes dictator demands exorbitant
kickbacks for the crap oil he sells from a bad location; however, he
has brought in the big money from big oil by serving up his nation's
resources in sweetheart deals.

The Stans (Kazakhstan, Uzbekistan, Turkmenistan, Kyrgyzstan)
knew how to make their fields seductive to Big Oil via Profit Sharing
Agreements (PSAs). Through PSAs, Western oil giants possess and
suck up oil fields without the untidy bother of seizing official ownership. National governments hold nominal titles to their fields,
which mollifies the patriotic citizenry; but the actual pumping and
piping of the crude, for an appropriate share of the take, is handed
over to what the paper calls "IOCs," the international oil companies.

But what is an "appropriate" share for the IOCs? (Note there are no

"LOCs" or local oil companies.) There's the happy case of Kazakhstan, which obtained more foreign investment in oil than any other former Soviet state, notes the *Options* report with favor. In 1996, the nation received a quick $120 million in the first sale of a production share to an outfit called "Hurricane Hydrocarbons." Not mentioned in the report is that, in 2005, Hurricane flipped its share to the Chinese government for $4.2 *billion*—a 35,000% gain. The Kazakh people got none of it. Mobil Oil (now ExxonMobil) also bought a share of the Kazakhstan action after, it seems, the company's broker bought a share of President Nursultan Nazarbaev. About half of Mobil's $51 million payment to the "broker" ended up, according to Justice Department papers, in the Swiss accounts of the president and oil minister. ExxonMobil says it acted "in an ethical manner," unaware of where its money ended up. ("Ethical" may have a special meaning in the oil industry.) The broker's defense is noteworthy: In 2006, his lawyers asserted that he was "working for . . . United States government agencies."

But woe to Iraq should it make its fields available for "profit sharing" with U.S. companies on terms less favorable than the lubricated deals with Kazakhstan and Azerbaijan. The *Options* committee has a stern warning against attempting to squeeze IOC profits:

> Countries that do not offer risk-adjusted rates of return equal to or above other nations will be unlikely to achieve significant levels of investment regardless of the richness of their geology.

In other words, give it up like Azerbaijan or eat your oil.

OPEC Enhanced

But the Iraqis know that. They know about the consequences of "inadequate regard for the risk borne by IOC contractors." Don't give IOCs fat "profit shares" and they walk. Iraqis don't need a report from Houston to tell them that. Inclusion of the point in the report was just an unfriendly reminder. The teeth and guts of the *Options* is focused on one directive: ensuring Iraq would establish an absolute government monopoly on oil exports. Why were the standard bearers of Western capitalism, Texas oilmen, so insistent on Iraq creating a state-owned national monopoly? On page 15, they get to the point:

> A single state-owned company . . . *enhances a government's relationship with OPEC.*

"Enhances a government's relationship with OPEC"? You can enhance your relationship with your wife with flowers, your children with affection and your God with prayer. But how does a government enhance its relationship with an oil cartel by creating a state-owned oil monopoly? Just one way: Only through the unique power of government monopoly can a nation hold back production to the OPEC quota.

U.S. oil majors get very excited when they see an OPEC member "enhance its relationship" with the cartel, and for good reason. The latest enhancement doubled OPEC's benchmark price for crude—which also doubled the price Exxon and its comrades may charge for crude pumped *from Texas and Alaska*, not just from Saudi Arabia. OPEC's 2006 prices produce a windfall of approximately $48 billion a year from sales of oil produced in the U.S. Altogether, the windfall for oil companies taken from U.S. customers totaled $305 billion over prewar prices in the first three years since "Mission Accomplished." "Enhancing" OPEC, then, strikes one as an odd recommendation for a U.S. policy guide. But then, the report was supposed to be confidential; and it was born and bred at James A. Baker's institute.

Rodeo Day and No Ideology

The James A. Baker III Institute is constructed a bit like a church or mosque, with a large echoing rotunda under a dome at its center, encircled by memorabilia and photos of the Great Man himself with the world's leaders, about evenly split between dictators and democrats. And there is the obligatory shot of a smiling Nelson Mandela shaking Baker III's hand. (Mandela is not so impolite as to remind Jim that he was Reagan's Chief of Staff when Reagan coddled the regime that kept Mandela imprisoned.)

For tax purposes, it's an educational institute, and looking through the alarm-protected display cases along the wall was unquestionably an education. You could virtually write the recommendations of the *Options for Iraqi Oil* report by a careful inspection of the trinkets of Baker's travels among the powerful.

There is the golden royal robe given Baker by Kazakh strongman Nazerbaev, the one who shared in the $51 million payment from ExxonMobil—a James A. Baker client—and alongside it a jeweled sword with a note from Nazerbaev, "Jim, there will always be a slice for you." (I made that up.)

Who is this James A. Baker III that he rates a whole institute, and one that will tell Iraq its oil future? Just some highlights:

- In 1990, as Secretary of State to Bush Sr., Baker sent a message to Saddam Hussein giving him the go-ahead to invade Kuwait.
- When Bush Sr. was unemployed, Baker found the ex-President work as an arms dealer. Baker found a job for Junior, too, before *he* entered the Oval Office.
- When fifteen Saudi Arabians flew airliners into American buildings, their victims' families sued the kingdom's Defense Ministry for indirectly buying the tickets for the terrorists. James A. Baker's was the first law firm in the courthouse . . . for the Saudis.
- And, not least, as Baker himself bragged in describing his fancy legal work for the Republican party after the 2000 vote, he fixed the election for George Bush in Florida—as Bush's lawyer. (See "The Best Little Legal Whorehouse in Texas," page 136.)

When I arrived in Houston, the planet-spanning man himself was away from his institute, doubtless at his other office at 1600

Pennsylvania Avenue. That's correct. You may be wondering how a lawyer for a foreign government gets his own desk next to the President's—as far as I know, it's never happened before. How it happened is worth a short chapter by itself, attached at the end of this one. (See "The Best Little Legal Whorehouse in Texas.")

No matter. Baker wouldn't soil himself with the details I needed. I was looking for the anonymous authors of Iraq's oil *Options*. When, after a year of schmoozing, I met one of the designers of Iraq's future, I found in Amy Jaffe a preppy, talky Jewish girl with a Bronx accent like a dentist's drill who, stranded in a cowboy world, poignantly wanted to be one of The Boys. She thinks she can accomplish this through fashion accoutrements—she showed me her alligator cowboy boots and rolled her eyes—"for *Rodeo* Day!" Lucky for me and my recorder, she did not learn from Baker and the boys Rule #1 for rulers: *Shut up.*

Who was anointed to tell Iraq its "options"? Besides the notable exclusion of Iraqis in drafting their fate, the usual neo-con experts were let nowhere near the report. I met Amy in March 2005, after my meeting with Ari Cohen at Heritage in Washington. Cohen already knew his neo-con team was slipping, "The Bush administration is on the brink of snatching defeat from victory," he told me, but he could lay these unfortunate events only to his "witches' brew" of Saudis and their State Department quislings. When I asked Cohen about the James A. Baker group's report he was clearly stunned by its existence and stung by his exclusion.

As to excluding Ari Cohen, Amy had already told me, "He's never been in the fucking oil industry and he doesn't know anything about the oil industry." The *Oil Options* group was no place for neo-con think-tank theorists. This was the real thing, laying out the real oil program for Iraq and putting it in the safe hands of a coterie of "consultants to the industry and retired oil company executives" and technicians.

I asked her about Big Oil's concern that neo-con plans for a sell-off of oil fields would fail to "enhance" OPEC. Amy added that U.S. oil companies also had a practical concern about privatization: They could get cut out of the action.

> There is no question that an American oil company or *any* [foreign] oil company wouldn't be enthusiastic about a plan that would make it so that they're going to privatize all the assets in Iraq with Iraqi companies and they [the IOCs] *might get left out of the transaction.*

So "left out" is something Big Oil isn't used to. If Bush leaves it to the Iraqis to vote on terms of a sell-off, the Iraqis might be foolishly tempted to keep the oil fields for themselves.

A bigger-than-life portrait of Baker III glowered down, but Amy continued on. I was picking up from her that democracy could get out of control. Western oil companies want to cut deals to drill in Iraq, but

> Under a democratic, privatized system, with private Iraqi oil companies, that might not have happened.

ExxonMobil and friends went through one big privatization and they didn't like it at all:

> I mean, why would American oil companies want to go through the same thing like they went through in Russia? They invested *billions* of dollars and have had their assets either stolen or diverted.

I see: Privatize the Iraqi fields, and it will be Russia Part 2, with cronies of our hand-picked regime sucking up the assets, with the big international players sliced out of the game. Nor did the Iraqis like how their oil ministry was run in the early days after the U.S. invasion:

> They don't want it to have it be that just five people are stealing all the money and giving out awards . . .

Big Oil didn't like pay-to-play. In fact, under U.S. law, they couldn't.

Where does bringing democracy to Iraq come into the picture? For the oil companies, it doesn't seem to.

> It's in the interest of the Western oil companies to have a *stable* government.

I thought of the Chairman of Entergy Corporation, the global power company, who said of investing in Peru, "They've got a good stable situation there, sort of a benevolent dictator, which means good, responsible leadership."

Not that the neo-cons are Jeffersonian democrats. As to Ari Cohen's plans for privatization, which the James Baker Institute crew totally excluded from their list of recommendations, she noted, "You have a country of 22 million people who believe the central government should control all the oil assets." Jaffe's the insider who complained to me about Wolfowitz shouting for democracy in Iraq while shoving privatization down their throats, "something that 99% of the people of Iraq wouldn't vote for."

Her own preference? She echoed Phil Carroll's allergy to ideologies:

> I'm working for James A. Baker [a Republican] and I used to work for Ed Morse [a Democrat]. . . . So whatever it is I'm telling you, I am telling you because I think it is right and *there's no ideology behind it.*

I didn't see in the *Options* report any option but forms of state-owned oil monopolies. As Jaffe had observed in our interview, however, lowering prices is not necessarily their objective.

> I'm not sure that if I'm the chairman of an American oil company and you put me on a lie detector test, I would say that higher oil prices are bad for me or my company.

But if you were the chairman of an oil company, Amy, you *would never* be put on a lie detector.

PART 4

JERKS, EUROS, THE HUBBERT HUMBUG AND MR. 5%

Why *Did* Saddam Have to Go?

It was a fine chat with Amy, but I still didn't have an answer to the question that was just driving me crazy, *what* about the oil? Why did the oil industry promote an invasion of Iraq to get rid of Saddam?

The question is basic but the answer is not at all obvious.

We know the neo-cons' answer: The ultimate target of their invasion was Saudi Arabia, which would be cut low by a Free Iraq's busting the OPEC oil cartel. But Big Oil wouldn't let that happen. The neo-cons' privatization scheme ended up an unnoted smear under Amy's alligator boot heels.

The Texas-Washington axis of authority wanted Iraq to stay a good member of OPEC and not overproduce. Saddam, under U.N. restrictions, couldn't bust his OPEC quota. So why get rid of him?

I tested several theories from both Left and Right. There was the "Euro" theory, as in, *Bush ordered up the invasion because Saddam threatened to switch oil sales from dollars to euros.*

Oh, *please.*

The goin'-euro theory, an Internet special, just won't die. *George Bush,* not Saddam, has been doing his best to push the dollar under the euro, and he succeeded (see "The Network" chapter for reasons why). There would be no point in Bush taking out Saddam for his boosting the President's own goal of devaluing the dollar.

The leading candidate for Cheney's reason to get Saddam: *We need Iraq's oil* and Bush and Blair sent us into Iraq to get it. In its most sophisticated form, this is the "Peaking Oil" theory. It's compelling, it's based on expert authority (the calculations of a top oil geologist, M. King Hubbert) and it's thoroughly wrong. However, before we learn what the oilmen were telling Dick Cheney in private as the reasons

Saddam had to go, we really should take a look at the theory that we went into Iraq to get its oil. A ride up "Hubbert's Peak" will allow a clearer view of the real topic of this chapter: the geo-politics of petroleum.

No Peaking: The Hubbert Humbug

On March 7, 1956, geologist M. King Hubbert presented a research paper that would, a half century later, become the New Gospel of Internet Economics, the Missing Link that would Explain It All from the September 11 attack to the invasion of Iraq.

In his 1956 paper, Hubbert wrote:

> On the basis of the present estimates of the ultimate re-
> serves of world petroleum and natural gas, it appears that
> the culmination of world production of these products
> should occur within a half a century [i.e., by 2006].

So get in your Hummer and take your last drive, Clive. Sometime during 2006, we will have used up every last drop of crude oil on the planet. We're not talking "decline" in oil from a production "peak," we're talking *completely gone*, kaput, dead out of crude—and not enough natural gas left to roast a weenie.

In his 1956 treatise, Hubbert wrote that Planet Earth could produce not a drop more than one and a quarter trillion barrels of crude:

> We obtain a figure of about 1250 billion barrels for the ul-
> timate potential reserves of crude oil of the whole world.

That's the entire supply of crude that stingy Mother Nature bequeathed for human use from Adam to the end of civilization. Indeed, our oil-lusting world consumed, by the end of 2006, about 1.2 trillion barrels of oil. Therefore, by Hubbert's calculation, we're finished; maybe in the very week you read this book we'll suck the planet dry. Then, as Porky Pig says, "That's all, folks!"

But the pig ain't sung yet. Planes still fly, lovers still cry and smogo-saurus SUVs still choke the LA freeway. Why aren't our gas tanks dry? Hubbert insisted Arabia could produce no more than 375 billion barrels of oil. Yet, Middle Eastern oil reserves *remaining* today total 734 billion barrels. And those are "proven" reserves—known and measured, not including the possibility of a single new oil strike or field extension. Worldwide, ready-to-go reserves total 1.189 *trillion* barrels—and that excludes the world's two biggest untapped fields, which could easily double the world reserve. (One is in Iraq, the other we'll get to in Chapter 4.)

In all fairness to the Hubbert Heads, there's a more sophisticated, updated version of Hubbert's theory. This is where the "peak" concept comes in. In this version of the Hubbert scripture, we ignore his dead-wrong prediction of total crude available and look only at the up-and-down shape of his curve, the "peak." The amount of oil discovered each year, Hubbert posited, will stop rising by 2000, then will crash rapidly toward zero when we will have used up our allotted 1.25 trillion barrels.

We haven't crashed or even peaked. Oil production has risen year after year after year and discoveries have more than kept pace. Nevertheless, like believers undaunted by the failure of alien spaceships to take them to Mars on the date predicted, Peak enthusiasts keep moving the date of oil apocalypse further into the future. In the new, revisionist models of Hubbert's prediction, the high point in the curve of discoverable oil on our planet will come in a decade or so. Though we have a reprieve, goes the new theory, still, *We're running out of crude, dude!* There's only another twenty years left in proven reserves! Oh, my!

"It's true that there's only twenty years' supply left—and that's been true for the last hundred years," Lewis Lapham told me over a decent sauterne at Five Points. (He more often sups at Elaine's, but I don't rate that.) Lapham of *Harper's* magazine is the only editor in the hemisphere with hard knowledge of the petroleum market, insight he inherited legitimately: His family helped found Texaco, now part of Chevron.

He asked, Why in the world would oil companies, or any company, announce that there's lots of its product out there? You'd bust your own market. It's better to say the cupboard's bare. As Lapham noted, we have been "running out of oil" since the days we drained it from whales.

OPEC's big headache before the war shut down Iraq's fields was that there was way *too much* oil. We were swimming in it and oil prices stayed low. The *last* thing oil companies want is more oil from Iraq, any more than soybean farmers want more soybeans from Iraq. Increasing supply means decreasing price.

This war is about the oil, but *what* about the oil? The Hubbert Peaksters think they know. They are convinced that Dick Cheney in his bunker is panicked that the world's supply of oil is about to run out, and so to Iraq we go, to seize the last of it. Here's the flaw in that argument: To believe that George Bush and Dick Cheney hustled us into Iraq to open up that nation's untapped bounty of petroleum is to believe that these two oil Texans in the White House are deeply troubled that the price of oil will rise unless they get us more crude. But Dick and George get a rise out of the rise.

Have we peaked? The planet is producing today twice as much as the maximum predicted in 1956 by the "Peaking Man." But the political use of *holy-shit-we're-running-out-of-oil!* has yet to peak.

Indeed, Bush and Cheney are more than happy to allow others to promote Hubbert Peak hysteria in the public. "We need Iraq's oil" is used as a good bogeyman to get the public behind an invasion that promises to get Americans a fill-up for the family gas guzzler for less than a hundred dollars. Anti-war progressives seized on the Hubbert humbug as proof that Bush's invasion was a war of "Blood for Oil." Nuns, professors and rock stars were outraged. But the average American thinks, *Blood for oil? That's a BARGAIN*.

The Shell Game

Hubbert's predictions may have been astonishingly wrong but his little forty-page research report is, nevertheless, astonishingly important in understanding the mindset of Big Oil.

Almost everything you need to know about Hubbert and the agenda behind his crucial 1956 study is contained on its cover page. The oil doomsday pronouncement is "Publication No. 95, Shell Development Company, Houston, Texas." Hubbert was the chief Consultant on general geology for Shell Oil and his "end of oil" paper was presented to the Texas meeting of the American Petroleum Institute. All else flows therefrom.

Every once in a while the landlords of the planet have to remind us to be grateful for their services. In 1956 it was Shell Oil's turn and Hubbert was their man for the job. It was not a happy time for the oilmen of Texas. Shell and the other Seven Sisters, as Big Oil was then known, faced a heck of a problem: crude was cheaper than dirt—$2.77 a barrel, that is, a nickel a gallon—and sinking. Worse, they were finding more of the stuff all over the planet, meaning prices would fall further.

In March of that year, Hubbert presented the solution to his fellow oilmen at the API in Houston. He unveiled this magical

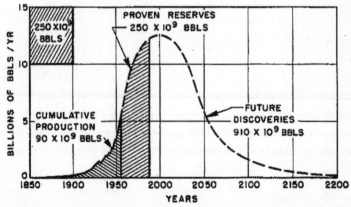

Hubbert's "Peak" Note: The *total* sum of oil is 1,250 billion barrels—which ran out in 2006. (This chart by Hubbert assumed a lower annual burn of oil than has occurred.)

chart, which I reproduce here in its original form as a public service:

Look closely. When Hubbert spoke, oil reserves worldwide were zooming heavenward. Despite the tide of petroleum rising around us, Hubbert declared that oil discoveries in the USA had begun to peak "as recently as 1951 or 1952" and that the world's reserves would follow not long thereafter. He didn't need to wink. His oil industry audience understood what oil giant Shell wanted America to believe: Oil isn't abundant, it's *a scarce commodity* and therefore . . .

1. *It's too cheap—so oil companies should, for the public's own good, raise the* **price** *to conserve this precious resource.*
2. *We need to find an abundant* **alternative** *to fossil fuel.*
3. *We need to protect our* **access** *to dwindling sources of crude, by force if necessary.*

Shell Oil, through Hubbert, sought, successfully, to change the way America thought of oil's price, alternatives to oil and access to oil.

PRICE: The problem of falling oil prices was solved for Shell, brilliantly, in four years, in 1960, by the creation of OPEC. On paper, OPEC was created by national governments. If oil *companies* had created this cartel to fix prices, that would have made it a criminal conspiracy—cartels are illegal. But when *governments* conspire for the same purpose, the illegal conspiracy turns into a legitimate "alliance" of sovereign states. OPEC's government cover makes the price-fixing perfectly legal, and Big Oil reaps the rewards.

ALTERNATIVES: As to replacing fossil fuels, Hubbert had the answer: limitless nuclear power. His 1956 paper is *not* called "Peak Oil." Its title is "Nuclear Energy and the Fossil Fuels." His let's-go-nuclear chart, call it "Hubbert's Plateau," is usually ignored. I'll reproduce it here opposite.

Note that Hubbert envisions a high, flat plateau of nuclear energy outstripping fossil fuels by the twenty-first century, providing us a comfy, electric economy for *five thousand years*. Hubbert's *Uranium Reich* was longer than anything the Führer could have imagined. Who would supply all this nuclear fuel? Lucky for us that Hubbert's

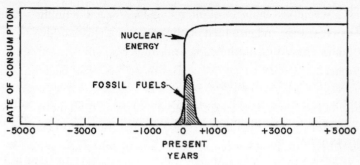

Hubbert's Plateau

company, Royal Dutch Shell, was about to announce the formation of its new mega-venture, "URENCO," a uranium enrichment consortium.

ACCESS: Protecting our access to petroleum, a "peaking" resource, was Shell Oil's urgent message. Hubbert's paper was published in June 1956, not long after the CIA overthrew Iran's Prime Minister Mohammed Mossadegh for having nationalized Shell's and BP's assets. The paper was released just one month before Gamal Abdel Nasser, Egypt's President, seized the Suez Canal, the oil tanker passageway, and just months before a British-French-Israeli invasion force took it back. Hubbert's Peak thinking helped provide a justification for war over this "strategic resource."

Have we peaked? Worldwide oil reserves continue to rise even faster than America and China can burn it. Since 1980, reserves, despite our binge-guzzling, have risen from 648 billion to 1.2 trillion barrels. Yet, weirdly, despite the rising flood of discovered crude, its price quadrupled between 2001 and 2005. Supply choked, yet there's no peak in sight. Behind this slow in the flow of crude:

- This bit of bother in OPEC's second-largest reserve (Iraq);
- Russian president Putin's cutting off financing to, then his seizing of, Russian producer Yukos Oil, reducing its output;

- U.S.-promoted sabotage of oil piping, loading and refining systems in Venezuela; and, not least of all,
- the Saudis sitting on their spigots.

The oil squeeze tightened after the Bush Administration, beginning with the energy bill of 2001, abandoned conservation and encouraged a monstrous jump of two million barrels a day in U.S. oil consumption.

So please *don't slander Mother Earth* and say she's run out of oil when it's man-made mischief to blame. Evil, not geology, has a chokehold on energy; nature is ready to give us crude at $12 a barrel where it was just a few short years ago.

Mr. 5% and the Red-Lining of Iraq's Reserves

World oil production today stands at more than twice the 15-billion-a-year maximum projected by Shell Oil in 1956—and reserves are climbing at a faster clip yet.

That leaves the question, Why this war? Did Dick Cheney send us in to seize the last dwindling supplies? Unlikely. Our world's petroleum reserves have doubled in just twenty-five years—and it is in Shell's and the rest of the industry's interest that this doubling *doesn't happen again*. The neo-cons were hell-bent on raising Iraq's oil production. Big Oil's interest was in *suppressing* production, that is, keeping Iraq to its OPEC quota or less. This raises the question, Did the petroleum industry, which had a direct, if hidden, hand, in promoting invasion, cheerlead for a takeover of Iraq to *prevent* overproduction? It wouldn't be the first time.

If oil is what we're looking for, there are, indeed, extra helpings in Iraq. On paper, Iraq, at 112 billion proven barrels, has the second largest reserves in OPEC after Saudi Arabia. That does not make Saudi Arabia happy. Even more important is that Iraq has fewer than three thousand operating wells . . . compared to *one million* in Texas. That makes the Saudis even unhappier. It would take a decade or more, but start drilling in Iraq and its reserves will about double, bringing it within gallons of Saudi Arabia's own gargantuan pool. Should Iraq drill on that scale, the total, when combined with the Saudis', will drown the oil market. That wouldn't make the Texans too happy either.

So Fadhil Chalabi's plan for Iraq to pump 12 million barrels a day, a million more than Saudi Arabia, is not, to use Bob Ebel's terminology, "ridiculous" from a raw resource view, it is ridiculous *politically*. It would never be permitted. An international industry policy of suppressing Iraqi oil production has been in place since 1927.

We need again to visit that imp called "history."

It began with a character known as "Mr. 5%"—Calouste Gulbenkian—who, in 1925, slicked King Faisal, neophyte ruler of the country recently created by Churchill, into giving Gulbenkian's "Iraq Petroleum Company" (IPC) exclusive rights to all of Iraq's oil. Gulbenkian flipped 95% of his concession to a combine of western oil giants: Anglo-Persian, Royal Dutch Shell, CFP of France, and the Standard Oil trust companies (now ExxonMobil and its "sisters.") The remaining slice Calouste kept for himself—hence, "Mr. 5%."

The oil majors had a better use for Iraq's oil than drilling it—*not* drilling it. The oil bigs had bought Iraq's concession to seal it up and keep it off the market. To please his buyers' wishes, Mr. 5% spread out a big map of the Middle East on the floor of a hotel room in Belgium and drew a thick red line around the gulf oil fields, centered on Iraq. All the oil company executives, gathered in the hotel room, signed their name on the red line—vowing not to drill, except as a group, within the red-lined zone. No one, therefore, had an incentive to cheat and take red-lined oil. All of Iraq's oil, sequestered by all, was locked in, and all signers would enjoy a lift in worldwide prices.

Anglo-Persian, now British Petroleum (BP), would pump almost all its oil, reasonably, from Persia (Iran). Later, the Standard Oil combine, renamed the Arabian-American Oil Company (Aramco), would limit almost all its drilling to Saudi Arabia. Anglo-Persian (BP) had begun pulling oil from Kirkuk, Iraq, in 1927 and, in accordance with the Red-Line Agreement, shared its Kirkuk and Basra fields with its IPC group—and drilled no more.

The following was written three decades ago:

> Although its original concession of March 14, 1925, covered all of Iraq, the Iraq Petroleum Co., under the ownership of BP (23.75%), Shell (23.75%), CFP [of France] (23.75%), Exxon (11.85%), Mobil (11.85%), and [Calouste] Gulbenkian (5.0%), limited its production to fields constituting only one-half of 1 percent of the country's total area. During the Great Depression, the world was awash with oil and greater output from Iraq would simply have driven the price down to even lower levels.[11]

Plus ça change . . .

When the British Foreign Office fretted that locking up oil would stoke local nationalist anger, BP-IPC agreed privately to pretend to drill lots of wells, but make them absurdly shallow and place them where, wrote a company manager, "there was no danger of striking oil."

This systematic suppression of Iraq's production, begun in 1927, has never ceased. In the early 1960s, Iraq's frustration with the British-led oil consortium's failure to pump pushed the nation to cancel the BP-Shell-Exxon concession and seize the oil fields. Britain was ready to strangle Baghdad, but a cooler, wiser man in the White House, John F. Kennedy, told the Brits to back off. President Kennedy refused to call Iraq's seizure an "expropriation" akin to Castro's seizure of U.S.-owned banana plantations. Kennedy's view was that Anglo-American companies had it coming to them because they had refused to honor their legal commitment to drill.

But the freedom Kennedy offered the Iraqis to drill their own oil to

[11]John M. Blair, *The Control of Oil* (New York: Pantheon, 1976).

the maximum was swiftly taken away from them by their Arab brethren. The OPEC cartel, controlled by Saudi Arabia, capped Iraq's production at a sum equal to Iran's, though the Iranian reserves are far smaller than Iraq's. The excuse for this quota equality between Iraq and Iran was to prevent war between them. It didn't.

To keep Iraq's Ba'athists from complaining about the limits, Saudi Arabia simply bought off the leaders by funding Saddam's war against Iran and giving the dictator $7 billion for his "Islamic bomb" program.

In 1974, a U.S. politician broke the *omerta* over the suppression of Iraq's oil production. It was during the Arab oil embargo that Senator Edmund Muskie revealed a secret intelligence report of "fantastic" reserves of oil in Iraq undeveloped because U.S. oil companies refused to add pipeline capacity. Muskie, who'd just lost a bid for the Presidency, was dubbed a "loser" and ignored.

The Iranian bombing of the Basra fields (1980–88) put a new kink in Iraq's oil production.

Iraq's frustration under production limits explodes periodically. In August 1990, Kuwait's craven siphoning of border-land oil fields jointly owned with Iraq gave Saddam the excuse to take Kuwait's share. Here was Saddam's opportunity to increase Iraq's OPEC quota by taking Kuwait's (most assuredly *not* approved by the U.S.). Saddam's plan backfired. The Basra oil fields not crippled by Iran were demolished in 1991 by American B-52s.

Saddam's petro-military overreach into Kuwait gave the West the authority for a more direct oil suppression method called the "Sanctions" program, later changed to "Oil for Food." Now we get to the *real* reason for the U.N. embargo on Iraqi oil exports. According to the official U.S. position:

> Sanctions were critical to preventing Iraq from acquiring equipment that could be used to reconstitute banned weapons of mass destruction (WMD) programs.[12]

---

[12]"Report for Congress, Iraq: Oil-for-Food Program, International Sanctions, and Illicit Trade," September 26, 2002, Code RL30472.

A History of Oil in Iraq
Suppressing It, Not Pumping It

1925–28   "Mr. 5%" sells his monopoly on Iraq's oil to British Petroleum and Exxon, who sign a "Red-Line Agreement" vowing not to compete by drilling independently in Iraq.

1948   Red-Line Agreement ended, replaced by oil combines' "dog in the manger" strategy—taking control of fields, then capping production—drilling shallow holes where "there was no danger of striking oil."

1961   OPEC, founded the year before, places quotas on Iraq's exports equal to Iran's, locking in suppression policy.

1980–88   Iran-Iraq War. Iran destroys Basra fields. Iraq cannot meet OPEC quota.

1991   Desert Storm. Anglo-American bombings cut production.

1991–2003   United Nations Oil embargo (zero legal exports) followed by Oil-for-Food Program limiting Iraqi sales to 2 million barrels a day.

2003–?   "Insurgents" sabotage Iraq's pipelines and infrastructure.

2004   *Options for Iraqi Oil*. The secret plan adopted by U.S. State Department overturns Pentagon proposal to massively increase oil production. State Department plan, adopted by government of occupied Iraq, limits state oil company to OPEC quotas.

How odd. If cutting Saddam's allowance was the purpose, then sanctions, limiting oil exports, was a very suspect method indeed. The nature of the oil market (a cartel) is such that the elimination of two million barrels a day *increased* Saddam's revenue. One might conclude that sanctions were less about WMD and more about EPS (earnings per share) of oil sellers.

In other words, there is nothing new under the desert sun. Today's fight over how much of Iraq's oil to produce (or suppress) simply extends into this century the last century's pump-or-control battles.

In sum, Big Oil, whether in European or Arab-OPEC dress, has done its damned best to keep Iraq's oil buried deep in the ground to keep prices high in the air.

Iraq has 74 known fields and only 15 in production; 526 known "structures" (oil-speak for "pools of oil"), only 125 drilled. And they *won't* be drilled, not unless Iraq says, "Mother, may I?" to Saudi Arabia, or, as the Baker/CFR paper says, "Saudi Arabia may punish Iraq." And believe me, Iraq wouldn't want that.

The decision to expand production has, for now, been kept out of Iraqi's hands by the latest method of suppressing Iraq's oil flow—the 2003 invasion and resistance to invasion. And it has been darn effective. Iraq's output in 2003, 2004 and 2005 was less than produced under the restrictive Oil-for-Food Program. Whether by design or happenstance, this decline in output has resulted in *tripling* the profits of the five U.S. oil majors to $89 billion for a single year, 2005, compared to pre-invasion 2002.

That suggests an interesting arithmetic equation. Big Oil's profits are up $89 billion a year in the same period the oil industry boosted contributions to Mr. Bush's reelection campaign to roughly $40 million. That would make our president "Mr. 0.05%."

Saddam Does the Jerk: Why He Had to Go

Every cartel needs one producer to stifle production, and that was Iraq's sorry role, under Mr. 5%, the IOCs and OPEC, for nearly a century. The last thing the oil industry wanted from Iraq in 2001 was a lot more oil. Therefore, we can rule out the West's desire for Iraq's oil as the decisive motive to invade Iraq. Neither Saddam's affection for euro currency nor panic over oil peaking ruffled the international oil industry. What, then, made Saddam, so easy to hug in the 1980s, unbearable in the 1990s?

Saddam had to go, but why?

They held meetings about it. Beginning just after Bush's Florida victory in December 2000, the shepherds of the planet's assets got together to plan our energy future under the weighty aegis of the Joint Task Force on Petroleum of the James A. Baker III Institute and the Council on Foreign Relations. The master plan makers included the Master Race of lobbyists expert at turning grasping self-serving industry demands dripping with give-me-more greed into selfless policy-speak advice for the new President. There was Bremer's and Kissinger's partner, Mack McLarty, CEO of Kissinger McLarty Associates; John Manzoni of British Petroleum; Luis Giusti, former CEO of the Venezuelan state oil company (until Chávez kicked him out); Ken Lay of Enron (not yet convicted, not yet dead); Philip Verleger of the National Petroleum Council, and other movers and shakers crucial to such bipartisan multi-continental group gropes—all chaired by Dr. Edward Morse, our man from Hess Oil Trading.

The final report detailed Saddam's crimes. Gassing Kurds and Iranians? No. James A. Baker was the Reagan Chief of Staff when the U.S. provided Saddam the intelligence to better target his chemical weapons. Weapons of Mass Destruction? Not since this crowd stopped selling him the components.

In the sanitary words of the Council on Foreign Relations' report (written by Amy Jaffe), Saddam's problem was that he was a "swinger":

> Tight markets have increased U.S. and global vulnerability to disruption and provided adversaries undue potential influence over the price of oil. Iraq has become a key "swing" producer, posing a difficult situation for the U.S. government.

Now hold on a minute: Why is our government in a "difficult" position if Iraq is a "swing producer" of oil?

The answer was that Saddam was jerking the oil market up and down. One week, without notice, the man in the moustache suddenly announces he's going to "support the Palestinian intifada" and cuts off all oil shipments. The result: Worldwide oil prices jump up. The next week, Saddam forgets about the Palestinians and pumps to the maximum allowed under the Oil-for-Food Program. The result: Oil prices suddenly dive-bomb. Up, down, up, down. Saddam was *out of control*.

"Control is what it's all about," Lapham told me. "It's not about *getting* the oil, it's about *controlling oil's price.*"

Within days of Bush's election in November 2000, the James Baker Institute issued this warning:

> In a market with so little cushion to cover unexpected
> events, oil prices become extremely sensitive to perceived
> supply risks. Such a market increases the potential lever-
> age of an otherwise lesser producer such as Iraq . . .

Falah Aljibury, an advisor to the Baker CFR group, put it this way: "Iraq is not stable, *a wild card*," as Saddam cuts production, or suddenly boosts it, playing games with the U.N. over the Oil-for-Food Program. The tinpot despot was, almost alone, setting the weekly world price of oil and Big Oil did not care for that. In the CFR's sober language:

> Saddam is a "destabilizing influence . . . to the flow of oil
> to international markets from the Middle East."

With Saddam out of control, jerking markets up and down, the price of controlling the price was getting just too high. Saddam drove the oil boys bonkers. For example, Saddam's games pushed the State Department, disastrously, to launch, in April 2002, a coup d'état in Venezuela.

I was in Caracas that month for BBC. I learned from Ali Rodriguez, OPEC's secretary general, what had panicked the U.S. into premature action against Chávez and why it failed. The OPEC chief told me that days before the coup, Libya's Gaddafi had contacted Rodriguez to say he was preparing, with Saddam, to launch a new Arab oil embargo. The U.S. State Department had certainly learned of it. Rodriguez tipped off his old friend, Venezuela's President Chávez, which allowed Chávez to prepare for the obvious U.S. response: a coup d'état. The plot collapsed, spectacularly, in 48 hours.

If you're wondering why Saddam's threat would lead the U.S. to remove Chávez, keep in mind that Venezuela, once the top exporter to the U.S., broke the back of the 1973 Arab oil embargo by replacing the oil withdrawn by Saudi Arabia. Chávez, despised by Bush, was not likely to save Bush's bacon by busting another embargo. Therefore, Chávez had to go *immediately*.

The Venezuela debacle, the failure of the coup, underscored the endlessly costly consequences of leaving Saddam in a position to rock the oil markets. Whether through his conspiracies with Libya or his games with the oil-for-food allotments, the Council on Foreign Relations concluded:

> Saddam Hussein has demonstrated a willingness to threaten to use the oil weapon to manipulate oil markets. . . . United States should conduct an immediate policy review toward Iraq, including military, energy, economic, and political/diplomatic assessments.

Saddam could light a match that would burn in Venezuela or Iran or Russia. This could not stand. Saddam delighted in playing cat-and-mouse with the USA and our oil majors. Unfortunately for him, he wasn't playing with mice, but a much bigger and unforgiving breed of rodents. *Saddam was asking for it.* It was time for a "military assessment."

The true motive to invade Iraq, Saddam's "manipulation of oil markets," was there, but not yet, in April 2001, the official excuse.

Not surprisingly, the desires of the "Project for a New American Century," the neo-con field of dreams, of remaking Arabia, was *not* in the Baker Institute-CFR plan. However, the conclusion, *Saddam must go*, matched the neo-con's policy demand, if for highly different reasons. The Baker-CFR panel had a limited concern: Get rid of the jerk, the guy yanking the market about.

Morse was close-lipped about who saw and used the 2001 Baker-CFR report, but Amy Jaffe could not help telling me that Morse reported its conclusions in a briefing at the Pentagon. More important, back in early 2001, the initial Baker-CFR report (another participant tipped me) was handed directly to Vice President Dick Cheney. Cheney met secretly with CFR task force members and other energy industry comrades to go over the maps of Iraq's oil fields. That, apparently, sealed it. Cheney took Morse's CFR/Baker recommendations as his own plan for dissecting Iraq, I'm told, beginning with the none-too-thinly-veiled take-out-Saddam "assessment."[13]

And whose plan was it? The membership of the Baker-CFR group was Big Oil and its retainers. But I was curious to know who put up the cash for drafting the extravagant report that was so protective of OPEC and Saudi interests. This 2000–2001 document was, after all, the outline on which the Bush administration drew its grand design for energy, from Iraq to California to Venezuela. According to Jaffe's introduction, the cost of this exercise in Imperialism Lite was funded by "the generous support of Khalid al-Turki" of Saudi Arabia. Did he who pays the piper call the tune?

It is worth underscoring that the Baker-CFR report duly inventoried Iraq's enormous untapped oil reserves—then carefully noted these riches must never be touched, nor Iraq leave OPEC, without inviting crushing punishment from Saudi Arabia. "Punish" is a term straight

---

[13]Another mystery solved, it appears. The Vice President fought like a she-wolf protecting her cubs when asked to turn over the names of the oil and energy executives he met with in March 2001. The Supreme Court sealed his papers. We've learned one participant in this meeting was electricity baron Ken Lay, an odd choice for a meeting over Iraq and Saudi Arabia—but not if you recognize Lay as a member of the Baker-CFR group. From the maps, the participants and the info they reviewed, it seems likely the meetings were to go over with Cheney the Baker-CFR global oil suggestions, "military assessment" included.

out of the report. From the Saudis' point of view, al-Turki's generosity was money well spent. The Saudis could, if provoked, economically devastate Iraq—which now had fair warning.

PART 5

WOLFOWITZ DÄMMERUNG: TWILIGHT OF THE NEO-CON GODS

The Decision from the Bunker

As the occupation slogged into 2004, there were still two competing plans for Iraq's oil: the OPEC-friendly state-owned oil company and privatization of the fields, Cohen's no-brainer, favored by Chalabi's Governing Council.

More was at stake than Plan A versus Plan B. This chapter, beyond Iraq and its oil, is about the flow and tides of power, centered on a struggle over two competing visions for the Middle East; on one side, the aggressive neo-con agenda for remaking Arabia as a Little USA (or better, another Chile); on the other, Big Oil and the State Department's history-hardened view of the Middle East as a giant gas station inhabited by creatures with inscrutable superstitions and violent habits best not disturbed.

Someone had to choose. It was time for the big man in Washington, sitting in judgment over the factions, to make a decision. And that would be, Ed Morse told me,

> The person most influential in running American energy policy, the Vice President.

In over four years of investigation, not one insider I spoke with suggested that George Bush weighed in *at all* on the decisions that would determine the fate of Iraq, the length of war or the price America would pay for oil.

The Pentagon crowd had hope: Cheney is a card-carrying member

S.P.R.

Cheney's Strategic Political Reserve

When the "oil-will-be-cheap" propaganda of 2003 ran into the reality of 2004, oil prices doubled to over $50 a barrel and gasoline closed in on $3 a gallon.

Neo-cons—joining, oddly, with Democrats—had a solution. They were pushing Vice President Cheney to use America's special weapon to cut down the post–invasion price spike: our Strategic Petroleum Reserve. Bill Clinton had done it, dumping oil from U.S. government stocks when oil threatened to bust above $30 a barrel. Clinton worked out this price-capping stratagem with the complicity and connivance of Venezuela's President Hugo Chávez, who, not incidentally, was also president of OPEC. Chávez got Clinton to agree to an implicit *floor* of $20 in return for agreeing to a *cap* of $30 per barrel. Clinton, by releasing or merely threatening to release oil from the Strategic Petroleum Reserve, maintained the Goldilocks not-too-hot-not-too-cold solution known as "The Band."

Cheney doesn't like Clinton and he doesn't like Chávez and he certainly doesn't want to play in their band. "We keep the Strategic Petroleum Reserve available to deal with true emergencies, *national crisis*," the Vice President said in a sneering comparison with Clinton. Cheney released oil only one time during the first Bush term. The "national crisis" was the hurricane that hit Florida in late 2004. Cheney released oil from the Reserve only and solely to refiners in Florida. This created a short-lived dip in gasoline prices in Florida just before the presidential election. The timing, doubtless, was coincidental.

For the Vice President, releasing reserve oil to bring down prices was Clintonesque impiety. The petroleum industry's freedom to price is as sacred to the Vice President as free speech to the ACLU. Cheney "thinks security begins by building an S.P.R. and letting prices follow where they may," Hess Oil Trading's Ed Morse told me. Oil at $50 a barrel? Cheney's response was, *Fill'r up!* He *added* to the reserve as prices jumped. The 2005 energy bill quietly authorized new purchases of 300 million barrels. In other words, Cheney dealt with higher oil prices by letting them go higher.

CHENEY ENERGY PLAN

Iraqi Oilfields and Exploration Blocks

Both the timing, this map and the few other papers pried from Dick Cheney's secret March 2001 meeting with Ken Lay and other oil and power company executives (whom he refuses to name) suggest its topics were taken from the Council on Foreign Relations / James Baker Institute joint recommendations for global energy control. (Lay was a member of the CFR-Baker group.) These recommendations include "military, energy, economic . . . assessments" of Iraq and other oil-producing states. (Map Source: Judicial Watch)

BUSH ENERGY PLAN

Turn Ordinary Tap Water Into Hydrogen Fuel!

This kit includes a sleek rocket that shoots 200 feet into the sky, using only ingenuity and a carefully concocted mixture of science and fun. Kids get to run through a four-point system check and do a countdown before hitting their remote ignition button. Uses six D batteries (not included).

Ages 12 and up

Hydrogen Fuel Rocket	*FG25112*	**$49.95**
Six D Batteries	*FG24033*	**$12.95**

"Turn Ordinary Tap Water Into Hydrogen Fuel!" In his 2003 State of the Union address, the President called for betting America's energy future on hydrogen. "A single chemical reaction between hydrogen and oxygen generates energy, which can be used to power a car," he said. I could not fathom where he got the idea. Then this arrived in the mail for my kids. (Toy and catalog listing from Mindware, "Brainy toys for kids of all ages." Mindwareonline.com 1-800-999-0398.)

of the Rumsfeld/Wolfowitz Project for a New American Century. But, in the end, said a confident Morse, the Vice President would never let neo-cons gun down OPEC nor bring down the industry that raised him.

A triumphal Morse told me (admittedly, in the conversation he said we never had):

> The VP's office [has] not pursued a policy in Iraq that would lead to a rapid opening of the Iraqi energy sector . . . so they have not done *anything*, either with pro-ducers or energy policy, that would put us on a track to say, "We're going to put a squeeze on OPEC."

The quotas were safe, OPEC was safe and Big Oil had won. But to put the industry's plan into place, the *Options* "so generously supported" by the Saudis, to create a permanent, all-powerful state oil company in Iraq, another regime change was necessary: Ahmad Chalabi and his oil ministry toy-boy, Bahr al-Ulum, had to go.

Day of the Long Knives

And they went. On May 20, 2004, Iraqi police raided Ahmad Chalabi's home in Baghdad and carted away his computers and files. Two days before, the CIA yanked his $335,000 monthly stipend for his front group and his White House sponsors launched the character assassination leak barrage they had previously practiced on General Garner. Chalabi was now hunted by his own government: The charge was espionage, no less, for Iran.

Chalabi was swapped for another CIA payroller, ex-Ba'athist Iyad Allawi, dubbed "Prime Minister" of the newly sovereign Iraq, chosen by an electorate made up of the occupying powers. New puppets, same strings.

Chalabi's Governing Council was shut down and, crucially, Bahr al-Ulum was yanked from the Oil Ministry. With Chalabi off the

"De-Ba'athification Committee," the way was clear for the return of Saddam's old *nomenklatura*, headed by oil industry favorites Mohammad al-Jiburi, brought back to Baghdad from Westchester, New York, as new Minister for Trade, and Thamir Ghadbhan, ex-Ba'athist technocrat, who was back on top as Oil Minister, replacing the man who had replaced *him*.

Sovereignty meant, if not an elected government, at least one that could quickly get back to the oil industry's *Options for Iraqi Oil*. In accordance with the Options plan, Ghadbhan rushed to announce to the *Financial Times* that he would establish a state oil company to own and control all reserves.

June 30, 2004: "Sovereignty Day." It was, as our president said, a peaceful transfer of power—but not to the Iraqi people. Rather, it was a passing of authority from the neo-cons to the IOCs, the international oil companies.

Completing that transfer would require still more regime change. Paul Bremer was made to walk the plank, replaced as our top man in Baghdad by the State Department's John Negroponte. Ambassador Negroponte was once a hero to the neo-cons because he allegedly turned a blind eye to the right-wing death squads in Honduras during the Reagan years. But he'd become a wizened State Department pragmatist, an early opponent, I'm told, of the neo-con's *totalen Krieg* in Iraq.[14]

---

[14]My late, brilliant comrade Jude Wanniski would take issue with this. He saw Negroponte as a closet neo-con, a Wolfowitz in establishment clothing, "proconsul for a Perle/Wolfowitz/Rumsfeld empire." Wanniski went back to Negroponte's days subverting sovereignty in Vietnam, the Philippines, Panama and Honduras during the Cold War when Wanniski himself ran with the wolves. "The fact that we were up to our keisters in the Cold War back then does excuse a certain amount of trimming, assassinations, death squads, etc., which we should try to forget about. Indeed, back then when I was associate editor of *The Wall Street Journal* editorial page, I stood shoulder to shoulder with Perle, Wolfowitz and Rumsfeld, and the rest of the gang." But Negroponte, like Wanniski, changed. I am assured that within the State Department, Negroponte, along with Richard Jones, formerly State's "oilman" in Saudi Arabia, abhorred Chalabi's and the neo-con's grand get-OPEC schemes. A top lieutenant of Hugo Chávez also informed me that Negroponte blocked neo-con nut cases from further attempts to overthrow the Venezuelan President, at least until after the U.S. elections of 2004. That doesn't give Negroponte angel wings, but it does make the non-ideological oil establishment comfortable with him.

What is left to the Iraqis? To them will go, after time, the shards of their economy, the industries not sold off or financially demolished, and the dead hand of the copyright laws and other free-market commandments that are the neo-cons' lucrative consolation prize.

Bremer was removed but his one hundred New World Orders stayed behind as Iraq's law in perpetuity. There is just no point in Grover Norquist arranging for Bremer to give Sony a 50-year copyright on Céline Dion's oeuvre if some later out-of-control Iraqi government is going to take it away. To prevent that, there's Order 100, Bremer's final commandment. Order 100 ensures that, "the interim government *and all subsequent Iraqi governments* inherit full responsibility for these [Bremer's] laws, regulations, orders, memoranda, instructions and directives," which effectively locks in the economic rules of occupation.

To make certain the latest sovereign government got it right, the U.S. State Department embedded Americans, nearly 200 of them, to sit right in the offices of each Iraqi agency to babysit the sovereign government's ministers.

Bremer departed with the words "The Coalition Provisional Authority will cease to exist on June 28, 2004. At that point the occupation will end" . . . except for the 200 government proconsuls and the 140,000 troops that will remain.

And the oil? In 2005, Iraq exported only 1.4 million barrels a day, less than under Saddam, less than half its old OPEC quota, less than a fourth of its ultimate capacity and light-years from Wolfowitz's promise. World prices leaped to reflect the shortfall. Oil executives, if wired to a lie detector per Amy Jaffe's tantalizing suggestion, would have to admit that Iraq has turned into a financial orgasmatron.

With neo-cons out, the long-term plan for Iraq's oil industry was settled. Though technically owned by the Iraqis through their state oil company, we can expect the crude to be gathered and controlled downstream by the same old hands, British Petroleum, Chevron and other IOCs that first drew that nation's borders, politely fulfilling Iraq's quota assigned by the Saudis, no more, maybe less.

For those Big Oil dreams to come true, more regime change would be required—this time in the USA, for which the Vice President sharpened his long knife.[15] On November 2, 2004, Bush-Cheney forces took Ohio. Then, as the Bush-Cheney second term began, neo-con forces, surrounded by the Vice President and the oil industry, surrendered. In January 2005, Undersecretary Douglas Feith announced his departure. Feith had created the Office of Special Plans, the neo-con's dream factory at the Pentagon. (His assistant there, Larry Franklin, would later plead guilty for passing classified documents to lobbyists.) At the State Department, John Bolton, the vicious, knuckle-dragging enforcer of neo-con orthodoxies, was booted from Washington to New York to the powerless post of United Nations Representative. With Bolton's removal to the U.N., the editor of the Council on Foreign Relations' journal crowed in triumph, "The realists have defeated the fantasists!"

Finally, on March 16, 2005, second anniversary of the invasion, Paul Wolfowitz was cast out of the Pentagon war room and tossed into the World Bank's presidency.

Only in BushWorld is an appointment to run the World Bank a punishment post but that's what it is for Wolfowitz, exiled from the testosterone-powered war-making decision center at Defense to the lending office for Bangladeshi chicken farmers.[16]

---

[15]On June 29, 1934, the Night of the Long Knives, Hitler had the seventy-seven leaders of his Brown Shirt shock troops, his most devoted doctrinaire followers, arrested and shot. Let's not, despite the hysterical imaginings of some of my colleagues, compare the flailing imperial impulses of the Bush Administration with the immeasurable horrors of the Third Reich. Nevertheless, the echo of the Führer's purge of his ideological spear-chuckers in the Bush-Cheney purge of neo-cons is too delicious to pass up; further evidence that history repeats itself, first as tragedy, then as farce.

[16]On April 1, 2005, I published an article, "Wolfowitz Turns Down World Bank Post, Neo-Conservative Accepts Blame for Intelligence Errors." The information in the article, I must now state, was incorrect. In fact, it was a complete fabrication. I am writing this note to apologize to the New Zealand diplomat who, swallowing the nonsense whole, sent copies around to the diplomatic community, then blamed me for his embarrassment when it became clear this was my misguided and ill-considered April Fools' Day joke.

Old Puppets, New Strings

But just when you thought the fat lady sang for the neo-cons, who should rise from his crypt but Ahmad Chalabi. Cutting a deal with Sheiks Sistani and Bahr al-Ulum, Chalabi rides, *mirabilis dictum*, the religious Shia vote back into office as Deputy Prime Minister *and* interim oil minister. The espionage accusations against him are dropped; the King of Jordan offers to pardon Chalabi for the $72 million missing from Chalabi's former bank; and Chalabi once again turns over his oil ministry to Sheik Bahr al-Ulum's son, "the nothing." The oil industry's favorite, Ghadbhan, is again kicked downstairs and Big Oil's Ambassador, Negroponte, is kicked upstairs, back to Washington as the new "Terrorism Czar."

Chalabi's maneuvers with the Shia mullahs open the path for a neo-con counter-coup, capped with Ambassador Negroponte's removal and replacement, in July 2005, by neo-con Zalmay Khalilzad, holder of the full deck of over-the-right-edge credentials: University of Chicago, Wolfowitz aide, RAND, Project for a New American Century. In 1997, Khalilzad, ever the gracious host, rolled out the red carpet in Sugarland, Texas, for the Taliban, winning their hearts and an agreement for his client, Unocal Oil, to run a gas pipeline from Turkmenistan to Pakistan by way of Afghanistan. Only a few years later, he was named the U.S. Ambassador to Afghanistan, land of his birth. Homeboy done well; but not all Afghan voices rose to praise the think-tank warrior who backed the Islamic berserkers that left Kabul a city of rubble.

In 2005, after two years of bringing democracy to Afghanistan (one warlord, one vote), Khalilzad was ready to show the Iraqis a thing or two about "sovereignty." While Iraq now had an "elected" government, Zalmay did not want any misunderstandings about who was in charge. On June 21, 2005, Zalmay was sworn in at an ambassadorial castle befitting his ambitions—an embassy of 3,000, the largest in world history (at least since the U.S. evacuated the one in Saigon in 1975).

Khalilzad immediately launched into ten days of backroom dicta-
tion to the new government, surfacing to announce the seven points
on which "we agreed" about the economy, politics, military and foreign policy of the nation. He began each point with "the U.S. and the
Iraqi government" or "we" or "I will." Quite an odd role for a foreign
diplomat. Old puppets, *new* strings.

The Conoco Petroleum/Halliburton man McKee, now that the
Options plan was complete, returned to Houston, leaving the ministry in the able hands of Mike Stinson, also from Conoco Petroleum.
On the day Chalabi returned to power, Stinson—from Houston—
announced to the press that the new government, despite the stated
position of the returning minister, would establish a fully integrated
state oil monopoly within the year. Nevertheless, Chalabi's man Bahr
al-Ulum began to offer licenses for private companies to export some
of Iraq's oil.

Bahr al-Ulum imposed the drastic domestic oil price hikes that the
World Bank imposed upon him. When the government gunned down
four Iraqis protesting the increases, Bahr al-Ulum lost his stomach
for the job, and in January 2006, handed the oil ministry back into
Ahmad Chalabi's hands. The neo-con's counter-coup was nearly
complete, though fleetingly temporary.

Rumsfeld remained on, holding his hollow title, the hand puppet
the Administration could hold up to take the political bullets. By the
end of 2006, the Rummy rag was shredded, his usefulness as a demo-
nized decoy no longer protecting the Administration, and he was dis-
carded.

A new glove puppet was slipped on in Rumsfeld's place as the Defense Secretary, Robert Gates, the former CIA chief who trailed behind
him unanswered questions about his secret assistance to Saddam Hussein's military in the 1980s. The shift to Gates was more than symbolic:
in the new Secretary's fingerholes was not the iron fist of Dick Cheney
but the dexterous hand of The Master himself, James Baker III.

Now that the allies of the oil industry pragmatists had publicly ad-
ministered the coup de grâce to Rumsfeld, titular head of the neo-con

faction, Baker, heretofore the *gris eminance* working Iraq policy from behind the curtains, was ready to step out to stage center. At the end of 2006, Baker arranged to put himself in charge of the "bi-partisan" Iraq Study Group (from which Gates had been elevated to the Defense post). In 2007, the new Democratic Congress, willing to do anything to avoid responsibility for handling this tar baby of a war, bowed before the counsel to ExxonMobil, pleading for Baker and his Group to show them the way.

And so the Iraq conquest a la Bush, the miasma created by the tug-of-war between Big Oil and neo-cons, staggered into its fifth year.

Getting Better

But don't worry, America. Ignore that man on fire. Carlos Arredondo didn't understand that, when he lost his son, our leaders were still tragically inexperienced at handling the globe and its oil. We can rest assured, as Rumsfeld's assistant Larry Di Rita explained, the more practice we get at invasions and occupations, the better we'll do:

> We're going to get better over time. The future of war is that these things are going to be much more of a continuum. . . . This is the future for the world we're in at the moment. *We'll get better as we do it more often.*

More often?

OIL WARS BONUS CHAPTER!

The Best Little Legal Whorehouse in Texas

© Robert Grossman

Looking for the *real* action in Texas? In Houston, stop by "Baker Botts LLP" and ask for "Jim."

The law firm of James Baker III, Secretary of State under George Bush the Elder, doesn't bat an eyelash at the kinkiest client requests. Right now, his stable is working day and night for the Defense Ministry of Saudi Arabia to prevent the families of the victims of the September 11 attack from seeking information on the Defense Ministry's funding of Al-Qaeda fronts. It's tough work, but Jim was ready for more when, in December 2003, President Bush the Younger announced that Baker would get the job of "restructuring" the debts of the nation of Iraq.

And who will net the big bucks under Jim Baker's plan? Answer: Baker Botts' client, Saudi Arabia, which claims $30.7 billion due from Iraq plus $12 billion in "reparations" from the First Gulf War.

Let's ponder what's going on here. We are talking about something called "sovereign debt." And unless George Bush has finally 'fessed up and named himself Pasha of Iraq, he is not their sovereign. Mr. Bush has no authority to seize control of that nation's assets nor its debts.

But our President is not going to let something as trivial as international law stand in the way. To get around the wee issue that Bush has no legal authority to mess with Iraq's debt, the White House crafted a neat little subterfuge. The White House told me the President did *not* actually appoint Mr. Baker, so Baker can assert that he is not, in fact, a White House employee. Rather, Mr. Bush was "responding to a request from the Iraqi Governing Council." That is, Bush acted on the authority of the puppet government he imposed on Iraqis at gunpoint.

The Bush team must have seen the other advantage in having the rump rulers of Iraq pretend to choose Mr. Baker: The U.S. Senate did not have to review nor confirm the appointment. If you remember, when President Bush asked Henry Kissinger to head up a commission to investigate the September 11 attack, U.S. Senators demanded to see Kissinger's client list, so Henry ran away with his consulting firm tucked between his legs. In the case of Jim Baker, our elected Congress had no chance to ask him who is paying his firm—nor even to require him to get off conflicting payrolls.

Or maybe there's no conflict at all. If you see Jim Baker's White House job as working not to protect a new Iraqi democracy but to protect the loot of the old theocracy of Saudi Arabia, the conflict disappears.

Fixed

Why is our President so concerned with the wishes of Mr. Baker's clientele? What does Bush owe Baker? Let me count the chads, beginning with the 2000 election.

"I fixed the election in Florida for George Bush," as Bush's lawyer

Baker told an audience of Russian oil industry oligarchs, bragging about his post-election legal work in 2000. That was reported to me by my somewhat astonished colleague at BBC Television in Moscow. I assume Baker was referring to his work as *consigliere* to the Bush family. He came up with the strategy of maneuvering the 2000 Florida vote count into a Supreme Court packed with black-robed politicos he helped appoint. Baker's claim to have "fixed" the election was not a confession; it was a boast. He meant, says our eyewitness, to dazzle current and potential clients about his Big In with the Big Boy in the White House.

Over the years, Jim Baker has taken responsibility for putting bread on the Bush family table. For example, among his other titles, Jim is "Senior Counsel" for Carlyle, an arms-dealing investment group that hired *both* Poppy Bush after he was booted from the White House and Junior Bush while his daddy was still President.

Bush Sr.'s job with Carlyle was to schmooze the Saudi royal family into buying weapons of major destruction. The sales pitch was made easy as one of the most powerful families in Saudi Arabia, the bin Ladens, were financial backers of the Bush-Baker Carlyle venture.

Bush Jr. was paid by Carlyle as a board member of its CaterAir unit. Sad for Carlyle, under George W.'s business stewardship, CaterAir swiftly took a terrifying financial nosedive. Not to worry. It was Carlyle that got President Bush Jr. to pay the "wind-down" money for its Muslim-mauling Crusader tank-and-bulldozer combo.

Invitation to Invasion

To Americans, the war in Iraq was sold as bringing democracy to the sands of Arabia. To Jim Baker's clients, the Saudis, it was more of an armed debt collection action. Saudi Arabia wanted billions in "war reparations" Iraqis owed them for Saddam's invasion of Kuwait. But who gave Saddam the idea he could get away with invading Kuwait, anyway?

Answer: Mr. Jim.

On July 25, 1990, Saddam asked U.S. Ambassador April Glaspie if the U.S. would object to an attack on Kuwait over the small emirate's theft of Iraqi oil. America's ambassador told him;

> We have no opinion on . . . your border disagreement with Kuwait. . . . The issue is not associated with America. James Baker has directed our official spokesmen to emphasize this instruction.

We have *no opinion*?! Glaspie, in Congressional testimony in 1991, did not deny the authenticity of the recording of her meeting with Saddam—which world diplomats took for what it was: Jim Baker's green light for Iraq to attack Kuwait.

Why did Baker turn on his buddy Saddam? The Kuwaitis had been sucking up that which wasn't theirs in the shared oil field on the Kuwait-Iraq border. Oil men Baker and Bush, long familiar with the etiquette of the Wild West oil fields of the Permian in Texas, knew the Texas response to such cheating was the proverbial baseball bat to the knees. Saddam had a right to invade, but, too full of himself, went too far, taking not just the oil fields but all of Kuwait, as Iraq's "nineteenth province." And that most certainly upset the fine political balances of OPEC and Saudi control. Baker and Bush suggested Saddam leave Kuwait, and with the 82d Airborne, they made Saddam an offer he couldn't refuse.

Who's Counting?

Baker was playing with an Iraqi debt totaling $120 billion to $150 billion, depending on who's counting. And who's counting is *very* important. Some of the so-called "debt" owed to Saudi Arabia was given to Saddam to fight a proxy war for the Saudis against their hated foe, the Shia of Iran. Should Iraqis today and those not yet born have to be put in a debtor's prison to pay off the secret payouts to Saddam?

James Wolfensohn, when he was president of the World Bank, said "No!" Wolfensohn has never been on my Valentine's list, but in this case he got it right: The Saudis and partners should be forced to eat their $120 billion "debt."

And that might have happened if the World Bank, not Baker, was given the task of dealing with the sheiks' shakedown of Iraq. In fact, the World Bank has always been put in charge of postwar debt restructurings. That's why the official name of the World Bank is "International Bank for Reconstruction and Development." One suspects that Bush rushed Baker in to preempt the World Bank's sticking with Wolfensohn's recommendation that Iraq tell the Saudis to take their "debt" and shove it.

28 Pages Missing

How did Baker Botts get that lucrative job as lawyer defending the Saudis from Americans? I got a hint in my wanders around the grandiose James Baker III Institute in Houston, checking out Jim's trophy case. Among Baker's notable jobs was Chief of Staff to President Ronald Reagan. The only memento of that job on display was Baker's personally notated tally sheet listing the names of the U.S. Senators he lobbied to vote in favor of selling "AWACS" to Saudi Arabia. In 1981, that was a big deal. AWACS is an incredibly sophisticated theater-of-war system given only to our most trusted NATO allies. Only through Jim Baker's arm-twisting did a slim majority of congressmen agree to this plain dangerous scheme to let the Saudis have these murderous machines. (The AWACS will come in handy for Osama when he knocks over the House of Saud.)

I don't want any readers thinking Baker's firm was hired by the Saudis as payback for the AWACS. There are many other tentacles of power worth renting from Jim Inc. and his business chums.

For example, in July 2003, Congress issued the official report on the September 11 attack. But the report made public was missing, it turns out, twenty-eight pages the White House didn't want us to see.

Apparently, it was all about Saudi Arabians' "charitable" donations to needy terrorists. Some nasty readers might think Jim Baker had a hand in censoring the info, but that's not fair. It was purely a U.S. government decision, likely reviewed by our Ambassador to Saudi Arabia, Robert Jordan, formerly partner in, uh, Baker Botts.

Rug Rat

By 2006, James III had enough of the job of puppeteer and stepped out from behind the curtain to take a bow as leader of the "Iraq Study Group." When, in December, Baker came down from the mountaintop with the ISG's Commandments, every news channel carried loafer-licking praise for the Master Fixer for having courageously drafted a "new" plan for Iraq—without a single mention anywhere of Baker's critical role in crafting the "old" plan, albeit from the shadows.

Notably, the "new" Baker plan smelled awfully similar to the "old" Bush plan—"stay the course," though the U.S. corps would be cut from 140,000 to 70,000 soldiers. You could call it, "Staying *half* the course."

Why keep any troops at all in Iraq in the middle of a Sunni-Shia civil war? The answer is: Saudi Arabia.

On November 25, 2006, Baker's client, Saudi King Abdullah, demanded Dick Cheney drop his Thanksgiving turkey and appear before the King's throne. The cover story was that Cheney rushed to Riyadh to discuss the Palestinian-Israeli conflict. But their ain't no oil in the Holy Land. The real topic was the King's making it crystal clear that the Saudis wouldn't tolerate the U.S. leaving Iraq, or the Saudi's Sunni brothers, or Iraq's oil, to a bunch of Shia controlled by the Saudi's arch enemy, Iran.

The King's wish was Cheney's command—and Baker's. U.S. troops would stay.

And the King got a bonus. The Baker report attacked Iran for funding the Shia killers in the civil war—but nary a word was said about the piggy bank financing the Sunni berserkers on the other side. According to a confidential memo written by the National Security Counsel to the President in November 2006, the money behind the Sunni mayhem makers comes via Saudi Arabia.

Most important, Baker's report states that, "President [Bush] should restate that the United States does not seek to control Iraq's oil." Much of the lengthy report is then devoted to details of exactly what Iraq should do with its oil, going public with the once-secret schema of Baker's gal Amy Jaffe.

What threat, we have to ask, would move the Bush boys to kowtow to the Saudi royals? Nawaf Obaid, our intelligence source, was impolitic enough to mention that the Saudis, if things don't go as they wish in Iraq, might cut the price of oil in half. ExxonMobil would not be amused.

So, if you've got the cash and are looking for a good time, but can't find the little red light out in front of the Baker Botts office in Houston, try his satellite office at 1600 Pennsylvania Avenue in Washington, DC. No kidding. Since the beginning of the war in 2003, our President has given Baker an office in the White House itself. This may be the first time in the history of our Republic that a lawyer in the employ of foreign sovereigns has an office in the presidential residence.

In fact, I've heard, though can't confirm, that Mr. Bush allows Baker to use the Oval Office desk while the President plays on the rug.

Another Day at the Office ©Winston Smith 1986

CHAPTER 3

THE NETWORK

The World as a Company Town

The holistic system of systems, petro-dollars, electro-dollars, the assassination of Hugo Chávez, Euro-nations and Mundell's Toilet and coming down from Hubbert's Peak. Mr. Friedman tees off.

"*Am I getting through to you, Mr. Beale?*" The Arabs have taken billions of dollars out of this country, and now *they must put it back*. It is ebb and flow, tidal *gravity*, it is ecological *balance*. You are an old man who thinks in terms of nations and peoples. *There are no nations*. There are no peoples. There are no Russians. There are no Arabs. There are no "Third Worlds." There is no "West." There is only *one holistic system of systems*, one vast and immense, interwoven, interacting, multi-variate, multi-national dominion of dollars! *Petro-dollars. Electro-dollars. Multi-dollars.* Reichsmarks, rins, rubles, pounds and shekels! It is the *international system of currency* which determines the totality of life on this planet. That is the natural order of things today. That is the atomic, and subatomic and galactic structure of things today. *Am I getting through to you, Mr. Beale?* You get up and howl about America and democracy. *There is no America*. There is no democracy. There is only IBM, and ITT, and AT&T, and DuPont, Dow, Union

Carbide, and Exxon—*those* are the nations of the world today. *We no longer live in a world of nations and ideologies*, Mr. Beale. The world is a college of corporations, inexorably determined by the immutable by-laws of business. The world is a business, Mr. Beale. And our children will live, Mr. Beale, to see that *perfect world in which there's no war or famine, oppression or brutality. One vast and ecumenical holding company, for whom all men will work to serve a common profit, in which all men will hold a share of stock, all necessities provided, all anxieties tranquilized, all boredom amused.* And I have chosen *you* to preach this evangel, Mr. Beale.

There is really nothing more to add to Paddy Chayevsky's script from the movie *Network* to understand The System, the ebb and flow, except to update the details. In the three decades since *Network* first screened, the "holistic system" has become more holistic: Neither reichsmarks nor Karl Marx exist except in grainy documentaries.

And "to preach the evangel" of a borderless, interconnected, tranquilized corporate utopian earth in which we all own shares of stock, Mr. Beale has been replaced, of course, by Thomas Friedman.

Petro-Dollars

Let's take the *Network* economics lesson a step at a time: the "multinational dominion of dollars"; multi-dollars, electro-dollars and first, petro-dollars.

The Arabs have taken billions of dollars out of this country, and now *they must put it back.*

Indeed they must. In April 2005, when George Bush drove the King-to-be of Saudi Arabia around the Crawford ranch in a golf cart, the President wasn't playing caddy to Abdullah because we need the

Saudis' oil. OPEC nations will always sell us their oil. After all, they can't eat the crude nor drink it and there's only so much Abdullah's harem can pour on his belly. George Bush's concern is that, in the first five years of his Administration, Abdullah and the oil-exporting nations sucked up over half a trillion dollars from U.S. consumers— $649 billion for their oil—and our President wants it all back. He needs it.

Why? Empire isn't cheap these days. Bill Clinton left office bequeathing a budget surplus projected to total $5.6 *trillion* for this coming decade. But George Bush blew it all, stone sober. Then Bush went another $4 trillion into the red. It's not just the Iraq war. We have to add in a trillion dollars over the next ten years to make up for the revenues lost from his repealing the inheritance tax. And we'll need another $6 billion for filling up the Strategic Petroleum Reserve, and don't forget his "Marines in a Tube" price tag: $64.7 billion. Then add in the Big One, taking over the pension obligations of U.S. corporations that have, with Bush's blessing, dumped their commitments on the U.S. Treasury: $142 billion.

To fund his binge spending, our President could have taxed us directly, say, a dollar a gallon tax on gasoline. But a gas tax is, politically, a no-go. Instead, our leader has arranged an *indirect* tax on gasoline: OPEC's $50-plus price for a barrel of crude, which translates roughly into an extra dollar a gallon at the pump.

Think of the gas pump price spike as a war tax.

Saudi Arabia and other OPEC nations take our billions and then they lend them back to us to fund Mr. Bush's deficit. In 2005, $243 billion in petro-dollars was collected from Americans at the pump (and in your heating and electric bills) and left the country. At the same time, it cycled back, and then some, as foreigners bought up nearly a third of a trillion dollars ($311 billion) in U.S. government debts. Mr. Bush spent every penny of it, and more.

Under the Bush Administration, the sum of Treasury bills on the market rose, by August 2005, to $4.11 trillion, with half of it ($2.06

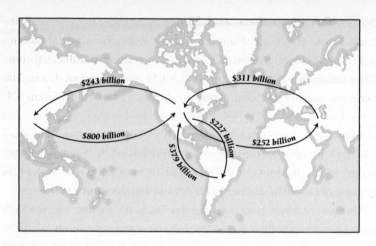

The Flow Map

The Arabs took $252 billion in 2005 for OPEC's oil—and put back $311 billion by purchasing U.S. Treasury bills, Latin America borrowed $227 billion at high interest—while lending the U.S. $379 billion at low interest. Americans bought $243 billion in stuff from China—while China holds nearly a trillion dollars ($800 million) in reserve to buy up the U.S.

trillion) lent to us from dollars held by foreigners. In fact, the Bush Administration has, on a net basis, borrowed the entire increase in Treasury debt from foreign sources. The only way to get that much money *in* is to let it bleed *out*.

That's the "petro-dollar cycle," Mr. Beale. It flows out; it comes back.

It's one heck of a deal for this Administration. All the goodies, from nuclear subs to tax cuts to war in Mesopotamia, appear to be "free" to the taxpayer. It's all just put on the tab, the national debt, including the interest on it. The actual cash needed to pay for these budget busters is first collected from U.S. consumers via the hidden oil tax for which Mr. Bush takes no blame.

Why would Abdullah give us our money back? Why wouldn't the Saudi royals and the emirs of the Persian Gulf use their trillion-dollar windfall to invest in the Islamic world, from Morocco to Palestine to Pakistan? Why do the Gulf States just hand the capital back to the banks of New York and London? The answer: *protection*. The Saudis may love their Islamic brothers, but they *fear* them more. The sheik-doms know they can count on the Bush family when a Saddam marches into Kuwait or Osama's cadres try to seize Abdullah's throne. They know they can count on the USA because they pay for it. The marching song of the Saudi Army is, after all, "Onward Christian Soldiers."

Every Gulf dictator (or "royal" if you prefer) knows that there's another advantage to parking their loot in the West. If "regime change" occurs in Saudi Arabia, if the House of Saud caves in, the bulk of its funds will be safely stashed in New York, London and Zurich.

Our petro-dollars go out, then come back, all of them, but at a high cost. First, there's the interest. Despite the Koran's prohibition on the charging of interest, the Saudis and other oil states demand no small pound of flesh. When interest rates rise to lure back our money from King Abdullah, the rest of us must pay higher interest as well. Between June 2004 and November 2005, the Federal Reserve had to hike interest rates twelve times. And, as we'll discuss further on, we pay the interest "vigorish" not just in higher credit card fees, we pay in jobs.

Because of Mr. Bush's deficits, U.S. federal government interest payments for 2002 through 2011 will total about $2.4 trillion. (If we had to pay only the debts Bill Clinton left us, the interest payout would have been just a fourth of that, $622 billion.) Mr. Bush's interest payments themselves are on the tab as well, rolled into the national debt. We pay a "shadow" cost for that too. Higher borrowing costs for business since the beginning of the Iraq war are bleeding manufacturing investment.

But then, manufacturing is *so*, like, twentieth century. Who wants manufacturing industries anyway?

The Other Saudi Arabia

The answer is, the *other* Saudi Arabia wants them: China. Two decades ago, trade with China was small potatoes. Look at the chart on p. 148, "OPEC Revenues vs. U.S. Trade Deficit with China." Look at the dotted line, the amount we bought from the Chinese less the amount they bought from us. The difference, the rising black line, is our "trade deficit." In 1985, our trade deficit with China was absolute zero: We sold them $3.9 billion in goods, they sold us $3.9 billion in goods in return. "Even Steven," as my kids say. Today, we no longer trade with China. We *buy* from China. And buy and buy. In 2004, we bought $197 billion in goods from the Chinese. They purchased only $35 billion from the U.S., for a net trade deficit of $163 billion. In 2006, our trade deficit with China broke through the stratosphere to $233 billion, nearly a quarter trillion dollars.

America's addiction to OPEC's oil ain't nuthin' compared to America's addiction to Chinese toys, lipstick, fake Christmas trees and slippers with bunny faces on them. "Sino dollars," the cash we export to China, has leaped ahead of petro-dollars, the money taken from the West by the oil exporting nations. Financially, China is the new Saudi Arabia, but bigger. Over the two terms of this Administration, we expect the net cash paid to China for its goods to reach one trillion dollars. And now, Mr. Beale, *we must get it back*. How?

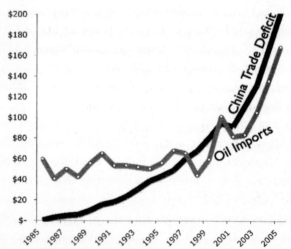

OPEC Revenues vs. U.S. Trade Deficit with China

China Floats, America Sinks

On July 22, 2005, the President, beside himself with idiot glee, took personal credit for China's "revaluing" its currency, the yuan. The press applauded, unanimously, and egghead-looking TV analysts in bow ties told us that this was a great boon for U.S. manufacturing employment.

Was it?

First off, most Americans haven't the least idea what "revaluing" China's money means. Let me put it in the language of economics: *The revaluation of the yuan didn't mean squat* . . . at least in terms of saving American manufacturing jobs. In simple terms, "revaluation" means that it takes fewer Chinese yuan to buy an American dollar. The White House peddled the line that this slight alteration of exchange rates makes our products cheaper for the Chinese and they'll buy more from us.

They didn't.

Why not? Currency Exchange Rate Economics Lesson Number One: You can't change the value of goods by changing the value of the currency on the price tag. The price inflates to compensate for the currency change. As my comrade the economist Art Laffer reminded me: "If cheap currency makes your products more competitive, all automobiles would be made in Russia." Driven a Lada lately?

Currency Exchange Rate Economics Lesson Number Two: Don't take economics lessons from George Bush.

By definition, *revaluing* the yuan means *devaluing* the dollar. Imagine if our President had put the news differently:

> My fellow Americans, today I am proud to announce that this Administration has successfully devalued the dollar. Dollars are now worth less compared to Chinese money. Your pensions are worth less, your savings have been shaved in value. Devaluation of the U.S. dollar leads to price inflation in the USA. Always. And get ready for this. We're going to have to buy our own money back from

China—and it will now cost us more. The U.S. Treasury
will have to raise interest rates to get the Chinese to return
the loot. So yes, there's an effect on manufacturing jobs.
Kiss them good-bye. And may God bless America.

Class dismissed.

Almost. There's another way to get the money back besides trying
to sell China more goods or by raising interest rates to borrow our
money back from them. If China won't buy our manufactured goods,
they can return our capital by *buying our manufacturers*. It is no accident that the very week China raised the value of its currency, the
Chinese state oil company made a cash bid for Unocal Oil of California. Raising the value of the yuan cut the price of Unocal to the Chinese by about half a billion dollars. The Bush Administration was
unhappy, but not about a foreign takeover of a strategic industry.
Rather, our Treasury Secretary John Snow flew to Beijing to demand
the Chinese hike their currency even higher, demanding the Chinese
further devalue the U.S. dollar.

Under Bill Clinton's Treasury Secretary Robert Rubin, the USA had
a "strong dollar" policy. In those Clinton years, the highly valued U.S.
currency lorded it over cheap euros and yuan. America owned the
world, literally. How things have changed. Now, it's America for sale.
Cheap. In 2004, for example, foreigners, flush with the cash the U.S.
sent to them, bought up $1.05 trillion of U.S. assets—stocks, real es-
tate, companies, whatever. That's on top of the sum lent to Mr. Bush
for his deficit. What's clear is that the new regime that came to Washington in 2001 brought a new agenda.

And what is that new agenda?

Yuan Your Social Security? The Soylent Green Solution

The year is 2036. Bill Gates, by now only a shriveled brain in a jar
wired to a blinking Vivitron, plays video games. Gates—or at least his
neurons—doesn't realize that he's poor, *kaput*, about to be unplugged.

George W. Bush remains in a persistent vegetative state. He laughs, he cries and he defends the privatization of Social Security. "The government can't take away your personal account," he repeats, pathetically, horrifically. When those private accounts were kicked off in 2012, the stock market, hyped up by two trillion dollars in new cash siphoned from the Social Security Trust Fund, took off like a bat out of hell. The Dow hit 16,000. Then, in 2030, the babies of the Baby Boomers retired and began to sell their stocks. And sell and sell. But there was no one to sell to. The boom of 2012 became the bust of 2036. The last Mekong Motors (formerly, General Motors) auto rolled off a U.S. assembly line and SinoSoft folded its Microsoft subsidiary.

Looking back, the 93-year-old Paul Krugman jumps over his walker, shouting, "I told you so!"

You have to love Paul Krugman. How he stays with *The New York Times* and keeps his soul is a great mystery. Krugman, bless him, has been riding up and down the East Coast for the last decade like a financial Paul Revere shouting, *"Privatizing social security is a fraud! Privatizing social security is a fraud!"*

Unlike columnist Thomas Friedman, Krugman does not pretend to be an economist—Krugman actually *is* an economist. But here, he may have let his patriotism gum up his calculator.

Let me explain. President Bush insists that every American will earn a bigger pension if only we invest our Social Security funds in the stock market rather than let the U.S. Treasury invest our retirement in Treasury bills. The market, says our President, will "outperform" Treasury bills (that is, win a higher return) forever and ever. It's money for nothing. Just shift your retirement fund from the Treasury bond market to the stock market.

There's a problem with our President's fishes-and-loaves sales pitch for Social Security privatization. First, the cold laws of finance tell us that the market cannot provide us risk-free returns above Treasury bills forever. If that were true, *no one* would ever buy a Treasury bill—and then how would Mr. Bush finance the debt?

Second, it's true the stock market zoomed over the last couple of decades. But the American economy is aging, and *those big gains are history, long gone.* Because our Social Security insurance payments purchase Treasury bills, our Social Security trust fund is, in effect, a giant bet on the U.S. economy. Our "profits" on this investment in ourselves, cautions Krugman, are "equal only to the rate of economic growth" in the USA. Think of the total value of all investments in the USA. Slice it any way you want—into stocks, bonds and Treasury bills held in private accounts or public accounts. Change the size of the slices or rename them from "public" to "private"—you can't increase the ultimate size of the America pie.

But then, who says Mr. Bush expects us to invest in *America*?

Remember: *There is no America, Mr. Beale. It is the international system of currency that determines the totality of life on this planet.*

The USA's economy grows by 4% in a very good year. But China is rising at 9% per year, twice as fast as America. There is one flaw in Krugman's calculations. Krugman's one error is that he's a patriot, and therefore cannot understand our rulers' cold agenda. As professor Joseph White of Case Western Reserve University explained to me:

> Social Security privatization is the realization that America's economic growth is at a plateau, on a flat line—whereas China and India and Malaysia are taking off—providing market returns twice that of U.S.-based industry.

In other words, Social Security privatization is about moving our capital from a dying economy (America) to rising economies, like China.

The money flows out, it flows back in, then it flows out again.

There is nothing new in this process of national abandonment. In the twentieth century, the elites of Argentina and other Third World nations sold their plantations and mines and infrastructure to foreign (i.e., American) multinational corporations. Argentina's "*ricos*" cashed out and moved to Miami. In the twenty-first century, it is America's elite that is cashing out, abandoning ship. They will maintain their condos in New York, but their capital will live abroad. Your Social

Security funds will subsidize their escape, leveraging their foreign ventures.

But what do we do with the old folk? While some of our Social Security tax goes to buy Treasury bills, most still goes to pay today's retirees. This is America's "pay-as-you-go" system. How do we keep up payments to those already retired, who've paid their insurance over a lifetime, if we withhold our money for private accounts? We can't. The privatizers in the Administration call this potential for disastrous collapse of old-age pensions a "transition issue." In fact, it's a debt of up to $3 trillion to current retirees. We must get it by borrowing or by cutting benefits or by taxation (in other words, a Social Security tax to replace the Social Security tax). There's only one way around this "transition" conundrum: The *Soylent Green* solution. I've heard the White House is carefully studying the transition method used in that old sci-fi classic: The elderly can be turned into a cheap source of protein.

The World Is Tilted

My own sequel to *Network* has an odd and unbelievable opening. The new Mr. Beale flies business class from Frankfurt, Germany, to Bangalore, India. On arrival, he is whisked off in an air-conditioned limo by a fabulously rich Indian dot-com CEO to a golf course. On the greens, Beale's replacement, "Thomas Friedman," has an epiphany: These eighteen holes on the Arabian Sea are just like the links in Stamford, Connecticut, which are just like the back nine in Palm Beach which are similar to the greens in Singapore. *"The world is flat!"* he declares, one large economic fairway, smooth and wide and freshly mowed, with no obstacles, no mountains to cross, no borders or fences between you and the flag sticking out of the hole. And every man and woman on the course is equal, an international brotherhood, at the tee-off.

Friedman imagines that, through some high-tech Internet abracadabra, all the greens will one day connect across the planet into one giant economic fairway. In his future, you will be able to play straight through from Bangalore to Boston to Bangkok to Berlin. But first, there will have to be some radical changes in the way business is done: Obsolete trade barriers between nations will have to come down, stodgy public industries must be sold into private entrepreneurial hands, the entangling weeds of business regulation must be slashed, the sand traps of nitpicky bureaucracies abolished, the obstructions of selfish labor union contracts cleared away and—*presto!*—prosperity and peace shall reign forever and ever. *Fore!*

Frighteningly, *Network's* sequel is not a movie. Thomas Friedman really did (he writes) fly business class to Bangalore, India, played eighteen holes with an olive-skinned CEO and on those links had the geomorphically suspect vision that led him to write *The World Is Flat*.

Friedman has spoken with people of all colors and genders around the world: the Chairman of Intel, the dictator of Malaysia, sweatshop owners, currency speculators and Silicon Valley magnates. And everyone in business class agrees that this brave new prosperity will at first require some sacrifices. Friedman announces who should do the sacrificing:

> Europe can no longer sustain its 35-hour workweeks and lavish welfare states because of the rising competition from low-wage, high-aspiration China, as well as from India and Eastern Europe.

And thus, Friedman concludes, China will snuff the torch of "European socialism." It's simple arithmetic, according to Friedman. Europeans can't "preserve a 35-hour workweek in a world where Indian engineers are ready to work a 35-hour day."

What he need not add is that if a 35-hour week is a frivolous luxury for the French, then the 40-hour week in U.S. law is hardly less extravagant. Luckily for us, it too will soon go. (See "The Grinch That Stole Overtime" in Chapter 5.)

Just as Europe's 35-hour week cannot survive global competition, and America's 40-hour week cannot survive, neither can India maintain a 50-hour week. The very month that Friedman's *The World Is Flat* hit the bestseller list, India's government lifted the limit on the workweek in textile sweatshops from 50 hours a week to 60. After all, Indians too have to compete against China. China's workweek? The clothes in Wal-Mart with the chilling label "New Order" are manufactured by the People's Liberation Army. What are the work hours of Chinese conscripts? If you know what's good for you, you won't ask.

Someone who did ask was Harry Wu, the only man I've ever met who broke *into* a prison. Born in China, jailed there, then exiled to America, Wu returned to his homeland and snuck into his former jail compound to document the brutal work conditions in China's prison factories, the world's largest pool of enslaved labor for hire. Wal-Mart, by the way, prohibits its Chinese suppliers from using shackled labor. However, the retailer can't inspect prisons and therefore, notes Wu, can't possibly know where all its goods come from. Little matter, all of China is a prison economy. Any Chinese citizen who challenges, as Wu did, working conditions have "high aspirations" beaten into them.

Like Thomas Friedman, I've also flown to Bangalore, admittedly not business class. And to tell the truth, I didn't even *know* there was a golf course there. Most Indians don't know that either. But that's nitpicking, I suppose. Friedman is correct in that I also found Indians willing to work a 35-hour day. And he could have added that, in Karnataka State, which includes Bangalore, Indian families are ready to sell their children as "temple dancers"—sex slaves—just to survive.

Friedman praises the New India, deregulated, privatized and freed of the shackles of Old India's socialist welfare state. I've seen the New India: Nearly a billion people in shacks supporting a teeny minority's right to shop in air-conditioned malls. It is a Fritz Lang film in Hindi. Just look at the numbers. India's productivity has exploded, tripling in two decades to the world's fourth largest in purchasing power. But not many Indians are doing the purchasing. The average Indian can't even manage eighteen holes on the weekend—79.9% of the population still makes under $2 a day. India's government could have addressed this imbalance with a progressive income tax. But that's so New Deal, so Round World. Rather, to the applause of the International Monetary Fund, India's free-market-mad central government figured out how to make the unequal distribution of wealth even less equal. The government now taxes those wages of $2 a day through a regressive sales tax, the VAT ("value-added tax").

The new "flat earthers" might say the two-bucks-a-day wage is a vestige of the Old India, of rural villages with oxen-plowed fields. What about the New India, the new manufacturing colossus that lifted India's gross domestic output by 48% per worker in just six years (1997–2003). In that same six years, wages in this modernized manufacturing sector went from 25 cents an hour to . . . 23 cents. Who got the gap? That is, who pocketed the value of the extra output, which, obviously, didn't go into wages? One hundred percent of the value of the new manufacturing output went to India's richest one percent, the new pashas of subcontinental industry, who've doubled their slice of the nation's income over the past decade.

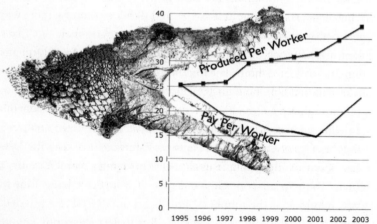

Flat World Tilted in India

From 1995 to 2003, national output in India grew by 48%, but manufacturing wages sank from 25 cents an hour to 23 cents. The extra national wealth rolled uphill into the pockets of the wealthy.

The avalanche of publicity about America's I.T. outsourcing to India features images of futuristic uplink satellite dishes shuttling code to Seattle. But the high tech sector employs barely one million Indians, about one-third of one percent of the workforce. Indian's Blakean Dark Satanic textile mills employ 38 million.

Doubtless, a new "middle" class of technocrats has profited. Yet, many of India's educated now find themselves, just like programmers in Palo Alto, in a murderous intercontinental competition to cut their wages in hopes of buying themselves a job in the new digital sweatshops.

As it is in India, so it is in China, parts of South America and most of Europe.

The world may be "flat," Mr. Friedman, but it is *tilted*. India's wealth, Europe's wealth, China's wealth, the entire planet's wealth, with precious few exceptions, is flowing from those who have a little to those who have a lot. Here are the stats:

- Since the fall of The Wall, Russia, formerly of the Soviet Union, has gone from zero billionaires to 36. What's wrong with that? Answer: There's no such thing as a free lunch—or a free billionaire. The transfer of wealth was paid for by demolition of the health care system. Spending on medicine and hospital care fell by two-thirds after the Soviet Union became Russia, and, according to the International Union for the Scientific Study of Population (Paris), "about half the [remaining] money spent on health care benefits an elite medical network that serves only the best connected 1%" of Russia's population. As a result, according to the Center for Disease Control in Atlanta, Russian life expectancy has fallen by 4 years. Unless you're an oligarch, you die young. Now *that's* pension reform.

- Poland, following free-market Pied Pipers after the implosion of the Soviet Union, had, by 2005, successfully unemployed 18% of its workforce. That's the official number, which would have been higher, except that herds of Poland's skilled workers have been

sent to rove Western Europe. The desperate droves of Polish workers were used as a tool for bending Germany's workforce into sub-
mission. From 1995 to 2003, the average German's pay was cut
4.7%.

- China, Mr. Friedman's heartthrob, is, he tells us, our future. How
looks it out there in The Future? In a single year, 2005, China's
richest forty businessmen saw their net worth rise by 44% to $26
billion. That's in U.S. dollars—obtained from U.S. pockets. And
they aren't sharing. Employees in their new entrepreneurial private
companies earn an average 8,033 yuan ($994) a year. Those work-
ers stuck in the "past"—the old state enterprises—earn nearly
twice as much: 14,577 yuan ($1,803) a year. The pay cut has slid
into the pockets of "entrepreneurs," the new factory owners, who
take home twenty-five times their average worker's pay.

Why Not Slip Into Something Less Comfortable?

The new Mr. Beale describes the latest fashion craze:

> The golden straight jacket is the defining political eco-
> nomic garment of globalization . . . tailored by Margaret
> Thatcher. Ronald Reagan sewed on the buttons.

And what does one have to do to shimmy into this attractive madhouse couture? Deregulate industry, drop trade barriers, free currencies, cut government spending, de-unionize, cut pensions, welfare
and subsidies, and make government whimper at the feet of the entrepreneurial gods and obey them.

But there's resistance. Not all the inmates want to be buckled into
the latest design, and Friedman/Beale just can't stand it:

> This is a bad time for France and friends to lose their ap-
> petite for hard work.

The Danes in particular have made sloth a policy. Blithely unaware
that Indians are working 35 hours a day, the Danes average 22 hours

a week. Partly that's the result of the "laziness" written into law: employers must provide a minimum of five weeks paid vacation. The official week is 37 hours, but non-vacation weeks average 28. Worse, there's paid maternity leave! The Danish minimum wage is $10 and health care is free. By Beale/Friedman economics, Danes should be falling off the edge of the flat world. But look at this: Danes earned an average $26 an hour in 2001, a solid 61% more than Americans. By 2006, the difference became even more embarrassing. And with a workforce 80% unionized, the nation is regulated to a fare-thee-well. Yet they do fare quite well.

Norwegians do even better than their Danish brothers. The workforce is wealthier, the wealthiest in the world. You could say that's because Norway has oil. But so does Russia, so does Nigeria, and so, for that matter, does the USA. But whose oil is it? In Norway, it's the Norwegians'—that is, the oil company is state-owned and its profits shared.

One has to ask why the Thomas Friedmans and Milton Friedmans want us to follow the goose-stepping example of Pinochet's Chile or the Darwinian horror show of China as economic guiding lights. Why imitate India and Poland, where more and more is produced by those making less and less, when far more successful examples shine under the midnight sun?

How did the Scandinavians get so rich? Norway and Denmark are, with Sweden, the least economically polarized nations on the planet: Almost no one's very rich and almost no one poor. The official international standard of economic inequality is called a "GINI" index. The Scandinavians are all at a low (i.e., very equal) 25. India is 33 and China a feudal 45. The USA lies uncomfortably close to China at 41.

The Organisation for Economic Co-operation and Development, OECD, which gathers these statistics, explains that Scandinavia's low hours and lots of rules produce big paychecks. In these nations, employers are forced to make their profits by investing more per worker to hike productivity. This is the opposite of the Chinese/Indian/Reaganized American model of making profits by cutting wages.

No wonder Scandinavians are in no mood to slip on Ronald Reagan's straightjacket. Other Western Europeans, from France to Holland, not so far behind Scandinavia, are also resisting.

Here's the problem for the owning class of this planet. The lackadaisical Danes and Swedes have the highest pay, best health care, longest vacations, and safest pensions anywhere on earth, and the French, Luxemburgians and other Europeans were, for decades, not far behind. How do you persuade the well-cared-for Europeans to give it all up?

Answer: Grab them by their currencies.

Multi-dollars, Euro-nations and Mundell's Toilet

> One vast and immense, interwoven, interacting, multivariate, multinational dominion of dollars! *Petro-dollars. Electro-dollars. Multi-dollars*, Mr. Beale.

"Multi-dollars"?

In 1999, Europe first adopted the "euro"—the multinational currency designed, as the movie *Network* predicted, to replace national coins: German deutsch marks, French francs, Spanish pesetas, Danish krone and the rest.

But the euro wasn't invented in Europe—it was created in the good old USA, in New York, by Robert Mundell. Mundell, called the Godfather of the Euro, won a Nobel Prize for it.

Who is this Mundell? The "golden straightjacket" is Thomas Friedman's madhouse fashion metaphor for "Reaganomics," the free-market, free-trade, government-free, dog-eat-dog economic free-for-all that also goes under the alias "supply-side economics." The inventor of Reaganomics, Thatcher-nomics and "supply-side" economics? Robert Mundell.

"Ronald Reagan would not have been elected President without Mundell's influence," wrote *The Wall Street Journal's* Jude Wanniski. Mundell was the guy whose brain stayed awake flattening the world while Reagan napped.

In the eighties, excepting Margaret Thatcher's Britain, Western Europeans saw no reason to make a mad dash to deregulate their economies. And this drove Mundell just crazy. It started with his toilet, Mundell told me. In a long chat we had in 2000, he told me about the travails of owning a castle in Tuscany. (Like many "flat world" supply-side economists, Mundell created prosperity—for himself.)

"They won't even let me have a toilet!" he said, which seemed like a mighty uncomfortable and unfair rule. His problem was that, to preserve the ancient structure, local officials wouldn't let him simply rip out a couple of walls to put in a tub and water closet. He concluded, "Europe is over-regulated." And he was going to do something about it.

He had other complaints. "It's very hard to fire workers in Europe," he said.

To solve the problems of putting toilets where you want them and firing workers when you don't want them, and in sum, to rip down the entire structure of employee protections enjoyed on the continent (minimum wage, lazy workweeks and all), he invented the euro. The euro is designed to be the battering ram to break down the entire edifice of worker protection rules and taxes on businesses that support the welfare state. The euro and free-market economics are as inseparable as flies and feces.

The Godfather of the Euro explained how it will work: "Monetary discipline forces fiscal discipline on the politicians as well." What he means is that every Euro nation must adhere to strict limits on borrowing (no more than 60% of GDP) and on deficits (no more than 3% of the government budgets). Furthermore, nations will no longer have their own central banks printing money. That's all quite extraordinary, really. No congress of a European nation may call on the key tools used to pull a nation out of a recession (increased government spending to create jobs, lowering interest rates to boost investment, printing more money to create demand through more liquidity).

National parliaments are castrated—their powers to affect their nation's economic destinies cut off. Isn't that a bit, uh, *un-democratic?* Forget it: *There is no democracy, Mr. Beale.*

If a nation can't control its own interest rates, borrowing, or money supply, how can it keep up employment? Answer: by stealing the jobs from their Euro neighbors, luring industry away by cutting out rules and slashing business taxes. Mundell foresees a Europe unburdened of unemployment compensation, minimum wages, chemical safety regulations and government medical insurance. Out they will go, as well as rules barring the landlord class from Euronating wherever the hell they like.

The Little Red Book of Chairman Rob

Denmark resisted the trend. It voted down the euro and held fast to its krone coins and its chill workweek. But for how long? The new Mr. Beale of the *Flat World* is warning them:

> I believe history will record that it was Chinese capitalism
> that ended European socialism.

Now we're getting to the *real* point of the New Order. The shorter workweeks, unemployment insurance, all that stuff that the French call "Le New Deal"—it's all got to go, Pierre.

Friedman's language is a bit odd, no? He defines "socialist" states as those with workweek limits, unemployment compensation and union work rules. The "capitalist" state, China, is the one where the state owns and controls what Marx, Lenin and Mao called, "the means of production." I'm sorry, you can call China a chicken but that won't fly. If China is now a capitalist free-market state, then I'm Paris Hilton.

The truth is that China's economy soared because it stubbornly refused the Friedman free-market mumbo-jumbo that government should stop owning, regulating and controlling industry. Its new inequality is not the engine of its success but the measure of the power of a thin elite that is sopping up the productivity gains.

China isn't buying Free Markets Uber Alles. Its markets are no freer than its press. The truth is that regulation and state control are its economic locomotives. For example, China's announcement that it would "revalue" the yuan covered over a more important notice that China would henceforth bar foreign ownership of its steel sector. China has built a powerhouse steel industry larger than America's or Europe's by directing the funding, output, location and ownership of all factories. And rather than freeing industry through opening its borders to foreign competition, the Chinese, for steel and every other product, have shut out in-bound trade except as it suits China's own needs.

China won't join NAFTA or CAFTA or any of those free-trade clubs, and joined the WTO only on the *sotto voce* condition it could ignore all of the rules. In China, Chinese industry comes first. And it's still the *People's* republic, where the state and army own an unknown number of Wal-Mart's 4,800 suppliers. In an interview just before he won the Nobel Prize in economics, Joseph Stiglitz explained to me that China's huge financial surge of 9.5% per year began with the government's funding and nurturing rural cooperatives while protecting fledgling industry behind high, high trade barriers.

It is true that China's growth also got a boost from ending the blood-soaked self-flagellating madness of Mao's Cultural Revolution. And China, when it chooses, makes use of markets and market pricing to distribute resources efficiently. However, Chinese markets are as free as my kids: They can do whatever they want unless I say they can't.

Yes, China is adopting select elements of "capitalism." That's the ugly part. Chinese capitalism appears to be limited to real estate speculation in Shanghai, making millionaires of Communist party bosses' relatives and to bank shenanigans worthy of a Neil Bush. But it is not the Shanghai skyscraper bubble that is allowing China to sell us $200 billion more goods a year than we sell them. By rejecting free-market fundamentalism, China's government can easily conquer American markets where protection is now deemed passé.

Am I praising China? Forget it. China is Stalinist in governance, capitalist in sales pitches and feudalist in the division of wealth and power. This is one rank dictatorship that brutalizes, terrorizes and

Recipe for a Better World Order

Kerala Meen Kootaan (Fish Curry)

You won't find this on the menu at The Palm or the Four Seasons or other feedlots for rulers of the New World Order.

Chances are, you've never heard of Kerala, and the economic carnivores want to keep it that way. While the free-market Mouseketeers peddle the blood-soaked fake "miracle" of Chile as their model, Kerala has thrived, notes Nobelist Amartya Sen, on the economic cooperative model, with expansive social services and universal education.

This tiny Indian state on the Arabian Sea has a population more literate than any American state's—its main export is PhD's for energy and computer industries. In 1995, I visited a fishermen's cooperative.

This is what they fed me:

KERALA MEEN KOOTAAN (FISH CURRY)

Ingredients

1½ lb. firm white fish (cod, halibut, sword) or tuna cut into 1-inch cubes

1 medium onion, chopped

1-inch cube ginger, shredded

7 cloves garlic, chopped

2 tsp. mild Kashmiri Red Chili Powder (or ½ tsp. hot red chili powder plus 1 tsp. paprika)

1½ tsp. coriander powder

1 pinch turmeric powder

4 pinches fenugreek powder

2 tbsp. canola oil or other light-flavored oil

½ tsp. mustard seeds

10–12 curry leaves (Note: Curry leaf is NOT the whole form of that English mixture called "curry powder.")

2 tsp. tamarind paste

Continued

1 cup water

salt

2 tsp. coconut oil (optional, for garnishing)

Method

- Cut and clean the fish.
- In a blender or small food processor, make a paste of the following ingredients with a little water: onion, ginger, garlic, chili powder, coriander powder, turmeric, and fenugreek powder.
- Heat oil in a frying pan and fry mustard seed and curry leaf.
- Add the paste and fry all this well (until the oil separates).
- Now add the softened tamarind, and pour in the rest of the water.
- Then add salt. After it boils, add the fish.
- Let it simmer until the gravy thickens and the fish is tender.
- Lastly, sprinkle the coconut oil, and leave it on the heat for a minute.
- Serve it with white basmati rice or with boiled tapioca.

Thanks to Santhosh Shyamsundar in Cochin, Kerala, for recovering the recipe, Linda Levy in New York for converting it to the Western kitchen and Oliver Shykles of Brighton, UK, for testing it.

tortures. All must kowtow to the wishes of Chairman Rob—Wal-Mart chief Robson Walton.

Can this planet imitate Chinese success without Chinese autocracy? Yes, there is another way. I found it in an India not visible from Bangalore's golf courses.

In 1995, I dropped in on a fishing village in Kerala, a jarring but stunning day-long railway journey from Bangalore. Most of the village's fishermen worked from motorless dug-out log boats. Their language is Malayalam, but a large banner slung between two coconut trees announced in English, "WordPerfect applications class today." After they brought in the catch, the locals practiced programming on cardboard replicas of keyboards.

What made all this possible was not capitalist competitive drive (there was no corporate "entrepreneur" in sight), but the state's investment in universal education and the village's commitment to developing opportunities, not for a lucky few, but for the entire community. The village was 100% literate, 100% unionized, and 100% committed to sharing resources through a sophisticated credit union finance system.

This was the community welfare state at its best. Microsoft did not build the schools for programmers—the corporation only harvested what the socialist communities sowed.

The economist Amartya Sen won the Nobel Prize in 1998 for predicting that Southern India, with its strong social welfare state, would lead the economic advance of South Asia—and do so without the Thatcherite sleight of hand of pretending that riches for the few equates to progress for the many.

The Electro-Dollar Riots in Ecuador

In April 2005, I was in the Andes Mountains, standing on the equator, when a condor flew over and dropped a document into my hands marked, "FOR OFFICIAL USE ONLY." There were other warnings. The document's contents "may not be disclosed" without authorization of the World Bank. In light of the Bank's concern, please do not look at this document on the facing page.

Nowhere is the world flatter or more tilted than that part of the world that hangs down perilously from Texas: Latin America. Mother Nature has stocked these nations with a wealth of resources from gold to oil to cropland to hydropower, creating an El Dorado richer than any in the most extravagant dreams of the conquistadors. Yet 132 million South Americans live on less than $2 a day; and just a couple of years ago you could find schoolteachers in Buenos Aires hunting through garbage cans for dinner. Why? Because one resource was mined from their land until it was exhausted: capital.

FROM: Vice President and Corporate Secretary

Republic of Ecuador
Structural Adjustment Program Loan
(Loan 7024-EC)

Second Tranche Release

Attached for information is the memorandum of the President with the tranche release document entitled "Republic of Ecuador - Structural Adjustment Program Loan (Loan No. 7024-EC) - Second Tranche Release".

Questions on this document may be referred to M_____ se_____ _____, Ms. Calvo (ext. 36337).

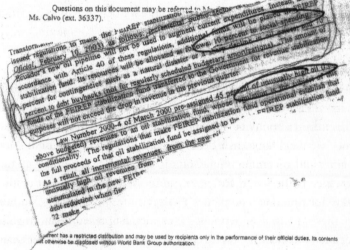

Transform_____ to make the FEIREP stabilizatio_ __ _____. Instead, and in issued regulations to fo_llows: increment_ p_ublic e_xpenditures will be pla_ce_ i_ FEIREP Oficial, February 10, 2003) as follows: increment_ p_ublic e_xpenditures w_ill be _____ in social spending. Th Ecuador's new oil pipeline will not be used to augment current expenditures. Instead, _____ accordance with Article 40 of these regulations, addition____ as fol_lows: 10 percent to _____. The amount of stabilization fund. Its resources will be allocated as follows: 10 percent for revenue stabilization percent to debt buybacks (not for regularly scheduled budgetary amortization. The amount of funds of the FEIREP stabilization fund transferred to the Government for revenue stabilization purposes will not exceed the drop in revenue in the previous quarter _____ of unusually high oil ri

Law Number 2000-4 of March 2000 pre-assigned 45 pe_____ ___ _____ _____ establis that above budgeted revenues to an oil stabilization fund, whose _____ __ FEIREP stabilization fund operational conditionality. The regulations that make FEIREP stabilization fund be assigned to th_ _____ the full proceeds of that oil stabilization fund from the new ___.

As a result, all incremental revenues from all unusually high oil revenues from the new FEIP___ accumulated in the new FEIP___ debt reduction when fisc___ 72 makes ___

In this confidential document, the World Bank orders Ecuador to give 90% of its increase in oil earnings to creditors, leaving only "10% to social spending."

I admit, I made up the bit about the condor. But I really did stand on the equator (a goofy, but obligatory, tourist stop for travelers to Ecuador) reading through a confidential document slipped to me by unhappy employees of the World Bank.

At the Ciudad Centro del Mundo, the City at the Center of the World, loudspeakers on poles scratch out some Inca-cum-New Age music while underdressed kids squat in the dirt selling gum. These great-great-grandchildren of the Inca have no water except what they can carry in jugs up hills. The national treasury cannot afford the $5 million for vaccinations the United Nations says these children must have.

However, their parents have been hit with electric bills of $30 to $60 a month. The bills are based on a price per kilowatt-hour that is twice the average paid by consumers in the U.S. That's one of the conditions dictated by the World Bank in the confidential agreement between Ecuador and the Bank. That's quite a price to pay in a nation where only a minority of the population earns the "minimum" wage of $153 a month. That's $153 a month U.S. money, and most items cost what they cost in the U.S. Try it out yourself for a month.

Why, in a nation so painfully poor, is the World Bank, an agency founded after World War II to help the helpless, requiring this nation to sock it to electricity customers? *Electro-dollars, Mr. Beale.* Electric utilities are marvelous cash cows. The costly systems are built with consumer and government funds, then "privatized" at pennies on the dollar. Electricity, water, and gas customers are hostages to the monopoly. To avoid the companies charging ransom instead of a fair price, these "natural" monopolies as economists called them, used to be regulated worldwide. Prices were set to match costs plus a strictly limited profit. No more.

Here's the secret condition set by the bank on Ecuador. If you want to see how the brave new globalization order works, forget code writers in India and iPods smaller than your pinky. This is what it's all about:

> The Borrower's [Ecuador's] Electricity Council has issued
> tariffs [that means 'set prices'] . . . at the longer marginal
> cost of electricity generation, transmission and distribu-
> tion calculated using a methodology acceptable to the
> Bank.

Let me translate from the Techno-Croatian. Charging at "cost"
sounds fine. But "cost" and "marginal cost" are two different animals,
especially by the "methodology acceptable to the bank." The cost of
producing electricity is cheap in Ecuador—they have water falling
right down the Andes for hydropower. But the "marginal cost" is
based on the world price of oil and gas—way, way above actual costs.
In effect, the Quechua families in Quito slums will be whacked with a
light bill based on the price of oil set by OPEC.[17]

And that's not all.

The Bank also required Ecuador to raise prices on basic foods.
What is behind such devastating cruelty—forcing Ecuadorans to
choose between lights and food? Always ask, *qui bono?*—who benefits?

Ecuador's bondholders in Miami, for sure. But first and foremost,
the privatized electric companies. Who are these guys?

There's Duke Energy (of the Carolinas), founded decades ago by
cigarette magnate James Buchanan Duke, which owns 51.5% of
"Electroquil," which, in 2004, demanded $30 million in back pay-
ments from the public. Duke's pathway into Ecuador's pocketbooks
was paved for them by the owners of "Emelec," the Spanish acronym
for its old name, American Foreign Power and Electric Corporation. It
was taken over by one of Ecuador's richest men, also the owner of one
of Ecuador's big banks whose assets, the deposits of half a million

---

[17]If you can handle a fuller academic discussion of the issue, read *Democracy and Regulation: How the Public Can Govern Essential Services,* by myself, Jerrold Oppenheim and Theo
MacGregor, a guide for regulators commissioned by the United Nations (Pluto Press,
2003).

customers, just seemed to evaporate. In 1999, that tycoon, Fernando Aspiazu, siphoned his Emelec shares out of his bank and dumped them into a Bahamas shell company to keep it out of government hands just before the police raided and seized the bank (and arrested Aspiazu, later jailed).

Aspiazu put a couple of front men in charge of selling the Emelec assets—now the government's claimed property—and sought Uncle Sam's political help. But Emelec was an Ecuadoran-Bahamian fugitive property by then, none of the business of the United States.

So the Bahamas shell obtained U.S. corporate citizenship through a tried and true route: The company's operators hired Henry Kissinger's lobbying firm, Kissinger McLarty Associates. The "McLarty" in this power duo is Mack McLarty, former Clinton chief of staff. The concerns of the Bahamian Kissinger-Americans suddenly became a crucial foreign policy concern of the U.S. Secretary of State Madeleine Albright, who personally put the screws to the president of Ecuador to get Emelec's complaints "resolved."

Welcome to the Flat World, Mr. Beale. In sum, the huge difference between electricity cost and price is a windfall for foreign owners, a windfall sucked right out of the Andes and sent straight to New York or to the Bahamas, or sometimes, simply pumped up the hill to the huge homes commanding the best views of Quito.

How that windfall is obtained is not always nice and rarely public. The World Bank, in its secret agreement with Ecuador, made sure the prices stayed sky high. *Electro-dollars, Mr. Beale*: one of the ways to squeeze dollar blood from the South American stone.

That was Margaret Thatcher's formula. If you want to seize a nation's economy, grab it by its lightbulbs. She used the terminology of military conquest, "seize the commanding heights," to describe the sale of public utility systems. "Privatize" and "deregulate" public services, starting with electricity, telephone and water systems, and the rest of the economy will soon be forced to adopt the free-market nostrums of "supply-side" economics. If the nation doesn't come along willingly, the World Bank, holding the nation's access to credit markets in its hands, will impose a "methodology" for pricing and privatization "acceptable to the Bank" and its stockholders.

The World Bank and IMF also required Ecuador to throw away its own currency and replace it with U.S. dollars. Those $60 electric bills, for example, must be paid by Quito residents *in U.S. currency*. As a result, Ecuador must borrow and pay interest on the U.S. dollar bills sitting in every Ecuadoran's wallet.

When Ecuador's currency was "dollarized," the wealthy took their crisp new bills with Alexander Hamilton on them and sent them, literally, to Miami. Ecuador's banks, like Mr. Aspiazu's, with their dollar reserves missing and stashed in the USA, collapsed. The IMF demanded the nation's treasury bail out the banks' private shareholders. That added a huge new debt to be paid by all Ecuadorans.

But Ecuador can afford it. Ecuador is rich. The vast nation of only thirteen million citizens sits on a pool of oil worth a quarter trillion dollars. The solution is painfully obvious: Let Ecuadorans keep their oil wealth, at least enough to keep the lights on and pay for their children's vaccines.

But that solution runs smack up against paragraph III-1 of the World Bank's confidential plan, the "Structural Adjustment Program for Ecuador."

New oil wealth from a new oil pipeline will be spent per World Bank orders as follows:

> . . . 10% to social spending; 20% for contingencies . . . ;
> and 70% to debt buybacks, not for regularly scheduled
> budgeted amortizations.

How generous: Ecuador gets to keep 10%. "Social spending" by the way, means schools and medicine. The codicil says the big bucks, 70% of its new oil wealth, will go to bondholders to buy back their bonds. (These payments are over and above interest payments.) Another 20% will go into an "oil stabilization fund"—that is, another reserve for the bondholders.

The bonds are held by speculators who, in most cases, purchased them for twenty cents on the dollar. The IMF plan calls for expediting payment at five times what these speculators paid for the bonds, a swift, neat 500% return. Who *are* these guys collecting the windfall? Who is squeezing Ecuador by the bonds? The nation's President says, "The tragedy is that we don't know who owns the bonds." The greater tragedy is that, according to a U.N. official I spoke with, the bonds are held by the same crew in Miami that bled the nation's banks dry.

The terms imposed by the IMF for new financing would make a loan shark blanch. Electricity prices would rise, as well as charges for cooking gas. And Ecuador would agree to open its delicate jungle areas to oil drilling by Chevron Oil, the company that named a tanker after a corporate board member, Condoleezza.

I traveled to Quito to meet with then-President, Alfredo Palacio, to discuss with him the confidential IMF terms. That was not easy. First, an aide to the President told me the U.S. State Department had warned Palacio against meeting with me. (It's comforting to know that *someone* in the Bush Administration is reading my reports.) Second, Palacio had taken office only days before, on April 20, when his predecessor disappeared out the back door of the Carondelet Palace to seek asylum in Brazil. Then-President Lucio Gutierrez was fleeing a crowd of one hundred thousand protesters, angry and hungry Quechua Indians from the hills, seeking his arrest.

"Sucio Lucio" (*Dirty Lucio*, a nickname I believe even his mother uses) had won election in 2002 promising to break away from the supposedly "voluntary" austerity plan imposed by the World Bank. Within a month of taking office, Gutierrez flew to Washington, held hands with George Bush (a photo now infamous in Quito) and received instruction from U.S. Treasury officials in the financial facts of life. Lucio returned to Quito, reneged on his campaign promises and acceded to every demand of the IMF to raise prices of basic necessities and cut services, from hospitals to schools. The public, after a dispirited three-year delay, revolted. Sucio fled and his Vice President, Palacio, was sworn in.

On April 25, 2005, when I arrived at the Presidential Palace, crowds were still there, chanting their suspicions that the new President would follow Sucio Lucio's path.

But Palacio saw no reason to adopt the extreme free-market path to economic asphyxiation. At his inauguration, Palacio suggested that Ecuador might keep a little of its oil wealth for health and education needs.

That's not what the Bush Administration wanted to hear. Secretary of State Condi Rice fired a diplomatic cruise missile, calling for new elections to get Palacio out of the way.

President Palacio seemed an unlikely target of U.S. official assaults. He comes off like a cardiologist you'd meet at an AMA convention. That is, in fact, what he is: a heart doctor who practiced in the USA for a decade. Affiliated with no political party, he was brought into the government to build a national health program.

Palacio is soft-spoken, conservative in his views and pro-American—but his patient, his nation, is ill from diving into an extreme form of free-market globalization ordered by the World Bank.

He just wanted to keep a few petro-dollars for the vaccines and general welfare. "Sick people," he told me, "are not going to produce anything."

I showed him the World Bank confidential agreement signed by his predecessor. He was obviously familiar with the terms.

"If we pay that amount of debt," he told me, "we're dead. We have to *survive*."

He was quite certain that Condi Rice, the World Bank and the foreign bondholders would listen to simple medical logic. "If we die, who is going to pay them?"

But they didn't listen. Getting off the petro-dollar cycle, or at least slowing it down, is not so easy. Just by Palacio's suggesting he might redirect some oil money, within weeks of Wolfowitz taking over the World Bank, Ecuador was cut off by both the Bank and IMF. Ecuador's bonds were facing a boycott.

The Quechua-speaking indigenous population, the ones who

drove out Sucio Lucio, were still unhappy. They reaped almost nothing from foreign corporations drilling their oil except poisoned water and a destroyed rainforest. In the summer of 2005, fed up, indigenous protesters occupied Occidental Petroleum's rainforest oil production facilities. The nation, starved for both cash and gasoline, fell into crisis.

Then, when hope seemed lost, in August 2005, a dark stranger rode into Ecuador, wrote a check for $200 million to buy up Ecuador's bonds and restore the nation's credit. The Stranger from Caracas also brought along two million barrels of crude oil, diesel fuel and naphtha to keep the nation moving. Then he rode on to Argentina with a check for nearly a billion dollars to bail out that nation's bonds.

Before we meet this Lone Ranger, let me explain why this chapter travels to Ecuador and Argentina. First, we need to illustrate that there's more to Latin America than cheap resources. There's cheap capital, mined from banks and public utilities, which is then lent back to them at a dear price. Second, if China is the new Saudi Arabia, offering up cheap, cheap labor, then Latin America will soon be the new China. The threat that the American dream is too costly in a Flat World is, at its core, the Haves telling you that they can hire Chinese textile workers and scientists for pennies. And therefore, you shall Have Not. Nothing has changed since railroad magnates imported Chinese workers to California during the Gold Rush to lay railroad track. Now Chinese labor is transported by Internet or in products on container ships.

But the scare of a "Yellow Peril" to U.S. and European workers has a short lifespan. In what may be one of the most important economic reports to go unread and unnoticed is a rare CIA public projection of China's economy, *Mapping the Global Future*. By 2020, says the CIA, China's GDP will be the world's second largest, but the headlines in that year will be about China's looming labor shortage and devastating population decline. The fanatic one-child-per-family diktats of the Communist Party will make it the *oldest* nation in world history. A third of a billion elderly retirees, encompassing 25% of a shrinking population, will create a production crisis beyond imagination. That leaves only one place with both a surplus working-age population and functioning infrastructure: Latin America. U.S. workers will then be kept in line with a new threat, a "Brown Tide" of employees in Ecuador and environs willing to undercut even China's wages.

Not all Latins have been willing to play coolie to foreign operators. Decades ago, Buenos Aires was the Paris of South America, and living standards were higher there than anywhere south of our border under a government in the hands of the nation's labor unions. But that came to an end with the thirty-year military dictatorship that began in 1955. In 1991, facing the problem of a temporary drop in its commodity prices and wild inflation, Argentina's elected "Peronist" government swallowed every pill in the free-market remedy bottle. The nation's electric systems, its "commanding heights," were sold off, as was Argentina's big state oil company. Both were gobbled up by operators from Spain and Chile. Now Argentina pays for its oil and power instead of selling it. Argentina effectively dumped its own currency by fixing it one-for-one to the U.S. dollar. It opened its borders to free trade and ended capital controls—permitting money to move in and out. Predictably, the money moved *out* and out. At least $189 billion of the nation's savings in its own banks, once freed from capital controls, floated north on the Money Gulf Stream to seek a safe haven in U.S. Treasury bills and other North American securities. In return for safety, Argentines accepted 4% and 5% returns on their U.S. investments. But then Argentina's government had to borrow it all back, paying, in 2001, a 16% interest rate to U.S. lenders. Out *to* the United States at 4%, back in *from* the United States at 16%, then out and in again—*the ebb and flow, Mr. Beale*—a financial suicide cycle that exploded, in December 2001, into riots in Buenos Aires, national bankruptcy and starvation in what had been South America's breadbasket.

In 1997, the World Bank and IMF had held up Argentina as the poster child, the proud advertisement, for the wonders of the Friedman/Beale free-market future. And what was the result of their handiwork in Argentina? Manufacturing wages averaging $4.03 per hour in 1997 dove to half that ($2.12 per hour) in 2003.

Despite the dismal results of their advice, even now the World Bank and its globalization twin, the International Monetary Fund, continue to demand more sell-offs, more deregulation from Argentina. But this time, a new president, Nestor Kirchner, has said, *basta!*—enough! He stopped payment on some of the most usurious bonds—and told the IMF and World Bank to go fly.

Resistance paid off. Since the new president's taking office in 2003, Argentine wages have begun to rise. Still, long-term recovery for Argentina, suffering from a capital boycott by the bond market, remained in question. Then the Lone Ranger arrived with his half billion dollars.

Who is this guy, a mini-IMF unto himself, breaking the cycle of ebb and flow?

The Assassination of Hugo Chávez

On August 26, 2005, the Lord spoke to His servant on cable television and His servant told the faithful watching in TV land:

> Hugo Chávez thinks we're trying to assassinate him. I think that we really ought to go ahead and do it.

Reverend Pat Robertson has a tough time with the separation of church and hate. But Pat Robertson is not crazy. He is, in fact, one of the most ingenious, *un-crazy* men I've ever met. And the most calculating and viperous. Those who dismiss him as some cornpone, Bible-thumping Elmer Gantry fruitcake have dangerously underestimated him and his reach into political and financial power centers in Washington and abroad.

He never speaks for himself. Whether he speaks for God, I can't say, but certainly Dr. Robertson uses his television platform to preach the evangel of the elite to which he was born. His father, U.S. Senator Absalom Willis Robertson, was the mentor of Senator Prescott Bush.

"I am not a 'televangelist,' " he told me. "I am a *businessman*."

And when he spoke of taking down Hugo Chávez, President of Venezuela, Robertson was all business. The hit the Reverend proposed was calculated for risks and rewards like any investment:

> It's a whole lot cheaper than starting a war, and I don't think any oil shipments will stop. This is a dangerous enemy to our South controlling a huge pool of oil that could hurt us very badly. . . . We don't need another $200 billion war. . . . It's a whole lot easier to have some of the covert operatives do the job and then get it over with.

When I met with President Chávez in Caracas, in April 2002, he offered to write the introduction to the Spanish translation of my last book. I'm not crazy about politicians endorsing journalists, but I agreed on condition he meet the deadline: He'd have to write it before he's dead.

Chávez wasn't overly concerned. "It's a game of chess, Mr. Palast. And I'm a *very* good chess player."

He's more than that. He is, as Robertson says, a dangerous man. But dangerous to whom?

> *Mr. Beale, the Arabs have taken billions of dollars out of this country, and now they must put it back. It is ebb and flow, tidal gravity.*

In October 2005, Hugo Chávez defied gravity and withdrew $20 billion of Venezuela's petro-dollars from the United States Federal Reserve and deposited the money in an account with the International Bank of Settlements for investment in Latin America.

> *There is no Third World, there are no nations, Mr. Beale, there is only IBM and Exxon.*

Maybe. At the beginning of 2001, Venezuela instituted a new "Law of Hydrocarbons." Henceforth, Exxon, British Petroleum and Shell Oil, the major oil extractors in Venezuela, would get to keep only 70% of the sales revenues from the Venezuelan crude they sold. The oil majors had grown accustomed to their usual take—84%. The reaction to the reduction in Big Oil's share of the Venezuelan pie was swift. Otto Reich, Assistant Secretary of State for Western Hemispheric Affairs, met with Venezuelan "dissident" billionaires and shortly thereafter, on April 11, 2002, Chávez was kidnapped. The President of Venezuela's Chamber of Commerce, an oil industry lawyer, declared himself President of the nation—giving a whole new meaning to the term "corporate takeover." The coup d'état against the elected president, Chávez, was endorsed by *The New York Times*.

On April 12, banking and oil industry chiefs held an inaugural party in Venezuela's Presidential Palace. The U.S. Ambassador rushed down to have his picture taken with his arms around the partying coup leaders. But within twenty-four hours, the party was over. I learned later that Chávez, geopolitical grandmaster, had expected the coup and planted commandoes inside secret passages of the Presidential Palace. When informed that Chávez had secretly moved his knights into kill position, the partygoers took off their custom-made Presidential sashes and costumes and returned the real President to his desk, without bloodshed, within 48 hours of his capture. The *Times* apologized.

But not the White House. Bush's spokesman conceded Chávez "was democratically elected," *but,* he added, "legitimacy is something that is conferred not just by a majority of the voters." I see.

Chávez was just warming up. Exxon had begun tapping into Venezuela's heavy tar oils in the Orinoco Basin. Despite rising oil prices, Exxon figured the government should be satisfied with a 1% tax on the profits. Chávez changed that to a 16.6% tax.

Shell Oil and other foreign extractors had made a habit of not paying taxes on their oil windfalls. Shell, when handed the back-tax bill, balked and was surprised to find itself, in 2005, bounced out of a lucrative natural gas project. Chávez redirected the gas, meant for export, back to Venezuela's own consumers.

Venezuela has landless citizens by the millions. It also has unused land by the millions of acres locked up in fallow plantations on which a tiny elite had squatted for four centuries. In 2001, a new law required selling untilled land to the landless. It was a program long promised by Venezuelan politicians at the urging of John F. Kennedy as part of his Alliance for Progress. Progress waited for Chávez.

Heinz Ketchup's Venezuela division didn't like the new terms for doing business and shut its plant in the state of Maturin. Venezuela seized the multinational's property and put the workers back to work.

Pat Robertson was not the first to suggest terminating Chávez with prejudice. In response to previous threats, the very good chess player instituted a kind of "assassination tax" on U.S. oil companies. Every time a new plot to shoot the President was foiled, Chávez's tax authorities would send another bill for those "back taxes." Shell was hit with a new $130 million tax bill and got the point. In June 2004, neocon Otto Reich, friend of the coup plotters, was dis-employed by the U.S. State Department.

And what does Chávez do with Shell Oil's tax money?

In Caracas, I met with a reporter for the TV station whose owner is generally credited with having backed the failed 2002 coup. She pointed to the "ranchos," the slums, above Caracas where shacks, most made of cardboard and tin, were quickly transforming into homes of cinder blocks and cement. "He gives them bread and bricks, so they vote for him, of course." She was disgusted. By "them," she meant the 80% of Venezuela that is "negro e indio" (Black and Indian). This poor, dark 80% had, until Chávez ran for President, left the running of government, and the spending of the nation's wealth, to the minority white 20%.

The bread and bricks, and jobs and new health clinics, are intimately tied to the "ebb and flow" of capital; and now Chávez was standing in its way. In early 2003, his government overturned the keystone of borderless globalization and imposed controls on the movement of capital. *The Wall Street Journal* reported, with surprise, that instead of economic doom:

> . . . the controls trapped liquidity within the economy,
> which in part led to reduced interest rates and helped
> boost economic activity.

Lots of economic activity. In 2005, their economy grew by 9.4%,
the highest in the Western Hemisphere, following a blazing 17.9% in
2004, with the biggest boosts occurring in the *non*-oil sector. Government services for health, education and food subsidies didn't drain
the economy, as "flat world" globalizers predicted, but added to economic demand and productivity.

Chávez then waded further into the rushing flow of international
finance to build another economic dam. His backers in Venezuela's
Congress voted to require all private banks to dedicate 20% of their
lending portfolio to "micro-loans" for small businesses and small-plot
farmers. As a result, a large portion of the oil wealth in Venezuela
would have to stay there, barred from flowing northward as is the cus-
tom with petro-dollars. Most important, 20% of the working class's
savings would be channeled back to it rather than rising upward to
fund the extravagant high-rises in Caracas.

There's no question that Chávez's largesse to the "negros e indios,"
for the bricks and medicine and loans abroad, is made possible only
by wildly high prices of petroleum. That still makes Chávez one of a
rare breed. After all, the new oil riches of Kazakhstan ended up, at
least $51 million of it, in the Swiss bank account of its President (ac-
cording to the bagman who deposited it). At the same time, pensions
in Kazakhstan are half of what they were in 1993. Despite the windfall of receipts from privatization of the Kazakh oil fields, the Red
Cross reports that the unequal distribution of the nation's oil wealth
has pushed "three-quarters of Kazakhstan's 15.7 million population
below the poverty line." Tuberculosis is now epidemic in the oil-rich
nation. Kazakhstan's manufacturing employment has fallen by 36%
and its GDP has imploded. Other developing oil states—Nigeria, Indonesia, Sudan—show just as little interest in distributing their petroleum wealth to the mass of their citizenry.

And, after all, Venezuela itself was a wealthy oil exporter long before Chávez, without much to show for it except massive international debts. Three decades ago, I wrote about the "peasants under the bridges in golden Caracas in shacks made of packing boxes." That was after the real price of oil hit $80 a barrel. Then, in the 1970s, in Caracas, no one passed out bricks and bread.

Chávez is called a Marxist and a socialist. He is neither. His reformist, cooperative and redistributionist program, and his handling of oil wealth, is clearly "Norwegian-ist." Chávez *is* a dramatist, calling his Scandinavian-style reforms the "Bolivarian revolution." It seems to drive Washington just crazy that brown people are demanding Nordic privileges.

It's one thing to be kind to poor folk, another to rearrange the global flow of petroleum. After bouncing Shell from one project, Chávez signed major development deals with the state oil companies of Brazil, China and India. Now, for the first time, a flow of crude would bypass the oil majors. Chávez was cruising for a bruising.

And it was Chávez, of course, who played Latin Lone Ranger to Ecuador and Argentina, writing checks to support their bond sales. And when Ecuador's indigenous population seized Occidental Petroleum's fields, it was Chávez who arrived in Quito with two million barrels of oil products in tow to keep the nation on wheels. The point was clear: Petroleum and petro-dollars could ebb and flow without Occidental or Chevron.

And without the IMF and World Bank. It was *The Wall Street Journal* that dubbed Chávez "a tropical version of the International Monetary Fund, offering cut-rate oil-supply deals and buying hundreds of millions of dollars of bonds from financially distressed countries such as Argentina and Ecuador." The un-tropical International Monetary Fund in Washington was not amused, nor were money center banks of New York and London. Petro-dollars are supposed to move from Venezuela to New York and only *then* return to Latin America as loans carrying interest rates up to 16%. Chávez, bypassing the side trip to

New York, showed that the costly financial cycle is *not,* Mr. Beale, "tidal gravity . . . an immutable law."

And to underscore the point, Chávez traveled to more Third World nations with gifts of low-cost oil: the Bronx, New York, and Chicago's West Side. In September 2005, Chávez offered these poor racial Bantustans within the USA (Hispanic neighborhoods in Chicago, African-American 'hoods in the Bronx) discounted heating oil through CITGO, the U.S. retail outlet of Venezuela's oil company. A public relations gimmick? Undoubtedly. But Chávez is making a point: The public, American public included, does not have to remain hostage to the Saudi-Houston cartel.

Chávez is a wily gamester. He pushes only so far. He may tax the oil majors, sell to their Brazilian competitors and spend oil loot in Ecuador, but his state oil company has, at strategic moments, waived most of the higher royalties and signed lucrative contracts with Exxon and Shell to extract offshore gas reserves. His government sells tantalizing morsels of concessions in the Orinoco Basin to keep industry majors mollified.

Nevertheless, Chávez has challenged the great ebb and flow of international finance capital and petro-dollars. If Chávez were president of Kazakhstan, he could play Robin Hood with his nation's oil money without incurring the fanatic wrath of the White House. Venezuela is a different matter altogether. Chávez is, correctly, seen as a class warrior, a crafty opponent of what George Bush calls "the impressive crowd, the Haves and the Have-Mores." Chávez wanted me to film him under the larger-than-life oil painting of Latin America's "Great Liberator," Simon Bolívar. Chavez sees himself as Bolívar, taking his class war beyond his borders, from Argentina to the Bronx, tilting the flat world back to level.

Can he? The difference between a grandiose nut and a grand visionary is the economic power to impose the vision. What makes Chávez's declaration of worldwide class war credible can be understood by returning to Hubbert's Peak.

Chávez Scales the "Peak"

We need to bring Guy Caruso back into this discussion. Caruso, you'll recall from Chapter 2, is the former CIA oil expert, now the Energy Department information chief, who gave Paul Wolfowitz's Pentagon the realistic projections of Iraq oil production that the U.S. public never saw.

In June 2005, Caruso flew to Kuala Lumpur, Malaysia, to present a series of charts to a select crowd of state oil chiefs.

One chart Caruso presented in Malaysia was a reproduction of Hubbert's famous 1956 "peak oil" graph. Caruso did not challenge Hubbert's total crude oil potential reserve figures. Rather, in two other charts, Caruso added to Hubbert's liquid oil reserves an additional sum for heavy oils, petroleum with a "viscosity over 10,000 centipoise"— that is, tar sands and tar oil.

The sums were significant. Canada holds 80% of the world's "bitumen" sands. The chart shows an even bigger pool of untapped oil, the super-heavy tar oils of Venezuela. And there's a lot of it: 1.36 *trillion* barrels in Venezuela, more oil than Hubbert suggested lay under the entire planet. Venezuela, warns Caruso, holds 90% of the earth's heavy oil reserves. *Ninety percent.* This reserve remains hidden, "off the books," unless and until the price of oil rises permanently above $28 a barrel, at which point the Venezuelan oil is worth pulling up.

Caruso didn't need to translate the charts into Arabic. Middle Eastern oil men in the room would have understood his message. At $14 a barrel, the long-term historic price of oil, Saudi Arabia holds the world's biggest reserve of oil. But at $30 to $40 a barrel, Venezuela is, by a long way, the oil reserve champ. Add Venezuela's liquid reserves to its "tar oil" and Saudi Arabia becomes a poor cousin, a bit player.

The geopolitical implications are monumental. Saudi Arabia's control of OPEC (and, by extension, the kingdom's control of world prices) depends on its overwhelming reserve superiority. If the Saudis insist on keeping the price above $30 a barrel for the coming decade, Caruso's chart suggests, the fulcrum of power in OPEC shifts back

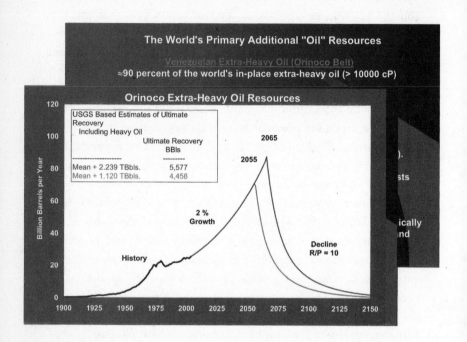

The World's Primary Additional "Oil" Resources

Venezuelan Extra-Heavy Oil (Orinoco Belt)
≈90 percent of the world's in-place extra-heavy oil (> 10000 cP)

Orinoco Extra-Heavy Oil Resources

USGS Based Estimates of Ultimate Recovery
Including Heavy Oil

	Ultimate Recovery BBls
Mean + 2.239 TBbls.	5,577
Mean + 1.120 TBbls.	4,458

2 % Growth

History

2055

2065

Decline R/P = 10

Chávez: Abdullah of the Americas?

Guy Caruso—former CIA, now DOE—presented this chart to oil industry and ministers in Kuala Lumpur, Malaysia, June 2005. Caruso warns that if oil stays above $30 a barrel, OPEC's power center shifts—to Venezuela.

west to the Americas; not to the USA, but to Venezuela—a Venezuela with a President who does not believe his country's petro-dollars, Mr. Beale, should ebb and flow but insists that this oil money remain south of New York.

This information, you can imagine, does not bring joy to the White House. Dick Cheney didn't invade Iraq to make Hugo Chávez the Abdullah of the Americas.

On September 15, 2006, addressing the United Nations General Assembly, Chávez responded to Reverend Robertson's assassination prayer with some theological musings of his own. "It smells of sulfur here," said the President of Venezuela. The Devil's perfume was left at the podium, implied Chávez, by a previous speaker, George Bush.

The diplomats were amused, the U.S. press got huffy, but the White House had heard worse—and said worse. The White House publicly brushed off Chávez' words, but privately, they could not brush aside Caruso's charts. At the UN, Chávez added, "God is with us." From the White House's view, the Venezuelan had with him something more significant than the Lord: more oil than Saudi Arabia.

Caruso's charts sharpened the question confronting Saudi Arabia and the White House: How can Hugo Chávez be stopped from becoming the Bill Gates of petroleum?

There are two methods to undermine Chávez's power. First, the unattractive choice: Cut the price of oil. Option two: Kill him.

Conventional Wisdom ©Winston Smith 2004

CHAPTER 4

THE CON

Kerry Won. Now Get Over It . . .

. . . because they're putting '08 in their pocket. Republicans just seem to have that winning spirit. They also have caging lists, felons of the future, rotting ballots, snuffed canaries, and a lock on the votes of Kissinger-Americans and the undead.

WARNING! There are cranks and kooks and crazies out there on the Internet who say that George Bush *lost* the 2004 election, like one titled, "Kerry Won" published on the TomPaine.com Web site two days after the election. I wrote it.

On November 11, a week after TomPaine.com published it, I received an e-mail from *The New York Times* Washington bureau. Hot on the investigation of the veracity of the vote, the *Times* reporter asked me pointed questions:

> Question #1: Are you a "sore loser"?
> Question #2: Are you a "conspiracy nut"?

There was no third question. Investigation of the vote was, for the *Times* at any rate, complete. The next day, the paper's thorough analysis of the evidence yielded this front-page story, "VOTE FRAUD THEORIES, SPREAD BY BLOGS, ARE QUICKLY BURIED."

As America's self-proclaimed Paper of Record had no space for the facts, I thought I'd share some with you here.

"Kerry Won" was not a two-day inquiry à la *Times*. It was the latest in a series of investigative reports coming out of a four-year team examination, begun for BBC Television's *Newsnight*, Britain's *Guardian* papers and *Harper's* magazine, dissecting that greasy sausage called American electoral democracy.

And, by the way, the answer to Question #1: *I* didn't lose, so I'm not sore. This investigation isn't about John Kerry. As a journalist, I don't give a toss which rich white kid won the game. But I'm not so blasé that I don't care about the disappearance of American democracy. And I really wanted to know how the Bushes swallowed the sausage.

How'd they do it? *Again.* And how will they do it in '08? The answer arrived just after midnight on October 8, 2004, three weeks before the official voting, in a series of extraordinary e-mails. The e-mails were intended for the chieftains of the president's reelection campaign in Washington. Strangely enough, they were misaddressed and ended up in my mailbox. Such things happen.

Night of the Uncounted: How to Disappear
Three Million Votes

But the e-mails and their technical attachments won't mean a thing unless you understand some arcane facts about elections American-style.

First, take a look at these two balls on the next page.

These are CNN's Ohio exit polls broadcast just after midnight after the voting ended on Election Day. They show John Kerry defeated George Bush among women voters by 53% to 47%. And among men voters, Kerry defeated Bush 51% to 49%.

So here's your question, class: What third sex put George Bush over the top in Ohio and gave him the White House?

Answer: the uncounted.

The nasty little secret of American democracy is that, in every national election, ballots cast are simply thrown in the garbage—

Exit Polls 1:05 AM, 11/3/04

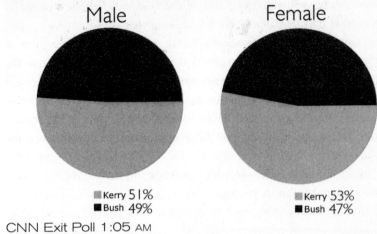

Male   Female

■ Kerry 51%   ■ Kerry 53%
■ Bush 49%   ■ Bush 47%

CNN Exit Poll 1:05 AM

millions of them. Most are called "spoiled," supposedly unreadable, damaged, invalid. They just don't get counted.

In Ohio, there were 153,237 ballots simply thrown away, more than the Bush "victory" margin. In New Mexico the uncounted vote was *five times* the Bush alleged victory margin of 5,988. In Iowa, Bush's triumph of 13,498 was overwhelmed by 36,811 votes rejected. In all, *over three million votes were cast but never counted* in the 2004 presidential election. The official number is bad enough—1,855,827 ballots cast not counted, reported to the federal government's Election's Assistance Commission. But the feds are missing data from several cities and entire states too embarrassed to report the votes they failed to count. Correcting for the under-reporting of the undercount, the number of ballots cast but never counted goes to 3,006,380. And there are certainly more we couldn't locate to tote up. *Why doesn't your government tell you this?* Hey, they do. It's right there in black and white on a U.S. Census Bureau announcement released seven months after the election—in a *footnote* to the report on voter turnout. The Census tabulation of voters voting "differs," it reads, from ballots tallied by the Clerk of the House of Representatives for the 2004 presidential race by 3.4 million votes.

This is the hidden presidential count, which, with the exception of the Census's whispered footnote, has not been reported. In the voting biz, most of these lost votes are called "spoilage." Spoilage, not the voters, picked our President for us.

Unfortunately, that's not all. In addition to the 3 million ballots uncounted due to technical "glitches," millions more were lost because the voters were prevented from casting their ballots in the first place. This group of un-votes includes voters illegally denied registration or wrongly purged from the registries.

Joe Stalin, the story goes, said, "It's not the people who vote that count; it's the people who count the votes." That may have been true in the old Soviet Union, but in the USA, the game is much, much subtler: He who makes sure votes *don't* get counted decides our winners.

In the lead-up to the 2004 race, millions of Americans were, not unreasonably, panicked about computer voting machines, "black boxes," that could flip your vote from John Kerry to George Bush. Images abounded of an evil hacker-genius in Dick Cheney's bunker rewriting code and zapping the totals. But that's not how it went down. The computer scare was the McGuffin, the fake detail used by magicians to keep your eye off their hands. The new black boxes played their role, albeit minor, but the principal means of the election heist—voiding ballots, overwhelmingly of the poor and Black—went unexposed, unreported and most importantly, uncorrected and ready to roll out on a grander scale in 2008.

Like a forensic CSI unit, we can perform a post mortem starting with the exhumation of more than 3 million uncounted votes:

- **Provisional Ballots Rejected.** An entirely new species of ballot debuted nationwide in 2004, the "provisional ballot." These were crucial to the Bush victory. Not that Republicans won this "provisional" vote. Republicans won by the rejection of provisional ballots that were cast overwhelmingly in Democratic precincts. The sum of "the uncounted" is astonishing: 676,676 ballots lost in the counties reporting to the federal government. Add in the missing jurisdictions and the un-vote climbs to over a million: 1,090,729 provisional ballots tossed out.

- **Spoiled Ballots.** You vote, you assume it's counted. Think again. These are the votes that bad machines fail to record. Your "x" was too light for a machine to read. You didn't punch the card hard enough and so you "hung your chad." Therefore, your vote didn't count and, crucially, *you'll never know it*. And you'd have lots of company. The federal election assistance agency toted up nearly a million ballots cast not counted. Add in states too shy to report to Washington, the total "spoilage" jumps to a rotten 1,389,231.

- **Absentee Ballots Uncounted.** The number of absentee ballots has quintupled in many states, with the number rejected on picayune technical grounds rising to over half a million (526,420) in 2004. In swing states, absentee ballot shredding was pandemic.

- **Voters Barred from Voting.** In this category we find that combination of incompetence and trickery that stops voters from pulling that lever in the first place. There's the purge of "felon" voters from vote registries that continues to eliminate thousands whose only crime is VWB, Voting While Black. It includes subtle games like eliminating polling stations in opponent's districts, creating impossible lines. No one can pretend to calculate a hard number for all votes lost this way any more than you can find every bullet fragment in a mutilated body. But it's a safe bet that the numbers reach into the hundreds of thousands of voters locked out of the voting booth.

Proportion of Ballots
That Were Not Counted
By Precinct, November 2000 Election

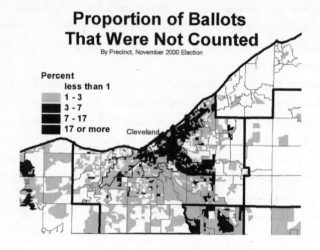

Percent
less than 1
1 - 3
3 - 7
7 - 17
17 or more

Cleveland

Percent African American
Persons 18 and Older, One Race Catagory

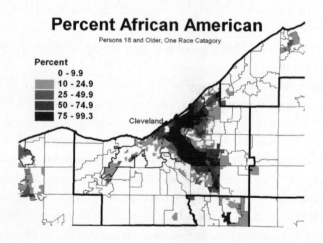

Percent
0 - 9.9
10 - 24.9
25 - 49.9
50 - 74.9
75 - 99.3

Cleveland

An Apartheid Vote Count? If the Boot Fits . . .

Maps by Mark J. Salling, PhD, Cleveland State University

Counting by Colors

So big deal. If the buried ballots split evenly, then Kerry voters didn't get the shaft. But that's not what happens.

Not everyone's vote "spoils" the same.

Look at the maps of Cleveland, Ohio (Cuyahoga County), on the opposing page. That boot-shaped stain on the top shows the precincts where ballots were thrown away, "spoiled." The vote spoilage boot makes a perfectly matched pair with Cleveland's boot-shaped ghetto shown on the bottom.

The maps tell us: Dive into the electoral Dumpster and you'll find that the ballots rotting away there are very Black.

But why pick on Ohio?

Look at the chart "Rejection of Votes by Race."

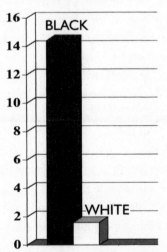

**REJECTION OF VOTE
BY RACE**

Black: 14.4% Cast not counted
White: 1.6% Cast not counted

This little gem is taken from an unnoticed appendix to a report by the U.S. Civil Rights Commission. There are two sticks. The short stick shows ballots of "non-Black" voters rejected: 1.6%. That is, just one in 63 ballots cast by white folk are tossed in the garbage.

Now look at the black stick: 14.4% of Black voters' ballots are tossed in the garbage, uncounted. One in seven.

This bar chart showing racially biased hanky-panky in the vote count is a statistical analysis of precinct-by-precinct data in Florida. Now let's do the arithmetic, class. Given the racial breakdown of Florida's population (13% African-American), that means that *over half* (54%) of the "spoiled" votes in Florida were cast by African-American voters.

So what? I'll tell you what, using the 2000 election as an example (no, I haven't gotten over it). Black folk cast 54% of the 179,855 ballots "spoiled" in Florida in that election. Given the nearly unanimous support for Democrats among those Black voters, candidate Al Gore undoubtedly was the choice of the vast majority of those votes thrown in the spoilage bin. Indeed, we can calculate, with high accuracy, that Gore's total vote in the state would have been higher by 77,000 if all spoiled votes had been tallied[18]—in a race officially giving the presidency to Mr. Bush by 537 votes.

I'm not saying that the Bush family "stole" the election, but that in Florida in 2000, Al Gore actually received at least 77,000 more of the votes *cast* in Florida than Mr. Bush.

They just didn't count them.

But that is the Florida of "Jeb Crow," a very un-nice name sometimes used for our President's brother Jeb, Governor of the Sunshine State. Other states are different, right?

Wrong. It turns out Florida is, statistically, terribly *typical* of the USA. Like Florida, 13% of the population of America the Beautiful is

---

[18]For the arithmetic of vote-fixing, see "Florida by the Numbers" at www.gregpalast.com/florida-by-the-numbersal-gore-won-florida-in-2000-by-77000-votes.

African-American, and if you're Black, the chance your vote will be "spoiled" is 900% higher than if you're white, same as in Florida. And that's not pretty.

Consider the effect of spoilage on the Kerry-Bush tally. Of the 1.4 million spoiled ballots cast and not counted in 2004, based on the racial difference in spoilage, we know that a bit more than half, about three-quarters of a million of those uncounted votes, were cast by African-American voters. And we haven't even gone over the horrendous "spoilage" rates among Hispanics and Native Americans. Altogether, nearly a million minority votes were lost in 2004, disappeared, just *fftt!*

Add to the 1.4 million spoiled votes the 1.1 million rejected provisionals, all of them race-loaded, and you've found the key to unlock the strange results of 2004, where voters told exit pollsters they voted "Kerry" but the official count said "Bush." Take a look at these states:

Voters Lie?

	Voters Said (Exit Poll)	Votes Counted (Official Tally)
Iowa	Kerry wins by 2%	Bush wins by 1%
New Mexico	Kerry wins by 2%	Bush wins by 1%
Ohio	Kerry wins by 4%	Bush wins by 2%

Nationwide, 51% told polling agents standing at the voting station exits that, only minutes before, they had voted for Kerry. Only 48% of those leaving the polls said they voted for Bush. But the voters were wrong: They had, said the official tally, voted just the opposite of what they told the polling agents. The official tally was: Bush 51%, Kerry 48%.

The exit polls differed from the official tally because:

a. voters had temporary amnesia,
b. voters lie or
c. not all votes were counted.

I went to sleep election night with the exit polls showing Kerry ahead in swing states. But between 1:05 AM and 6:41 AM the next morning, goblins went to work. By dawn, CNN's exit poll for Ohio showed Kerry dead even with Bush among women, and down by five percentage points among men.

Look at the balls now:

They've changed!

What happened? Were thousands of Bush voters locked in the voting booths, released at 2:00 AM, then queried about their choices? Not quite. The network's polling company applied a fancy algorithm, a mathematical magic wand, to slowly transform the exit polls to match the official count.

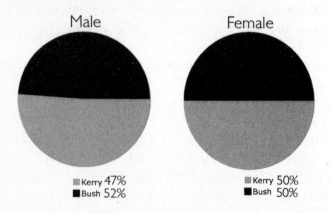

Exit Polls 6:41 AM, 11/3/04

Male

Female

Kerry 47%
Bush 52%

Kerry 50%
Bush 50%

CNN Exit Poll 6:41 AM The Day After the Vote

And that's bad. By quietly contaminating the exit polls, the networks snuffed the canary that would signal that something was deeply wrong about the vote count.

Hunting for a Democrat to defend the Twilight Zone between the exit polls and the "official" polls, media latched on to Dick Morris, Bill Clinton's old advisor. An expert at walking that fine line between minor criminality and psychopathic ambition, Morris knows which way his next client's wind blows. On CNN, Morris said:

> Exit polls are almost never wrong. So reliable are the surveys that actually tap voters as they leave the polling places that they're used as guides to the relative honesty of elections in Third World countries. To screw up one exit poll is unheard of. To miss six of them is incredible.

His opening was promising, suggesting the Ohio count was as phony as a Ukrainian primary. But then he switches into full Morris:

> It boggles the imagination how pollsters could be that incompetent and invites speculation that more than honest error was at play here.

So, Dick, you're telling us there was an evil cabal among six pollsters, competitors who don't even *like* each other, conspiring one dark night to make George Bush look like a vote thief?

There's another explanation for Kerry's leading the exit polls: Kerry won.

That is, either voters in Ohio (and nationwide) forgot whom they voted for just minutes earlier or, for a small but significant few, the ballots they cast were not counted. But *we* can count them: Add Ohio's 103,660 "spoiled" votes to the 33,998 provisional ballots rejected to the 15,519 absentee ballots never counted to the several thousand lost due to voting machine shortages (we'll get to that), and mix in the race of the voters who lost their vote and you have a recipe to cook an election, no matter whom the voters choose. The same

November 2, 2004

Night of the Uncounted

	Iowa	New Mexico	Ohio
Ballots "Spoiled"	18,847	21,084	103,660
Provisional Ballots Uncounted	7,368	6,593	33,998
Absentee Ballots Uncounted	10,596	4,217	15,519
Ghost Votes and Blocked Votes	unknown	2,087	85,950
Total Uncounted[19]	**36,811**	**33,981**	**239,127**
Bush "Victory" Margin	10,059	5,988	118,599

[19]Totals here include the ghost vote only for New Mexico, and the machine shortage only for Ohio. Registry purges, etc., would increase these total

went for Iowa and New Mexico in 2004, and possibly a half dozen others; the voters' choice was undone by the un-count.

We've got the body (the wounded elections), we've got the bullet holes (the missing votes), now where are the smoking guns? *How* does the GOP disappear the vote? And why do Democratic ballots spoil so much more readily than Republican ballots? How's it done?

But that little Bill O'Reilly in your head is screaming, *Get over it; let's move on already.* That's the point of investigation. What they tested in 2000 and practiced in 2004, they are preparing to roll out in 2008, big-time.[20]

---

[20]They've been at it a long time. Readers with sharp calculators and long memories will realize that not only did Al Gore win comfortably in 2000, but so did Hubert Humphrey when he defeated Richard Nixon in 1968—among the votes *cast*, but not votes *counted*.

In fall 2004, my editors wanted to know, *How do they keep doing it?* How could the Republican Party keep a million Black ballots from being counted in the face of all those voting reforms passed after the 2000 fiasco? We couldn't figure how they'd game it again. Then we got the e-mails.

PART 1

"CAGING LISTS": GREAT WHITE REPUBLICANS TAKE VOTERS CAPTIVE

John A. Wooden loves a good joke. We all do, but Wooden is special, because he's also Satan's best friend (if Bush was the Lord's candidate), a prankster and the man who answered a big part of our riddle. Not that he knew it at first.

Wooden runs the WhiteHouse.org site and GeorgeWBush.org. No, he doesn't have a special White House security clearance, he just owns sites with those names. What's fun is that all e-mails that end with "@GeorgeWBush.*org*" go to him. Unfortunately for the Republican National Committee, a clerk there did not know that confidential missives involving political conspiracy should be sent only to "GeorgeWBush.*com*" addresses. The clerk accidentally added dot-org to a name in the "copy to" line instead of dot-com. Wooden got them and giggled, then sent them to our offices.

Most of our sources are jittery insiders who drop off brown envelopes at the risk of their jobs or even their lives. So when our investigator Oliver Shykles called me after midnight on October 8, 2004, to say a joke site was passing on some inscrutable e-mails from the RNC, I assumed 1) we'd been set up, 2) Wooden was pulling our leg or 3) the e-mails were the usual worthless self-preening gasbag baloney that is sent around inside a campaign.

The e-mails were none of the above. They were hot stuff. The intended addressees were Brett Doster and Randy Kammerdiner. Brett directed the entire Bush-Cheney campaign in Florida; Randy, in

Washington, directed research ops for the Republican National Committee. Tim Griffin, Research Director and Deputy Communications Director for the Bush campaign, also received a copy. And attached to the first e-mail was a list of about 2,000 names and addresses on a spreadsheet, in a file named "CAGING.XLS." What made this list so special that it had to be flashed immediately to the top Bush campaign honchos?

After our team spent hours going over them, it became clear that virtually every list—GeorgeBush.org captured over fifty of them, with tens of thousands of names—were made up entirely of voters in African-American neighborhoods that we checked against ZIP Codes. The lists included the ghettos of Lauderdale, Pompano Beach and a town with the Gone-with-the-Wind name of Plantation, Florida. Why would the campaign chiefs want that?

With just a couple weeks to go before the vote, I flew to Tallahassee to show the list to Ion Sancho, the supervisor of elections for Leon County. A real straight shooter who favors no party, Sancho is looked on as the final word on voting procedure in the state. He confirmed my new suspicion. "The only thing that I can think of—African-American voters listed like this—these might be individuals that will be challenged if they attempt to vote on Election Day."

Sancho wasn't happy about the list we showed him. In his entire career of nearly two decades running elections in the capital area, the supervisor had not encountered a single Election Day challenge. He's made sure of that, pointedly warning political parties not to play that game. Moreover, it was known that legions of Black voters were expected to pour in for the 2004 vote, threatening to swamp polling places and build up lines that could cause hours of waiting. If the Republicans challenged thousands of voters, Sancho said, that would "wreck" the entire voting process. "It would discourage and intimidate legitimate voters." It would sabotage voting in Black precincts.

Did Republicans plan a giant ambush for Election Day, challenging and blocking citizens when they showed up to vote?

That would not be nice. And it could be, as well, *a crime*, a violation of federal voting rights law. BBC laid the lists before Ralph Neas, the famed civil rights attorney, who explained that you cannot challenge the rights of large groups of voters where race is a factor in your targeting, even if individual challenges have some legitimate basis. That's the law.

And political parties, until 2004, have long kept on the good side of the law. It had been decades since a political party had attempted to stop citizens from voting on Election Day. Half a century ago, the White Citizens Councils of the old Confederacy, mostly Democrats, had blocked African-Americans, using everything from "literacy" questions asked only of voters of color to the simple expedient of beatings and the hanging rope.

In the 1950s and early 1960s, Republicans too fielded a team in the Jim Crow "literacy test" game. But as the South was conceded to the Democrats, the GOP did its racial thing in the West: From 1958 to 1962, the Republicans used "Operation Eagle Eye" to menace Hispanic voters in Arizona to keep the wrong color folk from voting. A Republican lawyer would question every dark-skinned voter about their address and history, then read them a passage from the Constitution, challenging their right to vote if they did not provide a clear English interpretation of the passage.

"Literacy tests," "Operation Eagle Eye," all that was made illegal by the Voting Rights Act of 1965.

Nevertheless, in 1981, the Republican Party toyed with mass challenges of voters. They created a caging list of 45,000 folk in Black precincts of New Jersey—and swiftly got busted. Facing prosecution, the party signed a consent decree swearing in federal court never again to play the racial profile game anywhere in the nation, so help them God.

But now, in October 2004, this political party on legal probation appeared to slide back into its old ways.

The Tallahassee Lassie and the Bleaching of the Voter Rolls

If we were going to show the Republican's Black-voter caging lists on BBC Television we'd better make sure that we were not planted with false material. Were the documents bogus? The corpse of Dan Rather's career was still swinging from the Bush campaign's front gates after he used a questionable document in a basically solid story on the President's Vietnam war days.

So we went to the horse's mouth. Two weeks before the elections, our BBC crew flew to Washington to ask about the lists, but the Republican National Committee slammed the door on us. Back in Florida, we thought we'd ask Brett Doster, supreme commander of the Bush campaign in that state, straight up, "Brett, did you lose something? Is this your list? Do you and the RNC intend to block a few hundred thousand Black folk from voting on November 2?"

In Tallahassee, the path to Doster's door was blocked by a thick-armed blonde slurping on a supersize Coca-Cola: Mindy Tucker Fletcher, chief spokesmistress for the Bush campaign in Florida.

Brett, she said, couldn't speak for himself; he'd canceled our appointment. She would do the talking on his behalf. She smiled at me. It was not a ray of sunshine. Mindy Tucker Fletcher is one of those public relations flacks with that condescending faux-friendly manner who is always so glad to meet you but would prefer for you to die in pain.

After a little Q&A dance, I finally asked her if the Republican Party kept something called a "caging list" of voters.

Mindy: "I don't know what a 'caging list' is. I don't—I'm not part of that strategy."

That strategy? Hmm. I showed her the list. I can't say she started snorting cola out of her nose, but clearly, she was flustered.

She took the list inside the brick citadel, the George Herbert Walker Bush Republican Center, while I maintained a low-speed chase with her assistant, lobbing questions as he ducked into a stairwell.

Bleaching Blonde

Mindy Tucker Fletcher, spokeswoman for the Bush-Cheney reelection campaign, holding Republican "caging lists," which the party planned to use to bleach voter rolls whiter than white in Florida.

Half an hour later, Mindy, painted with fresh makeup, a retinue of jumpy PR men in tow, asked to speak to our cameras.

Suddenly, she was an expert on caging lists. She began, "Clearly you don't know a lot about politics if you don't know this term 'caging.'"

With the list in her hand she could not deny its authenticity, but there was an *explanation*. There is always an explanation.

Joseph Agostini, the Republicans' Director of Communications, nervously sputtered that the lists were made up of *potential donors* to the Bush-Cheney campaign. Really? On the one list we gave them were several residents at the Sulzbacher Center, a shelter for the homeless. "Do you get a lot of major donors from poor, African-American neighborhoods?"

Mindy cut Agostini off with a "shut it, fool" glare and stepped in with a different line altogether. "These are newly registered voters we mailed to, where the letter came back—bad addresses."

No kidding. No one sends campaign junk mail first class; it's too expensive—unless you had a reason to pay for a very expensive set of return addresses. Mr. Agostini, you wouldn't be preparing to challenge the votes of these Black folk, would you?

Agostini started jabbering. "You see, we wanted to save on the cost of postage for our campaign mailings so we wouldn't be sending to the wrong address . . ."

"You're telling me, Mr. Agostini, that you send clerical information, mailing address changes, to the chiefs of your state and national campaigns? You don't have an office clerk handle it?"

Mindy shut him down with another "shut your gap" look. It was time for the boss lady to take over.

"This is not a challenge list," Mindy said. "That's not what it's *set up* to be."

"So you won't use these lists to challenge voters on Election Day?

"Uh, that's not what they were *created* to do."

Three points for Mindy: well-crafted words. *Using* the list might be legal, but *creating* the list to bleach the voter rolls white is not.

"Will you challenge voters on Election Day?"

Mindy: "Where it's stated in the law, yeah."

She saw my eyes widen, so she added, "Every one does it, both parties, all the time. You can check."

We did. Everyone does *not* "do it." Certainly not in Florida. Our investigators called a dozen county elections offices. Not one of them could recall a single Election Day challenge in their career, especially since the enactment of the federal law in 1965.

More confidential RNC caging lists poured in: hit lists of African-American voters, including students of Edward Waters College, an African-American school, and the Jacksonville State Street Rescue Mission (more Bush campaign donors, Mr. Agostini?). Voters in Black precincts made the list if a first-class letter sent to them was returned—they could then be challenged based on an address change. We checked one list that included fifty black soldiers. We called one, Randall Prausa. His wife indicated that his address had changed because he was shipped overseas. Go to Baghdad, lose your vote. Nice. A Black soldier's vote gone. Mission accomplished.

On October 26, 2004, a week before the election, we broke the story on BBC Television's *Newsnight*. According to the network, it was the most-watched story around the globe that week. But not in the USA. Only one single U.S. television network mentioned what looked like a massive attack planned against Black voters. ABC Television's Web site informed its patrons that "The entire BBC story was more or less entirely incorrect." Really? ABC's source: Mindy Tucker Fletcher. For the USA, it was story over and buried.

On November 2, they did it as we feared. The Republican Party, despite the consent decree signed twenty-five years earlier, launched a massive multimillion-dollar campaign of mass challenges of voters in Black precincts, concentrating on Ohio, where the GOP worked from a list of 35,000 names. NAACP lawyers attempting to stop the party's racially weighted challenges were frustrated by Ohio's Secretary of State Kenneth Blackwell. The Republican claimed, with some justification, that the Ohio Republican party didn't break the law: The court order only barred racially targeted challenges by the Republican *National* Committee. In Florida, prudently, Republican operators did not carry the lists, because Democratic lawyers, who saw our broadcast, said they would file suit. But the Republicans challenged thousands nonetheless in Florida, as well as in Pennsylvania, Michigan and Wisconsin. The United States hadn't seen such a mass challenge to dark-skinned voters since Martin Luther King was jailed in Birmingham.

The caging memo distribution list makes clear the Republican National Committee was into it up to their necks notwithstanding the 1981 no-race-baiting consent decree and the Voting Rights Act. Protecting the "caged" was the job of Attorney General John Ashcroft. But Ashcroft did nothing. I should note that before Mindy became flak-catcher for the Bush campaign, she was press spokesperson for Attorney General John Ashcroft.

In fairness, I acknowledge that Republican lists did not target only Black people. In Palm Beach, they hit retirement areas for elderly Jews, another ethnic demographic that cussedly insisted on voting for Democrats.

The Ballot at the Back of the Bus

But a challenge to a vote does not itself block a citizen's taking a ballot or prevent its counting. Here's where scamming the vote gets truly complex and deliciously devious.

It comes down to something called a "provisional ballot," a whole new category of mischief created just for the 2004 race. "Provisional" ballots are baloney ballots, kind of a voting placebo. A provisional voter thinks his or her vote counted when it's likely to have been tossed in the garbage. A whole new category of "spoilage."

Like all bad ideas, provisional voting started out as a good idea. It originated with the Congressional Black Caucus reaction to the *Guardian* and BBC reports uncovering, in the 2000 election race, that tens of thousands of African-American voters were wrongly erased from Florida voter rolls just before the election. That story didn't make it to American TV, but Congressional Black Caucus members got the word and got real steamed. Rep. Corinne Brown of Jacksonville, minutes after watching the BBC film on video, marched onto the floor of Congress and denounced the 2000 election as "the United States' coup d'état." For that simple recitation of fact, the Republican majority voted to censure her, a rare punishment from which even thieves, scoundrels and senators have been spared.

Congresswoman Brown and the Black Caucus demanded a procedure that would allow a voter to get a ballot even if his or her name is missing from the rolls. The ballot would be kept aside, marked "provisional," yet would still be counted, on review, once the polls closed. Some states already had "affidavit" ballots and it was assumed that, like affidavit ballots, the provisionals would be counted

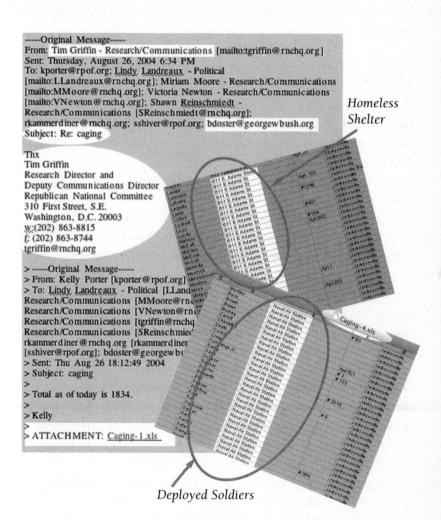

-----Original Message-----
From: Tim Griffin - Research/Communications [mailto:tgriffin@rnchq.org]
Sent: Thursday, August 26, 2004 6:34 PM
To: kporter@rpof.org; Lindy Landreaux - Political
[mailto:LLandreaux@rnchq.org]; Miriam Moore - Research/Communications
[mailto:MMoore@rnchq.org]; Victoria Newton - Research/Communications
[mailto:VNewton@rnchq.org]; Shawn Reinschmiedt -
Research/Communications [SReinschmiedt@rnchq.org];
rkammerdiner@rnchq.org; sshiver@rpof.org; bdoster@georgewbush.org
Subject: Re: caging

*Homeless
Shelter*

Thx
Tim Griffin
Research Director and
Deputy Communications Director
Republican National Committee
310 First Street, S.E.
Washington, D.C. 20003
w:(202) 863-8815
f: (202) 863-8744
tgriffin@rnchq.org

> -----Original Message-----
> From: Kelly Porter [kporter@rpof.org]
> To: Lindy Landreaux - Political [LLand...
Research/Communications [MMoore@rn...
Research/Communications [VNewton@rn...
Research/Communications [tgriffin@rnchq
Research/Communications [SReinschmied...
rkammerdiner@rnchq.org [rkammerdiner
[sshiver@rpof.org]; bdoster@georgewbu...
> Sent: Thu Aug 26 18:12:49 2004
> Subject: caging
>
> Total as of today is 1834.
>
> Kelly
>
> ATTACHMENT: Caging-1.xls

Deployed Soldiers

Caging Lists, Republican Party

unless there was evidence a voter was lying, an extremely rare occurrence.

So, the Black Caucus demanded provisional voting. Then, in 2002, something terribly suspicious happened: The Republicans agreed.

Why? A newfound commitment to civil rights by the party of Lincoln? Or an invitation by the spider to dine with the fly?

The "provisional" ballot was the Republican's come-on for the Congressional Black Caucus to support something called the "Help America Vote Act." The Black Caucus should have known: When the Bush family tells us they are going to "help" us vote, *look out*. George Bush signed it in 2002, grinning.

In the new law, the Black Caucus won the requirement that states *hand out* provisional ballots. The law requires states to give out the provisional ballots, but it does not require states to *count* them.

And they didn't. The number of provisional ballots handed out on Election Day 2004 was stunning, utterly unpredicted by its sponsors:

- The total number of voters shunted to provisional ballots was 3,107,490.
- And the number rejected was even more surprising: 1,090,729

It was breathtaking. A million votes trashed.

How could that have happened? That's where the "caging lists" and challenges came into play. The wild explosion of provisional ballots did not occur spontaneously. The massive, coordinated challenge campaign was the engine that dragged Black voters to the ballot at the back of the bus.

Two Hats, One Head

November 2, 2004, was a provisional ballot auto-da-fé, a bonfire of the ballot box. Ballots were rejected, effectively tossed away, by the hundreds of thousands. And once again, the provisional voters who were rejected had a dark hue; and there were just enough of these to create that margin of victory for George W. Bush in Iowa, New Mexico and Ohio.

Let's go back to that little bait-and-switch in the Help America Vote Law: giving ballots to any legitimate voter who requests one, but not requiring the ballot be counted. It was left up to each of the 50 Secretaries of State. And in Ohio, Secretary of State Blackwell announced an odd rule indeed, just days before the election. For decades before the 2004 race, Ohio voters could cast a provisional "affidavit" ballot in any precinct in their county. After all, it's the same president for everyone in Ohio. Under Blackwell's new rule, however, if they cast their provisional ballot in the "wrong" precinct, out it would go, uncounted. It was a terribly cute maneuver: In many cases, voters were told not to bother to go to the right precinct because they could vote on the provisional ballot. Often, the "right" precinct was simply another table in the same school gym where they were voting.

Voters left smiling. Then, even if it was later determined the voter was legitimately registered but in the "wrong" precinct, Blackwell, under his new rule, ordered their provisional ballots trashed.

In Ohio, we know of at least 33,998 provisional ballots tossed out, mostly because the voters appeared at the "wrong" precinct.

Did I mention that Secretary of State Blackwell was Co-Chairman of the Bush-Cheney reelection campaign in Ohio? Shades of Katherine Harris. In 2000, Katherine Harris was both Secretary of State of Florida, in charge of the voting machines there, and Co-Chairperson of the Bush-Cheney election campaign. It's a rule of both ethics and fashion that one shouldn't wear two hats unless one has two heads. Did Mr. Blackwell feel a wee uncomfortable reenacting both the creepy conflicts and two-hats-one-head methods of Katherine Harris? Blackwell himself felt very comfortable indeed. "Last time I checked," Blackwell said, "Katherine Harris wasn't in a soup line, she's in Congress." Well, hats off to them both.

On election night, I called Santiago Juárez, who shepherded the nonpartisan get-out-the-vote drive for the Catholic Church in Las Cruces, New Mexico, a state I knew to be whisker close. "They're handing out provisional ballots like candy to Mexicanos," he told me. Any pretext was used. Most important, officials refused to count 6,593 of them, more than Bush's New Mexico "victory margin."

And so on. In Colorado, poll watchers noted the extraordinarily high number of Hispanic voters hustled to the "provisional" booth. Twelve thousand provisional ballots were then voided by rulings from the Republican Secretary of State.

In Nevada, one of the closest states of all, where both Native Americans and Hispanics were deluged with provisional ballots, the Republican Secretary of State rejected an astonishing 60% of the provisional ballots. Some Nevada voters were handed the provisionals because their registration forms were not recorded—and then had their votes voided. They'd been collected by an outfit with the do-gooder name of Voter Outreach, which was funded by Arizona operatives of Sproul & Associates which, Congressional investigators discovered, was in turn funded by the Republican National Committee. They collected registration forms, all right, then, says an insider in a sworn affidavit, "Voter Outreach" recorded the Republican ones.

Spoiled Rotten

Let's get back into those Ohio "boots"—the "overwhelming" match of Cleveland area of ballots spoiled, not counted. The term "overwhelming" to describe the connection between race and ballots lost is not mine. That's the conclusion of Professor Mark Salling of Cleveland State University, the expert who first noticed the Black Stain of votes not counted in Ohio.

Even more interesting than Salling's finding is the year in which he reported his conclusion: 2003. In other words, the professor, looking into the historical records of voting in Ohio, sounded the alarm *before* the election. The academic's warning wasn't ignored. Secretary of State Blackwell, the man with two hats, wrote before the election,

> The possibility of a close election with punch cards as the state's primary voting device, invites a Florida-like calamity.

Blackwell appears here to be trying to *prevent* the "calamity." But appearances can deceive. In practice, the steps he took were making darn sure *it would happen again*. It did. What's he got against Black folk? Nothing. (In fact, his parents are African-American.) It's just that Republican Blackwell had to know that Black citizens "overwhelmingly" vote Democratic. Throw out dark-voter ballots and Republicans do a lot better. Bending elections isn't rocket science.

That is, the basics of a vote heist are simple: "Spoil" the other guy's ballots. But the details are obscure, little understood, rarely noticed and almost never discovered, and if discovered, well, *tough luck*.

How do votes spoil? Not by leaving them out of the fridge. The biggest spoilers are the "overvote" and the "undervote." Put a stray mark on a ballot—an "overvote"—and it's spoiled, tossed out. Fail to pop a hole deep enough through a punch-card ballot and your ballot is also ruined. This is an "undervote," which is also tossed out. And you, Mr. and Mrs. Voter, don't even know your vote was thrown away—so you can't complain about it. You was robbed, but you're not sure. And even if you knew it, the elections cop to call would be . . . Mr. Blackwell.

Now to Mr. Blackwell's comment about punch-card machines. Punch-card machines, which most states dumped after the 2000 race, are ballot-spoiling machines. It's absurdly easy to fail to punch through correctly, leaving "hanging chads" and "pregnant chads." It was those "hanging chads" and "overvotes" in overwhelmingly Black precincts that gave Florida to George Bush in 2000. And, in 2004 in Ohio, chads hung Kerry as well.

Did Blackwell really know that leaving those punch-card machines in place in the poorest precincts could give his man the election? Given Blackwell's pitched battle to keep those vote-mangling machines in place, one could be forgiven for being suspicious about his motives. A year before the election, the ACLU sued Ohio and half a dozen other states for dragging their feet on removing these machines known to lose votes. Every state but one—Ohio—signed a deal to replace or fix the busted machinery.

In Michigan, a temporary fix for the bad machines was absurdly easy. Punch-card reading machines were placed in each precinct. Just stick in your card and if your ballot shows no vote for President, it tells you and you get a new ballot—in Michigan. The ACLU said it would accept this cheap and easy solution for Ohio as well. But Blackwell said, in effect, *sue me*. Blackwell previously conceded that punch-card machines produced more spoiled votes, which, because of the disproportionate placement of those machines in minority districts, was an implicit concession that in 2004 they would eat mostly minority votes. It's not the kind of statement you'd make if you expect to win in court. But Blackwell knew he wouldn't have to win the case to win the election: The trial date was set for late November, three weeks *after* the election.

Delay was unnecessary. Blackwell won in court, though the ACLU, in 2006, is fighting on with an appeal. More enlightening, and frightening, was the judge's reason for tossing out the suit by African-American voters. The court concluded that the ugly number of uncounted ballots, the "residual vote," was due in part to "*income level of the voters*," not their race. The emphasis is mine. In other words, racial bias in the vote count is a no-no, but *class* bias is just fine.

This is crucial: You don't have to "fix" machines to rig an election, you just have to fail to fix the broken ones. Strategically. Like a good vulture, Mr. Blackwell just waits for his kill to die.

But Ohio was just practice. If you want to know what's coming for 2008, go out to where the deer and the antelope play.

PART 2

THE INDECISIVE INDIAN

Dig this: In November 2004, in early voting, in Precinct 13 in Taos, New Mexico, John Kerry took 73 votes. George Bush got three.

On Election Day itself, 216 in that precinct voted Kerry. This time, Bush got 25, and came in third. *Third?* Taking second place in the precinct, with 40 votes, was *no one at all.* Or, at least, that's what the machines said.

Precinct 13 is better known as the Taos Pueblo. Every single voter there is an American Native or married to one.

Precinct 13 wasn't unique. All over Indian country, on Election Day 2004, in pueblo after pueblo, on reservation after reservation in New Mexico, as well as in Arizona and Colorado, American Natives were seized by indecision. Indians by the thousands drove to the voting station, walked into the booth and then said, "Who cares?" and walked out without choosing a president.

On Navajo lands, Indian Indecision struck on an epidemic scale. They walked in, they didn't vote. In nine precincts in McKinley County, New Mexico, which is almost entirely (74.7%) Navajo, *less than one in ten voters picked a president.* Those who voted on *paper* ballots early or absentee knew who they wanted (Kerry, overwhelmingly), but the *machine-counted* vote said Indians simply couldn't make up their minds or just plain didn't care. On average, across the state, the machine printouts say that 7.3%—one in twelve voters—in majority Native precincts didn't vote for president. That's three times the percentage of white voters who appeared to abstain.

No Hee-Ah-Hoe

So I dropped in on Taos, Precinct 13, and asked Ruben Romero, who holds the grand title of Governor and War Chief of the pueblo, "*Why can't you people do something as simple as pick a president?*"

The War Chief ignored my deliberate provocation. Unflappable, in his slow rhythmic English, he explained, "We thought they knew about these sophisticated things, so we trusted them." By *them* he meant the local, politically hostile white officials from the county who wheeled in new machines before the vote. He was resigned to it. Nothing new on the rez.

Outside his window were ruins of an old steeple where, in 1847, the Taos Indians took refuge from the U.S. cavalry, trusting the soldiers wouldn't fire on a Catholic church. The troops, Romero told me, leveled it with artillery and left the Natives' bodies under the rubble. It remains the pueblo cemetery today. Beyond it, on the mesa ridge, you could see the second homes of Houston oil brokers. They bought them for $2 million each and spent another half million to make them look like the pueblo's adobe mud-brick houses. Down the pueblo's dirt path was the smokehouse, not the traditional cleansing hut, but a shack where Anglos could buy cheap un-taxed cigarettes, and beyond that, the reservation's big employer, its piteous little casino where workers from the nearby Wal-Mart lose their rent money. Which wasn't much. In 1999, my British newspaper surveyed starting wages for Wal-Mart cashiers: $6.50 an hour in most of the USA, but $4.50 near Indian reservations.

The "old" pueblo is old indeed—built five hundred to one thousand years ago. Its spirit houses are entered through holes in the roof. In these adobe dwellings stacked like mud condos, no electricity is allowed nor running water—nor Republicans as far as records show. Richard Archuleta, "Head of Tourism" (i.e., cigarette sales, gambling and the annual pow-wow), a pro-plumbing Native with gray pigtails and hands as big as flank steaks, taught me Tiwa for thanks, "Hee-Ah-Hoe." Of course, for all I knew, it could have meant my mom services sailors.[21]

---

[21]An annoying anthropologist I met told me she was so liked by the local Navajo, they honored her with the "beer baptism" ceremony, pouring cans of beer on her head. At least they hadn't drunk it first.

Richard Archuleta, Taos Precinct 13

Richard wasn't buying the indecision theory of the Native non-count. Indians were worried about their Bureau of Indian Affairs grants, their gaming licenses and working conditions at their other big employer: the U.S. military. Richard's dad and five brothers enlisted. It was just assumed, he said, if you're Native, you served in the Army or the Marines. A lot of red Indian blood was spilling in Falluja, and the pueblo, using little or no electricity, was not interested in Iraq's oil. On the pueblo's mud-brick walls there were several hand-painted signs announcing Democratic Party powwows, none for Republicans. Richard showed me where the Ketchup Queen herself, First Lady wannabe Teresa Heinz Kerry, had stopped and had lunch before the election. Laura Bush wouldn't do that. *Indecisive?* Indians are Democrats. *Case closed, white boy.*

The Color That Counts

It wasn't just Natives who couldn't seem to pick a President. Throughout New Mexico, indecisiveness was pandemic . . . at least, that is, among people of color. In Taos and Dona Ana counties, the same indecision virus that struck the Indian reservations also hit half a dozen majority Mexican-American precincts where less than one in ten voters chose a president. *Or so the machines said.* Across the state, high-majority Hispanic precincts recorded a 7.1% vote for nobody for president.

Here's the arithmetic. George Bush won New Mexico and its electoral votes by only 5,988 ballots. That's the official count. Yet, altogether no less than 21,084 ballots showed no vote for president in New Mexico in 2004.

Whose "unvotes" were these? I asked Dr. Philip Klinkner, the expert who ran stats for the U.S. Civil Rights Commission, to look at the New Mexico data. His solid statistical analysis discovered that if you're Hispanic, the chance your vote will not record on the machine was 500% higher than if you are white. For Natives, it's off the charts.

The Hispanic and Native vote is no small potatoes. Every tenth New Mexican is American Native (9.5%) and half the remaining population (43%) is Mexican-American.

I punched the "no-count" stats into the state's demographic profile and, with a little high school algebra, calculated that Hispanics, Natives and the tiny population of Black people in New Mexico cast no less than 89% of these no-choice votes. Let me repeat that: *Nine out of ten votes uncounted were cast by non-Anglo voters.*

Who would they have voted for?

Our team drove an hour across the high desert from the Taos Reservation to Española in Rio Arriba County. According to the official tallies, *entire precincts* of Mexican-Americans registered few or zero votes for president in the last two elections. Española is where the Los Alamos workers live, not the PhDs in the white lab coats, but the women who clean the hallways and the men who bury the toxins. They work through contractors so the government won't have to pay benefits. Job "security" is a joke. This was not Bush country, and the people we met with, including the leaders of the get-out-the-vote

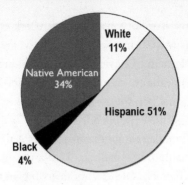

Whose Votes Don't Count?
Ballot "Spoilage" in New Mexico

operations, knew of no Hispanics who insisted on waiting at the polling station to cast their vote for "nobody for President."

The Bushes make a big deal about having lots of part-Mexican children. But, despite the Bush family photo ops, the huge majority of Mexican-Americans, especially in New Mexico, and a crushing majority of Natives (over 90%), vote Democratic. What if those voters weren't indecisive; what if they punched in a choice and it did not record?

Let's do the arithmetic. As minority voters cast 89% of the state's 21,084 blank ballots, that's 18,765 missing minority votes. Given the preferences of other voters in those pueblo and barrio neighborhoods, those 18,765 voters of color should have swamped Bush's "majority" with Kerry votes. But that would have required those votes be counted.

Disappearing Democrats of Area 51

My first call in New Mexico was "Little Texas," the group of mesquite-and-rattler-populated New Mexico counties tucked atop the snout of the Lone Star State. There Republican officials preside over Hispanic voters and the results are, let's say, *mysterious*.

I asked Mr. Dave Kunko, Chief Deputy Clerk in the Little Texas county of Chaves, what happened to the vote in the Hispanic precincts in his domain. Chaves is 42% Hispanic, yet carried for George Bush in 2000, thanks to a stunning number of blank ballots—up to 10% percent of all votes—in the Hispanic precincts of the county. Kunko, a white Republican, told me, "Well, there's a lot of these people who just *don't want to vote for president*."

Chaves is one big county—over six thousand square miles. Apparently, Hispanics drive notable distances to register their refusal to vote. I spoke with Kunko three months *before* the 2004 election—my editors reasoning it would be better to hunt for missing votes before they went missing.

I started off with Little Texas's counties of Chaves, Eddy and Curry because an old political hand in the state Senate had told me, "If this election's going to be stolen, it will be stolen in Little Texas." And he suggested I look at the registration stats. Democratic registrations should have been way up because of a big drive by the Catholic Church to register Hispanics. But here's what happened:

Chaves County: Registered Democrats drop by 10.6%
Curry County: Registered Democrats drop by 11.9%
Eddy County: Registered Democrats drop by 13.1%

Now how weird is that? We were told by a nice white lady in the Eddy County elections office that these Hispanic voters had switched parties—by the thousands. That would be unprecedented in the nation. People may switch their votes, but it just doesn't happen that, en masse, people file papers to switch party registrations. Santiago Juarez, lawyer with the Church voter-drive, registered Hispanic "low riders," the kids who drive chopped and jacked Chevys with neon trim under the sissy skirts. He doesn't remember registering many Republicans among them, and certainly he would have remembered someone switching from Democrat to Republican. There were none.

Where'd the registrations go? How do Democrats just disappear? Chaves County is home of Roswell and "Area 51," which more inventive minds believe houses the U.S. military's captured UFOs. Were the Democrats removed to Area 51? Mr. Kunko's office had a more straightforward explanation for the big-time plunge in Democratic registrations. His clerks had "cleaned up" the rolls under authority of the Help America Vote Act—lots of apparent "felons" and other suspect voters. That the cleansing had a political tinge, well, that's too bad, eh? I'm sure the purge was done fairly, but we'll have to take it on faith, as the state wouldn't release the purge lists.

The Great Brown Ballot Boycott?

Still, despite Kunko and his party's actions, many Hispanic Democrats remained registered on the books. But that didn't mean they would be allowed to vote.

According to Kunko's records, Mexican-Americans early on showed a blasé attitude toward the presidential election: Relatively few showed up for early voting. Of course, that may have to do with the fact that Kunko's office placed the only early voting booth in that mammoth-sized county in a white suburban shopping center. It was about an hour's drive from the slaughterhouses and dairies where the brown voters work. If they chose to make the long trek to the polling station, they would have had to drive fast, as the county closed the poll at 6:00 P.M.

To counter the inventive placement of the polling station, the Church organized a bus and caravan to take young, newly registered Chicano low riders to the Roswell poll. Santiago said many of his first-time voters were turned away for having the wrong ID. Maybe the middle initial was missing from the license, or "Jr." added. No perfect match, no vote. A *gotcha!* set of rules that seemed to apply only to voters of a darker hue. A young Chicana told Santiago she wouldn't return to try again; one round of humiliation was enough. "They don't want me there anyway," she said. And they don't.

On Election Day, despite Little Texas remaining half Democratic in registration, George Bush romped to a large and unexpected (if not inexplicable) victory, taking Chaves, for example, nearly two votes to one. Crucial to this "victory" was the apparent renewed "boycott" of the presidential choices by Hispanic voters.

In Kunko's county, for example, just about every white person chose a president—Bush. In the six whitest of white precincts (82% Anglo), less than one in a hundred ballots "spoiled," that is, showed no presidential choice. Indeed, the white folk of Chaves were so enthusiastic about our democracy that they appeared to vote more than once. Precinct 21 (83% Anglo) registered eight more votes for President than voters! The only other "extra-vote" precinct was also three-fourths Caucasian.

While in the white precincts there were more votes than voters, in the Hispanic precincts it was just the opposite—more voters than votes. In New Mexico overall, Hispanic ballots were five times as likely as white ballots to go unrecorded. But in the "brownest" precincts, those with a population more than 75% Hispanic, the vote loss was 900% higher than in 75% white precincts. Maybe Hispanics can't pick a president. Or maybe, just *maybe,* their votes vanished into dysfunctional, error-diseased machines.

Of course, Little Texas wasn't alone in experiencing a "boycott" by Hispanic and Native voters. In Quay County, Hispanic-heavy Precinct 6A recorded 115 votes for county commissioner, zero for President. In a dozen precincts in minority areas, 90% or more of the voters recorded no vote for President on Election Day.

The "unvote" added up. In the Bush-controlled areas, purges, ID games, spoilage, poll-location tricks and provisional balloting cost Kerry dearly. In those counties, the average recorded vote for Democrats compared to their registrations was an odd, dismal 44.2%, whereas Republicans tallied a vote equal to 103.2% of their registrations. Vote shifts of that magnitude are the stuff of dreams. But are they the voters' dreams or the machines'?

Democrats in Dreamland

Just because Kunko put down the missing Hispanic vote to some kind of racial indecisiveness doesn't make him a dumbbell, racist redneck Republican party hack. So I thought it reasonable to get a view of the vanished Hispanic vote from a Hispanic Democrat, the one in fact in charge of the vote statewide. I reached Secretary of State Rebecca Vigil-Giron on her cell phone while she was cruising through the desert between Albuquerque and the capital. This was still months before the 2004 election.

Ambitious, fast-talking, and chatty, Vigil-Giron said she would prevent another voting disaster like the one that occurred in 2000 when, for example, a Hispanic precinct in Española recorded zero votes for President.

I was intrigued by her relaxed investigative style. While the Secretary of State looked into that one case of a precinct with a zero vote and discovered—surprise!—*machine* error, she showed no interest in investigating the less dramatic vote disappearances throughout her state though they added up to thousands of vanished votes. She didn't have to examine other machines, she said, because she knew why votes weren't recorded. In Hispanic and Native areas, a loss of 10% to 14% in blank ballots, she told me, "is the normal *where people just don't want to vote for President.*" Kunko's Brown Boycott theory! I had to ask twice to believe it.

I was too dumbstruck to ask her why Mexicans and Indians like to drive to the polls and stand in line to register their ambivalence.

On November 2, 2004, three months after I spoke with the Secretary of State, the supposed Brown Ballot Boycott hit with a vengeance in Dona Ana County—64% Hispanic—in Little Texas. There were 207 ballots mailed in from overseas, mostly Mexican-American soldiers. *Not one* registered a choice for President. Or at least that's what the machines said.

I guess the Secretary of State was right: Our Chicano boys in uniform just don't give a damn who ends up as their commander-in-chief.

New Mexico ended Election Day 2004 with more uncounted votes than almost any state in America. Vigil-Giron had the authority to open the machines sealed right after the elections. In the face of the wacky returns, and with still-uncounted and missing ballots far exceeding George Bush's victory margin, the Democratic Secretary of State moved decisively: She turned down $114,000 from concerned voters who offered to pay for a recount and investigation of the machines. On January 12, 2005, Vigil-Giron ordered all machines wiped clean, thereby eliminating crucial evidence regarding the November tallies.

The Undead Vote for Bush

Your fevered conspiracy-prone brains are already saying, *Bush won because Kerry's votes weren't counted.* Yes, that's true. But what about the voters that *don't exist?*

Look at the map of Bernalillo County (Albuquerque) on the facing page. George Bush swept Precinct 512, winning 206 votes out of 166 ballots cast. That's right: Bush tallied more votes than voters.

Bush also won Precinct 558, where 178 absentee voters produced a remarkable 319 votes.

They don't call New Mexico the "Land of Enchantment" for nothing.

What makes these precincts special besides the large number of ballots cast by spirits? Answer: Three out of four ghost votes were tallied in *Bush* precincts.

Kerry wasn't so lucky. Democratic Precinct 14 reported 114 out of 207 ballots showed no mark for President. Democratic stronghold Precinct 46 had a vanishing vote problem—half the absentee ballots recorded no choice for President.

Almost every precinct recording more votes than voters went for George Bush; whereas almost all precincts with huge votes uncounted are Kerry's. Every case, every time. Extra votes—Bush's. Votes lost—Kerry's. Just look at the map.

The official poltergeist vote in New Mexico was 2,087. But normal "undervoting" masked the total of "extra" votes. Statistically corrected, the ghost vote was higher—a small sum, true, but about half of George Bush's "victory" margin in the state. Before you leap to conclusions, let's just say that George Bush is very popular among the undead.

Push-Button Smallpox

What happened to the missing votes?

I'm not going to pretend this was the most difficult investigative story I've worked. We didn't need to call on Sherlock Holmes. In

Ghost voters for Bush in Albuquerque

Precincts with extra votes shown as ghosts. The white zones are Republican majority precincts. (Data mapped by Prof. Sonja Klveck Elison and Walther Eric Elison. County map courtesy Bernalillo County, New Mexico.)

Ohio, the Black Stain of spoiled votes traced directly to bad punch-card machines in the ghetto. In New Mexico, the Red-Brown Tide of spoiled votes corresponded directly to the *type of machine* used in Native and Hispanic precincts.

The old push-button ballot boxes made by Sequoia did just awful. One in ten Native Americans faced with these cheap push-button machines appeared to make no choice for President. But give New Mexico's Indians a new iVotronics machine and suddenly their indecision disappears. A handful of Native precincts were given some of the newer, flashy machines and, behold! only one in 200 Natives using the upgraded equipment failed to make a choice for President.

Same for Hispanics. Put them in front of an old "Shouptronic" push-button machine and 7.4% of them (one in 13) do not register a vote for President. But, the stats tell us, give a Chicano a good optical scanning machine to use, and 399 out of 400 will choose a President.

This suggests an alternative to the Kunko–Vigil-Giron theory that these citizens waited in line to register their non-vote. Maybe the machines dumped into Native and Hispanic communities are crap. Maybe they don't work right. And maybe some politicians *know* they don't work right and like it that way.

So who got the easy-to-use machines and who got the cheap castoffs? We don't wipe out Indians anymore by giving them blankets infected with smallpox. We just let them vote on obsolete Shouptronics.

No-Count Champs

If we're talking machine spoilage, we have to return to Florida to speak with the champ, Dick Carlberg. While the entire state of New Mexico in 2004 had 21,000-some spoiled votes, a *single county* in Florida, Duval, had a stunning 27,000 ruined ballots in the 2000 election—11,000 of that total from just five precincts.

I should say, "five *Black* precincts," 72% African-American according to the Census. Jacksonville is a city more divided than Berlin when the wall was up. The acting elections supervisor in that race, Dick Carlberg, from the white side of the wall, was in charge of counting the vote on the Black side. Those votes were cast on some ancient punch-card machines. At the elections office, Dick was happy to explain to me how he counted those votes. In a voice sticky sweet with Southern charm, he explained that he put the cards through an automatic reader, which just doesn't read too well if a card isn't "clean punched." He ran the cards through once, and thousands indicated no vote for President. When he ran those through again, the punches opened a little more and Al Gore picked up another 160 votes, George Bush just 80.

Bush officially won Florida by 537 votes. Carlberg knew the count was whisker-close when he did his second run. Then he stopped counting.

"So, Dick, if you ran the 'blank' ballots through a few more times, we'd have a different President," I noted. The Republican gave me a big, wide grin and wouldn't answer.

On a per-voter basis, another county did worse on the count in 2000, far worse. It wasn't Palm Beach where the strangely designed "butterfly ballot" switched Democratic votes to the Brown Shirt candidate, Pat Buchanan. The TV networks crawled all over Palm Beach where reporters can "investigate" while sipping piña coladas on the beach and filling their dispatches with "honey shots" of the toned and wealthy sporting thong bikinis. Well, yes, I did that, too. But our BBC crew also traveled to beachless Gadsden, the Blackest and poorest of Florida's sixty-seven counties where one in twelve votes spoiled. In the county seat we found a Black township that would have fit well in South Africa, with busted-out storefronts—and busted voting machines.

Here's how it worked. Gadsden used optical scanners to read the paper ballots. Any stray mark, easy to make, and *zap!*—the vote was trashed. How odd. In upscale Tallahassee, next door, they used paper ballots and in the last election did not lose one single vote! The difference is as simple as Black and white. Make a stray mark on a Tallahassee ballot, and *zap!*— the ballot *returns* to the voter.

But with all the new loot available for new machines, the public screaming for "reform," how do you keep the Gadsdens, the Rio Arribas and the Taos Pueblos from having their full vote recorded? The machines changed but the ballot-count apartheid has remained. How does it happen?

It's easy: Launch Jim Crow into cyberspace.

PART 3

JIM CROW GOES DIGITAL

Sharp readers notice that I've avoided a lot of the talk about computer voting and evidence that those computer "black-box" machines were just plain fixed. That's because we have a less dramatic answer at hand for missing votes: "There's this Hollywood idea of stealing them [elections] . . . this sexual thing where, 'Ah, man! We caught 'em!' and they were switching votes on the computer and stuff like that," Santiago Juárez told me, frustrated that Anglo "reformers" cared more about the unknown dangers of touchscreen machines and couldn't give a rat's ass about IDs for low riders. "But actually, elections are stolen in ways that aren't elegant—they're not Hollywoodish—but they are real effective at suppressing the vote."

But computers can add a high-tech touch to the old game: Generating lots and lots of digital spoilage; and unlike punch cards, it's hard to detect, impossible to correct.

And the Lords of the Voting Universe know it, and that drives Ion Sancho just nuts. The dean of Florida's elections supervisors is the one who posted the zero-spoilage perfect election count in 2002. He knew all about the Gadsden "Black-out" machines *before* the 2000 election and warned Governor Bush and his Secretary of State Katherine Harris.

Katherine, as her last act before moving to Congress, ordered all counties to switch to computer "touch screens." Now, that's downright odd, says Sancho, because:

1. Computer touch screens produce unrecorded votes at a rate 600% higher than paper ballots with "try it again" scanners.
2. Computer touch screens cost 400% more than the paper-and-scanner combo.
3. With paper, you can recount the vote, check the vote and see with your eyeballs how the voter voted. With computers—*forget it*.

So, why in the world would politicians rush to put in the system that costs a whole lot more, loses many more votes and can't be audited?

Could the answer be that it's not *their* votes that are lost? The giant differential in spoilage between paper and computer is far higher in minority precincts than white ones, by a factor of three. And someone likes it that way. One such someone is Governor Jeb Bush. After the 2000 embarrassment, Governor Bush appointed a high-sounding "Select Task Force on Elections Procedures." Apparently, Jeb Bush didn't select carefully because these experts, to his dismay, called for using paper ballots statewide. They rejected computers. Never mind. Bush overruled them.

You can't recount a computer vote—something the Bush family finds attractive. Florida's statutory right to a recount in close races was frustrating Jeb's desire to digitize democracy. The problem was overcome by Jeb Bush's replacement for Katherine Harris, Republican Glenda Hood. She helped her boss by issuing a fiat, voiding the right to recount ballots for counties with computer voting.

Leon County elections supervisor Sancho objected. Hood replies that Sancho is "not a team player." He certainly isn't. Just for fun, and calling on my rusting skills as an adjunct professor of statistics, I asked Sancho, prior to the 2004 election, to calculate with me the number of Florida votes that would be spoiled because of computerization. The prediction proved accurate in November 2004, with over

25,000 votes lost in computers in the counties where 53.6% of the state's African-Americans vote.

Governor Jeb gave computers a test run in 2002 in Broward County. The computer system was chosen over the objections of Broward's Democratic elections supervisor, Miriam Oliphant. On the day of the 2002 gubernatorial primaries, the new computers crashed, machines wouldn't boot up into operating mode and, all agree, thousands of African-Americans lost their vote. In other words, the test was a success and the vote-eating system was immediately rolled out statewide.

(In response to the computer fiasco, Jeb Bush fired the supervisor who had objected to their use. He replaced her, a Black Democrat, with a Republican who would become, as we will see, very helpful to George Bush in the 2004 race.)

If computers were good enough for Florida, they were good enough for America. Brother George's Help America Vote Act pushed $3 billion at the states to go digital.

Ignore That Man Behind the Screen, Dorothy

There are good reasons why the Lord wrote down the Ten Commandments on stone tablets and not on a computer chip. He didn't want Moses choosing just his favorite six.

The sun had not set on Election Day when *The San Jose Mercury News* gave us the good news:

> No Major Glitches Reported with Electronic Voting Machines.

I was glad to hear that! But I had a question for the *Mercury* and all the other papers that had repeated this happy news, "*How do you know?*" Exactly *what tests* of the computer processors did you conduct, what *electronic log audit* did you review, what *paper trail* did you follow? Exactly how, my journalist comrades, did you conclude that the new touch-screen voting machines recorded the vote as voters intended?

If the computers are hacked, if the central tabulators in far-off locations are messed with, what exactly did you expect to see—smoke rising from the computer tabulators? A siren going off with a metallic voice screeching, *I've been hacked! I've been hacked!?*

Why is it that America's media elite nearly broke its collective legs in rushing to report that all was A-OK with the touch-screen machines used by 36 million voters? The voters themselves, at exit polls, said they voted for Kerry, but the computers tell us they were lying: The computers said that more people secretly voted for Bush. The computers never get it wrong, are never messed with, never crash.

We hope.

I'm not going to tell you that the computers were hacked on November 2. I don't know. But for the Media-Bush Axis to pronounce that all went well, that no one toyed with our tallies, without taking twenty minutes to check out the weird data leaking out, is journalism that would have made *Pravda* proud.

There's too much evidence of systematic anomalies and problems to say, "All's well, sleep tight."

A month after the election, I flew to Columbus, Ohio, and met with investigators Bob Fitrakis and Harvey Wasserman. Unlike the *Mercury* and the rest of the media's see-no-evil gang, Fitrakis and Wasserman thought they should actually get these basic documents that backed up the touch-screen tallies. As was their right under the states' Freedom of Information Law. They petitioned officials in the state to produce their voting-machine backup logs. The first reply was none too comforting.

> The backup tapes have been destroyed so as not to conflict
> with the official tally and create confusion.

Huh? The computer logs were *different* than the "official" totals . . . so the county did the right thing: threw the evidence in the garbage.

Wasserman and Fitrakis were gob smacked—not just because the true vote was tossed out but because, as a lawyer, Fitrakis told me that chucking voting records is a *crime*. But heck, if a presidential election can be shoplifted, early recycling of some official papers seems like pretty small stuff.

What about the other counties? Once the two activists started raising a stink, the other counties simply refused to hand over the records.

I'd feel a whole lot better about democracy-in-a-box if I could get a receipt for my vote. I get a receipt for a Slurpee, I get a bank statement on my ATM withdrawals, why not a receipt for my choice for president? And by "receipt," I don't mean something you take out of the voting booth. That wouldn't do much good. The "receipt" is a printed copy of your ballot with all choices marked. Put that printed paper ballot in a locked box at the polling station and—*voilá!*—any questions about the computer can be answered by matching them to the ballots it printed.

But, we were told, that can't be done.

But it can be. Maybe not in Third World places like Florida or Ohio, but it was accomplished in Venezuela. There, President Hugo Chávez, facing a recall vote, feared that opposition governors would steal the election. All the voting booths in the nation were converted to computers that printed paper ballots—so you could see and touch your ballot (or smell and taste it, if you wished). Chávez won by a million votes—and when the Bush Administration yowled at the outcome, Chávez said, "Well, recount the votes." A fair election with verified paper audit: one more reason to hate Hugo Chávez.

By the way, Venezuela's computer vote machines that could, astonishingly, print out ballots, were made in Florida.

Back in the USA, Sequoia Voting Systems, Inc., the company with the funky push-button machines that ate the Chicano vote in New Mexico, was busy rolling out its new computer democracy machines.

Three months before the 2004 election the company showed off its new touch-screen box to the California State Legislature with a way-cool button that could switch the screen from English to Spanish. It worked perfectly—until you counted the votes. The choices of those who used the English-language screen tallied just fine. But if a voter hit the "Español" button, it turns out, their vote didn't add to the machine's totals. The company said it was just a glitch they would fix. Maybe they did, but *¿quién sabe?*

Voting's Private Parts

Before the voting in November 2004, New Mexico's Secretary of State assured me that the voting machines were A-OK and would work perfectly. After the voting, she declared she would clean up the mess she promised could not occur. For the cleanup she hired Ernie Marquez.

Ernie certainly had experience with electoral disaster: He had been the elections director of McKinley County—you remember, the Navajo county with the highest vote loss in the state, if not the country. Ernie's first task was to deal with questions about the handling of the 2004 vote tally by a private company, AES, Automated Election Services. Ernie knew all about AES. Between his misplacing Navajo votes in McKinley County and taking over the entire state's elections system, he worked for . . . AES.

The Secretary of State likes Ernie and AES. And they like her. Enough so that, state records show, in 2002 when Ernie was at AES, the company printed, gratis, the Secretary of State's campaign literature.

This was just too much affection for Holly Jacobson. Holly's a soccer mom with a heightened sense of justice and a nose for baloney. She gathered some locals with similarly bad attitudes and good computer skills, pooled some cash, registered themselves as "Voter Action New Mexico," and teamed with a big-shot elections lawyer from California. Now, the Secretary of State was hit with one nasty lawsuit to investigate the poltergeist votes and missing ballots. The case continues.

Holly's crew asked Ernie for the "canvass" reports of vote details from each machine in the state. Ernie didn't have it in his state office. The vote totals were kept by his old employer, AES.

Note what's happening: "privatization" of the voting system. States have been purchasing more than touch screens. They are outsourcing the blood and bones of vote *counting*. In New Mexico, AES tallies the count from hundreds of machines at a remote location. Their work is mysterious, proprietary and beyond the scope of public scrutiny. Effectively, the privateers call the winners. Hopefully, the voters influence their choices.

In New Mexico, AES had sole control of the tally files for the presidential election. So what? Here's what: Holly's group through sources already had gotten their hands on one canvass report of the presidential vote, machine by machine. When they finally got the state's official files from AES, something had disappeared: Some of the ghost votes had vanished.

Ghosts do that, I suppose.

But if ghost votes could disappear so easily, just like magic, from the private company tallying the votes of the state's machines— maybe other votes could disappear, votes from dogcatcher to votes for President of the United States. And if done on Election Day, no one would know.

But I'd rather not think about that.

Mystery Machines

Santiago Juárez nailed it—provisional ballots, spoilage, registration games—the crude stuff bends the elections. But that doesn't mean that theft "Hollywood-style," by computer, can't happen.

Albuquerque speech therapist Joyce Bartley tried to vote for the Democrat running for Congress on the 2004 ballot. In fact, she tried several times on several machines in the same precinct. "I pressed the circle next to the name," she told our investigator Matt Pascarella, "and his check mark went into the circle of the other candidate." Hours later, a court clerk, Terry Ashcrom, also tried and couldn't get the machine to accept the Democrat. Ashcrom told us, "Someone in the line said, 'You're a Democrat, right?' and everybody laughed." The other voters gave in to the machine's preference for Congress rather than lose their ballot entirely.

In Sandoval County, a *Republican judge* found he couldn't vote for himself. The machine manufacturer explained that the problem was "an inconsistent stream of electricity." Well, OK then. The company: Ernie Marquez's old employer AES.

The Republican judge complained and got results, but when Bartley complained to the Democratic Party, even filling out a sworn affidavit about her anti-Democrat machine, the party's headquarters told her, "Why do you want to do this? This is over. We're moving on."

Now why would the Democrats say that? Hold that question.

Some games are crude: In one precinct, Kerry's name was simply left off the tally sheet. The machine appeared to work so voters were

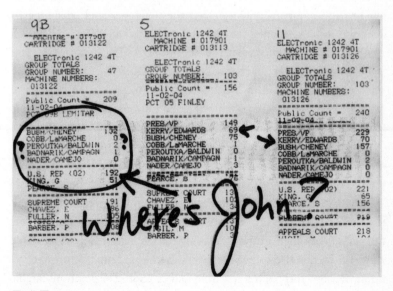

Poll Tape

Poll Tape Without Kerry Listed as Candidate Choice

clueless that their choice didn't tally. If you think that's easy to catch, forget it. An election official slipped it to the Voter Action crew who gave it to me, fearful he'd lose his job if discovered as our source.

None of this requires a grand conspiracy. If you know that bad machines eat Native votes, and you don't change the machines, you know damn well what will happen. "Strategic neglect" is crucial.

"Strategic neglect" wasn't invented in New Mexico. It's as old as Jim Crow and as widespread. For example, in Georgia in 2002, Congresswoman Cynthia McKinney, who was in a tough primary, found Diebold's new computerized touch screens froze, batteries died and votes were lost. "Diebold said that the machines don't perform well in the heat," the Congresswoman told me. She let that sink in, then added, "Well, give me a break! What do you think you have in July in Georgia other than heat?"

The Black Congresswoman knew, but didn't have to say, the answer: In the poor districts, in the sweltering school gyms where Black folk voted, it was Southern-fried hot. In the air-conditioned offices where the Secretary of State tested the machines and in suburban Georgia's air-conditioned schools, the Diebolds work just fine.

The Voting-Industrial Complex

New Mexico's Secretary of State seemed curiously uncurious about Hispanic precincts where only one in ten voters chose a president.

But who was I to second-guess Secretary Vigil-Giron? After all, she was a big shot, President, no less, of the National Association of Secretaries of State, the top banana of all our nation's elections officials.

After the election, rather than schlep out to investigate among the iguanas and Navajos in some godforsaken hole in the desert, she left the state to officiate a dinner meeting for her national association. It was held on a cruise ship. The tab for the moonlight ride was picked up by touch-screen voting machine maker ES&S Corporation. Breakfast, in case you're curious, was served by touch-screen maker Diebold Corp.

The Lineup

And there's undervote that's unreported. You can give your opponents' precincts bad voting machines—or don't give them machines at all. In Jacksonville, Florida, the Republican elections supervisor, knowing of the long lines expected in 2004 in Black precincts, removed several of them. In Ohio, with the high turnout expected, the same trick was repeated, leaving Black people and students in suspiciously selected precincts to wait in line for seven hours or more. It was systemic and measurable.

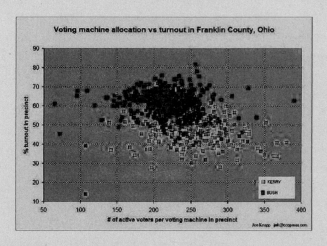

The chart above looks like a dark, ugly bacterium devouring a defenseless cell. This is statistician Joe Knapp's "scattergram" of the suspicious placement of voting machines in Franklin County (Columbus), Ohio, confirmed by a nearly identical finding by Elizabeth Liddle of the University of Nottingham in Britain. The attacking splotch represents the Bush-majority precincts, the white ones getting eaten, Kerry's precincts. In fancy math, it tells us what any bonehead knows: Make people wait seven hours and some will have to leave. The result by Knapp's precinct-by-precinct calculation was no less than 17,000 votes lost, cutting Kerry's net vote by 9,971 in Columbus alone. Congressional investigators, albeit Democrats, thought "hundreds of thousands of votes" were lost statewide. My own estimate is far more conservative, 85,950 frustrated voters. The trick is, as

Knapp and Liddle's bug-war chart shows, the machines were strategically allocated, with the rich getting machine-richer, and the poor getting machine-poorer polling stations. Kerry lost 71,542 votes versus 14,408 lost to Bush.

The point is not the quibbling over the number, higher or lower. The issue is, who's watching the machine allocation in 2008? Like an Agatha Christie mystery, we get to guess where vote boxes will disappear next.

Not that Vigil-Giron was satisfied with New Mexico's voting machinery. She wanted the state to rush into the arms of her meal tickets, the touch-screen computer makers. And like other politicians who have fallen in love with computer voting machines, she found her affection reciprocated. The Secretary of State is a big booster of computers by ES&S and Sequoia. And they boost her. Company executives were on the list of her top ten campaign contributors.

Let's not single out the New Mexicans. For ES&S, it's "all in the family" nationwide. They hired the husband of the supervisor of elections in Pinellas, Florida, and the husband of the state legislator representing Broward County, the place where, in 2002, non-operating ES&S machines locked up and lost African-American votes. Florida's county officials endorsed ES&S machines on the recommendation of their advisor, Sandra Mortham, who, balancing a second hat on her one head, was also lobbyist for ES&S.

It's 10:00 PM: Do You Know Where Your Absentee Ballot Is?

Voters wary of balloting by computer went postal in 2004: In some states, mail-in ballot requests were up 500%. The probability that all those votes—over 19 million—were counted is zilch.

Those who mail in ballots are very trusting souls. Here's how your trust is used. In the August 2004 primaries in Florida, Palm Beach Elections Supervisor Theresa LePore (aka Madame Butterfly Ballot) counted 37,839 absentee votes. But days before, her office told me only 29,000 ballots had been received. When this fishes-and-loaves miracle was disclosed, she was forced to recount, cutting the tally to 31,138. Could LePore know who was voting for whom? Any experienced politicians can tell a voter's politics with fair accuracy from the ZIP Code. In Palm Beach it was easier: The voter's party was printed on the outside of the return envelope.

Had a few thousand votes disappeared instead of more of them miraculously appearing, there would be almost no way to figure it out.

We had our eyes on LePore, but who was watching Arapahoe County, Colorado? Three times more absentee ballots mailed to Democrats "failed to return" as compared to Republican ballots, a bias in return rates I found in many Republican-controlled counties. The difference was not accounted for in the number of Dems versus Reps asking for the ballots. Maybe Democrats don't have the saliva to make the stamp stick. I refuse to speculate on the fate of the missing ballots.

Democrats by the millions, not trusting county elections officials to operate computers without tampering with them, mailed their ballots to these same officials on faith they will be acknowledged, opened, accepted and properly tallied. Absentee balloting in the USA is the greatest expression of mass faith since the Hebrews walked across the Red Sea bed trusting the Lord would keep the waters parted. The difference is, in 2004, the absentee voters mailed their ballots to Pharaoh's clerks.

If they don't like your signature, the envelope you use, the pencil size or the postmark or your ZIP Code, you lose your vote. Pharaoh decides.

Here's an example. In San Diego, in 2004, the Democratic candidate for mayor lost by 2,108 votes—after 5,551 absentee ballots with her name clearly written in (she was a write-in candidate) were tossed out. The Republican elections officials determined that, while the five thousand voters wrote in her name, they failed to *check the box next to* her name.

Unusual? Not by a long shot. In 2004, from official reports, we can calculate that half a million (526,426) absentee ballots were received but not counted. And that's just the ones they acknowledged receiving.

Doing a bit of arithmetic on the precinct-by-precinct reports discloses that, *believe it or not,* in strong Kerry precincts, voters were 265% more likely to have their absentee ballots tossed out than voters in Bush-majority precincts. Behind this statistic is Jim Crow: the rejection of Black voter absentee ballots ran 316% higher than rejections of white voters' ballots.

Mail-in voter registration forms are protected by federal law. Absentee ballots are not. Local government must acknowledge receiving your registration and must let you know if there's a problem (say, with signature or address) that invalidates your registration and you can fix it. But your mail-in vote is an unprotected crapshoot. How do you know if your ballot was received? Was it tossed behind a file cabinet—or tossed out because you did not include your middle initial? In most counties, you won't know.

You don't need Einstein to bend the absentee vote. Remember how Jeb Bush removed the "incompetent" Black Democrat Oliphant as elections supervisor in Broward County, Florida? In 2004, her competent Republican replacement sent out nearly 60,000 absentee ballots too late to return. The majority of belated ballots were intended for Democrats. The "Broward problem" was pandemic across America.

Democrats, who once excelled at voting absentee for Chicago's dead, are now way behind in the new game. Or maybe they are just suffering from "battered party syndrome": beaten mercilessly by Republicans but unable to break off the relationship.

Detective Doug

Once you've got the caging lists, you can get creative. Besides challenging voters of color on Election Day, you can, if the scent of racism doesn't bother you, intimidate them.

Forget the burning crosses, that's passé. This is "Doug." From his all-black SUV, he took telephoto shots of each Black voter as they went into the Jacksonville early-voting station—every day, all day. That type of creepy KGB stuff is a no-no under civil rights law and the Justice Department agreed to look into the matter—after the election was over. What the detective didn't know was that as he was filming the voters, our BBC cameras were filming *him*. He said his name was "Doug," a licensed detective, and he assured us that he was paid a pretty penny to take photos of the voters day after day. He just couldn't say who was sending him the check. And he seemed to forget his last name. So we're including his photo here to see if any of our readers can identify him.

PART 4

OLD DOGS, OLD TRICKS

Felons of the Future

Back in the dark days before our President decided to Help America Vote, I was sitting in my kitchen in London watching election returns from my homeland. That night, November 6, 2000, and the next day, a parade of African-Americans told our BBC television crews they couldn't vote—their names were missing from the voter registries. Conspiracy nut that I am, I began to imagine there was some kind of computer program that systematically hunted down Black voters and wiped their names off the registries.

Within weeks, I had the program on two CD-ROM disks from inside the office of Florida Secretary of State Katherine Harris. If you read my last book, you know it was a list of bad people—57,700 criminals who had registered to vote despite Florida's lifetime ban on felons voting, including, I noticed, Bernice Kines, convicted on July 31, 2009.

2009? Ultimately, we obtained lists of 94,000 targeted by Harris. At least 91,000 were innocent of any crime, except for 325, like Kines, who were convicted in the future.

However, 54% were guilty of being African-American. Katherine Harris, on Jeb Bush's command, ordered them removed from the voter rolls before the election. The scrub list was four-to-one Democrats. And that's how Bush "won" Florida in 2000.

But you knew that. You saw the "felon" report—that is, if you swam to London with your TV, converted its voltage and watched our BBC story or read the London papers. Or you picked it up on samizdat Web sites or from out-of-control radio broadcasters like Randi Rhodes. After a CBS News producer told me in December that her network decided to kill the voter-purge story (we'd fed CBS our material), we used one last desperate trick to get it picked up in the USA: Gave it to a fat guy with a chicken suit.

I admit that *The New York Times* did report the story of the ethnic cleansing of Florida's Black "felons"—but four years later, in 2004, and only to assure us that all was now corrected.

But it wasn't. In April 2004, in complete secrecy, Governor Jeb Bush personally ordered a new purge of 45,000 voters . . . including that felon of the future, Bernice Kines.

I called Jesse Jackson in Chicago who, within days, hopped a

At a press conference in Boston, Michael Moore holds up my computer displaying evidence of the illegal purge of Black voters from registries. This photo is included here to convince progressive-minded Americans of the importance of buying this book, one of several creative and craven marketing ploys I use to overcome American resistance to information not channeled through celebrities.

Photo: Matt Pascarella, Globalvision 2004

plane to Atlanta and demanded CNN expose the new voter scrub. And, applause for CNN, they did. But the Rov-atrons were ready. On October 20, 2004, a smarmy little American Enterprise Institute spinmeister named John Lott announced on CNN's *Lou Dobbs Tonight* that the U.S. Civil Rights Commission "was not able to identify even one person" wrongly disenfranchised by Jeb's Black-out operation. At the same time, the same line was repeated nearly word for word by John Fund in *The Wall Street Journal*. Fund was Vigil-Giron's special guest speaker to the National Association of Secretaries of State.

Well, Messrs. Lott and Fund, meet Willie Steen. I found Steen working at the Florida Orthopedic Center in Tampa. Odd that: You can't work in a hospital in Florida if you have a felony conviction. (See "Mr. Lott, Meet Mr. Steen.") And after you've apologized to Steen, we have a print-out of several thousand others you can meet if you're ever visiting the ghettos of Tampa or Jacksonville.

After our 2000 report, the NAACP sued Jeb and the creators of the racially stained "scrub" list, ChoicePoint, Inc. (the War on Terror profiteers we met in the Fear Chapter). The Bush team confessed to its "error" and agreed not to do it again.

In 2004, my British network thought it a nice touch, now that Governor Jeb would let Black folk vote, to film the newly reenfranchised Steen finally casting his ballot for president. In October 2004, we called the Hillsborough County supervisor of elections to find Steen's early-vote polling place. A clerk looked up his name and said, "Steen can't vote. He's a felon."

A repeat offender!? Well, in that case, we'd film Willie getting the heave-ho again. The Republican supervisor who'd had Steen scrubbed the second time, advised of our filming, showed up at the polling place. His clerk told us, "Wow, this is extraordinary! Steen's status was just changed this morning!" Willie got his ballot. God bless America. It's comforting to know that Republicans will put away the electoral hanging rope when the cameras are rolling.

Mr. Lott, Meet Mr. Steen

John Lott, American Enterprise Institute, Washington, DC
"I think a lot of the discussion about disenfranchising African-American voters . . . they weren't able to identify even one person."

Willie Steen, Florida Orthopedic Center, Tampa, Florida
"I went into the place to vote and I was with my son and there were about 40 to 50 other people around and I got up there to vote and they told me I was a convicted felon. I told the young lady that I had never been arrested. I've never been arrested in my life. I was in the military for four years and have been in the medical field ever since. You can't even work for a hospital being a convicted felon . . . I was in the Persian Gulf War in '91. It's pretty screwed up how they did me, but what can I say?

"I was upset. I was ashamed—with 40 people around—it made me feel real bad. And I'm just hoping I get a letter stating, hey, you can vote again, Willie.

"I really feel it was bad for African-Americans—but hey, what can we do sometimes? What can we do?"

Florida 2000 was the wave of the future. The urge to purge went national. In 2004, Ohio purged thousands, though their law *allows* ex-cons to vote. Texas, which also allows almost all ex-cons to vote, somehow found 525,967 of them registered illegally. Every one was wiped off the voter lists, but, strangely, none busted for the crime of illegal registration. Not to worry. If any voter was wronged, they could ask for a provisional ballot. However, it would not be counted.

My favorite is Colorado. Just weeks before the 2004 election, Colorado's Secretary of State Donetta Davidson removed 6,000 supposed felons from the state's voter rolls. In Colorado, convicts lose their vote only while serving time. There's *not one* verified case of a Colorado con voting illegally from the big house. It is unlikely that Davidson's list contained many, if any, potential illegal voters. But it does contain Democrats, overwhelmingly so. And the timing of Davidson's operation is more than a bit suspect. Federal law bars purges within 90 days of a presidential election to allow a voter to challenge his loss of civil rights. To exempt her action from the federal rule, Republican Secretary of State Davidson declared an "emergency." However, the only "emergency" in Colorado seems to have been George Bush's running dead even with John Kerry in the state's opinion polls.

"Caging" lists, fake felon purges, forged registration forms, evidence tampering, "Black arts" surveillance ops, disappeared absentee ballots, cracked computers. Whatever happened to simply persuading the voters you've got the best candidate?

Smooth Criminals?

Voter snuffing really is illegal, Mr. President.

For those who think that Florida's ballot machinations may have been criminal, there is some official corroboration. On July 15, 2004, the United States Civil Rights Commission requested I testify about BBC's and *Harper's* evidence (I don't turn over notes or

Republican High

The GOP seemed to get awfully lucky with registration switches to the Republican Party in critical counties in swing states. There were the switches in "Little Texas" in New Mexico, and an amazing number of Florida college students, at least 4,000 of them, mostly African-American, who switched to the Republican Party a month before the November 2004 election.

However, Ion Sancho, the non-partisan elections supervisor in Tallahassee, became suspicious when he received a registration switch from one new Republican: his stepdaughter. Look at this signature; it's not a bad forgery. The students, it turns out, thought they had signed a petition to legalize use of marijuana for medical purposes. Covered over by the "legalize pot" sign-up sheet was a registration change form. The form requires two signatures. The second signature was forged, copied from the one obtained by the "pot" fraud. The students, doubly registered, then lost their right to vote altogether. Elections supervisor Sancho immediately called the cops, but Governor Jeb Bush's state police informed him that they would be too busy to investigate until after Election Day. They never did.

In Ohio, it was much simpler. Statistician Anthony Fairfax discovered that Black voters were twice as likely as white voters to have their mail-in registrations simply rejected. In Congresswoman Katherine Harris's district in Florida, Democrats found that, though they submitted registration forms on time, they were entered on the voter rolls only after the deadline, barring them from voting in the Presidential race.

sources) on the felon purge. The Commissioners then voted to request a federal investigation into whether Florida's highest officials "engineered," in their words, a racially bent scrub of voter rolls.

The vote to dig into "the possibility of criminal violations" of federal law was proposed by Civil Rights Commissioner Chris Edley who is Dean of the law school at the University of California at Berkeley.

Justice triumphs! Almost. The Commissioners can't conduct their own criminal probe, which, by law, is handled for them by the Justice Department. They formally requested Attorney General John Ashcroft send investigators to Florida. A year after the election, the Commission was still waiting.

It would be unfair to say President Bush ignored the Commission's request. Shortly after his reelection, the president replaced Edley, the law school dean, and got rid of Mary Frances Berry, who chaired the Commission and who voted with Edley to investigate the President's brother.

PART 5

DEMOCRATS CONCEDE 2008

Think of the new computer black boxes as a convenience: You may already have voted in 2008, they just haven't told you how.

New Mexico '04 is America '08

When Jeb Bush and Katherine Harris rustled Election 2000, I couldn't get American editors interested in Florida. In 2004, I couldn't get them off it. Like generals refighting the last war, their eyes were glued to Jeb's latest ballot-bending games in the Sunshine State. I just couldn't sell sending a crew to film low riders in Rattlesnake, New Mexico, or worse, Columbus, Ohio, the dullest city in the USA.

The real topic of this chapter is Election *2008*.

As they prepare for 2008, the GOP is deeply concerned about voting rights: the fewer the better. In 2006, Republican Governor Bobby Taft, fresh from his conviction on a handful of ethical crimes, signed off on roughly one hundred changes to Ohio's voting laws. His legal trim job won't stop Democrats from voting in 2008; it's just that fewer of their votes will count.

But for the real action in 2008, go west, young man. Just as wiping out Black voters in Florida in 2000 was practice for Ohio in '04, New Mexico '04 is the test site for disenfranchising the new demographic goliath, the Hispanic vote, that will decide '08. Republicans, who have turned the American Dream into American Mean, are surprised that Mexican-American voters still don't feel welcome in their party. Therefore, the voting machinery must be adjusted to correct for these voters' error in judgment.

Provisional Democrats

The Democrats' concession speech for 2008 is written in the provisional ballots of New Mexico. I said at the outset of this tale that

21,084 ballots were not counted in the Land of Enchantment. In addition to these votes spoiled, 6,593 of those new-wave "provisional" ballots—more than Bush's margin—were rejected. They might as well have been tossed in the garbage can.

Easily the worst county in New Mexico was McKinley, with a population three-fourths Navajo, where 6% of the voters were shunted to provisional ballots. An extraordinary 60% of these were effectively dumped in the bin.

After Navajo country, the next highest boatload of provisionals were unleashed on Dona Ana County, where two-thirds of the population is Hispanic. Our research team pored through the arcane stats and found that, in the Chicano precincts of Dona Ana, voters were at least 1,200% more likely to be pushed to a provisional ballot than voters in white majority counties. What's frightening is that New Mexico is horribly typical of the American West. Its higher total of missing votes simply reflects its huge "minority" population.

But hold on a minute. Where were those legions of Democratic lawyers I'd read about, ready to fight to the death for the right to vote?

In the ten days after the polls closed, the lawyers showed up all right: *Republican* lawyers, a phalanx of expensive suits lined up to challenge the rights of thousands of darker-skinned voters to have their provisional ballots counted. These provisional ballots held Kerry votes, no question, and the Republican suits wanted them trashed. That's no surprise. Across the table, they faced the opposition of . . . no one. The Democratic Party, $51 million left unspent on Election Day, refused to send in its A-team to defend the rights of the challenged voters. Instead, the Green Party sent out a frantic e-mail note to its activists for emergency enlistment of volunteers. The Greenies' ponytail crew didn't stand a chance, and the Democrats lost the votes that would have changed the election.

Why did the Dems just roll over? Hold that question.

Lord, Save Us from "Reform"

Native votes are eaten by bad machines, Bush is picking up votes from the dearly departed, voters named "Rodriguez" and "Hernandez" get those bouncing provisional ballots, absentees go absent and New Mexico's politicians are right there with the fix: A major "reform" bill that will require voters to show photo IDs at the polling station. Say *what?*

Dear Lord, save us from "reform." Almost every evil, devious little improvement in vote-bending originates in some voting "reform" law. The requirement for a photo ID, a hot item for Republicans in almost every state of the Union, was another vote-heist horror show masquerading as reform and voter protection.

The sales pitch for requiring ID is to prevent someone illegally voting by using someone else's name. The notable thing about this crime is that *it doesn't happen.* You are more likely to encounter ballot boxes that spontaneously combust. There are voters struck by lightning, some die after mailing in their ballots (there were a dozen in Arapahoe County, Colorado), but out of tens of millions of votes cast, it's quite a hunt to find a single criminal case of a bandit stealing someone's identity merely to cast a vote for the local school board.

So I was amazed to hear that New Mexico state legislator Justine Fox-Young (that's really her name) claimed to have "several" specific cases of vote identity rustling. Like Joe McCarthy waving his list of Communists in the State Department! I called Ms. Fox-Young.

Q: Justine, you've uncovered felony criminals. Do you have the names?

A: Oh, yes!

Q: Really? Wow! Did you turn these names over to the Attorney General of New Mexico or U.S. Attorney?

A: Well, no, someone . . . well, no, but someone did. I should say there were no convictions.

Q: You had evidence of a crime and you didn't have the bad guys arrested?

A: Not *exactly*. There were cases monitored by the FBI.

Of course, dear. And she promised to fax me the names and evidence the next day. That was exciting: If I turned them in, maybe I would get a reward. I'm still waiting.

She called two days later saying that, despite having been unable to send me the evidence, an Assistant U.S. Attorney, a Republican, could back her story. Now, here's a woman who reportedly flapped documents in the air—*here is the evidence!*—showing ID theft. First, her fax machine appears to be broken and now I'm sent to the U.S. Attorney. So I dialed her man, Assistant U.S. Attorney Norm Cairns.

After he told me the FBI is conducting *lots* of investigations surrounding allegations about the elections, I finally jumped into the deep, wide flow of bullshit to ask Norm,

GP: In other words, you can't back her story?
U.S. Attorney Norm: Well, yeah, uh, I guess you'd say that's true.

I guess I will say that, Norm.

GP: And how many people have been indicted during this crime wave of voter identity theft while you've been on the job?
U.S. Attorney Norm: None.

Still, what's wrong with asking people to show their ID? I threw that at Santiago Juárez—and he exploded.

"You know"—Santiago put on a cop voice—" 'show me your ID!' You have Mexicanos that are born here that are stopped by the police and say, 'Do you have your papers?' It's another emotional clamp of a society where you are never invited.

"In Roswell," he explained, "I grew up with signs that said, *'No Mexicans, niggers or dogs allowed.'*" In Roswell today, Kunko-land, signs are more subtle. PHOTO ID REQUIRED gives the same "not allowed" message to Chicano voters who don't have the plastic and club memberships that thicken the wallets of the Albuquerque suburbanites of Fox-Young's Northeast Heights district.

But, I challenged Santiago, Ms. Fox-Young's fear is that someone could rig an election by having their supporters vote under others' names.

Santiago replied, "How do you organize thousands of people to vote twice? Hell, it's hard enough organizing them to vote *once*."

The Dangerous Christian

In 2004, *three-quarters of a million* provisional ballots were thrown out—supposedly illegal voters, yet not one arrest. In seven states, lack of the correct ID card was the key reason for trashing a voter's provisional ballot. Not a *lack* of ID, but the "wrong" one.

And who had the "wrong" IDs? The EAC reports that almost all provisional ballots rejected were from twenty-five "urban" areas. Any guesses about the color of the "urb"?

But this creates a dilemma for the Republican National Committee. With rejections that high, how can you go higher? Answer: new ID requirements. Next problem for the GOP: Could they find Democrats to front the newest scheme?

There were plenty. For example, in 2005, enough Caucasian Democrats in Georgia's legislature joined Republicans to pass a law requiring a special ID card to vote. If you had no driver's license, you could get a voter ID card—for $20. But you'd need an ID to get the ID.

There was an impediment to Georgia's new ID law: the U.S. Constitution. The Twenty-fourth Amendment bars "poll taxes," a fee used in Jim Crow days to keep Blacks and poor Catholics from voting. The Amendment was added in 1964 after America was made ill by photos of Georgia gentlemen beating the crap out of African-American voting-rights workers. (During those one-sided battles, one Georgia gentleman used ax handles to stop desegregation of his diner. He was elected governor of the state.) In 2004, George Bush's Justice Department approved Georgia's new ID scam but federal judges quickly enjoined it as an ill-disguised poll tax.

In light of the court's resistance to voter ID cards, the Republicans would need a Democratic cat's paw to sell IDs as nonpartisan "reforms." It was not easy for the Republicans to find a dupe of the stature required.

James Earl Carter, who succeeded the axman as Governor of Georgia, is a born-again Christian. God help us. A grown man who calls himself "Jimmy," he finds something good in everyone.[22]

As sincere as he is witless, former President Carter was perfect for the Republicans' ID plan. George Bush had in 2001 already named Carter and ex-President Gerald Ford to head an earlier blue ribbon panel to "reform" elections. That panel came up with reasonably good recommendations including ending the entire game of "purging" ex-felons from voter rolls. However, eliminating ex-felon purges would give two million Democrats back their voting rights (93% of all former prisoners vote Democratic if given a chance). Bush's reaction to giving them the vote? I cannot say if Bush had Karl Rove ritually burn the Carter-Ford report or merely let it suffocate in a file cabinet.

In 2005, the GOP, having ignored the first panel, started over with a second. Bush again appointed Carter, but this time, the nice Jerry Ford was pushed down the stairs and replaced as co-chair of the new panel by . . . James Baker III. *No one* calls James Baker "Jimmy."

By September, the deed was done and the Baker-Carter Election Reform Commission issued its report. Gone was the recommendation to end the ex-con purges. In its place: A mandatory national voter ID

---

[22]I remember, while investigating the horrific Liberian civil war in the early nineties, that Carter had the warlords, baby-slicers and cannibals *hold hands* together so they could *feel their oneness*, that they were all God's children sharing together their love for Liberia. True, Jimmy got them to end their civil war—by divvying the nation into several kleptocracies. When Liberians demonstrated against Carter's Murder Inc. solution, Jimmy simply blessed Cut-Throat #1, Charles Taylor, a prison escapee from the U.S. who became President for a short time before he fled Liberia to avoid arrest for war crimes and embezzlement.

card. Some skeptical panel members noted that, for a century, matching voters' signatures to their registration signatures had, without costing votes or money, stopped identity theft. But Carter, with Baker's hand in his finger holes, wrote, "We think citizens would prefer to get a free photo ID"! Certainly, ChoicePoint, Inc., of Georgia would prefer it. The new national ID card required only a little expansion of the PATRIOT act, the un–civil rights law.

Jimmy Carter once said, "America deserves a government as good as its people." Unfortunately, that's what we get.

The Kissinger-American

Kerry won New Mexico—if you counted the votes. I could see how the non-count could happen in the plantation lands of Little Texas. But one fact drove me straight nuts: In the end, this state and its damaged elections were in the hands of a Democrat and a *Mexican-American* one at that.

Or maybe not. I knew it was not a polite question, but it was really bugging me, so I asked Santiago Juárez, "Exactly how does a Mexican get the name *William Richardson?*"

Governor Richardson's dad, he explained, was a Citibank executive assigned to Mexico City. There he met Governor Bill's mom, and—*milagro!*—a Mexican-American was born. Richardson gets big mileage out of his mother's heritage, and that makes him, legitimately, a Mexican-American, a politically useful designation. But it's just as legitimate to say that Richardson is a Citibank-American.

But Governor Richardson is more than that. Between leaving Bill Clinton's cabinet where he was Secretary of Energy and grabbing a Hispanic-district seat in Congress, Richardson became a partner in (Henry) Kissinger and Associates. That would make Richardson a Kissinger-American as well.

In New Mexico the issue of uncounted votes is more than skin deep. Lots of Mexican-American votes don't tally, but Citibank-

American votes never get lost. Kissinger-American votes always count. The story of America's failed elections is not about *undervotes*. It's about *underclass*. Disenfranchisement is class warfare by other means. It just happens that in New Mexico, the colors of the underclass are, for the most part, brown and red.

Class War by Other Means

As Santiago told me:

> You take away people's health insurance and you take their right to union pay scales and you take away their pensions—taking away their vote's just one more on the list.

Some New Mexico Democrats have no trouble at the voting booth. In Santa Fe, you find trust-fund refugees from Los Angeles wearing Navajo turquoise jewelry and "casual" clothes that cost more than my car. Each one has a personal healer, an unfinished film script and a tan so deep you'd think they're bred for their leather. They're Democrats and their votes count. Voting—or at least voting that gets tabulated—is a class privilege. The effect is racial and partisan, but the engine is economic.

The second- and third-highest undervotes in New Mexico were recorded in McKinley and Cibola counties—85% and 72% Hispanic and Native. But the undervote champ is nearly the *whitest* county in New Mexico: DeBaca, which mangled and lost 8.4% of ballots cast. White DeBaca, whose average income hovers at the national poverty level, is poorer than Hispanic Cibola. No question, disenfranchisement gives off an ugly racial smell, but *income* is the real predictor of vote loss.

And what about those Bernalillo ghost voters for Bush? Those spirits are, it turns out, quite well-to-do, haunting the mesas west of Albuquerque where the real estate provides unobstructed views of Georgia O'Keeffe sunsets.

This was my third investigation in New Mexico in twenty years. The first time, the state's Attorney General brought me in to go over the account books of Public Service of New Mexico (PNM), a racketeering enterprise masquerading as an electric company. Too young to understand what I wasn't supposed to know, I proudly mapped out the sewerage lines of deceit connecting the gas drillers, water lords and political elite of New Mexico. The AG's office handed me a nice check—which I took not as a reward, but as a payment to leave the state. After a decade away, I returned as a reporter, to look into prisons-for-profit outfit Wackenhut Inc. In September 1999, a company insider told me, Wackenhut was cutting costs at its New Mexico jails by sending guards alone into the cell blocks. Ralph Garcia of Santa Rosa, who'd lost his ranch to drought, took the $7.95-an-hour job guarding homicidal neo-Nazis and Mexican mafia thugs in the local Wackenhut lock-up. Inexperienced, untrained and alone, he was stabbed to death by inmates just two weeks after the insider's warning.

So that's how Garcia became one more impoverished Chicano who lost his vote. No question, that's not your typical case of voter disenfranchisement, but that's the reality of the "Land of Enchantment." New Mexico is the New America, where growing income inequality is creating a feudal divide between the prison-owning class and the prisoner-and-guard class.

Vote spoilage is the owning class's weapon of choice.

Whose flag does Bill Richardson carry in the nouvelle class war? When I was checking out the New Mexico vote in 2005, my old friends Public Service of New Mexico hit the front page, sued by the State of California for conspiring with Enron to rig the California power market. It is still in court. It was a scam called "Ricochet." Enron and PNM say it was not illegal. It played out about the time Garcia was walking the cell block. Where was Richardson? He was in Washington, Clinton's Secretary of Energy, playing chubby cheerleader for PNM's plan for "deregulation" of the energy market. Deregulation made PNM's games possible—and Richardson's employment by Kissinger inevitable.

Richardson, Ready for Takeoff

What about all those suspect spoiled votes in Hispanic and Indian precincts stuck inside the machines? Why didn't this Mexican-American Democrat ask for a recount? It didn't just slip Richardson's little mind: He actively did everything in his power to *stop* a recount. I was told that it was Richardson himself who encouraged Secretary of State Vigil-Giron to reject the $114,000 payment from pissed-off Democrats and the Green Party. The Governor was too busy to speak with me about this.

Halting the 2004 recount wasn't enough for Governor Bill, however. He demanded the legislature pass a "reform" law that would require anyone wanting a recount of a suspicious vote to put up a bond of over one million dollars. As a result, "free and fair elections" are now effectively outlawed in New Mexico. You can have a choice of a "free" election or a "fair" election, but not both. Want fair? Then you have to pay a million to recheck the ballots. In other words, it's against the law to buy votes, but in New Mexico not against the law to buy the vote count.

On his phony reform law, Richardson was called out by a fellow Democrat, State Senator Linda Lopez—an act of indiscreet defiance that would not be forgotten by the Governor's circle.

The centerpiece of the law signed by the Governor: Ms. Fox-Young's proposal to require photo ID for new voters. Maybe the former Cabinet Secretary and United Nations Ambassador Richardson couldn't imagine that photo IDs would be a problem for some voters. After all, Mexican-Americans in Little Texas may have trouble producing acceptable IDs, but it's no problem at all for a Kissinger-American like Governor Richardson. The Governor and Jimmy Carter both have passports, they have credit cards and they have chauffeurs who will vouch for them.

Richardson wouldn't speak with me about the 2004 vote fiasco. Instead, he busied himself with his space program. He announced the state would chip in $200 million to build a "spaceport" to land private rocket ships that will be launched beginning in 2009 by Richard Branson, the British billionaire. Passengers have already bought tickets for $200,000 each (round trip, they hope).

A Bullet for Lopez Takes Out Kerry

Class issues aside, why didn't the Democratic Party leadership defend those provisional ballots cast by Democrats or hunt for their missing votes?

One possible answer was delivered to me by a computer whiz who likes to play with spreadsheets through the night. He sent me several giant canvasses of color-coded voting data explicating the maddeningly complex numerology of New Mexico politics.

Now here's a bit of arcana you shouldn't need to remember after you're done with this paragraph: *The number of delegates to the Democratic Party county convention from each precinct is determined by that precinct's vote for the Democratic candidate for President.* Got that? Now, it so happens that there was a factional battle royal within the Democratic Party (so what's new?); and it so happens, that the *lower* the recorded vote for Kerry in Hispanic districts, the lower the number of delegates who oppose Richardson's faction.

Remember Senator Lopez, Ms. Trouble? She was the party's county chair and a pain to the Governor's allies. After the 2004 election, she was voted out as Chairwoman. Ensuring "her" voters got counted was hardly Priority One for the Democratic bosses. The bullet they shot at Lopez hit Kerry between the eyes. Didn't the party care about Kerry's count? Forget it: To those involved in the political infighting, preserving New Mexico's electoral votes for Kerry was as valuable as a bag of chicken feathers.

"All politics is local" is one of those clichés so accurate you tend to dismiss it. Only those who've been inside local campaigns know what I mean: Control of the White House is esoteric stuff that doesn't mean a thing to a hack trying to keep his patronage post in the local dogcatcher's office.

When Boss Daley delivered Illinois for Jack Kennedy in 1960 with a suspicious number of Democratic votes, the old scoundrel couldn't care less about the Presidency—the vote theft was all about his political machine keeping control of the county prosecutor's office, a post that monitored local corruption (and jailed Daley's cronies).

Had all the Native votes been counted in McKinley County, those Democrats would have earned 14 delegates to the state party convention, another hothouse of backbiting intrigue. Instead, they earned only 12—and the state party, messing with the formula, and assuming no one would notice, assigned the Indians only 10 seats. Indeed, no one noticed.

"All Politics Is Loco"

The petty party mud wrestling in New Mexico—Democrats always arrange their firing squads in a circle—echoed the loopy dynamics of the national party.

Like most liberalish Joes, I wondered why the national Democratic Party hadn't stood up to the election thieves in 2000. Maybe it was structural. Democrats don't stand up for the same reason jellyfish don't—they're invertebrates.

I thought I'd ask the jelly-in-chief, Terry McAuliffe, the party's chairman at the time, about protecting the vote. In 2002, I dropped by the Democrats' national headquarters, located in a dull Washington office cube. While waiting to meet Chairman McAuliffe, I watched political desk-warmers and expert infighters scurry this way and that, their day planners stuffed with losing battle plans, surrounded by force fields of unshakable self-importance. It had the feel of the French colonial office, circa 1950, in Vietnam.

There was no sense badgering McAuliffe over Gore's 2000 concession. My question was more pointed: Why were the Democrats about to throw *2004*? It was two years before the election and you could already see Florida's snakes—registry purges, vote challenges, ballot-eating machines—slither into two dozen other states under the guise of voting "reform." Black and brown votes were in jeopardy; in other words, a whole lot of Democrats were at risk.

I asked the party's chief how he would stop the hemorrhage. McAuliffe said he knew the Republicans were gaming the voting systems but, he said, "We just don't have the staff or resources to track this and fight it in fifty states."

Maybe not. But on November 2, 2004, within hours of the polls closing, the party threw in the towel with that $51 million left in its war chest.

I can't say the Dems made no preparations to stop another steal. I was assured that "we have a team of lawyers"—literally *thousands* of them "ready for Election Day." It was a very Democratic response. By Election Day 2004, the vote-spoiling machines were already in place, the "caging" lists already active in Florida and Michigan, the polling stations already removed from Black precincts in Ohio. Election Day was too late for lawyers; the fix was already in. And when it happened as predicted, a heartsick official in the NAACP Voter Protection Fund told me (anonymously, of course) that McAuliffe's captains gave the order to those thousands of lawyers to stand down.

Why Kerry Caved

Add up the spoiled and provisional ballots lost in Ohio, New Mexico and Iowa, and John Kerry would have overtaken George Bush's teeny lead—if all the votes were counted.

But Kerry conceded, and not without reason. Ohio was the key, and, let's face it, just as Katherine Harris stopped the count of spoiled punch cards in Florida in 2000, Ohio's Blackwell would likely have done the same in 2004.

Still, the Democrats could have stood before the Supreme Court

Democrats Eat Their Young

But what about in those hopeful days of 2002, when the Democrats could have protected the vote while it could still be protected? I pointed out to party Chairman McAuliffe that some of the most questionable games were being played in Georgia. He shrugged. "Each state has its local issues."

Indeed they did. In Georgia that year, the Democrats' leadership was directing big bucks to defeat not a Republican but Congresswoman Cynthia McKinney, the Atlanta Democrat. McKinney had, unknown to the wider public, opened a congressional investigation into a gold-mining company accused of horrendous misdeeds from Tanzania to Nevada. It was also a company that paid golden fees to George Bush Sr. as well as Vernon Jordan and Andy Young, the Atlanta Democratic power player. That was her mistake. Meanwhile, Georgia's own Democratic Senator Zell Miller was heading up a political lynch mob against the Black Congresswoman.

Defeating McKinney meant keeping down the Black vote. For the white rulers of Georgia's Democratic Party, not a little frightened of a Black-majority party, this was not a problem. One DNC staffer, on condition of anonymity, said that Senator Miller had threatened McAuliffe that if the party stood behind McKinney, he, Miller, would walk away from his Senate seat, leaving it to the Republicans.

You know the ending: McKinney went down to defeat (taking quiet note of the busted computer touch screens in her precincts). Her defeat alienated Georgia's Black voters from the Democratic Party, and so, in the general election, Democratic candidates for governor and Senate went down in flames. And Zell Miller? Despite his alleged promise, he gave up his Senate seat and, though remaining a Democrat by registration, endorsed George W. Bush for reelection.

I can't but feel sympathy for the Democratic Party. They've had a presidential election swiped out of their hands—*twice*. But then, any political party that embraces a brain-damaged vulture like Zell Miller deserves every beating it gets.

and argued, as Martin Luther King said, "Until justice rolls down like waters and righteousness like a mighty stream." Kerry's attorney could have told the Justices, and the world, that this election brought back the methods of the White Citizens Councils and the hoodless Klan tactics of Operation Eagle Eye, outlawed forty years ago. But before justice could get flowing, any well-read civil rights attorney would know that the man identified as "Bill" who directed the voter harassment teams of Operation Eagle Eye back in the 1960s was, by 2004, none other than William "Bill" Rehnquist, Chief Justice of the United States Supreme Court. Case dismissed.

59 Million Pinheads on Parade

Now you've got the facts: Kerry won, but his votes weren't counted. And that fixed it; fixed by purging, blocking, intimidating voters of color, mangling and dumping their ballots, sending their registrations and absentee ballots to the Bermuda triangle. What the Republican Party did would have made a Grand Dragon proud except, instead of doing the deed in white sheets, they did it in spreadsheets. Lynching by laptop.

This Jim Crow operation was far more effective than the racism of some Klansman redneck and immeasurably less excusable, because it was cold and passionless, with gleeful evil joy at pulling a fast one. I think of Bush's spokesmistress Mindy Tucker Fletcher's calculating eyes, standing in front of the George Bush Building, looking at the lists of homeless Black men and Black soldiers, "caged" and ready for electoral elimination—and she couldn't stop smirking.

I don't think for a minute Mindy is a racist, nor Dubya nor the RNC pooh-bahs. They couldn't care less about these voters' race; the registrants could have been purple. They knew only they were mostly poor, unliked, undefended even by their own Democratic Party—easy pickings for ballot box bullying. The escapade was all the more delicious because, in Ohio, Bush reelection front man Blackwell shared the victims' skin tone. Well, there's always a slave ready to serve Pharaoh. Nothing new in that.

Mindy knew some bald reporter for British TV could ask all the questions he wanted, but it wouldn't mean a thing—because the information would simply never make it past America's media border guards. And she was right. We broadcast the stories in Europe and Africa, printed the reports on the London *Guardian's* front page, warning that the election was about to be "caged." We might as well have stuffed the news in a time capsule and shot it to the moon. Either way, it never made it to American shores.

So, here's to you, Mindy, Kenny and George. You won.

In another world, in which all votes are counted, J. F. Kerry would have gathered all those arcane chits called "electoral votes" and would be sitting in the Oval Office today. But, dear reader, there's one cold statistic Kerry voters must face: 59 million Americans marched to the polls and voted for George W. Bush. The fact that Republicans monkeyed with the votes in swing states doesn't wash away that big red stain.

If Osama doesn't scare you, *that* should.

Because if 59 million Americans agreed with George Bush that every millionaire's son, like him, shouldn't have to pay inheritance taxes; that sucking up to Saudi petrocrats constitutes a foreign policy; that killing Muslims in Mesopotamia will make them less inclined to kill us in Manhattan; that turning over Social Security to the casino operators that gave us Enron, WorldCom and world depression is smart economics; then, fine, Mr. Bush deserves the job. But most Americans, bless 'em, don't actually believe *any* of that hokum. *Yet half still voted for him.*

What we witnessed on November 2, 2004, was a 59 million strong army of pinheads on parade ready to gamble away their pensions so long as George Bush makes sure that boys kill each other, not kiss; who feel right proud that our uniformed services can kick some scrawny brown people in the ass in some far-off place when we're mad and can't find Osama; who can't bring themselves to vote for a guy with a snooty Boston accent who's never been to a NASCAR tractor pull and who certainly thinks anyone who does is a low-Q beer-burping blockhead.

In his vulturous, brain-damaged way, Zell Miller was right: Stand up for Black voters and the redneck boobs will take their revenge. So the election came down to this: Nitwits who think Ollie North's a hero not a conman, who can't name their congressman, who believe that Saddam Hussein and Osama bin Laden were going steady, who can't tell Afghanistan from a souvlaki stand and, bloated with lies and super-size fries, clomped to the polls 59 million strong to vent their small-minded hatreds on us all.

I fear the election was an intelligence test that America flunked.

ELECTIONS CHAPTER BONUS!

The Necklace-ing of Dan Rather

You aren't stupid, they just talk to you that way.

It's 2004. Falluja's on fire, your pension's burning away, the last General Motors worker is turning out the lights in Detroit—and the biggest issue of the election, aside from Christians who don't want homosexuals to have families, was whether some elderly news celebrity, Dan Rather, had besmirched the reputation of our President, a former Naval Aviator.

They can't get you to ignore that man behind the curtain, Dorothy, unless there's a fascinating show on stage to distract you. And, for the final days of the presidential campaign, they gave us the lynching of Dan Rather.

We know George Bush was a Naval Aviator because it says so right on his toy box. Actually, he never was a Naval Aviator and never once landed a plane on the deck of an aircraft carrier. During the Vietnam War, our future President flew in the Texas Air National Guard protecting Houston from Viet Cong attack.

Our President obtained that job the same way he got the current one: The fix was in. Congressman Poppy Bush, said Rather, put in the fix for his son, despite Junior's too-dumb-to-fly test scores, by putting in a call to the head of the Texas Air Guard via Texas Lt. Governor Ben Barnes. That's what Dan Rather reported on *60 Minutes*, that Bush Jr. got the Texas top gun post, and thereby dodged the draft and the bullets of Vietnam.

It was a hell of a scoop and his network rewarded him and his producer, Mary Mapes, by firing their sorry asses. That wasn't enough.

The president of CBS, Leslie Moonves, bullwhipped his network's stars and, with his own spit, polished the soiled war record of our President, declaring that Rather's producer:

> . . . ignored information that cast doubt on the story she had set out to report—that President Bush had received special treatment thirty years ago, getting to the Guard ahead of many other applicants.[23]

Really? Well, Mr. Moonves, look at *this* evidence:

"His [George W. Bush's] dad called then–Lt. Gov. Barnes to ask for his help to get his son not just in the Guard, but to get one of the coveted pilot slots which were extremely hard to get. [Barnes, through a "cut-out," a third party,] contacted General Rose at the Guard and took care of it. George Bush was placed ahead of thousands of young men, some of whom died in Vietnam."

This is from a letter which had remained locked for years in the file cabinets of the U.S. Justice Department prosecutor in Austin, Texas. How I got it does not matter. Our War President has not challenged authenticity. And its contents, Mr. Moonves, were confirmed by the "cut-out" himself, the man who made the call to the Texas Air Guard for young George. (Would the cut-out, a major figure in the Lone Star State, allow BBC to film his statement? He said, "*Do I look like the dumbest Texan on the prairie?*")

But you knew that, if you're not American. At the *Guardian* and on BBC we also reported, before the presidential election, that Lt. Governor Barnes had put in the fix for George Jr. at the Air Guard. We reported that in 1999, before Bush's *first* run for office.[24]

---

[23]In January 2005, at the Sundance Film Festival, I publicly offered the CBS president $100,000 if he could produce this startling evidence. It was a cheap and shameless publicity trick for the BBC documentary, as I knew full well that Moonves had neither the information nor the inclination to bother with a sum he uses to tip his chauffeurs.

[24]For more details on George Bush Jr.'s high-flying days, watch the "War Hero" segment from the BBC film *Bush Family Fortunes*, at www.gregpalast.com.

War Hero or War Zero?

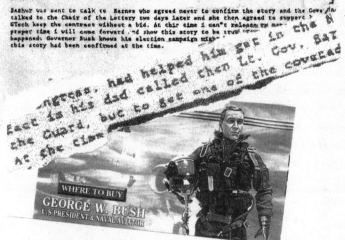

U.S. Attorney
Don Mills
816 Congress
Austin, Tx 78701

In light of all of the questions about the Lottery, I think it is important to reveal some information that should be disclosed.

Several months ago many of us felt that the Lottery Commission should rebid the Gtech contract when it came up for renewal. Leaders of the Republican Party strongly supported rebidding and I believe the Chair of the Commission also wanted to rebid. It is now time to disclose at least one reason why it was not rebid. Governor Bush thru Reggie Bashur made a deal with Ben Barnes not to rebid because Barnes could confirm that Bush had lied during the 94 campaign. During that campaign, Bush was asked if his father, then a member of Congress, had helped him get in the National Guard. Bush said no he had not, but the fact is his dad called then Lt. Gov. Barnes to ask for his help to get his son not just in the Guard, but to get one of the coveted pilot slots which were extremely hard to get. At the time ████████████████████ contacted General Rose at the Guard and took of it. George Bush was placed ahead of thousands of young men, some of whom died in Viet Robert Spellings also knew about this and began telling the story which made a lot of people nervous. I am told that Spellings was also an aide to Barnes at the time this to place.

Bashur was sent to talk to Barnes who agreed never to confirm the story and the Gove talked to the Chair of the Lottery two days later and she then agreed to support GTech keep the contract without a bid. At this time I can't release my nam proper time I will come forward and show this story to be true because happened. Governor Bush knows his election campaign migh this story had been confirmed at the time.

WHERE TO BUY
GEORGE W. BUSH
U.S PRESIDENT & NAVAL AVIATOR

"His dad called then Lt. Gov. Barnes . . . to get his son . . : in the Guard. . . ." The BBC obtained this memo in 1999 from the Justice Department U.S. Attorney's Office in Texas.

Justice for Miers

But there's much, much more to the story than Rather had *cojones* to report.

Barnes had two tasks—one, to get little George into the Air Guard and the other was to *shut up about it*. Keep it quiet. Barnes's good deeds and long silence were, indeed, well rewarded.

Barnes, who left office under a cloud of impropriety, stayed on in Austin as a big-fee lobbyist. And the biggest fee he received, maybe the biggest ever in the history of the lobbying art, was at least $23 million for representing a company called GTech when it got the contract to operate the Texas lottery. GTech's creepy ways of doing business caught up with it in 1997, when, after questionable payments to the Texas lottery director's boyfriend were exposed, GTech lost its contract by order of the new, uncorrupted, lottery director. The lottery work was put up for bid and GTech's replacement chosen.

But then something quite extraordinary happened: The new state lottery director was fired, the bids tossed out and GTech given back the lottery work—no bidding required. The governor at the time: George W. Bush.

Now, let's go back to the letter buried at the U.S. Attorney's Office in Austin:

> Governor Bush thru [another cut-out] made a deal with Ben Barnes not to rebid because Barnes could confirm that Bush had lied during the '94 campaign. During that campaign [for Governor of Texas], Bush was asked if his father . . . had helped him get in the National Guard. Bush said no he had not, but the fact is his dad called then–Lt. Gov. Barnes. . . .

Silence has a price and Barnes, the letter says, got his: safety for his client GTech, with whom he maintained hidden ties. I can't imagine that Barnes would make such a raw demand on Bush. But the war hero Governor's team made damn sure that no harm came to Barnes and his business associates.

> The Governor talked to the chair of the lottery two days later and she then agreed to support letting GTech keep the contract without a bid.

Did Governor Bush put in the fix for GTech as alleged? I wasn't on the phone when he spoke to the lottery board Chairwoman. Maybe they talked about their newfound faith in the Lord, which they both discovered together at the same time. The Chairwoman? Harriet Miers.

We don't know if Miers gave the overpriced GTech its contract back to help the governor keep his Air Guard secret a secret or simply because she liked GTech's record of high costs and corruption. In 2005, George W. Bush's attempted appointment of Miers to the United States Supreme Court surprised the U.S. media and even the President's own supporters. But I wasn't surprised at all.

The Shredder-in-Chief

Loose lips can sink presidential ships. And there was a whole lot more to be silent about. Once in the Guard, there were questions about the Congressman's son showing up for duty. When asked if he, in fact, had gone AWOL during the war, our President said, "Ask my commander," whom, he knew, we would have trouble interviewing. His commander was dead.

When Dan Rather faced the predictable jackal attack on his Bush draft story, Rather did the courageous thing: blamed someone else.

In this case, Rather and his producer, Mapes, loaded their corporate guilt on a guy you've probably never heard of before, rancher Bill Burkett of Abilene, a retired Lieutenant Colonel from the Texas Air National Guard. Burkett had given CBS a memo, which had been passed to him, which had nothing to do with the main story about Bush's dodging the draft. It was a teeny side story—whether young Bush had asked his commander if he could skip a drill. No question,

Rather should not have aired it without telling the audience, "We can't fully authenticate this memo." Frankly, it wasn't worth airing at all.

But back to Lt. Col. Burkett. Once Rather and CBS hung out their source and painted a target on him, Rove-ing gangs of media hit men finished him off. Burkett's an evidence "fabricator," "Bush-hater" and even, suggests William Safire in *The New York Times*, a felon ready for hard time.

Let me tell you about this Burkett "criminal." In 2003, I dropped by his ranch while filming a BBC documentary. It's a place halfway to nowhere, in tumbleweed land. He has cows (or cattle—I'm too much of a New York–London boy to tell the difference). Burkett a "Bush-hater"? "George W. Bush was an excellent pilot," Burkett told me. "He had the right leadership skills, he had the 'Top Gun' approach."

But I didn't go interview Burkett to chat about our President's days when he flew high. The Guardsman had an important story to tell that is far more important than some memo asking for a day off from drill. It has to do with a phone call and a shredder.

In 1997, Burkett was working at Camp Mabry with Major General Daniel James when a call came in from Joe Allbaugh, Governor Bush's Chief of Staff. Bush was about to get a political polishing up for his White House run, with a ghostwritten autobiography. Allbaugh, according to Burkett, stated that Bush political operative Karen Hughes would be dropping by the Air Guard offices to look at the war record and wanted to "make sure there's nothing in there that'll embarrass the Governor." According to Burkett, the General and his minions took this as an unsubtle hint to "clean up" the boss's record. (Bush, as Governor, was also Commander-in-Chief of the Texas Air Guard.) Lt. Col. Burkett, both curious and disturbed by the call, wondered how his fellow comrades-in-arms would respond. His answer was in the trash-to-be-shredded bin: George Bush's military pay records. "I saw what are called LES (leave and earnings statements), which are pay documents. I saw retirement points documents and other administrative information."

He did not see their content, only Bush's name, and therefore cannot answer The Big Question: Did those records, now "missing," indicate that our President went AWOL from the Air Guard? Other soldiers who failed to show up for duty twice lost their Air Guard posts and were then subject to the draft and shipment to 'Nam. Here was a whole new matter: Not just whether Bush got into the Guard on a family fix, but whether Bush, once in, failed to show up for duty.

Weirdly, when we checked at Camp Mabry, Austin, where Air Guard duty records are kept, Bush's were gone. That was extraordinary: Military records don't go AWOL by themselves. Were these the files Burkett said he saw in the shredder? Destruction of military records is serious business. However, the U.S. press, which belatedly launched a hunt into Bush's war record in 2004, has dropped the story, and Bill Burkett in particular, as radioactive because of Burkett's supposedly fabricating the memo used by Rather.

But he hadn't. Burkett is as capable of master forgery as I am of painting a passable Picasso. William Safire in *The New York Times* demanded the government prosecute Burkett for allegedly fabricating the document. Darned right they should have—if he did it. They haven't. Why not? Maybe they don't want to check into this "fake" document because maybe it's not fake.

So where are they now, the alleged polishers of Bush's war record? They're doing quite well, thank you. After a month in office, in February 2001, Bush made Allbaugh chief of FEMA, the Federal Emergency Management Agency, the agency whose main job is preparing for hurricanes and other disasters. To make way for Allbaugh, Bush dumped the technical expert in charge of disaster planning. Allbaugh didn't think FEMA should worry so much about hurricanes and he redirected FEMA's main efforts to the War on Terror. In 2003, Allbaugh quit and took up work as a registered lobbyist for Halliburton Corp.

Karen Hughes, who reviewed the clean and shiny Bush files to ghostwrite his autobiography, went on to glory as Bush's White House "Manager of Communications and Media Affairs." In April 2002, Hughes left to write a book, *Ten Minutes from Normal,* telling other women that there's more to life than politics. She appeared on a blizzard of TV shows chatting about how she decided to give up the public life and spend time with her family. It was a real affirmation of "Bush Family Values." However, once her book fell off the bestseller list, she dumped her family and went back to work on Bush's campaign full time. Her mission accomplished (Bush's reelection), she selflessly gave up a return to her family to accept, in July 2005, the title of Undersecretary of State for Public Diplomacy. The charming Ms. Hughes's job is to change the image of America among Arabs so they won't want to kill us. Lord, help us.

"They Hated His Guts"

And what about George W. Bush: war hero or war zero? In all the hullabaloo about CBS's "counterfeit" memo, no one asked, *Did he serve his country?*

I talked with an unassailable source: a former Guardsman and current compatriot of Bush. In strict confidence, he told me about Bush's flyboy days. It seemed that the other airmen had strong feelings about Bush. "*They hated his guts.* As far as they were concerned, he was a goof-off and a coward"—because Bush refused to volunteer for combat missions. According to Bush's comrade in the Guard, Little George was one of the only airmen who ran from combat. While Air Guard flyers were *not required* to fly combat runs in Vietnam, nearly all did, voluntarily, except for George.

Darkness at Noon at Black Rock

CBS and the U.S. media could have cleared up the entire business by simply asking the President point-blank, "Did you or did you not ask your commander to get out of drill?" Better yet, "Did you, as Governor, call 'Justice' Miers to restore the lottery contract to Mr. Barnes's associates?"

But CBS didn't ask. They had an execution to attend to, Rather's.

But before the execution, they had to hold a trial. To judge Rather and the veracity of his story that Bush Sr. had helped his son dodge the draft, CBS put together an "independent panel."

"Independent," my ass.

The "panel" was just two guys as qualified for the job as they are for landing the space shuttle: Dick Thornburgh and Louis Boccardi.

Remember Dickie Thornburgh? He was on the Bush 41 Administration's payroll. His grand accomplishment as Bush Sr.'s Attorney General was to whitewash the investigation of the *Exxon Valdez* oil spill, letting the oil giant off the hook on big damages. Today, Thornburgh earns fat pay as counsel to Kirkpatrick & Lockhart, the Washington law-and-lobbying outfit which promotes his services by hawking his former job as a retainer of Bush Sr. "Independent"? Why not just appoint Karl Rove as CBS's grand inquisitor and be done with it?

Then there's Boccardi, not exactly a prince of journalism. This is the gent who, as CEO of the Associated Press, spiked his own wire service's exposure of Oliver North and his treasonous dealings with the Ayatollah Khomeini. Legendary AP investigative reporters Robert Parry and Brian Barger found their stories outing the Iran-Contra scandal in 1986 stopped by their bosses. They did not know that Boccardi was on those very days deep in the midst of talks with Lt. Col. Oliver North, strategizing on how to get the hostages, one of whom was an AP reporter. Parry later discovered a 1986 e-mail from North, which gleefully notes that Boccardi "is supportive of our terropism [sic] policy" and wants to keep the story "quiet." The AP demoted journalist Barger and forced him to quit over the offense of trying to report the biggest story of the decade. This is "Spike" Boccardi's qualification to pass judgment on working journalists.

Why did CBS need the Stanlinesque show trial, the Moonves confession, dead-wrong resurrection of the President's war record, and the ritual slaughter of the network's own star?

The answer is more likely to be found, not at Blackrock (the unpleasant nickname for CBS headquarters), but in a distant corporate tower. The network's famous eyeball logo is now just a pimple on the corporate rectum of media monolith Viacom Corp. And when Viacom winks, the CBS eyeball blinks. And what did Viacom want?

> From a Viacom standpoint, the election of a Republican administration is a better deal. Because the Republican administration has stood for many things we believe in, deregulation and so on. . . . I vote for Viacom. Viacom is my life, and I do believe that a Republican administration is better for media companies than a Democratic one.

That was the voice of Sumner Redstone, Chairman and CEO of Viacom, speaking just weeks before the 2004 presidential election. It looks like Viacom needed George Bush to stay in the White House and some over-the-hill journalist who makes less than Redstone's dry-cleaning bill wasn't going to screw it up with some cockamamie story about the Texas Air Guard.

Decades ago, CBS's competitor, RCA/NBC, had a logo of a little dog listening to a phonograph record, responding happily to "its master's voice." CBS didn't have to put an old vinyl disk on the Victrola to hear its master's voice.

Silence of the Media Lambs

Quiz time. Who said this?

> What is going on to a very large extent, I'm sorry to say, is a belief that the public doesn't need to know, limiting access, limiting information to cover the backsides of those who are in charge of the war. It's extremely dangerous and cannot and should not be accepted, and I'm sorry to say that up to and including this moment of this interview, that overwhelmingly it has been accepted by the American people. And the current Administration revels in that, they relish and take refuge in that.

Dan Rather said it in 2002, but to a British audience, on BBC TV's *Newsnight,* the show that carries my reports. But in the USA, he said:

> George Bush is the President! He makes the decisions. He wants me to line up, just tell me where!

Good boy, Dan. Good boy.
But across the ocean, Dan slipped his leash:

> There was a time in South Africa that people would put flaming tires around people's necks if they dissented. And in some ways the fear is that you will be necklaced here [in America], you will have a flaming tire of lack of patriotism put around your neck. Now it is that fear that keeps journalists from asking the toughest of the tough questions.

In 2004, he knew exactly what would happen when he finally asked those questions. He had already delivered his own eulogy.

The lynching of Dan Rather is a cautionary tale of how news is made in the USA—and unmade—and topics permissible during an election. The story that cannot be reported is not about George Bush's special treatment but about the special treatment of the specially privileged. The real story, for me, is that Little George was just one of a dozen privileged princelings saved from the dangers of their powerful daddies' wars. Barnes did not give help to Bushes only. The man who actually made the call to the Air Guard for Little George at Barnes's request also confirmed that at Barnes' request, he also put in the fix for sons of Democratic big-wigs, Governor John Connally and Congressman, later Senator, Lloyd Bentsen. Vietnam was one front in a class war, and only one class was sent to fight it. I don't blame Congressmen Bush Sr. or Bentsen for keeping their sons out of Vietnam. I do blame them for sending other men's sons in their place.

New World Disorder (Detail) ©Winston Smith 2002

CHAPTER 5

THE CLASS WAR

Hope I Die Before My Next Refill

Dispatches from the war of the movers and shakers against the moved and shaken, including No Child's Behind Left, the Grinch That Stole Overtime and the Chávez of Louisiana. Welcome to 1927.

This is an impressive crowd: the Haves and the Have-Mores.

—Presidential candidate G.W. Bush
Waldorf Astoria, $800/plate dinner
October 2000

You don' geddit, Palast, do you? They din' screw up. They *love* it. What's Cheney's old Halliburton business? *"Oil services"*—that means drilling platforms and pipes and all that. "Emergency services" too. And I been working "infrastructure A.E."—architecture-engineering, my friend, with Brown & Root. Well, Cheney's hit the trifecta with this one, "the biggest reconstruction project since the pyramids"—oil, emergency repairs, bridges, levees, canals, power plants. You know it and I know it: Dick Cheney's the only guy in America who'd rather have a hurricane than a blow job.

—Fishhead, Ninth Ward, New Orleans, September 2005

America went through a terrible year. The levees broke in New Orleans. When bodies floated in the streets, the Republican Congress saw an opportunity for more tax cuts and consolidation of the corporatopia they had created for their moneyed donors. The Democratic Party was clueless, written off, politically at death's door.

The year was 1927.

Back then, when the levees broke, America awoke. Public anger rose in a floodtide, and in that year, the USA entered its most revolutionary period since 1776. The thirty-four-year-old utility commissioner of Louisiana, Huey P. Long, conceived of a plan to rebuild his state based on a radical program of redistributing wealth and power. The ambitious Governor of New York, Franklin D. Roosevelt, adopted it, and later named it The New Deal. America got rich and licked Hitler. It was our century.

It's 1927 again.

But this time, the Haves and Have-Mores have something better for you than a New Deal. They are offering "opportunity"—a lottery ticket instead of a guarantee. Like double-or-nothing in the stock market instead of Social Security—will the suckers go for it? There's one born every minute. I can't believe they're the majority, but at last count, they numbered over 59 million. And they vote.

Years from now, in Guantánamo or in a refugee relocation "Enterprise Zone," your kids will ask you, "What did you do in the Class War, Daddy?"

We may have to admit that conquest and occupation happened before we could fire off a shot.

The trick of class war is not to let the victims know they're under attack. That's how, little by little, the owners of the planet take away what little we have.

As both a journalist and economist (trained by Milton Friedman and Art Laffer, no less), I think of myself as a war correspondent in the class conflict. The point of this chapter is to find out, from the trenches, what happened that left the average American in peril. It will take us from the Peninsula Hotel in Beverly Hills to *Larry King*

Live to Japanese swine-feed microbe thieves and back to "The City That Care Forgot," New Orleans.

Tomorrow's Bacon

So who's winning? It's a crude indicator, but let's take a peek at the Class War body count.

If you thought I have nothing nice to say about George W. Bush, look at this: The World Bank reports that *the USA has more millionaires than ever—7.4 million!* And over a decade, the number of billionaires has more than tripled, 341 of them! And, if they're lucky enough to die before the inheritance tax break expires, *they won't have to pay taxes on any of it.*

If that doesn't make you feel like you're missing out, this should: You, Mr. Median, are earning, after inflation, a little less than you earned when Lyndon Johnson reigned. Median household income—and most of us are "median"—is down. *Way* down.

The chart below represents a typical Bush year.

Mr. Bush and friends are offering us an "ownership" society. But he didn't mention who already owns it. The richest fifth of America

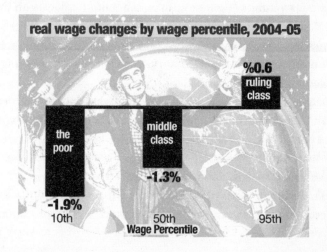

owns 83% of all shares in the stock market. But that's a bit misleading because most of that, 53% of all the stock in the market, is owned by just *one percent* of American households.

And what does the Wealthy One Percent want? Answer: more wealth. Where will they get it? As with a tube of toothpaste, they're squeezing it from the bottom. Median paychecks have gone down by 4% during the current regime, but Americans in the bottom fifth have seen their incomes sliced by 20%. And CEO pay at the Fortune 500 has bloated by 51% during the first four years of the Bush regime to an average of $8.1 million per annum.

When Reagan took power in 1980, the One Percent possessed 33% of America's wealth as measured by capital income. By 2006, the One Percent has swallowed over half of all America's assets, from sea to shining sea. One hundred fifty million Americans altogether own less than 3% of all private assets.

Yes, American middle-class house values are up, but we're blowing that gain to stay alive. Edward Wolff, the New York University expert on income, explained to me that, "The middle class is mortgaging itself to death." As a result of mortgaging our new equity, 60% of all households have seen a decline in net worth.

Is America getting poorer? No, just its people, We the Median. In fact, we are producing an astonishing amount of new wealth in the USA. We are a lean, mean production machine. Output per worker in America has zoomed by 19.5% over six years through 2006. Problem is, as the chart shows, although worker productivity keeps rising, the producers are getting less and less of it.

The gap between what we produce and what we get is widening like an alligator's jaw. You should recognize the chart on the next page: It's nearly identical to the pattern in India and China. The same jaws—productivity widening over wages—open here because they open there as workers, not products, compete.

The more you work, the less you get. It used to be that as the economic pie got bigger, everyone's slice got bigger too. No more.

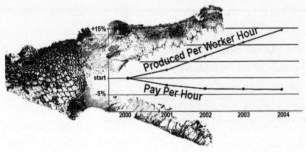

U.S. Productivity vs. Wages

The One Percent have swallowed your share before you can get your fork in.

Of course, there are killjoys who cling to that Calvinist-Marxist belief that a system forever fattening the richest cannot continue without end. Professor Michael Zweig, Director of the State University of New York's Center for Study of Working Class Life, put it in culinary terms: "Today's pig is tomorrow's bacon."

The Grinch That Stole Overtime

What we see is that the richest get richer not by "creating wealth" but by taking yours. How? In their "jaws" they are eating up America's productivity like a salami, a slice at a time. And when they're really good at it, really subtle and sly, you don't even know the knife is going in.

Here's a significant example. America's 40-hour workweek? Well, forget it, it's gone—for 2.7 million workers, at least. The rest of us are next. I'm sure you've already caught that interesting little item on page 15,576 of the 2003 *Federal Register*.

According to the *Register,* where the Bush Administration likes to place its little gifts to major campaign donors, those 2.7 million workers will lose their overtime pay. What this means is that nearly 3 million workers receiving time-and-a-half by law after they've worked 40 hours will no longer get the extra. It's a change in the Wage and Hour Law, blowing a big hole through the 60-year-old rule that established America's workweek, cornerstone of FDR's New Deal. The idea of that law was to discourage wage-slave hours and encourage hiring additional staff. And it worked. Now it won't.

The Bush Administration dropped this little piranha into the *Register* just before Labor Day 2003. Are these guys droll or what?

Look on the bright side. In the *Register,* Mr. Bush's Labor Department says the change in the Wage and Hour Law will produce a "benefit" of $1.53 billion. I put "benefit" in quotes because, in the official cost-benefit analysis, the amount employers will now be able to slice out of workers' pockets is tallied on the *positive* side of the rules change.

Mr. Bush has a good cover story. In September 2004, at the Republican Convention, the President announced he was changing overtime rules to give workers "comp time" off instead of pay, so we could spend more time with our families. Thanks, Mr. President. He forgot to mention that a few days before, on August 23, 2004, his Labor Department had already put in half the plan—eliminating overtime pay, the page 15,576 scheme—while failing to put into the regs one word about comp time. In the pre–September 11 days, we called that "lying."

We're not talking high-level executives or lawyers here; they've always been exempt from the 40-hour-week rule. We're talking mostly restaurant-chain workers.

Nevertheless, workers getting their pay snipped shouldn't complain, they will all be receiving promotions to management, because all an employer has to do is reclassify his worker bees as "managers" and they lose the legal right to overtime. Would you be surprised to learn this new rule was slid into law at the suggestion of lobbyists for the National Council of Chain Restaurants? You've met their "managers"—they're the ones in the beanies and aprons whose management decisions are "Hold the lettuce on that."

My favorite little rules change that sneaked into the *Register* would also reclassify as "exempt professionals" anyone who learned their skill in the military. In other words, thousands of veterans will now lose overtime pay on their return. For life. Now *there's* a veterans' benefit.

In fairness, I must add that, according to Labor Secretary Elaine Chao's press office, the rules changes will *extend* overtime benefits to 1.3 million burger-flippin' managers. How does that square with the billion-dollar "benefit" to business owners? Simple: The Chao hounds at the Labor Department suggest that employers *cut wages* so that, added to the new "overtime" pay, the employees won't actually take home a dime more.

I can hear the moaners and bleeding hearts saying this sounds like the Labor Department is telling Big Business how to evade the law. Yep, that's what the Department is doing. Right there on page 15,576 of the Federal Register it says:

> Affected employers would have four choices concerning potential payroll costs: . . . (#4) converting salaried employees' basis of pay to an hourly rate that results in virtually no changes to the total compensation paid those workers.

And in case some employer is as dense as a president and doesn't get the hint, Comrade Chao repeats, ". . . The fourth choice above results in virtually no (or only a minimal) increase in labor costs." For decades the courts have thrown the book at cheapskate bosses who chisel workers out of legal overtime by cutting base pay this way . . . but now they'll have a new defense: Bush made me do it.

But then, there likely will not be any cases against employers anyway, since Secretary of Labor Chao herself is the labor cop whose job it is to stop paycheck theft by chiseling employers. She's well qualified for her job. Her resumé reads, "Married to Republican Senator Mitch McConnell of Kentucky." I called her press office to ask if she qualifies for overtime, but they'd left the office early.

On Labor Day weekends, our President likes to play a few holes of golf. These labor law changes contain some good news for our sporting President. Under Chao's new rules he need not worry if he wants to replay that hole. "Exempt professionals" who cannot earn overtime—once defined as doctors, lawyers and those with specialized college degrees—will now include anyone who provides skilled advice . . . like caddies ("You might try the other end of the club, Mr. President").

No Deal

What's at stake here is the New Deal, Franklin Roosevelt's 1933 program that guaranteed what he called "Freedom from Fear and Freedom from Want." It was not, as misrepresented today, a program just for pulling America out of an economic depression, but a vision of government that takes ultimate responsibility for protecting its citizens' lives and livelihoods from misfortune and injustice. That was one hell of a radical program then. Before Roosevelt, if you got old and starved, well, *tough luck*. If you lost your job or your home blew down in a hurricane, *too bad, Jack*. If the power company charged you half your wages for your light bill; or the grain monopoly refused to buy your crop for more than the price of dirt; or if you worked 60 hours in the steel mill with no overtime pay; or if you joined a union and got busted over the head, it was *that's business, buddy*.

In his first one hundred days in office, Roosevelt tried to break the back of the *that's business, buddy* monopolists, passing through Congress a firestorm of legislation including the Wage and Hour Law, Social Security and the National Reconstruction Act.

And the current crew in Washington just *hates* it. This chapter, indeed this book, is all about how they are taking these American rights away, stripping them off you one by one, from the Wage and Hour Law's 40-hour week to the Clayton Antitrust Law to the False Claims Act to the laws that keep your lights on and your pensions protected. Many are laws that you've probably never heard of, like the Public Utility Holding Company Act. But, take my word for it, you'll miss them when they're gone.

These Little Piggies Went to Market

Honolulu, Hawaii. Four men in a hotel room. Unaware of the camera hidden in the bedroom lamp, they begin to share their most intimate secrets, as they had so many nights before, about pig food.

It's not a Paris Hilton video, but the FBI's grainy film of the chiefs of the world's pig feed industry is weirdly fascinating. Listen to Terry Wilson, a vice president of Archer Daniels Midland, the biotech food giant that NPR News calls "Supermarket to the World." In the 1994 Hawaii meeting, Wilson stood up to preach passionately ADM's customer relations philosophy to Japanese and European competitors:

> We are gonna get manipulated by these goddamn buyers.
> They are *not* your friend. They are not *my* friend. All I
> wanna tell ya again is, *let's put the prices on the board,* let's
> all agree that's what we're gonna do and then walk out of
> here and *do it!*

And they did it. They literally drew lines through a map of the planet and marked up which corporation got which slice of the world market for different products, including Vitamin C and lysine, the pig-feed additive; then they set the price. They kicked up the price of the pig food from $0.70 a pound to $1.20.

We have the tape of the Hawaii price-fixing confab (and a dozen others recorded in Paris, Tokyo and Mexico City) only because the FBI got lucky. The head of ADM's Frankenstein foods (bioengineering) division at the time, Dr. Mark Whitacre, is a self-confessed swindler and psychopath who enjoyed recording 237 meetings in which delegates bickered over the boring details of the administration of a billion-dollar conspiracy.

On the tapes, you can see how ADM easily got Roche, the Swiss drugmaker, on board, but the Japanese were squirrelly. So ADM's Vice Chairman, Mick Andreas, made the Japanese an offer they couldn't refuse. Borrowing from the Saudi Arabian playbook for cartel creation, ADM built a lysine plant in Illinois with enough capacity to fatten every pig on the planet—and bankrupt every producer world-wide. With this reserve he could tell competitor Ajinomoto of Tokyo: Either the Japanese agree to fix prices and market shares or ADM will open its lysine reserves and drown the globe in swine food.

When the Japanese executives questioned ADM's ability to produce the biotech food in such quantities, Andreas took them on a tour of the enormous U.S. plant. The Japanese came away awed by ADM's technology. (They also came away with proprietary microbes which they had stolen by wiping handkerchiefs on machine railings.)

On June 27, 1995, a team of seventy G-men raided ADM's Chicago headquarters. The company, along with Japanese firm Ajinomoto, Roche and Bayer, was charged with conspiracy to fix prices, a felony. Several executives did jail time: Mick Andreas, Wilson and Whitacre.

But ADM had prepared its defenses. The company's Chairman (Mick's dad), Dwayne Andreas, a friend of President Clinton, was known as the single largest contributor to *both* the Democratic and Republican parties (until Ken Lay took that honor away). Andreas *père* once left an envelope in the Oval Office for Richard Nixon containing $100,000 in cash—funds that ended up paying for the break-in at the Watergate.

The ADM cabal may have cuddled and coddled our lesser presidents, but Teddy and Franklin Roosevelt's laws that made fixing prices a felony remained on the books to nail Andreas's son. In 1999, ADM paid $195 million in fines and Mick Andreas was sentenced to break rocks on a chain gang (and, weirdly, Roche even flew in an executive to serve time with Mick). Then U.S. lawyers for consumers hit ADM and conspirators for $800 million in restitution.

Truth, justice and the men with shiny badges win. So it seemed, but something was bugging me. Swiss, French and Japanese executives had cashed in with ADM, and paid something to the U.S. Treasury and American customers. But except for Roche's designated fall guy, the other European and Asian conspirators were still skiing the Alps and sucking sushi in style, spending the ill-gotten loot they'd drained from their designated monopoly slices of the planet. The European

Union didn't touch a hair on their heads or a dime in their bank accounts.

Then I remembered what an acquaintance, Stanley Adams, had told me. He said that Roche had been running a multibillion-dollar price-fixing ring decades before the FBI started recording the world carve-up sessions. Adams should know: He was in charge of enforcing the price-fixing scheme as head of Roche's North and South American Bulk Vitamins division.

The conspiracy upset him, and he blew the whistle in February 1973, or tried to, by mailing evidence to European authorities. But the law's a little different over there. In Switzerland, giving up a corporate secret is a crime. And Adams had given up quite a secret about Europe's biggest corporations. The Swiss jailed him—incommunicado, without trial. When his wife, Mariléne, tried to locate him, she was told he would be held in solitary confinement, without any communication allowed with the outside world, for twenty years. The 31-year-old Mariléne wrote that, despite their three children, she could not face this future, and hung herself. Shortly after, Adams made an extraordinary escape to Britain. Last time I heard from him, he was in a men's boardinghouse in England, penniless. European authorities wagged their fingers at Roche, officially warned the company to stay out of trouble, then winked while Roche prepared a more effective conspiracy with ADM.

Not every whistle-blower gets the Adams treatment. In 2005, Swiss drugmaker Serono SA was caught selling a useless medicine to AIDS victims. Lots of it, $704 million worth. Horrified insiders called some lawyers, the Feds swooped in and the company will now give back every penny it collected and pay the whistle-blowers and the AIDS Healthcare Center a $75 million reward.

In other words, the Swiss company was nailed in the USA where such frauds are crimes, where price-fixing is a crime, and crucially, where *customers can sue the bastards.* Believe it or not, customers overcharged by a price-fixing conspiracy in Europe can't get their money back, even if the companies confess. And what we call "private rights of action"—your ability to go to court to get your money back—and "class actions" where you get *everybody's* money back, just don't exist in most of the world. The guy who came up with the idea of the whistleblower reward? Abraham Lincoln. He signed the False Claims Act when he became fed up with Big Business profiteering during the Civil War. It was a proclamation of emancipation from corporate greed.

After U.S. lawyers won ripped-off customers over a billion from the vitamin-price-fixing ring, the Euro-American operators dropped out of the Vitamin C business and cheap Chinese manufacturers stepped into their shoes. They not only took over the business, taking 80% of the world market, "they stepped right into the shoes of the European vitamin conspirators and set up a new conspiracy," says attorney William Isaacson, who is suing them for a billion dollars. But it's quite an unusual conspiracy: The companies posted some of their price-fixing meetings on the Internet. The in-your-face methods of the Chinese, and their few public statements, suggests that they operated with at least the knowledge, if not the blessing, of China's government. And that could be a big problem for Isaacson, who, in 2006, is seeking a billion dollars or so on behalf of U.S. customers: The Chinese could use the "OPEC" defense, that is, argue their price-setting confabs are a sovereign right of the Chinese dictatorship.

Americans read a story like this, the difference between America and the rest of this sad planet, and feel darn proud of the USA. But before you and the kids start marching around the living room singing "The Stars and Stripes Forever," I have to tell you that the owners in the Washington plantation house have decided it's time to end our rebellious ways. Read on.

"Just Put Down That Lawsuit, Pardner, and No One Gets Hurt"

There are 200 million guns in civilian hands in the United States. That works out to 200 per lawyer. Wade through the foaming Web sites of the anti-Semites, white supremacists, weekend militiamen and Republicans, and it becomes clear that many among America's well-armed citizenry have performed the same calculation. Because if there is any hope of the cease-fire that they fear, it will come out of the barrel of a lawsuit.

First, the score. Gunshot deaths in the U.S. are way down—to only 83 a day. Around 80,000 lucky Americans were treated for bullet wounds each year; 30,000 unlucky ones die, including a dozen policemen by their own weapons. For Americans, America remains more deadly than Iraq.

But, hey, that's business for you. And what a business it is. Guns, ammo and accessories are a $6-billion-a-year honeypot for several corporations: Glock, Smith & Wesson, Colt and others. But, the gun-o-philiacs say, what does po' widdle Smith & Wesson have to do with a mugger who uses his gun in an unsocial manner?

This cop-out drives Elisa Barnes crazy. Barnes thought it was just too convenient for gun makers to blame the criminal alone. Criminals are a much-valued, if unpublicized, market segment sought out and provisioned by these upstanding manufacturers.

Her statistics, which she worked on for years, are compelling. Gun companies dumped several million weapons into outlets in states with few curbs on purchases, super-saturating the legal market, knowing full well that the excess will flow up the "Iron Pipeline" to meet black-market demand in New York and other big cities. Like Zig-Zag, which sells rolling papers in quantities far outstripping sales of legal tobacco, gun manufacturers have a nod-and-wink understanding of where their products end up.

Every year, federal Alcohol, Tobacco and Firearms agents send the companies about 800,000 requests to trace guns recovered from crime scenes. You'd think that after the first half-million reports, the CEOs would realize that a large hunk of their market was made up by persons with little interest in bird hunting.

One of the gun-makers' customers bagged a Fox—Steven Fox. Steven can describe feeling pieces of his brain fly from his skull after the mugger shot him. Fox is permanently paralyzed.

So, this lady with the statistics, Barnes: Is she some kind of do-gooder freak with nothing better to do than wipe the blood off serial numbers on gun barrels? No, Barnes is a parasite. A bloodsucker: Stephen Fox's greedy, wheedling *lawyer.* At least that's how she and other plaintiffs' attorneys are played by something called the "Tort Reform" movement.

"Tort reform" has nothing to do with saving prostitutes from a life of sin. Rather, "tort reform" is a deliberately bland but sly little trope meant to disarm you politically. When the owner class owns governors, regulators, Congress and the law enforcement machinery, you still have that unique American right to haul bad guys' butts into court just like Stephen Fox did.

Or did until July 29, 2005, when the U.S. Senate voted to grant immunity from lawsuits to gun manufacturers. Not schoolteachers: gun makers. The new law was a quite effective bullet in the head to Fox's chance for financial recovery—his case was thrown out. The shoot-to-kill coalition was led by Wild Bill Frist, M.D., then the Republican majority leader, and his simpering sidekick, Democratic leader Harry Reid. What got Frist's posse all riled up was that a jury found several makers of .25-caliber handguns guilty of negligent distribution and ordered them and the shooter to compensate Steven. But Steven was just collateral damage. Frist and Reid were gunning for the City of New Orleans and the NAACP, because the city and the civil rights group had the effrontery to file a class action suit against the gun makers asking them to alter marketing plans to keep their products out of the hands of killers.

"Class action" is aptly named. Corporations don't file class action suits. Billionaires, dictators, and captains of industry don't file class action suits. Class actions are filed *against* them by the victim class, the working class. The point of a class action is to take the claims of thousands, sometimes millions, of victims of asbestos poisoning, baby carriage mangling, Nazi slave camp torture or electricity bill overcharges and join their claims together. That way, the victims who can't possibly afford to take on Hitler's bankers or Enron alone can, on paper, create a human pyramid that can meet the big boys eye to eye in court.

Class action is class warfare intended to channel, in a positive manner, Americans' instinct for seeking justice (see gun sales, above). "Tort reform" is all about taking away your day in court. I'm using the example of gun peddlers run amok, but the list of ne'er-do-wells who need to be reformed by a tort action is quite lengthy—a job requiring a plaintiff's lawyer.

For example, when Jeb Bush and Katherine Harris used the fake felon list that fixed the 2000 election, a bunch of bloodsucking, tort-toting lawyers for the NAACP sued Governor Jeb and his co-conspirator, ChoicePoint. If it weren't for these plaintiffs' attorneys, Jeb would never have agreed to stop the lynching by laptop.

As long as the tort reformers are gunning for evil plaintiffs' lawyers, they won't want to miss Nancy Vurner. You remember Kimberly Haeg, the young, paralyzed woman fighting for breath. Her insurer, Empire Blue Cross, refused to pay for full-time nursing. The company had just a few years ago converted itself into a for-profit operation, and obviously, Kimberly is not a profit center. Lawyer Vurner challenged the corporation on behalf of the Haeg family and, in 2006, got back the payment for nurses.

I spoke with the attorney for the City of New Orleans and the NAACP in the gun case, Mike Hausfeld, who'd just returned from beating Hitler's war machine. In a class action against Mercedes-Benz and other multinationals, his firm won $1.2 billion to compensate Polish prisoners enslaved by the producers of war materiel for the Fuhrer. Hausfeld argues that gun-maker Glock, like the Nazi defense contractors, owes their profits from sales to criminals to the victims of their crimes. Likewise, New Orleans should receive compensation for buying extra body armor for their cops.

But when Bush signed the new immunity law, "We were only taking orders" (for more guns) became a Bush-blessed defense. The City of New Orleans and the NAACP were kicked out of the courtroom.

Republican Leader Frist made no big deal about being a doctor. He must believe the Hippocratic oath changed from "First, do no harm," to "Shoot first, then run for President."

Frist's majority in the Senate had other victims of evil class-action tort lawyers to protect. His Senate Republicans tried to immunize medical-device manufacturers against class actions, like Pfizer (who knowingly sold badly made heart valves). About 800 valves burst and the wearers' hearts exploded. I can't help thinking that "tort reform" would die if, instead of exploding hearts, Pfizer's other big product, Viagra, also caused its target organ to detonate.

When Ahnold Got Lay'd

The consumer protection striptease is usually planned behind closed doors by a Washington coven of Grover Norquists (the super-lobbyist, you will recall, whose small, soft hands rewrote Iraq's tax laws). But once in a while, a note marked "confidential" comes through my fax machine that lets us eavesdrop on a politically de-bauched ritual of the rich in one of their natural habitats, for exam-ple, the Peninsula Hotel in Beverly Hills.

May 17, 2001. In a room at the Peninsula, the Financial Criminal of the twentieth century, not long out of prison, met with the Finan-cial Criminal of the twenty-first century who feared he may also have to do hard time. These two, bond-market manipulator Mike Milken and Ken Lay, not-yet-indicted Chairman of Enron Corporation, were joined by a select group of movers and shakers—and one movie star. Arnold Schwarzenegger had been to such private parties before. As a young immigrant without a nickel to his name, he put on private dis-plays of his musculature for guests of his promoter. As with those early closed gatherings, I don't know all that went on at the Peninsula Hotel meet, though I understand "Ahnold," this time, did not have to strip down to his Speedos. Nevertheless, the moral undressing was just as lascivious, if you read through the 34 pages of notes that ar-rived at our office.

Lay, who convened the hugger-mugger, was in a bit of trouble. En-ron and the small oligopoly of other companies that ruled California's electricity system had been caught jacking up the price of power and gas by fraud, conspiracy and manipulation. A billion here, a billion there, and pretty soon it was real money—$6.3 billion in suspect windfalls in just six months, May through December 2000, for a half-dozen electricity buccaneers, at least $9 billion for the year. Their skim would have been higher but the tricksters thought they were limited by the number of digits the state's power-buying computers could read. When Ken met Arnold in the hotel room, the games were far from over. For example, in June 2003, Reliant Corporation of Houston simply turned off several power plants, and when California cities faced going dark, the company sold them a pittance of kilowatts for more than gold, making several million in minutes.

Power-market shenanigans were nothing new in 2000. What was new was the response of Governor Gray Davis. A normally quiet, if not dull, man, this Governor had the temerity to call the energy sellers "pirates"—in public!—and, even more radically, he asked them to *give back all the ill-gotten loot*, at least $9 billion. The state filed a regulatory complaint with the federal government.

The Peninsula Hotel get-together was all about how to "settle" the legal actions in such a way that Enron and friends could get the state to accept dog food instead of dollars. Davis seemed unlikely to see things Ken's way. Life would be so much better if California had a governor like the muscle guy in the Speedos.

And so it came to pass that, in 2003, quiet Gray Davis, who had the *cojones* to stand up to the electricity barons, was thrown out of office by the voters and replaced by the tinker-toy tough guy. The "Governator" performed as desired. Soon after Schwarzenegger took over from Davis, he signed off on a series of deals with Reliant, Williams Company, Dynegy, Entergy and the other power pirates for ten to twenty cents on the dollar, less than you'd tip the waitress. Enron paid just about nothing.

Power Outage Traced to Dim Bulb in White House

Arnold's agreeing to the sweetheart deals for the state would not prevent the federal government from ordering a larger refund. Lay had

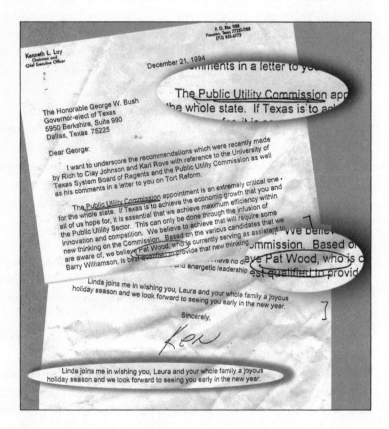

Ken Lay asks Santa George to wrap him a utility commissioner for Christmas.

prepared for that possibility years earlier. The agency that could order the refund is the Federal Energy Regulatory Commission, FERC. Its Chairman was Pat Wood III, former chairman of the Texas utility commission, a job Wood picked up after Governor-elect George W. Bush received this note in 1994:

> The Public Utility Commission appointment is an extremely critical one. We believe that Pat Wood is best qualified. . . . Linda joins me in wishing you and Laura and the whole family a joyous holiday. Sincerely, Ken.

That's *chutzpah*; first, because Ken Lay was claiming the right to pick the guy who will regulate his company; and second, because "Ken" uses a very familiar tone with the Governor-elect despite Bush's statement, years later, that at that time he didn't know "Kenny-Boy" Lay. Someone is fibbing, but let's not dwell on it. The key thing is, Ken Lay wished it, and it was so: Wood got the job as Texas' chief power industry regulator.

Under Lay's handpicked regulator and, for that matter, handheld Governor, Texas electricity customers got whacked for a special $9 billion surcharge collected by the state's power companies, one of many electricity price hikes that resulted from the Lay-Wood-Bush "deregulation" of the Texas power market.

But Christmas was not yet over for Lay and Enron. In 2000, weeks after Bush won the White House, the Enron Chairman secretly requested that Wood move to the chief regulatory post in Washington. And again, it was done. That put Ken Lay one up on Al Capone. Little Caesar had to *buy* off the top cops; Ken Lay simply had them appointed. Chairman Wood may have been as honest as the day is long, but on his watch, Enron and the industry treaded through the power market like Godzilla through a kindergarten. For example, one California utility commissioner fumed to me that Federal Regulator Wood had winked at a little game called "kilowatt laundering," in which power companies would pretend to send power out of California, then "import" it back to the State (on paper) at a higher price. And there was "Ricochet," the game played between Enron and its market playmate, Public Service Company of New Mexico.

Lay had more wishes for his fairy god-president. In letters to Bush and Cheney, he recommended, as an alternative to Wood, industry favorites Nora Brownell and Joseph Kelliher. Bush wowed Kenny-Boy by appointing all three.

What was so evil about Lay getting his people on the regulatory commission? If the mob picked all our judges, there'd be a bit of reticence by courts to punish criminals. Lay's favorite regulators re-created the commission in a manner most pleasing to the industry. A FERC "law judge" ruled that California consumers should receive nothing and their victims should pay the companies a few billion *more*.

But the utility magnates still fretted. You can name the commissioners who enforce the law, but the law remained on the books. Most troublesome was FDR's Public Utility Holding Company Act that banned speculation in the power market and—horrors!—outlawed political donations by the biggest utility corporations. So Lay and the industry set out to fix that too—a political heist done under cover of darkness . . .

On August 14, 2003, a third of the nation, from Ohio to New York, went black.

The three power companies that blew out the lights were the Ohio and Pennsylvania units of a holding company called "First Energy," and a New York operator called Niagara-Mohawk Power ("NiMo"). It happens that, some years ago (1986–92), I investigated all three companies at the request of the three state governments. The issues were gross financial mismanagement—there was plenty—and, in New York, NiMo was also accused of fraud and conspiracy.[25] So I'm not surprised that the Three Stooges of the power industry knocked their heads together and blacked us out. What's surprising is that the U.S.

---

[25]All three companies paid, through rate reductions, nearly a billion dollars for "management imprudence." NiMo's alleged coconspirator, Long Island Lighting (LILCO), but not NiMo, was found liable by a federal jury for civil racketeering. Later, after an appeals court throw out the verdict, LILCO settled for a payment of $400 million.

media kept America in the dark about how Larry, Moe and Curly blew out our nation's electronic lifeline and how they were rewarded for it.

The Great Blackout of '03 began with a power surge at First Energy Corporation's Ohio unit, which, short staffed, did not react quickly enough to shut off the correct systems. The surge passed to its Pennsylvania sister company, also short staffed, which passed the surge to Niagara-Mohawk Power Corporation (NiMo), which, shorthanded as well and unable to cope, simply shut down and took out the entire New York State power grid. Why was everyone "shorthanded"? In NiMo's case, the company was recently bought by a foreign outfit that sliced maintenance budgets, got rid of 800 workers and pocketed most of their wages—a $90 million windfall carted off to European stockholders. "Creating value," as Ken Lay would call it.

In the olden days before "deregulation," you couldn't do that. Government bureaucrats enforced stiff budgets and profit caps on power companies. The public paid for maintenance, the public got it. Furthermore, there was no power "market." Engineers in a "dispatch" center sent the power where it was needed, efficiently. Now, juice follows the money, and electrons fly about the grid in crazy-ass chaos determined by "traders" for whom "blackout" means "bonus." The power pirates who blacked out Ohio and California had first practiced their power market tricks abroad. "Deregulation" was first road-tested by these same companies in Brazil (by Reliant and Entergy), India (by Enron), and, as we know, in Ecuador (by Duke). You could call "deregulation" the "Third Worlding" of America.

Nevertheless, *regulation* was tagged the villain—and no less a power expert than Dick Cheney said so. It took two years from lights out to payout for First Energy, Niagara-Mohawk and the other power pirates, but they finally reaped their reward for a job well done. Deregulation gone wild caused the blackout, but the Administration would cure the problem with *more* deregulation. On July 29, 2005, Congress voted to repeal the Public Utility Holding Company Act, last bulwark of regulatory protection left to us from the New Deal.

The President Explains Everything You Need to Know About Social Security

Still, fragments of the New Deal have withstood the onslaught. They can't take away your Social Security. Yet. But, they can make you in-secure.

Franklin Roosevelt didn't call Social Security "Old Age Pension" because he saw this as an insurance program that would ultimately provide birth-to-death security, Denmark-style. Americans deserved, he said, "Freedom from Fear." By contrast, our fear salesman in the White House undermines your faith in the system with a good dose of financial terror, to create social *insecurity*.

On February 4, 2005, the President explained how he would "save" Social Security.

> *Because the—all which is on the table begins to address the big cost drivers. For example, how benefits are calculate, for example, is on the table; whether or not benefits rise based upon wage increases or price increases. There's a series of parts of the formula that are being considered. And when you couple that, those different cost drivers, affecting those—changing those with personal accounts, the idea is to get what has been promised more likely to be—or closer delivered to what has been promised. Does that make any sense to you? It's kind of muddled. Look, there's a series of things that cause the—like, for example, benefits are calculated based upon the increase of wages, as opposed to the increase of prices. Some have suggested that we calculate—the benefits will rise based upon inflation, as opposed to wage increases. There is a reform that would help solve the red if that were put into effect. In other words, how fast benefits grow, how fast the promised benefits grow, if those—if that growth is af-fected, it will help on the red.*

Got that?

So, go ahead, answer the President's question: *"Does that make any sense to you?"* And $50 to the first reader who can make it make sense to *anyone*. It doesn't make sense, of course. (So I pocket the $50.) And that's the point.

They are pretending to tell you their plan. But their plan has to do with the ebb and flow of international finance, the revaluation of the Chinese yuan, and the shift from America the Product Maker to America the Planetary Speculator. One can't divide the future of Social Security from the grinding forces of globalization. (See "Yuan Your Social Security" in Chapter 3: The Network.) Rather than tell you that, you're told nothing in as many words as possible.

Oil Wars and Class Wars

Three things happened in the fall of 2005 or, in the New Order's way of measuring things, the third quarter of Exxon's fiscal year:

1. The CEO of Delphi Corporation, Steve Miller, gave his 33,000 union workers a choice: Give back two-thirds of your pay or give up your pension. On the same day, he announced additional bonuses for Delphi's top 486 managers totaling $88 million cash up front, plus $400 million on its way.
2. General Motors' union workers, though entitled by their contract, voluntarily gave up $2 billion in annual health care benefits.
3. Exxon Oil pulled in $9.9 billion in net earnings, more profit than any company had collected for a three-month period in the history of mankind.

You got a problem with that? You might wonder why Delphi's CEO Miller would reward managers who, after all, had run their company into bankruptcy. But bankrupting the company was their job, what they were hired to do. Let me explain.

Delphi is only a few years old, a new baby on the corporate block, spawned by General Motors in 1999. It was a hollow shell into which GM dumped its former auto parts division, Delco. This was the way

GM could slice off a big hunk of its union workforce, nearly 40,000 people, and the huge pension and health insurance liabilities that GM auto parts workers had accrued over a lifetime at the job. GM management dumped the costly workers and its pension obligations to them—a $12 billion liability—on the leaky Delphi ship and watched, with a sly grin, as its Delphi "spin-off" sank under the financial waves. Then GM turned on its remaining workers in 2005, demanding, *your health insurance or your job*. Witnessing their Delco brothers drown, autoworkers coughed up the $2 billion out of their own pockets.

Sharper readers will be asking, How will Delphi managers collect their juicy $400 million bonus, averaging double their salaries, if their company is in bankruptcy?

Not to worry, Wilbur Ross will take care of them. More than thirty U.S. auto parts manufacturers have gone into bankruptcy court since Team Bush took office. They don't die and go to auto parts heaven, they go to Wilbur Ross, a financier adept at picking up the best pieces and repackaging the lot as a new moneymaker. Wilbur saved the American steel industry, which is now thriving as part of the international steel trust controlled by the Mittal family of India. I should note that the *industry* was saved, but the workers were not. America now produces nearly as much steel (over ninety million tons) as we did two decades ago, but the number of unionized steel workers has declined from over 400,000 to under 40,000 on its way to zero. Wages and benefits have gone from the envy of the world to the pity.

Wilbur is often called a "vulture," but I prefer to think of him as a gift wrapper. Prior owners, like LTV Steel, break down their workers, often via a trip through bankruptcy court, which allows companies to rip up union contracts. The pensions are dumped on the U.S. taxpayer (through the Pension Benefit Guaranty Corporation). Then several once-competing companies are tied into one price-lifting monopoly. For his services re-creating steel into a metallic Wal-Mart, Wilbur picked up a quick profit of somewhere over a billion dollars. All Wilbur does is tie the pieces together and wrap it up for delivery;

and, given the rake-off of the wage takeoff, his take is reasonable. (I've called on Wilbur's services myself, but that's another story.) Wilbur's said he's ready to do it again in auto parts. He envisions a $30 billion auto-parts behemoth, an auto parts OPEC (AUPEC?). If all goes to plan, the Delphi managers will get their half-billion slice of Wilbur's reorganizational windfall funded by the wage cuts that will bring the union workers' salary to $50 a year below the poverty line. In other words, the managers will simply receive their reasonable share of the spoils of the class war.

War isn't pretty. You have to accept collateral damage. Just ask the Sago mine workers. Wilbur purchased Sago of West Virginia in November 2005 through another one of his lucrative industry makeover operations, International Coal Group. In the first six weeks under his company's ownership, Sago's mine suffered two roof collapses. The billionaire said, "We were comfortable, based on the assurances from our management that they felt that it was a safe situation." Safe financially, maybe, but a third roof collapse in January 2006 caused twelve miners to suffocate. In light of the tragedy, Wilbur is asking Americans to donate to victims' families. I don't know, however, if you should send your money to his home in Palm Beach or the one in the Hamptons or the one on Fifth Avenue.

The same earth-flattening machinery that flattens the Third World has returned to the USA with a vengeance. And as China, India and Ecuador are tilted, so is the new America.

You can't separate the GM workers' $2 billion give-back and the Delphi workers' give-up from Exxon's miracle quarter, the $9.9 billion profit gusher. You could almost hear the *whoosh* as the loot rolled down from the cold Lake Michigan shore to Houston.

The cold cruelty of GM/Delphi managers was impelled by the "ebb and flow," the transcontinental in-and-out of petro-dollars and free trade across a borderless, flattened earth. There were four knives at GM's back:

1. *Health insurance.* GM, even after cutting Delco workers adrift, still pays $5.6 billion a year for worker medical coverage. And that's nothing compared to the required long-term cost of funding health care for their retirees: $80 billion. The cost of health insurance per GM car: $1,500.

2. *"Free" trade.* America imports $26 billion more in parts than we export. Our biggest competitor is Canada, where the government, not automakers, provides the medical care. Pretty sneaky of those Canucks, eh? Canadian car parts flow tax-free to the States because of NAFTA, the North America Free Trade Agreement. Free to whom? Not GM employees. But China is quickly replacing Canada, with China's sales to the USA rising 300% in a single year (2003). Free trade with a slave state. Delphi *USA* didn't stand a chance. But Delphi's China subsidiary is expanding as fast as you can say, "Independent unions are banned in China by law." Of Delphi's 167 factories, only 34 remain in the United States. General Motors has cut its U.S. workforce from half a million at peak to the shattered cadre of 80,000 survivors who will remain according to GM's plan for 2008.

3. *High interest rates.* Remember, Mr. Beale, that real interest rates must rise to entice back those petro-dollars that sailed to Arabia. Higher interest made GM's borrowing to modernize more costly. In just two years, GM's borrowing cost ballooned from $480 million to $2.48 billion—an interest hit equal exactly to the sum GM workers gave back to their company. General Motors the carmaker is dying, but GM *the bank* is doing quite well. Its GMAC unit, one of the biggest financial institutions in America, is rolling in loot from the interest spike and expects to fetch *mucho* billions if sold off.

4. *The Iraq War oil spike.* Ultimately, Delphi was gunned down in Baghdad. It could have survived the triple onslaught of health insurance costs, foreign competition and high interest rates. But it could not survive the higher oil prices that hammered the market for GM cars.

Crude at $60 a barrel ($2.50 a gallon at the pump) puts General Motors auto division dancing with the death's-head of bankruptcy. And the concomitant spike in the cost of jet fuel has financially hijacked U.S. airlines and driven 30 of them, including every full-service carrier, into Chapter 11.

What's going on here? Put it together: Exxon's profit meant Delphi's death. The murderously high price of oil created an effective "gas tax" on auto workers, which rolled down from Detroit to Houston, into the pockets of the oil-industry owner class, its managers and stockholders.

No wonder they're breaking out the champagne in Dick Cheney's bunker. The United Auto Workers and the airlines' International Association of Machinists provided the muscle and finances for many a Democratic campaign. Now their union membership is impoverished, reduced to a fraction of its former number, and dispersed from the "blue" Democratic state of Michigan.

Dick Cheney, the man who has his hands on the oil valves of the Strategic Petroleum Reserve, has his foot on the life-support lines of the auto and airline industries.

Did this Administration invade Iraq to eliminate union stronghold industries? No. Like vultures, they just have to stand by silently watching their prey die.

Remember the unguarded words of insider Ed Morse:

> The VP's office [has] not pursued a policy in Iraq [nor] done *anything,* either with producers or energy policy, that would say, "We're going to put the squeeze on OPEC."

Hot wars abroad can assist class war at home.

Dems in Drag

Let's be honest about it. George Bush didn't kill Delco and the United Auto Workers, he only attended the funeral. (OK, he unplugged the life support of cheap interest rates and cheap oil.) Auto parts and other thing-makers were mortally wounded by the prior administration. It began in 1992, when the Democratic Party was seized by the Democratic Leadership Council, a group of business-class collaborators who believed the party could be saved if Democrats stripped off those New Deal ideals and dressed up in something a little more Republican.

The pro-business platform didn't win many votes—the Bill Clinton–Al Gore ticket won a dismal 43% of the vote, but still won the presidency. In fact, it was a wipeout. George Herbert Walker Bush was pulverized, receiving the lowest percentage of votes (37%) of any Republican since Alf Landon lost to Franklin Roosevelt.

The difference between the Clinton/Gore low vote and the Bush lower vote was the Reform Party, the 19.7 million votes for Ross Perot. America hadn't seen anything like it since 1860, when Abraham Lincoln's new party destroyed and replaced the Whigs.

Perot, a quixotic billionaire, had fired up the resentment of his 19.7 million—and millions of sympathizers more—by a focused attack on "NAFTA," the North American Free Trade Agreement. In 1992, seven years before the "Battle of Seattle" at the World Trade Organization confab, Perot went after "free trade," the cornerstone of the new economic Darwinism. Perot alerted the nation that the wealthy had joined forces to cut your jobs and wages, to pit Detroit against Juárez in a competition to the bottom. His message woke up working-class Republicans by the millions; those guys in the mailroom and behind the lunch counter who voted Republican because of the corporate party's platform of no abortion, no flag burning, no homosexuals and lots of country music. Perot told them to "think jobs" instead.

The night of November 9, 1993, a year after the election, Vice President Gore had the opportunity to change history. He was to debate Ross Perot on *Larry King Live*. It was the most-watched cable program ever. Here was the Democrat's once-in-a-generation chance to win over that 19.7 million that was now up for grabs, to realign the entire party structure as Roosevelt had done in '32 and, like FDR, create a working people's majority led by the Democratic Party that could rule for decades.

Instead, I watched a swaggering, self-congratulatory Al Gore, snickering at the uncouth Perot's warning of a "giant sucking sound" of jobs draining to Mexico. I felt my political soul rise up off the sofa— this was an out-of-body political experience. Perot and his 19.7 million workers who feared for their pensions and union cards were called ignorant fools, suckers for labor union fearmongering, confused, economic dummies, and cowards before history, trying to hold on to their shitty little jobs at Zenith Electric when the future awaited in writing computer programs for Microsoft.

Gore laughed at Perot, he guffawed, he mugged at the camera, snidely dismissing Perot's prediction of a shift in the balance of trade. Gore, the rich prep-school kid, looked so pleased with himself, taunting the funny little man who'd made his way up from the working class. And 19.7 million Americans knew Gore was making fun of them, too, telling textile workers losing their health insurance they were unsophisticated little schmucks who understood nothing about economics. The Vice President knew jobs wouldn't be lost. In fact, if we embraced the free-trade treaty . . .

> We can create hundreds of thousands more [jobs]. We know this [free trade] works. If it doesn't work, you know, we give six months' notice and we're out of it.

Gore singled out the auto parts industry: Delco workers would win big. More jobs were coming.

Here's what happened: The border was erased, the economic levees burst. In 1992, the year before NAFTA's passage, the USA had a $5.6 billion trade *surplus* with Mexico. In 2004, under the free trade pact signed by Bill Clinton, it reversed, and with a vengeance. In 2004, $45.1 billion more in goods came in from Mexico than the U.S. sold to Mexico, an unprecedented $50.7 billion swing to deficit.

And auto parts? I noted that China's sales of auto parts to the U.S.

(and purchase of almost none) had risen 300% in one Bush year, but China's total remains relatively small. The $26 billion single-year tidal wave of auto parts that drowned the Delco/Delphi workers came overwhelmingly from the NAFTA nations, Mexico and Canada.

The macroeconomic modeling I did in my old academic days suggests that, very roughly, such a loss of income to the USA costs half a million jobs. You can quibble with the estimate, call it 300,000 jobs or 900,000. But a $50.7 billion crocodile is difficult to disguise as a pet gecko.[26]

American workers could have done worse, of course, and they did. The trade deficit with Canada went from a small $8 billion before NAFTA to a Katrina-sized $73 billion in 2005.

The giant sucking sound was not, as Perot predicted, so much the jobs gone south, but the sound of cash vacuumed from the workers' pockets in both nations to the owner class as workers in Juárez competed with workers in Detroit. Both lost. Real wages fell on *both* sides of the border, or, more correctly, all three sides, as U.S., Canadian and especially Mexican production wages were hammered. In Mexico, laborer's pay per hour dropped 40% in the first seven years after NAFTA's passage. At the same time, the wage-wealth jaw opened wide in all three nations as productivity rose, lifting the value of owners' equity by several trillion dollars.

Wal-Mart's own study, by the way, determined that the company had depressed U.S. wages by 2.2%. (This is offset, Wal-Mart quickly adds, by toasters and other goodies now costing, they claim, 3.3% less. That's quite a bargain.)

Gore followed his put-down of labor unions, which unanimously opposed NAFTA, with praise for Rush Limbaugh as a "distinguished American" (really) and accolades for NAFTA-backer Lee Iacocca,

---

[26]Other economists would disagree. I've seen some pretty slick economic legerdemain attempting to transmogrify trade deficits into job gains. My favorite, the November 2005 report, which got a lot of media play, by a consulting firm called "Global Insight" concludes that exporting jobs creates employment. The study, "The Economic Impact of Wal-Mart," was funded by . . . Wal-Mart ☺.

Sam's Club on Pennsylvania Avenue

In the debate over NAFTA with Ross Perot, Gore lauded Wal-Mart's opening in Mexico to sell "American products." But 83% of Wal-Mart's products, even then, were *not* made in the USA. Did Gore know that? Certainly, the former member of the board of directors of Wal-Mart, watching the debate from the White House, knew it. Sam Walton used to call his board member, attorney Hillary Clinton, "my little lady."

Perot thought free trade with a police state a bit problematic.

> I am deeply concerned about workers who, when they go on strike, U.S. companies [operating in Mexico] call in goons, bring in the state police, shoot several workers, kill one, injure dozens, put the workers back to work and cut wages 45 percent. Those are things that are wrong.

Sam Walton's kind of place. A folksy guy, he liked to chat with his Arkansas workers one-on-one . . . to personally threaten their jobs if they voted union. That's illegal, but he had a good little attorney. Of 3,705 Wal-Mart stores in the USA today, zero are unionized. And NAFTA keeps it that way. The three-government NAFTA board itself reports that 62% of U.S. industrial companies threaten to leave the country or shut operations when faced with union recognition votes.

We don't know what the future Senator Clinton thought of the Gore-Perot debate. But I'm quite certain what Sam Walton was thinking in Heaven: *Mission accomplished.*

Chairman of Chrysler Motors. Gore didn't mention that Iacocca had moved Chrysler engine assembly work to Mexico in anticipation of NAFTA. But the unemployed Chrysler workers knew that.

And they didn't forget. On November 2, 1994, a stunned Bill Clinton, incoherent and lost before the TV cameras, could not explain what had happened the day before. He and Al had dressed up in Republican drag but the 19.7 million Perot voters, given the choice of the Rich Man's Party or the Richer Man's Party, returned to "social" issues and the security of the Republicans' pledge against gun control. Clinton had done what no Democratic President had ever accomplished: lost 70 Congressional and Senate seats—and both houses of Congress—to the Republicans. Maybe forever.

Admittedly, the entire decline in real wages can't all be laid at NAFTA's door. Clinton's granting "Most Favored Nation" trade status to China was the bullet to the head of the U.S. textile industry. And the drop in real wages did not begin when trade laws were replaced by the laws of the jungle. But honesty requires that we recognize that a Democratic Administration rolled up the border and watched Delco jobs slide into the *maquiladora* trench.

November 9, 1993, was the Democratic Party's "Munich,"[27] the date on which the DLC's stalking horse, hoping to appease the chambers of commerce, loosed the dogs of class war upon America's hourly workers. I cannot get out of my mind how different our world might be today if Al Gore had listened to those 19.7 million, and instead of lecturing them, had invited them into the Democratic Party. But that was a Democratic Party he did not want to join himself, the New Deal Party. Gore's Rasputin, his guide, was Republican Dick Morris, the guy who in 2004 dissed the polls showing Kerry won. He wrote Gore's speeches, and it's known that one time Morris tested out the words on one of the hookers he patronized. (I can't imagine what a call girl would charge to listen to an Al Gore speech.) How would history have been different if a prep-school kid, his way into the Ivy

---

[27] *A pedagogical note:* As I travel around the USA, I'm just horrified at America's stubborn historical amnesia. Americans, as Sam Cooke said, don't know squat about history. We don't learn the names of a nation's capital until the 82nd Airborne lands there. And our ruling junta prefers it that way. For example, leaving Huey Long out of our history books is a premeditated crime against class self-knowledge. We'll fix some of that here. By the way, "Munich" refers to British Prime Minister Neville Chamberlain's 1939 attempt to "appease" Hitler by handing him Czechoslovakia. Hitler responded to this kindness by invading Poland.

League and into politics slicked by oil money and Daddy's connections, became president? Yes, there's a difference between Gore and Bush. Gore's oil money, unlike Bush's, came from Occidental Petroleum, the jungle marauders in Ecuador.

Maybe that's a bit over the top. It's personal jealousy and resentment, I suppose. Al Gore never had to fluff his own pillow or worry himself sick over losing a job he hated. I grew up near the GM-Chevy plant in Van Nuys. My dad sold Frigidaire refrigerators, then made by General Motors. If not for dumb luck, I'd be working there—or would have until the shutdown a few years ago.

In 2000, Gore won the election, but lost the presidency. Bush could swipe it only because the vote was so close. It shouldn't have been close, but Gore lost the NAFTA-wounded states of Ohio and Missouri. Should you run into Al Gore, and he repeats his line that NAFTA didn't cost American jobs, you might remind him, "It cost you yours."

No Child's Behind Left

They take away your overtime, your 40-hour week, your regulatory protection against corporate marauders, your right to courtroom justice, your protection against unfair trade, even the right to get your ballot counted. But there's always hope. Hope is the last thing to go. And your hope is your kids, that they'll have an opportunity you didn't have. On January 21, 2004, the President told you they'd have to take that away too.

On that night, deep into his State of the Union sermon to Congress, when sensible adults had turned off the tube or kicked in the screen, our President opened a new front in the class war. And like the one in Iraq, it began with a lie.

> "By passing the No Child Left Behind Act," our President told us, "We are regularly testing every child . . . and making sure they have better options when schools are not performing."

"And at Daddy's Polo Club, the Waiter Is Called A . . ."

The core of No Child Left Behind is the early-age test. And here's what they're testing. The following is taken from the actual practice test given eight-year-olds in the State of New York in 2006. The test determined which children should advance, which should be left behind in the third grade. Ready, class?

> The year 1999 was a big one for the Williams sisters. In February, Serena won her first pro singles championship. In March, the sisters met for the first time in a tournament final. Venus won. And at doubles tennis, the Williams girls could not seem to lose that year.

And here's one of the four questions:

> The story says that in 1999, the sisters could not seem to lose at doubles tennis. This probably means when they played
>
> A two matches in one day
> B against each other
> C with two balls at once
> D as partners

OK, class, do you know the answer? (By the way, I didn't cheat: There's nothing else about "doubles" in the text.)

For your information, I got this from a school in which more than half the students live below the poverty line. There is no tennis court. There is no tennis court in any of the poverty area schools of New York. But out in the Hamptons, *every* school has a tennis court. In Forest Hills and Westchester there are as many tennis courts as the schoolkids have live-in maids.

Which kids are best prepared to answer the question about "doubles tennis"? The eight-year-olds in Brownsville who've never seen a tennis match or the kids whose mommies disappear for two hours every Wednesday with Enrique the tennis coach?

Is this test a measure of "reading comprehension"—or a measure of wealth accumulation?

If you have any doubts about what the test is measuring, look at the next question, based on another part of the test, which reads (and I could not make this up):

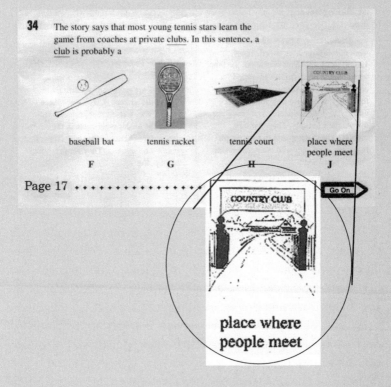

34 The story says that most young tennis stars learn the game from coaches at private clubs. In this sentence, a club is probably a

baseball bat   tennis racket   tennis court   place where
                                                             people meet

F   G   H   J

Page 17 ◆◆◆◆◆◆◆◆◆◆◆◆◆◆◆◆   Go On ▶

COUNTRY CLUB

**place where
people meet**

Helpfully, for Puerto Rican kids, it explains that a "country club" is the "place where people meet." Yes, but *which* people?

Class war dismissed.

He said it. And then that little tongue came out; that weird way our President sticks his tongue out between his lips like a little kid who knows he's fibbing. Like a snake licking a rat. I saw that snaky tongue dart out and I thought, "He knows."

And what he knows is this: There are no "better options" for failing children, but there are better *uses* for them. The President ordered testing and more testing to hunt down, identify and target millions of children too expensive, too heavy a burden, to educate.

Here's how No Child Left Behind works in the classrooms of Houston and Chicago and New York. Under the No Child Left law, millions of eight-year-olds are given lists of words and phrases. They try to read. Then they are graded like USDA beef: some prime, some OK, many (most in fact) failed.

Once the eight-year-olds are stamped and sorted, the parents of children with the test mark of Cain await fulfillment of the President's tantalizing promise, to "make sure they have better options."

But there are none. In the delicious doublespeak of class war, when the tests have winnowed out the chaff and kids stamped failed, No Child Left results in that child being left behind in the same grade to repeat the failure another year. And another year and another year.

Hint: When decoding politicians' babble, to get to the real agenda, don't read their lips, read their budgets. And in his budget, our President couldn't spare one thin dime for education, not ten cents. Mr. Big Spender provided for a derisory 8.4 cents on the dollar of the cost of primary and secondary schools. Congress appropriated a half penny of the nation's income—just one-half of one percent of America's twelve-trillion-dollar GDP—for primary and secondary education.

President Bush actually requested *less*. While Congress succeeded in prying out an itty-bitty increase in voted funding, that doesn't mean the cash is actually given to the schools. Fifteen states have sued the federal government on the grounds that the cost of new testing imposed on schools, $3.9 billion, eats up the entire new funding budgeted for No Child Left.

I can't say that Mr. Bush doesn't offer "better options" to the kids stamped "failed." Under No Child Left, if enough kids flunk the tests, their school is marked a failure and its students win the right, under the law, to transfer to any successful school in their district. You can't provide more opportunity than that. But Bush does not provide it, he *promises* it, without putting up a single penny to make it happen. In New York, in 2004, a third of a million students earned the right to transfer to better schools—in which there were only 8,000 places open. New York is typical. Nationwide, only one out of two hundred students eligible to transfer manage to do it. Well, there's always the army. (That "option" did not go unnoticed: No Child has a special provision requiring schools to open their doors to military recruiters.)

There's not a lot of loot for schoolkids in the No Child Left law, but Barbara Bush's kids made out just fine.

Her youngest, Neil Bush, jumped into the No Child biz big time. A company he founded in 1999 in Texas, Ignite! (exclamation point included), promotes robo-teaching. Instead of teachers, kids are plunked in front of a TV screen and blasted with automated lessons. It's cheap and, I'll admit, quite effective for communicating rote information and preparing children for a world in which they cannot deviate from the orders coming from machines and screens. This may have been what attracted the education ministries of Saudi Arabia and the Persian Gulf to purchase the robot teaching system, though one wonders if the sheikdoms see non-educational bonuses in dropping a few petro-dollars in a Bush child's pocket.

Neil also found an education reform soulmate in exiled Russian tycoon Boris Berezovsky, who met with Neil in Riga, Latvia, in September 2005. Berezovsky is advising Ignite! with a particular eye to the Russian market, where he himself cannot go because of some trouble with the law. (The meeting won't be repeated, at least in Riga. When the meeting between the First Brother and the fugitive was disclosed, the Latvian government banned Berezovsky's reentry.)

No Child Left does provide help to underfinanced schools in the form of Supplemental Educational Services (SES). In the old days, this was called "tutoring," but that's when we energized community volunteers. Today, it's big business for millions. If several students in a school fail tests, the federal government requires schools to hire tutors from these for-profit outfits. Our President's federal contribution to these "supplemental services"? Zero. So, how is it funded? A school must pay out 20% of their "Title 1" fund, their tiny federal subsidy, to hire tutors from private companies. That is, schools must cut back their own teaching staff to pay for the contracts with private tutoring companies.

And who are these tutors? By federal law, teachers must be credentialed, trained and tested—but not the tutors who replace them. Their qualifications are . . . well, there's the handyman in my apartment building. He was hired by schools-for-profit operator Princeton Review to teach high school math. They contracted to give him the high school math job after he passed a fifth-grade arithmetic proficiency test.

Handyman "Joe" (I promised not to use his real name) is quite a bright guy, who in fact knows geometry and trigonometry. But, he said of his fellow tutors, "Half of them about to be sent to high schools could barely handle it—the fifth grade arithmetic." The Princeton crew gets 20 hours of training versus a minimum of 1,000 hours for the teachers they replace.

But teaching isn't the job. Selling is. "Joe" told us:

> Last night I accidentally showed up at a training for site directors who are supposed to be educational specialists acting as principals over their teacher-tutors. The site directors were being prepped for "Operation Rapid Deployment." I shit you not. The Princeton Review now has two weeks to "sell" the "product" to as many "clients" as possible, which means all sorts of promises about one-on-one tutoring (that may or may not be forthcoming). The

imperative is to hire as many local kids and parents as possible, all who get paid per student signed up.

And the charge is taken out of the school budgets.

The more failures, the more cash for the privateers. And the most cash is had when a school fails continuously for five years. Its "option" then is to fire all its teachers or to turn the school over to a private company.

This privatization is a money tree for Edison. Not Thomas Edison, the lightbulb guy, but Edison Schools, Inc., a company that lifted the brainy man's name to put over their scheme to eliminate public education in favor of for-profit "charter" schooling for all.

Edison Inc. claims their teach-for-the-money theories proved successful in Sherman, Texas, the full-takeover contract they landed in Gov. George Bush's test run of privatization in 1995. The company advertised worldwide that it boosted the little Texans' test scores by 5%. But I talked to Sherman's superintendent of schools, who, the company fails to mention in its sales pitch, ran them out of town in 2000. The superintendent, Phillip Garrett, told me, "They were more about money than teaching." A lot more money. Sherman schools had to pay an additional $4 million to cover Edison's unpaid bills for local services. The promise of better education at no extra cost, the ultimate Free Lunch of the school privatizers, was bogus. And the "5%" improvement was called "dishonest" . . . by Edison's own president, Benno Schmidt. (Schmidt, in an interview, told me that anyone who claims student improvement with less than five years' experience is "dishonest"—not realizing he was commenting on his own company's sales material.) And Sherman's superintendent said Edison kids fell behind other Texans—no small feat.

The President offers one more "option," one more magic trick left for the rubes in front of their tubes to make them believe that the privileged will share the advantages of education with the rest of us: The Great School Voucher Hoax.

The Great Voucher Hoax

What's better than free money? Nothing, except maybe immortality or three wishes from your fairy godmother. Or, say, a "voucher" to send your kid to a big-shot school like Phillips Academy, where our President got so smart.

The centurions of the better classes love vouchers. On April 1, 2005, *The Wall Street Journal* ran an editorial, "Educational Nirvana." Nirvana, in case you don't know, is a wonderful place, kind of a Hindu heaven. Buddha's there. But the *Journal* wasn't talking about the place where good Buddhists go; it was talking about Arizona. What made Arizona heavenly in the *Journal*'s view is that the State Senate voted to give a "school voucher" to all parents who want one to pay to send their kid to any school they want. No more would parents be stuck with Arizona's horrid, failed, crappy schools. And what a godsend for poor kids stuck in dead-end districts brutalized daily by known members of the teachers' union.

And what will this cost the taxpayer? Nothing! Less than nothing, in fact, because the vouchers will cost only $3,500, while the state currently spends $7,000 per pupil in their current no-good schools. Parents, say *The Wall Street Journal* and voucher advocates, should have a "choice" of schools, not one chosen for their kids by bureaucrats. The proposal meant to build on the "success" of a five-year-old Arizona program that now provides $1,000 school vouchers.

OK, class: What is wrong here? Umm, well, it's not so easy to find a good school that will teach your kid for $3,500 a year, and there are exactly none for $1,000. In other words, your school voucher doesn't get you into school. You can give a poor kid a $3,500 voucher, but it won't get him into Phillips Academy. Little Antonio can use his voucher for about four weeks of Phillips ($33,000 per school year), at which point he'll have to go back to picking broccoli outside Phoenix.

In other words, the Arizona "voucher" program, like every other school voucher program proposed in the USA, is not a voucher at all. A voucher is a coupon that lets you get something for no cost. An

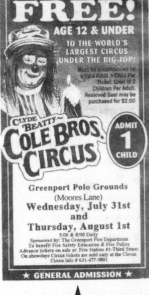

DISCOUNT COUPON **VOUCHER**

Vouchers vs. Coupons

(Source: Cole Brothers Circus)

airline screws up your ticket, you get a hotel voucher, you don't pay for your room. However, the Arizona "voucher" is nothing but a discount coupon, the kind you get in the mail every day and toss in the recycle bin.

So who benefits from this "free" private school program? According to No Child Left expert Scott Young, 76% of the money handed out for Arizona's voucher program has gone to children already in private schools. In other words, the $1,000 check from the state turned into a $1,000 subsidy for wealthy parents, a $1,000 discount on private schools for the privileged. How astonishing: A program touted as a benefit for working-class kids that turns into a subsidy for rich ones. You're shocked.

What about little Antonio? He returns with his unused voucher to his wretched under-financed local school in Apache County, Arizona. Unfortunately, there are no new textbooks, because the $1,000 voucher has been pocketed by a few parents who are already sending their kids to private school. The tab for the free lunch for the privileged kids is picked up by Antonio and friends: 20% of the local school districts' federal funds must be used to pay for the buses to transport privileged voucher students.

What I don't understand about the Arizona legislature is why, having discovered this formula for better education for less money, they don't apply it to other products as well. Why not car vouchers? "Everyone in Arizona should have a choice of cars! Why should the average Joe be stuck with an old beater when he can have a Mercedes?" All the state has to do is issue "Mercedes" vouchers backed by $3,500 from the state. It doesn't matter that there's no Mercedes dealer who will give you the car for $3,500.

I've never encountered a single opponent of school vouchers, of *real* vouchers where you choose the school and the state pays. But that ain't going to happen. You know it. I know it. And the clowns who are selling these counterfeit "vouchers" know it too. *So what's their game?*

The answers are in the test, class. The fifteen states that complain that the testing required by No Child Left exceeds the entire federal layout for the program miss the point. Testing is the heart and soul of No Child Left Behind.

The new world requires highly educated workers, but not too many. We saw how rising productivity created gargantuan wealth worldwide in the past two decades for a few. Maintaining the rise of productivity and riches through new technology requires a skilled, imaginative, highly educated, well-trained workforce. In India, very highly skilled workers account for one million jobs—about 2% of the workforce. America can afford to make it 10%. But no more. What about the other 90%? Someone's got to unload the goods shipped in from China, stock Wal-Mart's shelves and ask you, "Do you want fries with that?" In this flat, tilted new world, we have to adopt the methods used by emperors of Confucian China: *Test for the best, cull the rest.*

Of course, not everyone takes the same test. Only "Title 1" schools must test students: working class and poor schools. The wealthiest suburban districts are exempt and all schools where students wear designer blazers.

It's true that our President took a test to get into Yale. It had one question: "Is your grandfather, Prescott Bush, a Yale Trustee?" His answer, "Yes," gave him a perfect score.

No Child Left offers no "options" for those with the test score Mark of Cain—no opportunities, no hope, no plan, no funding. Rather, it is the new social Darwinism, the marketplace jungle brought into the classroom. This is educational eugenics: Identify the nation's loser class early on. Trap them, then train them cheap. Someone has to care for the privileged. No society can have winners without lots and lots of losers. And so we have No Child Left Behind—to provide the new worker drones that will clean the toilets at the Yale Alumni Club, punch the cash registers color-coded for illiterates, and pamper the winner class on the higher floors of the new economic order.

Hope I Die Before My Next Refill

How did this happen? How did Americans fall backward into the jaws meant to chew the Third World and the Old World. Who took away our New Deal?

I was in the drugstore today out here in Southold just down the road from the Terrorism Vulnerability Point. Some old guy in front of me was picking up his little paper bag of prescription medicine. The lady behind the counter handed him a credit card slip and said, "I'm sorry."

She was sorry because the bill was over $1,200. The old man stared at the charge card receipt and stared at it some more. Hesitating, he signed, then said, "I hope I die before I have to pay for the next refill."

He wasn't joking. The lady behind the counter said, "Oh, don't ever say that." And she said it in such a way that it was clear that she'd heard the same thought before, in different words, from too many of the old folk that come by.

And I was thinking, "I wonder if he voted for Bush."

I mean, did he vote for the man who would stop boys from kissing boys, who would allow big stone icons of the Ten Commandments in the Southold courthouse, who would get Saddam before he got us? In other words, was he a blind soldier in Karl Rove's army of the angry who would rather vote against themselves, for deadly high drug prices dictated by Big Pharma, for no national health insurance, in return for a promise from George Bush that he will be the malicious defender of their prejudices?

The polls tell us that Americans are in an ugly mood: too many jobs leaving for China, too many body bags returning from Iraq, and a bad feeling about a president grabbing for Grandma's Social Security check.

America is hurting, but what really hurts is that the wounds are self-inflicted.

1927. Again.

The National Public Radio news anchor was so excited I thought she'd pee herself: The President of the United States had flown his plane down to 1,700 feet to get a better look at the flood damage! Later, I saw the photo of him looking out of the window of *Air Force One*. The President looked very serious and concerned.

That was on Wednesday, August 31, 2005, two days after the levees broke and Lake Ponchartrain swallowed New Orleans. The President had waited the extra days to stop first at the Pueblo El Mirage Golf Course in Arizona.

I'm sure the people of New Orleans would have liked to show their appreciation for the official Presidential photo-strafing, but their surface-to-air missiles were wet.

I don't want to give the impression the President did nothing. He swiftly ordered the federal government to dispatch to New Orleans 18 water purification units, 50 tons of food, two mobile hospitals, expert search teams, and 20 lighting units with generators. However, that was President *Chávez*, whose equipment was refused entry to the disaster zone by the U.S. State Department. President Bush also flew in generators and lights. They were used for a photo op in the French Quarter, then removed when the President concluded his television pitch.

The corpses floating through the Ninth Ward attracted vultures. There was ChoicePoint, our friends from Chapter 1: The Fear. They picked up a contract to identify the bodies using their War on Terror DNA database. In the face of tragedy, America's business community pulled together, lobbying hard to remove the "Davis-Bacon" regulation that guarantees emergency workers receive a minimum prevailing wage. The Rev. Pat Robertson got a piece of the action. The Federal Emergency Management Agency's Web site encouraged those wanting to help victims to donate to the charities he controls. Within the week, the Navy penned a half-billion-dollar contract for reconstruction work with Halliburton. More would come.

Our President, as he does in any emergency situation, announced additional tax cuts. He ordered immediate write-offs for new equipment used in rebuilding. That will likely provide a relief for Halliburton, but the deductions were useless to small New Orleans businesses which had no income to write off. The oil majors, the trillion-dollar babies, won a $700 million tax break.

Don't think of hurricanes as horrors, but as opportunities. For the schoolchildren among the refugees, instead of schools, our President promised school "vouchers" on a grand scale.

And there was a bonus. Louisiana had been a "purple" state—neither a solid Republican Red nor Democratic Blue. It was up for grabs politically. With a Democratic Senator and a new Democratic Governor, Louisiana was ready to lead the South out of the GOP.

Louisiana's big blue Democratic splotch was enclosed within the city below sea level. On August 29, this major electoral problem for the Republican party was solved. I'm not saying our rulers deliberately let New Orleans drown. But before they would save it, the lifeguards boarding Air Force One had to play a few more holes.

In 1986, I was hired by the City of New Orleans to check out suspicious doings by a corporation called "Entergy." I flew in to meet City Councilman Brod Bagert, who is also New Orleans's top trial lawyer and its most accomplished poet. Over beignets and chicory coffee at the river, he said, "You want to know what this city's about, Mr. Palast? I'll show you." He drove me to a concrete bunker, banged on the metal door, and greeted a guy named Fishhead, who brought me into the belly of a horrendously loud, gargantuan and astonishing apparatus. "This here, Mr. Palast, is a pump. Forget Bourbon Street. This is all you have to know about New Orleans: *We are under water.* Below sea level, sir, and the only thing that keeps the river from pouring in over our heads are these pumps. You got that, son?"

Outside flowed the Mississippi. America's toilet. The poisoned expectorations of a hundred cities dumped into it or leached from suburban lawns and from factories when no one is looking, come out here in the tap water. A couple years ago, we buried our friend activist Gary Groesch, aged 50, of some mystery disease. "The City That Care Forgot" is their motto. The City That *Everyone* Forgot, a Bantustan where the forgotten can be ignored except for the jazzy minstrel shows for tourists.

I called Bagert four months after the flood. Nearly half the city is still in the dark.

The electric company, New Orleans Public Service, "NOPSI," is owned by a holding company, Entergy, the company Bagert, Groesch and I investigated in 1986. Here's what we found. In 1986, the New Orleans company was going broke because of the eye-popping cost of buying wholesale power—four times normal—from a company called Middle South Energy, charges they were passing right on to their captive customers in the city. Middle South is 100% owned and controlled by, you've guessed it, Entergy. But these were the days of government regulation, and government ordered an end to the shell game.

Then came deregulation and the siphoning restarted with a vengeance. Busy shuffling loot from pocket to pocket, Entergy had neither the concern nor funds to harden their system against a hurricane.

But from the looks of it, and my own review of their accounts, their plan in case of the long-expected flood came down to "turn off the lights and declare their subsidiary bankrupt," which they did three weeks after the hurricane. Negligent damage liabilities and rebuilding obligations were thrown into the Dumpster of the bankruptcy courts, and the holding company walked away. But don't worry, Entergy the holding company is doing quite well, posting a big 24% leap in earnings for the third quarter, a profit it attributes to "weather."☺

So who's to blame for losing New Orleans? That's easy. It was Franklin Roosevelt. New Orleans was the victim of the New Deal, according to *New York Times* columnist John Tierney, in "Losing that New Deal Religion." The free market flat-worlder's argument goes like this: The idea that government's job is to protect you is gone with the wind, drowned in the Mississippi. Government's the problem, and the solution is . . . Wal-Mart. Turn FEMA into WEMA, the "Wal-Mart Emergency Management Agency." That's a quote. Let the market do it, let the market save us. Louisiana's Republican Senator David Vitter was so excited by the idea of selling off the government, "privatizing," that he introduced a bill at high tide to do just that, "privatize" emergency planning.

But Senator Vitter, didn't Joe Allbaugh tell you? New Orleans hurricane planning *was* privatized.

You should remember Allbaugh from Chapter 4: The Con. It was Allbaugh, as Governor George Bush's Chief of Staff who, in 1997, handled the Governor's personal emergency: His office allegedly called the Texas Air Guard to let them know that Karen Hughes would be dropping by to "make sure there's nothing in there [Bush's war file] that'll embarrass the Governor."

Under Bill Clinton, the Emergency Management Agency was run by emergency managers. That was the dull way to do it. In 2001, Bush made Joe Allbaugh FEMA's chief and the two of them converted the agency into something more exciting, a front-line command center in the War on Terror, dissolving the agency into the Department of Homeland Security. And that's when the unexciting emergency planning work was put up for sale. (Allbaugh quit in 2003 and turned the Wal-Marted FEMA over to his old college roommate, Michael Brown, an executive with the Arabian Horse Association.)

It wasn't in the *Times,* but a year before the hurricane, the Department of Homeland Security and FEMA signed a half-million-dollar contract with a private operator to write up "a catastrophic hurricane disaster plan for the City of New Orleans," says the press release. Their plan was innovative. We know it was innovative because the work was handed to a company called "Innovative Emergency Management."

Innovative Emergency Management, said a company release, had "teamed" with expert James Lee Witt, the renowned Clinton FEMA chief, which was good news for New Orleans. The bad news was, it wasn't true. Witt, despite IEM's press release, said he was not part of the Innovative "team."

No matter. Innovative Emergency Management's founder, president and CEO, Madhu Beriwal, I believe, owns an umbrella *and* she's an exceptionally experienced donor to the Republican party. She has more campaign committee citations, including donations to Senator Vitter, than evacuation plans to her name. Maybe she has extraordinary credentials for saving a city from flood, but when we called seeking her experience and credentials, we got nothing.

IEM's press release, besides the fib about Witt, made this utterly truthful point:

> Given this area's vulnerability and elevation . . . a plan that
> facilitates a rapid and effective hurricane response is critical.

Amen to that. So I called IEM in Baton Rouge to see their critical and innovative plan that was supposed to be complete well before Katrina's landfall. The Wal-Mart of disaster prep couldn't get me a copy. In fact, they couldn't say if they had it. Nor if the City of New Orleans had it. Or if Senator Vitter or anyone had it or if it existed. Could they tell me the name of someone at FEMA who had the evacuation plan? They hesitated, so I prompted, "Well, who do you call if there's an *emergency?*" The question stumped them. And it stumped FEMA, which wouldn't provide me a copy. The problem, I was informed, was that they couldn't confirm it existed.

There is nothing new under the sun. A Republican president going for the photo op as the Mississippi rolls over New Orleans. It was 1927, and President Calvin Coolidge sent Commerce Secretary Herbert Hoover, "a little fat man with a notebook in his hand," who mugged for the cameras and promised to build the city a wall of protection. They had their photos taken. Then they left to play golf with Ken Lay or, rather, the Ken Lay railroad baron equivalent of his day.

In 1927, the Democratic Party had died and was awaiting burial. As depression approached, the coma-Dems, like Franklin Roosevelt, called for, of all things, balancing the budget.

Then, as the Mississippi waters rose, one politician, the state's electricity regulator, stood up on the back of a flatbed truck rigged with loudspeakers, and said, roughly, "Listen up! They're lying! The President's lying! The rich fat jackals that are drowning you will do it again and again and again. They lead you into imperialist wars for profit, they take away your schools and your hope, and when you complain, they blame Blacks and Jews and immigrants. Then they drown your kids. I say, Kick'm in the ass and take your share of the wealth you created."

Huey Long was *our* Hugo Chávez, and he laid out a plan: a progressive income tax, real money for education, public works to rebuild Louisiana and America, Social Security old age pensions, veterans' benefits, regulation of the big utility holding companies, an end to what he called, "rich men's wars," and an end to the financial royalism of the One Percent. He even had the audacity to suggest that the poor's votes should count, calling for the end to the poll tax four decades before Martin Luther King succeeded in ending it. Long recorded his motto as a musical anthem: "*Every* man a King." The waters receded, the anger did not, and, in 1928, Huey "Kingfish" Long was elected Governor of Louisiana.

At the time, Louisiana schools were free, but not the textbooks. The elite liked it that way, but Long didn't. To pay for the books, the Kingfish levied a special tax on Big Oil. But the oil companies refused to pay for the textbooks. Governor Long then ordered the National Guard to seize the oil fields in the Delta.

It was Huey Long who established the principle that a government of the people must protect the people, school them, build the infrastructure, regulate industry and share the nation's wealth—and that meant facing down "the concentrations of monopoly power" of the corporate aristocracy—"the thieves of Wall Street," as he called them.

In other words, Huey Long founded the modern Democratic Party. FDR and the party establishment, scared witless of Long's ineluctable march to the White House, adopted his program, albeit diluted, called it the New Deal and later the New Frontier and the Great Society.

America and the party prospered.

What happened to the Kingfish? As with Chávez, the oil industry and local oligarchs had few options for responding to Governor Long's populist appeal and the success of his egalitarian economic program. On September 8, 1935, Huey Long, by then a U.S. Senator, was shot dead. He was 42.

And now is the moment, as it was in '27.

Huey P. Long

"Share the Wealth" Sign-up Form

To: Huey P. Long

United States Senator, Washington, D.C.:

This is to inform you that a share-our-wealth society has been organized here with _____ members. Address and officers are as follows:

Post office _____   State _____

Street address _____

President _____

Secretary _____

I will go to people who know me and who personally know of the work I have done for the money that it will take for the expenses I will have to bear in this work, because, if any such thing as dues were collected from members for such expenses, the thieves of Wall Street and their newspapers and radio liars would immediately say that I had a scheme to get money.

—Huey P. Long.

Long's original Share-the-Wealth sign-up form. Source: US Social Security Administration.

Neanderthals Attacking the Constitution ©Winston Smith 1985

THE END
The House I Live In

America is a nation of losers. It's the best thing about us. We're the dregs, what the rest of the world barfed up and threw on our shores.

John Kennedy said we are "a nation of immigrants." That's the sanitized phrase. We are, in fact, a nation of *refugees*, who, despite the bastards in white sheets and the know-nothings in Congress, have held open the Golden Door to a dark planet. We are not imperialists and that's why Bush lies and Cheney lies and, yes, the Clintons lie.

Winston Churchill didn't lie to the Brits about their empire: He said, These lands belong to the Crown, we own'm and we'll squeeze the value from them. "Imperialism," as Karl Marx complained, was a *good* word in Britain, a word that got you elected in Europe until too recently.

Ignore the fey university hideouts of Europe. Go to Vietnam or to Brazil or to Morocco or to Tibet and you'll find the same thing: America's music, America's freedom of speech, freedom of religion and freedom of spirit and the heartfelt friendship of Americans for others have made the USA truly "the light unto the nations." Americans are not liked worldwide, but loved—sometimes I find that weird, but it's true—and that drives Osama to bombs and madness.

We are a nation conceived in liberty and dedicated to the cause that all men and women are created equal. It's silly and precious to point out that these ideals have been mangled, abused, ignored and monstered by those with plans to make us an empire. We know that. Now, *what are you going to do about it?*

America is indeed exceptional. That's not a boast, that's a *job* we have to do. George Washington and Thomas Jefferson burdened us with that exceptionalism in crafting the most important international law signed up until the Geneva Convention: The Alien Torts Act, in which the USA takes onto itself the right to bring civil penalties against any act of torture, political murder and piracy that occurs anywhere in the world. It is now being used in suits brought against Chevron Oil in Ecuador and against IBM for the death of slave laborers in Nazi Germany.

Damn right America is exceptional. It is America that defiantly walked out of the first "world trade organization," known as the British Empire, announcing, "We hold these truths to be self-evident that all men are created equal and are ENDOWED BY THE CRE-ATOR with INALIENABLE rights, and AMONG THESE are life, liberty and the pursuit of happiness."

Now, think about that. These rights don't come from Congress or Kings or Soviets, they come from The Creator, that is, we are *born* free—and "we" are Sri Lankans as much as Minnesotans. Our rights are "INALIENABLE": no one, *NO ONE*, may take them away, not the Ayatollahs of Tehran or Generalissimo Negroponte at the Department of Homeland Security or the kill-o-crats in Baghdad pre- or post-Saddam.

Will the snarling closet imperialists try to turn America from its cause and soul? Damn right they will. That's why two U.S. military lawyers resigned from their posts at the Guantánamo prison camp. They wouldn't put up with Bush-niks tearing up their Constitution. ("We the people" own it, not "them the Republicans.") In Iran, these two guys would have been shot, in Britain arrested. In America, Bush fears *them*—that their story would come out—as it did. Only in America could that happen. No question, the USA holds itself exempt from the legal standards of this world—which are execrable. Whose standard should we adopt? China's torture standard? Britain's Secrecy Act as a standard? Switzerland's Nazi-money-protection standard?

Only in America would a Lyndon Johnson order federal troops to protect Black school kids' right to attend class. You don't have to tell me that Johnson then ordered the slaughter of three million Vietnamese—I know, I went to jail to oppose it. But go to Vietnam today and ask what people they most admire? Mention Russians, they laugh; mention Chinese, they may hit you; mention Americans and they say (to my astonishment, I'll admit), "We love Americans."

They *don't* love Bush. That's because *George Bush is not an American.* Look, I didn't think much of Bill Clinton, and he dropped into some of the worst quasi-imperial habits of the New World Trade Order. But Clinton is also more popular worldwide than the pope and pizza combined because he represents that American sense of giving-a-shit, empathy and sincere friendship which are hallmark's of America's Manifest Destiny.

Yes, America does have a Manifest Destiny—to Let Freedom Ring—which the evil and greedy and pernicious would twist into a grab for land and resources and ethnic cleansing. And so the Manifest Destiny of the journalists in our shitty little offices in New York and London is to expose these motherfuckers.

Ronald Reagan said, "America is the shining city on the hill." And he *hated* it, doing his best to turn it into a dark Calcutta of the helpless. And when that didn't work, George II tried to drown us in the Mississippi.

Go back to Taos Precinct 13. What you'll find there is Pueblo Native war veterans who raise the flag every day and will fight and die for it knowing full well that the fight must also be taken to the pueblo's racially biased voting booths.

Howard Zinn, a shining historian on our hill, reminds us,

> It should be understood that the children of Iraq, of China, and of Africa, children everywhere in the world, have the same right to life as American children.

Damn right, they do. That's what Jefferson meant by "inalienable." And they won't get their rights to life and liberty from Osama's Caliphate of oil states or China's money-crazed "Communism" nor half of Africa's neo-colonial presidential Draculas or the puppet princes installed today in Iraq by George Bush.

Bush is so far away from his refugee loser roots that he just doesn't get what it is to be American. So he steals the one thing that every American is handed off the boat: a chance. When they take away your Social Security and overtime and tell you sleeper cells are sleeping under your staircase, you don't take a chance, you *lose* your chance, and the land of opportunity becomes a landscape of fear and suspicion, an armed madhouse.

You want to say that George Bush is an evil sonovabitch? I'd go further: he's UN-AMERICAN.

And that's why he lost the election. TWICE.

So, I'm asking you again. *What are you going to do about it?*

Do not fight for a dying regime. It is not worth your life.

—President George W. Bush

AFTERWORD

BUSTED

... and How to Steal Back Your Vote

Since the initial release of *Armed Madhouse* in June 2006, much has changed in America.

The Department of Homeland Security, after a five-year hunt for Osama, finally brought charges against . . . Greg Palast.

As America crawled toward the fifth anniversary of the September 11 attack, Homeland Security charged me and my U.S. producer Matt Pascarella with violating the anti-terror laws.

Don't you feel safer?

And I confess: We're guilty.

On August 22, 2006, we were videotaping Katrina evacuees still held behind barbed wire in a trailer park encampment a hundred miles from New Orleans. It had been a year since the hurricane and 73,000 POWs (Prisoners of Dubya) were still in mobile home gulags. I arranged a surreptitious visit with Pamela Lewis, one of the unwilling guests of George Bush's Guantánamo on wheels. She told me, "It's a prison setup"—except there are no home furloughs for these inmates because they no longer have homes.

You can't film there. FEMA is part of Homeland Security and its camps are off-limits to cameras. We don't want Osama to know he can get a cramped Airstream by posing as a displaced Black person.

To give a sense of the full flavor and smell of Kamp Katrina, we wanted to show that this human parking lot, with kids and elderly, is close by Exxon Petroleum's Baton Rouge refinery. The area goes by the quaint sobriquet, "Cancer Alley."

So we filmed it. Uh-oh. The refinery, like the Indian casino parking lot in Chapter 1, is a CAVIP—Critical Asset and Vulnerable Infrastructure Point. Apparently, you can't film a CAVIP.[1]

As to the bust: The positive side for me as a reporter was that I got to see Bush's terror-trackers in action. I should note that it took the Maxwell Smarts at Homeland Security a full two weeks to hunt us down. And we're on *television*.

Frankly, Matt and I were a bit scared that, given the charges, we wouldn't be allowed on a plane into New York for the September 11 commemoration. But what scared us more is that we *were* allowed on the plane.

Once I was traced, I had a bit of an otherworldly conversation with my would-be captors. Detective Frank Pananepinto of Homeland Security told me, "This is a 'Critical Infrastructure' . . . and they get nervous about unauthorized filming of their property."

Well, me too, Detective. In fact, I'm very nervous that extremely detailed satellite photos of this potential chemical blast site can be downloaded from Maps.Google.com.

Detective Pananepinto, in justifying our impending arrest, said, "If you remember, a lot of people were killed on 9/11."

Yes, I remember "a lot" of people were killed. So I have this suggestion, Detective—and you can pass it on to Mr. Bush: *Go find the people who killed them.*

---

[1] I'm writing this on the ferry to the Indian casino—Southold, New York's designated CAVIP. A sign on the gambling cruiser says, "Journalists must register before boarding." Why reporters should register, I'm not certain. It strikes me that they should require *terrorists* to register.

Eighteen Missing Inches

Before the Big Bust, we learned a little more about how New Orleans drowned. Given my line of work, I'm not shocked at much. Yet, this one got to me. An insider told me,

> By midnight on Monday the White House knew. Monday night I was at the state Emergency Operations Center and nobody was aware that the levees had breached. Nobody.

The charges were so devastating—the White House's withholding from the state police the information that the city was about to flood—that from almost any source, I simply would have dismissed it. But this was not just any source. The whistle-blower was Dr. Ivor van Heerden, deputy director of the Louisiana State University Hurricane Center, and the chief technician advising the state on saving lives during Katrina.

That Monday night, August 29, 2005, the sleepless crew at the state Emergency Operations Center, directing the response to Hurricane Katrina, were high-fiving it, relieved that Katrina had swung east of New Orleans, sparing the city from drowning.

They were wrong. The Army Corps of Engineers, FEMA, and the White House knew for critical hours that the levees had begun to crack, but withheld the information for a day and night. The delay was deadly.

Van Heerden explained that levees don't collapse in a single bang. First, there's a small crack or two, a few feet wide, which take hours to burst open into visible floodways.

Had the state known New Orleans' bulwark was failing, it would have shifted resources to evacuate those left in the danger zone. From my interview with the professor:

> Dr. Van Heerden: FEMA knew at 11 o'clock on Monday that the levees had breached. At 2 p.m. they flew over the 17th Street Canal and took video of the breech.

Question: So the White House wouldn't tell you that the levees had breeched?

Dr. Van Heerden: They didn't tell *anybody*.

Question: And you're at the Emergency Center?

Dr. Van Heerden: I mean *nobody* knew. Well, the Corps of Engineers knew. FEMA knew. None of *us* knew.

The prevarications continued all week.

Van Heerden said, "I went to the Governor's on Tuesday night and I said this, 'There's a lot more breeches than one.' They said, 'Whatever you need, go find out.' I got in an airplane, I flew. I counted twenty-eight breeches."

The White House had good reason, or at least political and financial reasons, to keep mum. A hurricane is an act of God, but catastrophic levee failure is an act of the Administration. Once the federal levees go, evacuation, rescue, and those frightening words—responsibility and compensation—become Washington's. Van Heerden said that this was "not an act of God, but catastrophic failure of the levee system" would mean that, at least, "these people must be compensated."

Not every flood victim in America gets the Katrina treatment. In 1992, storms wiped out 190 houses on the beach at West Hampton Dunes, home to film stars and celebrity speculators. The federal government paid to completely rebuild the houses, and hauled in 4 million cubic feet of sand to restore the tony beaches and guaranteed the homes' safety into the coming decades—after which the "victim's" homes rose in value to an average $2 million each.

But in New Orleans, instead of compensation, 73,000 have been sentenced to life in FEMA's trailer parks in Louisiana. Even more are displaced to other states. I asked van Heerden about the consequences of the White House's failures, the information about the levee being just one of a list.

"Well, fifteen hundred people drowned. That's the bottom line."

But why did the levees fail at all if the hurricane missed the city? The professor showed me a computer model indicating the levees

Grand Bahamian-style Dream House
Westhampton Dunes, New York

PROPERTY INFORMATION
Location: Westhampton
Dunes, New York

Price: $2,850,000 USD

Type: Single-Family
Residence

This oceanfront dream house sits on 80 feet of beachfront. With
five bedrooms, four full baths, and one half bath, the home also
boasts rich woods, fine stone, and exquisite detailing throughout.
The property features an oceanfront pool and a glorious deck
from which to enjoy spectacular views and mesmerizing sunsets.
This fabulous island getaway is just 90 miles from Manhattan. ■

While the federal government failed to rebuild New Orleans, Westhampton Dunes, New York, was extensively rebuilt after storm damage.

were a foot and a half too short—the result of a technical error in the
Army Corps of Engineers' calculation of sea level when construction
of the levees began in the 1930s.

And the Bush crew knew it. Long before Katrina struck, the White
House staff had sought Van Heerden's advice on coastal safety. So
when the professor learned of the eighteen-inch error, he informed the
White House directly at least a year before the flood. But this was advice they didn't want to hear. The President had already sent the levee
repair crew, the Army Corps of Engineers, to Afghanistan and Iraq.

Eighteen inches may not seem like much, but the LSU computer
models, available to FEMA before the flood, show this was the difference between the levees holding and their system-wide collapse.

I had one last question for Van Heerden. In the last chapter, I noted
that in 2004, a year before the flood, the Bush Administration had
taken the extraordinary step of contracting out New Orleans' hurricane
planning. What did the LSU experts know about this private contractor, Innovative Emergency Management (IEM), that was handed the
job of drafting an evacuation plan?

Van Heerden never heard of them until they were given the lucrative planning gig—and I mentioned they couldn't seem to find the
plan after the flood. (Maybe it got wet.)

But Van Heerden suggested they may have had good reason to let their New Orleans evacuation proposal get lost. The plan was, he said, that when a hurricane hit, everyone in the Crescent City would simply jump into their cars and get the hell out. It seems that the IEM/FEMA crew didn't remember that 127,000 people in the city didn't have cars. But Van Heerden remembered. LSU had drafted computerized maps locating these no-car people and knew how to get them out. Dr. Van Heerden offered this life-saving information to FEMA before the flood. They wouldn't touch it. Then, a state official told the professor to shut up, back off—IEM was upset with his meddling—or there would be consequences for Van Heerden's work. The state official now works for IEM.

So I dropped in on IEM. In their office down the road from LSU, IEM's spokeswoman assured me that company CEO Madhu Beriwal had "a lot of experience with evacuation"—but couldn't name a single city Beriwal had developed a plan for before getting the FEMA contract for New Orleans.

I showed the IEM folks the long list of her donations to the Republican Party and asked if that was the experience that won the contract. A short-necked guy standing at her side, a self-described "bioterrorism expert," suddenly put his hand over our camera lens and said, "We've called security." I took that to mean the interview was over.

Had the interview not been cut short, I would have asked about those residents without cars. Stephen Smith is one. He lost his home, and his children now live in Baton Rouge while he works in Houston. Smith told me that on the fourth day after the flood, still stranded with starving families in the brutal heat on an Interstate 10 overpass, an elderly woman asked him to close her dead husband's eyes. He had collapsed, perishing from dehydration after giving his last bottle of water to his grandchildren.

Well, it won't happen again. Mr. Bush's FEMA has hired a consulting firm to evaluate what went wrong with the failed evacuation plan. The contractor? A Baton Rouge company named Innovative Emergency Management, IEM.

FOX INVESTIGATES HENHOUSE

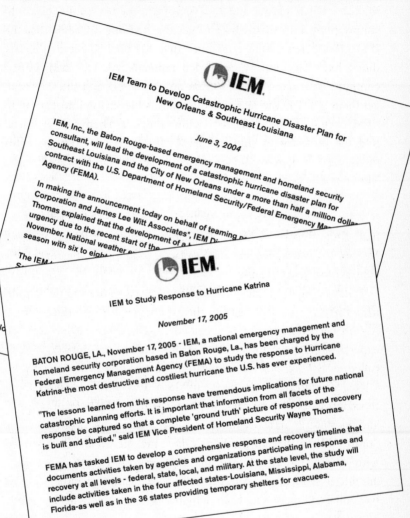

IEM Team to Develop Catastrophic Hurricane Disaster Plan for New Orleans & Southeast Louisiana

June 3, 2004

IEM, Inc., the Baton Rouge-based emergency management and homeland security consultant, will lead the development of a catastrophic hurricane disaster plan for Southeast Louisiana and the City of New Orleans under a more than half a million dollar contract with the U.S. Department of Homeland Security/Federal Emergency Management Agency (FEMA).

In making the announcement today on behalf of teaming partners Innovative Emergency Management Corporation and James Lee Witt Associates*, IEM Director of Homeland Security Wayne Thomas explained that the development of a catastrophic hurricane plan is of high urgency due to the recent start of the hurricane season, which runs from June through November. National weather experts are predicting another active Atlantic hurricane season with six to eight...

IEM to Study Response to Hurricane Katrina

November 17, 2005

BATON ROUGE, LA., November 17, 2005 - IEM, a national emergency management and homeland security corporation based in Baton Rouge, La., has been charged by the Federal Emergency Management Agency (FEMA) to study the response to Hurricane Katrina-the most destructive and costliest hurricane the U.S. has ever experienced.

"The lessons learned from this response have tremendous implications for future national catastrophic planning efforts. It is important that information from all facets of the response be captured so that a complete 'ground truth' picture of response and recovery is built and studied," said IEM Vice President of Homeland Security Wayne Thomas.

FEMA has tasked IEM to develop a comprehensive response and recovery timeline that documents activities taken by agencies and organizations participating in response and recovery at all levels - federal, state, local, and military. At the state level, the study will include activities taken in the four affected states-Louisiana, Mississippi, Alabama, Florida-as well as in the 36 states providing temporary shelters for evacuees.

In June 2004, Republican Party donor IEM announces a FEMA contract to develop a "Hurricane Disaster Plan for New Orleans." In 2005, after Katrina proved the plan a disaster, FEMA hired to firm to investigate what went wrong: IEM.

VICTORY IN NEW MEXICO

On March 3, 2006, a star appeared in the sky above New Mexico. Two wise men and a woman followed it to a golden manger at the State Capitol where they held a press conference to announce the birth of a new era of election reform. I hoped this was a sign that things had improved on the election front since the first edition of *Armed Madhouse*. The three wise-persons, Governor Bill Richardson, his Secretary of State Rebecca Vigil-Giron and her sidekick, elections official Ernie Marquez, were staging the signing of a law, the first in the nation, to require the use of paper ballots in every county in the state. "Black Box" Becky and the Governor, once fanatic defenders of touch-screen voting, would now lead the nation in a battle to ban voting on computer.

It was, unequivocally, a huge victory for the activists. Through grassroots action, they had put the powers of the state up against the wall and made them swallow their vote reform medicine. A couple of New Mexico radio hosts even credited my noisy investigation for *Armed Madhouse* with making this democratic dream come true. I blushed.

The voter activist chat rooms were on fire with self-congratulations. Maria Leyba wrote, *"Alrighty now!!! Woohoo!!!* Finally some *accountability."* Phillip Muñoz crowed, "It prevents the theft of an election like the last two." A New Mexican, Jessica Sanchez, posted the simple and sweet, "I love my Gov."

And that's when I realized: So *this* is how the GOP has stolen the election of 2008.

THE THEFT OF 2008 . . . AND HOW TO STEAL BACK YOUR VOTE

The Republican Party won the 2008 presidential race on January 1, 2006. It was a private affair, so the Democrats wouldn't recognize the GOP had put the ballots in the bag a couple years ahead of the voting.

But before I tell you how they stole it, I'm going to tell you how they *didn't* steal it . . .

The Black-Box Distraction

I know I'm going to get burned at the stake for saying this. It's pure heresy, but someone's got to say it: The Republicans aren't stealing the 2008 election by monkeying with your touch-screen vote.

Am I saying the computers machines are *safe?* No. Pay attention, damn it. They'll jerk the machines, for sure. They did it in 2006. But that's not the key to how they'll steal it in 2008.

The 2000 election was certainly stolen; so was the 2004 election— but *not* by computer. And in 2008, they won't steal it by computer either. But they'll steal it nonetheless, by methods more insidious, more certain . . . in fact, they've already done it. Millions of citizens' votes have *already* been snatched.

In 2000, it was theft by secret "scrub": by Katherine Harris and Jeb Bush targeting 94,000 innocent voters, mostly Black men, for elimination from the voter rolls.

Exposing Jeb's little "felon" scam seems to have kicked off an entire industry of writing about vote thievery and jump-started a growing movement of activists out to prevent the heist of our democratic franchise. That's good. What's bad is that many in this enthusiastic army of the aroused are marching the voter protection movement straight into the open jaws of Karl Rove.

We saw this in 2002, when activists signed off on the Help America Vote Act, creating a "provisional" ballot that, instead of helping voters, helped Republican operatives shunt 3 million voters to this newfangled baloney ballot two years later in 2004. One in three ballots were then legally tossed away.

And we saw it in 2004. In Ohio, there weren't enough touch-screens in place to have fixed that election. Only 14.6% of precincts had installed the computer ballot boxes. Rather, that November, John Kerry's votes were lost in a blizzard of hanging chads in the state with the greatest number of ancient punch-card voting machines—Ohio. Go ahead and shoot me for saying this, but Secretary of State Blackwell

was more than happy to have white folks campaign against placing
Diebold computers into inner-city voting booths. That let him keep
the chad-hanging machines in place. As mentioned in Chapter 4,
Blackwell had confidentially written to fellow Republican chiefs that
keeping the old punch-card machines would spoil thousands of ballots. They did. Two years after the election, a physical inspection of
the punch cards by a team led by lawyer Bob Fitrakis disclosed
22,000 suspiciously spoiled and uncountable ballots in what the experts called "high-performance Democratic precincts." Ohio was a
decidedly low-tech heist.

And now we're doing it again, making it easy for the vote burglars
to snatch the 2008 election by placing all our hopes and efforts onto
one single, incredibly narrow matter: making war on touch-screen
electronic voting machines.

And there's no better example of how the other side is using this
fear of computer voting to beat us to death than New Mexico. There,
the Republicans in the State Legislature agreed to Governor Richardson's law requiring paper ballots in return for a whole new set of
weapons to use against voters of color, most particularly, a new requirement for voters to produce ID cards.

And it didn't take long. Just before the 2006 midterm elections, the
Secretary of State of New Mexico was swamped with 200,000 returned, missent voter ID cards principally from the Albuquerque region. That is, the *Democratic* region.

And it didn't take long to claim a Democratic seat. In that 2006
midterm election, Democrat Patricia Madrid, running in New Mexico's First Congressional District, epicenter of the ID card disaster,
"lost" her race by 875 votes out of nearly a quarter million cast.

The Democrats, giddy with a snout full of congressional victories
nationwide in 2006, walked away from challenging that one loss in
New Mexico. They didn't even ask for a recount. While guzzling
their victory champagne from those midterm elections, Democrats
seemed to take little notice that, nationwide, half a million citizens

lost their vote in 2006 under the widening "Where's-your-ID?" rules.

. The Democrats, by not raising a protest in 2006, may find in 2008 that ID card tricks, not the voters, will choose our president.

But the new ID games are nothing. Here's how . . .

The Republicans Won 2008 on January 1, 2006

On that New Year's Day, unnoted in U.S. newspapers, a new provision of the Help America Vote Act (HAVA) became law. This sneaky little codicil allows each of the fifty Secretaries of State to reject voter registrations. In years past, Secretaries of State like Katherine Harris and Kenneth Blackwell skirted legal limits to say, in effect, "You can't vote" to a couple of hundred thousand U.S. citizens who happened to be Black Democrats. In 2006, this law-breaking came to an end—not because of a change in officials' behavior, but because the officials changed the law.

Beginning on January 1, 2006, the HAVA law gave Secretaries of State the right—in fact, *required* them—to reject any registering voter whose exact name and "identity numbers" (driver's license, Social Security, passport numbers) did not match up against a state "verification" list.

It sounds like pretty arcane stuff and not too treacherous, but if you think I'm getting wound up over a nitpicky matter, consider this: When HAVA gave state politicians this power to reject registration forms nationwide, the official hacks told one in three Americans attempting to register, "*Get lost!*" Most states used the rejection power with a mad vengeance. For example, at the beginning of 2006, California rejected 40% of registrants.

Does it really make a difference? Each year, about *24.3 million* Americans attempt to register or re-register. At the current rejection rates, it won't take long to clean out the voter rolls of undesirables— that is, undesirable to the Secretaries of State.

The key question is, of course: *Who* is tossed out? Overwhelmingly, it's folks with names like García-Marquez, Yao Ming, and Mohammed, according to Justin Levitt at the Brennan Center for Justice at New York University's School of Law. "Unusual names," he explained. Unusual for *Republicans*, that is.

Well, if they aren't legal voters, then we can't complain. However, a case-by-case review in one state, New York, disclosed that 71% of the registration forms rejected were tossed out as the result of data-entry errors by the government's own clerks.

And that's the point. There is not one scintilla of evidence of an attempt by thousands of citizens to vote illegally. However, in the California case, the thousands of rejected were guilty of "VWH," Voting While Hispanic. In Los Angeles, where a Democratic Chicano mayor and his allies have no interest in wiping out the Chicano vote, county officials went back through the local list of the 40% of applicants rejected. By simply contacting those voters and correcting obvious clerical errors on the forms, they reduced the rejection rate from 40% to nearly *zero*. In other words, the rejected were, in fact, legitimate voters. That was L.A. But for those given the boot in whiter counties, it was, "*tough luck, José.*"

So what's wrong with checking a would-be voter's ID against a verification list? The problem is that the system doesn't work. Indeed, it's *designed* to not work. Voters without driver's licenses, without passports, and without boat permits—in other words, low-income urban Democrats—must fall back on their Social Security numbers for registration. Sounds fair enough, but it's not. The Social Security Administration fails to verify an astonishing 46% of voters submitted by states. Evidence of a tsunami of fraudulent registrants? No, the databases are simply not capable of completing the checks. And there are some politicians who could not be happier with the political result. In Alabama, in 2006, the Democratic Party sued over the Republican Secretary of State's disastrous flaws in the verification database leading to the wrongful rejection of African-American voters by the thousands. The U.S. Justice Department came up with a solution: It convinced a judge to appoint a "special master" to expertly review the procedures. The expert appointed? Governor Bob Riley, the state's Republican Governor.

Los Angeles presented that rare case of officials attempting to protect voters. But across the USA, *millions* are getting the registration heave-ho with barely a peep from the press. In the bad old days of Jim

Crow, Black folks attempting to register were beaten or worse. Today, their forms are taken with a smile, then effectively tossed away.

But not always without a fight. The Brennan Center for Justice and a coalition of labor and civil rights groups successfully sued the state of Washington for having rejected nearly one out of three newly registered voters in urban Seattle. In that case, the victims were, in suspiciously large numbers, those with Chinese or Filipino names who suffered double the rate of rejection as did residents of the suburban and rural (i.e., white Republican) areas.

But the state of Ohio has so far outfoxed the legal watchdogs by keeping Ohio's methods and rules a foggy mystery. It's hard to sue a fog, and in this case, the fog-maker was then–Secretary of State Kenneth Blackwell. Up through the 2006 midterm election, Republican Blackwell refused to reveal Ohio's criteria for rejecting voters, the method of verification, or even how many voters were given the HAVA heave-ho. Blackwell, it's worth noting, got an early start in the registration rejection business. Leading up to the Bush-Kerry race, Blackwell attempted to reject thousands of applicants who filled out forms on paper that was not, in his opinion, the correct thickness. He backed down when caught on that gimmick. Nevertheless, Blackwell still managed to reject 36,251 new registrations before the 2004 election.

In 2006, the Blackwell Blockade of voters paid off for the GOP. In Ohio's second and 15th Congressional districts, the Republicans saved those two seats in Congress by less than 1% of the vote in the midst of an anti-Republican ballot-box tsunami.

Blackwell was one of the first to test the limits of the citizenship-destroying powers granted by HAVA. But he wasn't alone. Buried deep in the raw data of the government's National Voting Rights Act reports is this nasty statistic: Nationwide, in the two years leading to the Bush-Kerry race, 3,815,000 registration forms were officially thrown in the electoral garbage can on technical grounds. We know from the L.A. experience that minor filing flaws can be corrected—assuming officials want these voters to vote. They don't. And now, under the

2006 HAVA changes, the sky's the limit on rejections. In effect, this new federal "reform" law has become the cover for keeping the voter rolls as exclusive as a Georgia country club.

And why? What on earth required our Congress, four decades after the end of Jim Crow registration rules were abolished, to suddenly add a new weapon to the vote-heist arsenal? The official excuse is summed up by Republican legislator Russell Pearce of Mesa, Arizona:

> There is a massive effort under way to register illegal aliens
> in the country.

Really? Holy cow! A conspiracy to flood the voter rolls with the Brown Hordes of Juarez who've swum the Rio Grande just for a chance to vote for Hillary Clinton!? I called the legislator to ask him how he uncovered this grand cabal—to get a few names of the "massive" number of illegal voters and the perps behind the effort. I suggested that he turn over these ne'er-do-wells to the Justice Department for prosecution. But the Arizona politician didn't have a single name of a single convicted noncitizen voter. Nor could he tell us the names of the evil-doers who are behind this criminal conspiracy, orchestrating the "massive illegal" registration.

I asked the pol exactly how many alien voters have infested our system and the pol's public relations flak put it at 5 *million*.

Wow! It should be easy to find them, given that we have their addresses and driver's license numbers. The calculation came from a Republican Party website extrapolating from 500 residents of one town near the Mexico border who refused jury duty because they were noncitizens. Turns out jury lists are taken from voter files and driver's license records. These were legal residents, Mexican citizens, who were *driving*—not voting—in Arizona.

Other than in Republican Party website wet dreams, where are the millions of criminal alien voters? It's a myth—a myth that is politically very useful. The legend of the illegal alien voter is the basis of a slew of new laws to prevent a crime *that doesn't happen*—but which will result in a *real* crime: citizens wrongly denied the right to register to vote. Given that these new rules are tripling registration rejection rates, even after some voters successfully reapply, we can expect the number of citizens annually barred from voter lists to double from 1.9 million to 3.8 million. Count on it.

Crime Scene Investigation

Before I took up the questionable career of journalism in my late forties, I was, for two decades, an investigator. My specialty: "forensic economics." The job was to cut into evidence and figure out the scams by following the money and piecing together the statistics.

That's what's needed here. Vote rustling is a game of numbers, of probabilities, of shaving a percentage point here, a point there. The winners at this game understand that victory is in those "nega-votes," something polls don't catch: stopping your opponent's voters from voting or preventing their vote from counting.

So let's pause here for a bit of Fun with Forensics.

Begin by ignoring the media myths and bull crap about Black and Brown people being too lazy to register and vote. Look coldly at the numbers. Despite what we hear, African-Americans are as likely to vote as white voters, a notable nine out of ten Blacks who are registered (87%) vote, virtually the same as white voters (89%). (The difference, though small, is completely accounted for by the higher number of Black voters *denied a ballot* at the voting station.)

The big difference is in registration. Three-fourths of the white population is registered (75%), but only 69% of African-Americans. If Blacks registered at the same rate as whites, there would be another 1,630,000 African-Americans on the rolls, enough to change control of both houses of Congress and the White House.

But Blacks *do* register at the same rate as whites. *Huh?*

What I should say is that Black people *attempt* to register, fill out forms, at a slightly *higher* rate than the white population. Roughly 78% of African-Americans attempt to register versus 77% of whites. But the rate of minority applications *rejected* is so much higher, as is the rate of removal from voter rolls (purging), that the percentage of African-Americans *allowed* onto the rolls and allowed to stay on is so much lower than the percentage of white voters.

The bias in rejection and purges is not small stuff. For example, when I totaled up the number of wrongful purges in Florida before the 2000 race (where race is marked in registration files), I found that an innocent Black voter was *nine times* as likely to get the ax as an innocent white voter.

In other words, minority "culture" is not at fault for low registration. It ain't the culture, it's the *vultures*, the vote suppression predators.

Why are minority registrations under attack? One Republican pundit, John McWhorter, debating me in Harlem, suggested that people of color would not be targeted for such ugly vote repression tactics if they'd only stop voting for Democrats. I'm certain he's correct.

While African-Americans are victimized, the wipeout of Hispanic and Asian registrants, targeted immigrant groups, is even more severe.

In the spring of 2006, millions of Hispanics took to the streets to demand immigrant rights. Little noted by the press was the push for the rights of Hispanics who are already legal citizens. Their leaders announced that they would register a million new Hispanic voters. That should have been easy given that there are 7 *million* unregistered Hispanic, legal U.S. citizens. At the same time, the Black community was also signing up new voters like crazy. Reverend Jesse Jackson and other ministers collected literally hundreds of thousands of registration forms at Black churches and rallies.

But despite these registration drives, minority registration rates stay weirdly low. And now we know why: They're filling up a leaky bucket. The more registrations added, the more are rejected or purged.

Hispanics and Asians, given the chance to vote, do so in nearly the same numbers as white voters—over 80% of Hispanic and Asian registrants actually vote. But the percentage of those *enrolled* to vote is dismal, 47% of Hispanics and 44% of Asians who are currently eligible *citizens*. And for 2008, Republicans intend to keep it that way, punching more holes in the registration bucket, beginning with the hunt for . . .

Real Murkins

Arizona Representative Russell Pearce's posse isn't satisfied with HAVA's open door to voter-list manipulation. The pol went a step further promoting what I'd call the ultimate "José Crow" law: Proposition 200.

Prop 200, which became law in Arizona in 2006, requires proof of citizenship in order to register. That sounds fair: You can't register unless you can prove you're, as George Bush says, "a 'Murkin." The problem is that there are only three proofs of citizenship in most states: a certified original birth certificate, naturalization papers, or a passport. These are not easily available to a large chunk of those of us born in the USA. In most states, a driver's license won't do.

Many elderly and poor were never issued an official birth certificate, and almost no poor and working-class Americans have passports. In fact, only 23% of U.S. citizens have passports. The effect of this "prove you're American" rule is to make it darn hard to vote if you arrived from the rural South and were born outside a hospital, but darn easy if you've just had your passport renewed to ski in the Alps.

The aim must be to change voter registries from profiles of the nation to guest lists for the select.

And it's working. In the first year after Proposition 200 went into effect in Arizona, one-third of new Phoenix-area residents were denied the right to vote. An ACLU monitor determined that rejections were concentrated among "the poor." In Arizona, that means "Hispanic." Yet, if these rejectees, more than ten thousand of them, are, in fact, illegal immigrants, shouldn't they be busted and deported? That should be easy because they've *given their addresses* on the registration form.

So I called Arizona Secretary of State Jan Brewer—the state official charged with overseeing this Proposition 200—to ask how many illegal immigrant voters she's nabbed. No one in her office could come up with a single instance of uncovering an illegal alien among these rejected voters. (I should mention that Ms. Brewer was also Arizona cochair of the Bush reelection campaign.)

Watching the Big Brown-Out in Arizona caused by Proposition 200, Republicans in Washington began to salivate like hound dogs under a rotting rump steak. Congressman Henry Hyde (R-Ill), never one to let democracy get in the way of a fresh ballot-bending scheme, sponsored a bill that would impose on all fifty states the requirement that *every* voter, not just new registrants, produce proof of citizenship *and* a photo ID in order to cast a ballot. It's such an obviously mad, biased, and blatant attack on the right to vote that it passed overwhelmingly in the Republican-controlled House. Our nation should be grateful that the Senate, as of this writing, is still dawdling over the matter.

The Crusade Against the League of Women Voters

To make certain that do-gooder groups don't fix the fall in registrations through voter drives, the past four years have seen the rise of new rules to block registration campaigns among the poor. Florida is typical of Republican-controlled states. There, Sue Cobb, the Secretary of State appointed by Jeb Bush, threatened to enforce these new, twisted state laws and issue the League of Women Voters and individual volunteers with fines running to thousands of dollars for errors in submitting registration forms. That threatens to put the little ladies with the clipboards out of business. The League says it can't take the risk: just fourteen forms misplaced by a volunteer would bankrupt the organization. Political parties themselves are exempt from the fines.

But don't assume it's always the GOP that holds the electoral lynching rope. In Georgia, in 2006, then–Secretary of State Cathy Cox imposed a set of roadblocks to voter registration drives, disallowing all bundled registration sheets, barring groups from helping voters fill out the complex forms, outlawing photocopying of forms (necessary for groups to track if voters are rejected), and preventing anyone who is not "deputized" by the state from collecting a form.

Cox is, like her former Senator, Zell Miller, a nominal Democrat. Like Zell, her actions suggest that she has a deep-seated fear of a Black majority within her own party.

Luckily, a state judge could smell the old Jim Crow tactics a mile away and slapped down most of Cox's anti-voter tricks as unconstitutional. Still, there were enough roadblocks thrown up to new Black voters by the Cox wing of the Democratic Party to successfully defeat their targeted Congressperson. Unfortunately, their target, incumbent Cynthia McKinney, is a Democratic, though much despised by the party's elite. The blockades to Black voters registering helped defeat the renegade Congresswoman, but this "triumph" cost the Democratic leaders some races where those missing Black votes might have made the difference. Among the losers: gubernatorial candidate Cathy Cox.

Ultimately, barriers to registration are not about race or even party. Registration blockades are simply a new front in the class war. Registering to vote is rapidly turning into an exclusive privilege of the privileged. The percentage of Americans with incomes under $15,000 registered to vote has, for the first time in memory, dropped below 50% of those eligible. This is not, as the media have it, because low-income Americans don't give a damn about voting, but because their applications are quietly chucked in the reject pile.

Or, when no one's looking, the registrations are simply erased from the voter rolls altogether, a very common occurrence in . . .

Purgistan

If a poor or dark-skinned voter somehow makes it onto the registration list, staying there is another matter. The second prong of the Republican-led attack on democracy is the purge.

The phony Florida felon purge of 2000 wasn't just an ugly moment in history, it was a practice run for the national GOP. The 2002 HAVA law now *requires* Secretaries of State to "correct" their lists, an invitation to suspect purges.

Civil rights lawyers are getting hip to the faux "felon" purge game, so politicians are finding new grounds to scrub the lists. For example, in 2006, using the new HAVA powers, Kentucky's Republican Secretary of State discovered that 8,000 residents of his state were also registered in another state, intent on voting twice. He wiped their names off the voter rolls—and did not even bother to notify these double-dippers. Oddly, he couldn't identify a single case of someone actually voting in two states, but hey, he stopped them before they could carry out their double-voting scheme.

Or maybe he didn't. It appears he only discovered that, in a nation of nearly a third of billion people, several have the same name and birthday. An artifact of slavery is the commonality of names among African-Americans. This makes Black voters especially vulnerable to purges based on simple database name matches. Did the Kentucky Secretary of State, a Republican, know he'd nail thousands of innocent Black voters? A judge *did* notice and reversed the purge as unconstitutional (albeit *after* the election).

There's as many ways to purge a voter list as a Secretary of State can dream up, including purges for "suspect addresses"—the grounds for several hundred thousand challenges secretly orchestrated by the Republican National Committee in 2004. As you'll recall, a suspect address is one housing a Black soldier shipped to Baghdad or wherever our President sends our Hummers for a fill-up.

But the granddaddy of purges, the tried and true method first given a road test by Katherine Harris, the purge of alleged "felons," is still with us. It's not small stuff, either. In June 2006, Georgia's Secretary of State Cox purged 80,000 voters as convicted felons. That's stunning. Given that an ex-con registering in Georgia is committing a new felony, the state must have been in the grip of an unprecedented crime wave. Yet Cox busted not a single one of these recidivist criminals. On the day of the big purge, I flew down to Atlanta and was told by fuming lawyers for Operation PUSH that, as in Florida in 2000, the felon purge directly hit citizens Voting While Black.

In Georgia, it was a boll weevil Democrat who did the purge work, but, as is usually the case, it's the Republicans who grin and reap the electoral windfall.

The Uncle Wiggily Strategy

I *loved* playing Uncle Wiggily when I was five years old. The Bush posse loves to play it *now*. Except that *we* are their tokens, the pieces they move around the elections board.

Let's stop a moment and take a look at what's going on here.

First, they block the registration drives. Then, if you still get a registration form, they reject it. If you get past their rejection gauntlet, they purge your registration.

These are the first moves of what I call the Uncle Wiggily Strategy. In this old 1916 board game, players have to get past bunny-eating squids, down through rabbit holes, and out of traps and thickets to get to Dr. Possum's house. It's an obstacle course where winning is based on a roll of the dice.

In the 2008 election edition of Uncle Wiggily, the dice are loaded against players who are Hispanic, Black, poor or "itinerant" (i.e., students). It's the crowd without too many passports, otherwise known as "heavily Democratic voters."

For those looking for The Trick for 2008—mucking with computer touch-screens—forget it. It's not one trick, it's an entire game. The program is to create a series of hurdles where, at each stage, another small percentage of colored voters (that is, the Democratic Blue ones), lose their rights.

So far we've talked about HAVA's roadblocks to registration. But the obstacle course has hardly begun.Those voters that succeed in registering and avoid the purge monsters are still a long way from Dr. Possum's polling station.

Today, there are new obstacles between you and the voting booth. Then, if you do make it into the poll, there are several new, sophisticated barriers to getting a real ballot. Then, if you manage to get a ballot, there's a darn good chance your vote simply won't get counted.

The Cast-Your-Vote Obstacle Course

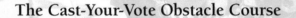

Oh, no! You're not the "verification list"! *Registration rejected!*

Oops! You've got the same name and race as a felon! *You're "scrubbed"!*

Sorry! You've got the wrong ID! *Take a provisional ballot!*

Ha-ha! You're provisional ballot's *rejected!*

Oh my! Machine error. Your ballot is "spoiled." *It doesn't count!*

Too bad! You're on a "caging list." Your absentee ballot is *voided!*

Tough Luck! Electronic voting: You can't get a re-count.

How to make 6 million voters disappear!!

	2004 Election actual	2008 Election projected
Registrations rejected	1,614,196	2,400,000
Voters wrongly purged	*est.* 300,000	300,000
Voters turned away—wrong ID	300,000	600,000
Ballots cast and not counted:		
Provisional ballots rejected	1,090,729	1,500,000
Ballots "spoiled"	1,389,231	1,000,000
Absentee ballots rejected	526,420	600,000
Total votes disappeared	**5,220,576**	**6,400,000**

2004 figures based on U.S. Elections Assistance Commission data. See Chapter 4 for 3 million ballots cast but not counted in 2004. Projecting the future "nega-vote" is tricky business, but some reasoned estimate is worth doing. Given the 2006 HAVA change, we can conservatively estimate registration rejections rising by 50%; new state laws should easily double voters rejected for wrong ID—another 300,000 will receive provisional ballots thereby accounting for the projected increase in provisional ballots rejected. Absentee ballots rejected should remain as sizable as in 2004—though new voting machines should *reduce* ballot spoilage (including unintentional under- and over-vote). Don't like my figures? Well, what're *yours?*

Obstacle Course Democracy

Once voters get past the registration blockade and somehow cling on to the registry, there's still the matter of actually getting a ballot.

Some of the tricks are just raw. More effective than giving "enemy" voters suspect touch-screen voting machines is to give them none at all. In 2004, in Chaves County, New Mexico, Republicans placed the only early voting station in a white shopping center, an hour's drive from the Hispanic neighborhoods. In Jacksonville, there was, astonishingly, only one early voting station, placed a long way from the Black townships of what is, in square miles, America's largest city.

In Ohio, the "No Colored Voters" operation was far more scientific. In Chapter 4, we calculated with grim accuracy that Democrats lost 85,950 votes to long lines. What we've learned since our first edition, thanks to the stellar sleuthing of investigators Bob Fitrakis and Harvey Wasserman, is that Republican operatives deliberately *removed* one in four voting machines from key Democratic precincts, guaranteeing six- and seven-hour waits on Election Day. The smoking gun is appended here. The numbers you see there are

Columbus	4	D	11507
Columbus	4	D	11508
Columbus	4	D	14208
Columbus	4	D	[redacted]
			4
Columbus	5	A	11539
Columbus	5	A	11540
Columbus	5	A	[redacted]
Columbus	5	A	14221
			4
Columbus	5	B	11769
Columbus	5	B	12666
Columbus	5	B	12667
Columbus	5	B	[redacted]
			4
Columbus	5	C	11543
Columbus	5	C	11556
Columbus	5	C	11559
Columbus	5	C	[redacted]
			4
Columbus	5	D	11541
Columbus	5	D	11542
Columbus	5	D	14298
Columbus	5	D	[redacted]
			4
Columbus	6	A	11519
Columbus	6	A	11520
Columbus	6	A	14276
Columbus	6	A	[redacted]
			4
Columbus	6	B	11521
Columbus	6	B	11522
Columbus	6	B	11533
Columbus	6	B	11534
Columbus	6	B	[redacted]
			5

Who crossed out these machines –

Someone removed one machine per precinct in Democrat-heavy Columbus, Ohio. Fewer machines=longer lines.

serial IDs for voting machines in Black precincts. Note that a line was drawn through one machine serial number in each precinct—evidence of a deliberate program to reduce the number of voting machines to create those impossibly long lines.

ID: Can You Prove That You Are You?

Now that you've made it to the polling station, *show me your ID, buddy.*

Are you *you*? Can you prove it?

Andrew Young, the former Atlanta mayor, said, "requiring ID can help poor people." Martin Luther King called Young, "my favorite Republican." He's not mine. Young served on the board of the Barrick Gold Corporation of Canada—he took George Bush Sr.'s post—one of the world's top-paying board memberships. I don't know which poor owners of Barrick's gold mines he polled to reach his conclusion, but African-American voters in Louisiana, for example, are only one-fifth as likely as white voters to have the photo ID that would qualify them to vote under proposed legislation. That figure may be too optimistic; it came from a survey by the U.S. Justice Department taken before the voters' IDs got washed away by Hurricane Katrina.

I'm not going to repeat the stories of Chapter 4 about the games that can be played with ID to knock out voters of the wrong racial or political tint. I must remind you that 300,000 voters were turned away from polls because of a challenge to their ID in 2004. (Notably, none of this crew of "illegal" voters was charged with attempting to vote illegally.) Since the 2004 test run of ID disenfranchisement tricks, a dozen states, including Louisiana and Florida, every one a presidential swing state, passed or are expected to pass new photo-ID requirement laws, tripling the number of voters getting carded. If the same rejection rate applies to all the new states adding ID restrictions, we can also expect to see a tripling of the number of voters turned away at the polling station. That is, it would not be unreasonable to expect 1.2 million voters to lose their vote in 2008 due to ID challenges.

If you have any doubt about who these laws are aimed at, just look at whom the law does *not* apply to. Some states with tough ID requirements (most states have none) allow what I call the "Good Ol' Boy exemption." Alabama, for example, gives a voter without any ID a ballot if he's "identified by two poll workers," as in, "Oh, that's Clem, he's a good ol' boy—just give him a ballot." If you aren't in Clem's club, well, buzz off.

Provisionally Caged

You've jumped past the man-eating registrars, waited two hours in line, and finally get your ballot. But it's *provisional,* that HAVA-created placebo ballot meant to fool you into thinking you have a vote.

Not everyone gets a fake-o ballot. Provisional balloting was almost unheard of in suburbs except among voters with "unusual" names, as the Brennan Center politely puts it. For example, John Brakey of the Arizona poll-watching group AUDIT AZ told us that on Election Day 2004, "One voter had the name Juarez. The poll workers looked it up as a W and then pushed him over to a provisional." Brakey recorded one after another Hispanic getting the Brown-ballot provisional treatment. He filed a complaint with Secretary of State Jan Brewer, but she must have been too busy running the Bush for reelection campaign to act on his findings.

Lucas County, Ohio, is a typical case. In 2004, just four wards of inner-city Toledo, with only 7.8% of the county's voters, accounted for nearly half of all provisional votes in the county. These provisional ballots were shoved onto voters, almost all of them African-Americans with "suspect addresses." Maybe the addresses were "suspect" because 86% of the residents of those districts voted Democratic.

The problem with provisional ballots is that a third of them *don't get counted.* They are tossed out by partisan Secretaries of State on arbitrary "gotcha" rules. In Ohio in 2004, poll workers gave desperate voters, some waiting three, five, or seven hours in the rain, the option of filling out provisional ballots if they had to leave. The Republican Secretary of State then barred counting them.

In 2008, the rise in provisional ballots will be the new version of the "caging lists," the secret scrub sheets that the RNC used in 2004 to challenge new Black voters. Many of those challenged for voting from "suspect" addresses, you will recall, were Black soldiers assigned overseas. First-class letters sent by the RNC to their homes, when returned, were then used as evidence to block the counting of their votes.

Will the Republicans use these racially poisoned hit sheets again? After the BBC uncovered this smelly plan in October 2004 to whack Black voters by the hundreds of the thousands, U.S. media reacted with deafening silence. As a result, in most states, the challenge game went unchallenged. So you can bet they'll do it again, adding "suspect citizenship status" to their "suspect address" lists. Black and Hispanic soldiers in Baghdad will be more likely than ever to have their mail-in votes blown away.

In 2004, those provisional ballots could have been counted, and the presidential vote for Bush overturned in Ohio, New Mexico, and Iowa, but the Democratic Party stood down its attorneys in those states, believing it wouldn't "make a difference" in the outcome.[2]

However, the Democrats' general failure to confront the rejection of provisional ballots in 2004 bit them in the behind in 2006. Democrats lost North Carolina's Eighth Congressional district by a ridiculous 329 votes—after Republicans were able to shift more than 1,000 voters to provisional ballots. Failure to defend provisional voters will undoubtedly make a difference in 2008, because so long as Republicans know they won't be challenged over their provisional gaming, it

---

[2]I must acknowledge that Florida Democratic Party lawyers threatened to enjoin the Republicans using their challenge lists in that state—a rare bit of hell-raising that was partially successful. As a journalist working the story for the BBC, I couldn't give them the help they requested, but I can applaud their efforts to protect voters' civil rights.

would be fair to expect the GOP to increase their "caging" and challenge operation. Don't be surprised to see the 1.1 million provisional ballots rejected in 2004 to rise to 2 million in 2008.

Absent-minded Voting

Some fed-up citizens may try to avoid the long lines and challenge lists by mailing in their votes "absentee." But Uncle Wiggily doesn't always read his mail. A record three-quarters of a million absentee ballots were rejected in 2004.

These mail-in ballots were lost with nary a peep from the national Democratic Party. Unchallenged, we can expect the Rove-bots will be thinking of new ways to dump absentee ballots in the dead-letter file in 2008. Here's one: HAVA now requires states to demand ID from new voters who didn't provide verified ID when registering. That's just about every Black and Brown voter registered in those church-sponsored drives. If the absentee ballot is mailed in without proof of identity or, in some states, citizenship, the ballots will be tossed out when challenged. And believe me, they will be challenged.

The Digitally Disappeared

You're halfway through the shoots and ladders of the voting game-board, safe in that voting booth. You hold your breath, close your eyes, and make a choice.

Now the real fun begins. You know you voted, but does the machine know? As they found out in the pueblos of New Mexico, you can pull the lever until your arm hurts and punch that card in Ohio harder than Muhammad Ali, and still you're recorded as an "undervote"—no choice recorded. Or in the county offices, the optical scanner finds your ballot "unreadable" as we discovered in Gadsden, Florida. Oddly, as we've explained, this "spoilage" happens almost exclusively (88% of the time) in minority and low-income areas.

And it will happen again, but with a digital twist. As touch-screen voting replaces democracy, spoilage will take a new form: machines that jam, zap, and send your vote to outer space. Just because I've said that touch-screen voting isn't danger #1 doesn't mean it isn't a danger nonetheless. The biggest threat, however, is not in suspect software (which you have good reason to lose sleep over), but in the oldest trick in the book—machines meant to confuse voters, frustrate them, or simply not work.

And that's how the Republicans held on to Katherine Harris' Congressional seat in the 2006 midterm election. (Harris had already given up that post to run—and lose—for Senate. The Republicans put up Vern Buchanan.) Harris' Sarasota district was in a bad mood, angry about the war; so angry, in fact, that 17,846 of them drove to the polls, waited in line, then cast their ballots for . . . *nobody* for Congress. The "Indian Indecision" we saw in New Mexico in 2004 seems to have spread.

At least that's what the computers said: One out of six voters, according the print-outs, simply did not make a choice in the hottest Congressional race in the nation. And so the Republicans declared victory by a dinky 369 votes—not counting those 17,846 supposedly "blank" ballots.

Funny thing about those 17,846 people who waited in line not to vote for Congress: Most of them were Democrats. I'm not guessing about that. The fifty-two precincts with the highest Democratic registration matches nicely with the fifty-two precincts with the highest number of missing votes.

Obviously, a recount is in order. But that's not possible. For the first time in Sarasota history, all Election Day voting was done on touch-screen computers. So it's physically impossible to check those supposedly blank ballots—they're floating lost in cyberspace. Forever.

The votes disappeared on touch-screens called the "iVotronics." One of Harris' final acts as Florida Secretary of State was to demand all counties adopt the iVotronics machine—the only electronic machine she certified for elections. In Sarasota, 14,000 local voters signed a petition to reject touch-screen voting. This was *before* the 2006 midterm election. Sarasota's Republican Elections Supervisor Kathy Dent made a special presentation to the county Republican Committee to resist the public's demand for paper ballots. She pleaded that the party should back her decision to use ballots that cannot be recounted. Why?

So what went wrong in Sarasota? Or, should I say, if you're a Republican, "What went right?" I contacted the top independent expert on the iVotronics computers used in Sarasota. Professor Douglas Jones at the University of Iowa told me that the strange differences between the reported look of the screens in some Democratic precincts could be explained by "corruption" of the "ballot image file." That's a fancy way for saying that the virtual buttons on the screen may not align with the touch-sensitive electronic targets behind them. Think of what you see on a touch-screen machine as a Halloween mask covering a real face underneath. You touch the eye hole, but the mask is misaligned, and you're actually touching someone's nose. You can touch, punch, or slam the square "button" for your candidate, but the computer won't feel it or record it unless you touch the screen, say, a half-inch farther to the right.

There was another possible "glitch" on the iVotronics robo-ballot, a horribly designed "graphic user interface," which made it hard to find, let alone correct, errors in voting in the Congressional race. Elections Supervisor Dent was warned of this "glitch" at least two weeks before Election Day and steadfastly refused to take timely action.

Elections Supervisor Ion Sancho of Leon County (Tallahassee), that rare nonpartisan voting official, told me, "If you're going to have a glitch bend an election, this is one way you could do it" (graphics and image file corruption) without getting caught deliberately finagling the results. Ignoring the misalignment of virtual buttons is a much more subtle way to bias the vote count than much-feared tampering with software that turns votes for Democrats into votes for Republicans.

Now note that it is not in any way necessary for an official to take deliberate, conspiratorial action to bend the vote. What's at work here is "vulture opportunism"—just ignoring, willfully, problems that happen to benefit your candidate. In Florida, whether it's crashed computers in Sarasota in 2006 (and Broward County in 2004) or error-filled "purge" sheets, the fix seems to come well after the election, if at all, when it's Democrats who lose their votes.

Of course, the problem in Florida could have been that, for some reason, computers prefer Republicans.

Now I don't want to imply that there was something wrong with the machines. After all, after the election, Dent certified that voters did not encounter technical problems in voting. Furthermore, the state elections board accepted her certification. The board is headed by Governor Jeb Bush.

But Florida isn't America. Or is it? Nationwide, the number of ballots cast blank in Congressional races in the 2006 midterm election— glitches, I'm sure—approached *one million*. But hey, who's counting?

Expect to see more of the unfortunate accidental breakdowns that, as we saw beginning in 2002 in Florida's Broward County, only seem to happen with computers in Black precincts. This technical failure game, first practiced in 2002, was perfected in 2004 and 2006, and will reach disaster levels in 2008 as the avalanche of new untried machines rolls in. It will be an "accident." It always is an "accident."

But it's not all grim. Because of crusading groups like Voter Action and the ACLU, we can expect to see a major decline in the number of unrecorded votes ("undervotes") and ruined ballots ("spoilage") in 2008, compared to the 1.4 million ballots that "disappeared" in 2004. With fewer chad-making punch-card machines and the replacement of busted-lever machines, the result of lawsuits and progressive political action, there should be half a million fewer undervotes in 2008. So we *don't* lose 'em all—but we haven't won it yet.

In 2004, I've noted, 3.6 million ballots were cast and never counted—undervotes, spoiled votes, plus rejected provisional and absentee ballots. That sum was calculated from the raw data of the

Federal Elections Assistance Commission, which, at this writing, has not yet divulged the "nega-vote" data for the 2006 midterm elections.

But there's another way to find out how many ballots ended up in the Bermuda Triangle. Ask the voters. The exit polls of the '04 presidential race implied that 3.5 million ballots were never tallied. That matched the noncount in the federal data. (Voters telling exit pollsters how they voted don't know if their vote was counted, so it's reasonable to expect the difference between exit polls and the official count to equal to the "undervote.") Statistician Steve Freeman of the University of Pennsylvania calculated that the 2006 exit polls suggest an additional 3.9% vote for Democratic candidates for Congress that did not show up in the official vote tallied. That suggests 3 million Democratic votes were lost somewhere—glitches, spoilage, undervote, rejections, the whole lot. The trend is not promising. The presidential race of 2008 will bring out many more voters than the 2006 midterms, roughly 120 million citizens. A 3.9% glitch rate would mean 4.7 million votes will simply go *fffft!*

Democracy in a Box: Dangers Down the Wire

We've made it past the registration roadblocks, jumped the provisional ballot turnstile, and we hope we've not been "spoiled," but then we still have to total up the votes.

With all the panic about touch-screen voting, not many voters realize that most computerization—and the opportunity for shenanigans—is happening "down the wire." You may vote on a paper ballot fed into a scanner. The ballot is paper, but the vote is *tabulated* on a computer receiving a message from the scanner. The good old system of calling in the vote to government offices while TV cameras roll is pretty much defunct.

Now the vote count is privatized, propriety and secretive. And sometimes the private operators hired to gather and total votes make errors, like leaving John Kerry's votes off some precinct totals as we saw on the tabulation sheet reproduced in Chapter 4. Tabulating votes by hand, done worldwide, is cheap, efficient, visible, and subject to public scrutiny. Why use the expensive, complex, and opaque high-tech methods to count the vote? Maybe some politicians see an advantage in black-box vote counting.

One official who saw an advantage in electronic voting is Franklin County (Columbus) Ohio Elections Director Matthew Damschroder. Damschroder enthusiastically took a check for $10,000 from a Diebold Corporation lobbyist in 2005 made out to the local Republican Party, which the elections director chairs. That was against the law—but only because he accepted the check in the elections office. Had he simply stepped outside the door, as other elections officials had, it would have been perfectly okay. After a thirty-day suspension from his post, Damschroder has returned to preside over the integrity of the Columbus voting system for the 2008 race. Damschroder pushed to buy electronic voting machines. I'm not saying the ten grand from the machine maker influenced his decision.

You Can't Recount If You Don't Count in the First Place

The fight over the "recount" of the Florida vote of 2000 was not, in fact, to count ballots a second time, but to force officials to look again at the "spoiled" or allegedly "blank" ballots that were never counted in the first place. Over 27,000 flawed ballots from the Black precincts of Jacksonville could not be read by machines—but humans could have read them if Secretary of State Katherine Harris had not barred it.

(Notably, when Republican chads are left hanging, the Red Party gets creative. In GOP-controlled Delaware County, lawyer Cliff Arnebeck discovered that officials gave the ballots to a mentally disabled "chad scraper" to scrape off the dangling votes so they could be counted. The frustrated attorney told me that it is quite difficult to depose a mentally handicapped man about his ballot-scraping methods—nor ask who directed this strange activity that helped decide the presidency of the United States.)

Florida eliminated that problem of a difficult recount by eliminating the right to an automatic recount in close elections.

There is no sense complaining about the new Florida law, because, with the introduction of touch-screen voting, there is nothing to recount. Demands to force a "recount" in electronic races are sad acts of self-delusion: You can't recount electrons. We should all be grateful that our Founding Fathers wrote the Bill of Rights on paper. Had they recorded it only on a touch-screen computer, Dick Cheney now would be telling us the Bill of Rights begins with the Second Amendment.

Paper ballot elections are feasible and cheap: 40 million Mexicans voted for President by paper ballot in July 2006.

Commitment to the Count

Of course, that Mexican election was stolen blatantly, grossly, violently. Which simply tells us that paper ballots are not a guarantee of democracy.

There's no sense in having the security provided by paper ballots unless someone actually counts the ballots. They weren't all counted in Old Mexico in 2006, reminiscent of the failure to count all the votes in New Mexico in 2004. The latter case was a decision by Governor Bill Richardson not to review the allegedly uncountable ballots. In a little-noticed ruling, the New Mexico Supreme Court smacked Richardson for refusing to "recount" those 2004 presidential votes. Not counting the votes was unconstitutional. But their ruling came two years after the fact. Bill Richardson's advisor said that Kerry would have lost anyway; it didn't matter. Didn't matter to *whom*, Bill?

Had Richardson agreed to a recount, which would have certainly handed New Mexico to John Kerry, I will admit it would not have overturned the federal election. Undoubtedly, those black-robed bandits called "the Supreme Court majority" would have figured out a way to frustrate the result. Fine then, *make* them steal it.

If they know you won't demand a recount, they won't count the votes in the first place. And that's what will happen in New Mexico in 2008 and Arizona, Nevada, Louisiana, Colorado, and other states where 2008 will be stolen.

So, *what are you going to do about it?*

First Thing You Do Is . . . *Steal Back Your Vote*

After I published the first edition of *Armed Madhouse*, I was just stunned at the number of readers who told me,

> So what's the *point?* If they're going to steal the election, steal the Treasury, and then put duct tape over the media's eyes and mouths, *what can we do?*

Until they open the Air America wing at Guantánamo, there's something we *can* do: vote.

But why the hell should I bother voting if the creeps are just going to steal my vote anyway?

Answer: Because that's exactly what they *want* you to say—that you're ready to give up, to let them have it. Just put out the silverware in front of the door, with a sign: BURGLARS, PLEASE TAKE. Just because ChoicePoint's out there hawking your identity doesn't mean you should write your MasterCard number on the mirror in the men's room at JFK International Airport.

Did Ben Franklin tell Thomas Jefferson to go fly a kite? When Martin Luther King had a dream, he didn't go back to sleep—he went into action. He didn't say, "I guess they don't want us to vote, so let's just skip it."

In 2006, filming in the Lower Ninth Ward of New Orleans, a year after the flood, still a wasteland of houses turned to driftwood, I found one stubborn old character, Henry Irving Sr., rebuilding his home in the middle of the ruins. Officialdom wants the Black neighborhoods sealed off and abandoned, but Mr. Irving was pounding nails and planting hydrangeas. Why? He said, "If two centuries ago, the

Founding Fathers had given in to the King of England without a fight, today we'd all be speaking English!" (He added, "Well, you know what I'm saying"—and we do.)

I didn't write this book with the idea that it would be an excuse for you to put your thumb in your tailpipe and whistle, "Don't Worry, Be Happy."

I think about the young Chicana in Little Texas, who said in tears, when her ID was rejected, "They don't want me to vote." That's exactly why she *should* vote—because they don't want her to. And why *we* should vote, because they won't let her vote count.

So if they're going to steal your vote—and they will—the first thing you do is, *steal it back.*

Here are a few dirt-simple steps.

1. Vote Early and Vote Often

Every state now lets voters cast ballots in designated polling stations and at county offices in the weeks before Election Day. Do it. Don't wait until Election Day to find out you have the wrong ID, your registration's "inactive," or you're on a challenge list. By Election Day, there's little to do but hold up the line.

And bring a posse. Voting, like bowling and love, is something you shouldn't do alone. "Arrive with five," as Jesse Jackson says. (The cost of that rhyme, by the way, was that Black voters in Florida were busted for excess passengers in a vehicle. I kid you not.)

2. *Don't Don't DON'T* Mail in Your Ballot

The *American Slang Dictionary* defines "going postal" as "a form of insanity," an appropriate description of voting by mail. In 2004, millions of progressives went postal, mailing in their ballots in that weird hope that they could avoid touch-screen computers and with their mail-in ballot, create a "paper trail." In 2004, in swing states like Florida, mail-in ballot requests were up 500% compared to the 2000 election.

For those of you who mailed in your ballot, please tell me, *what happened to it?* You don't know, do you? I can tell you that officially, three-fourths of a million absentee ballots were never counted, on the flimsiest technical excuses. And you won't even know it.[3]

Furthermore, tens of thousands of ballots are not mailed to voters in time to return them—in which case you're out of luck. Most states won't let you vote in-precinct once you've applied to vote absentee.

Every time I hear of a voter going "absentee" to avoid computer screens, I want to "go postal" myself. And maybe that's what it takes, a threat of violence. So here it is: *Just put down that postage stamp and no one gets hurt.*

3. Register and Register and Register

Think you're registered to vote? Check online with your Secretary of State's office or call your County Board of Elections. Then register your girlfriend, your wife, your mailman, and your mommy. Contact Operation PUSH, the League of Women Voters, and your local party organization, and commit to a couple of days of door-to-door registration, especially in minority neighborhoods or at social service agency offices. Instead of a condom, include a voter registration form in every Valentine's chocolate box.

In Ohio, as in some other states, the creepy new regulations used to hinder drives apply only to *paid* registration gatherers, not volunteers. The inexcusable shame is that the Democratic Party has to employ mercenaries to gather registrations. So go out and register voters. What are you doing this Thursday that's more important?

[3]Yes, there are exceptions: when in-station voting is impossible or in Oregon. That Left-coast state distinguishes itself from all others by notifying mail voters if their ballot has a problem and allowing a correction.

4. Vote Unconditionally, Not Provisionally

In 2008, they'll be handing out provisional ballots like candy, especially to Hispanic voters. If your right to vote is challenged, don't accept a provisional ballot that will likely not get counted no matter what the sweet little lady at the table tells you. She won't decide; partisan sharks will. Demand adjudication from poll judges on the spot; demand a call to the supervisor of elections; or return with acceptable ID if possible.

And be a champ: defend the rights of others. If you've taken Step 1 above and voted early, you have Election Day free to be a poll watcher. You'll need training and credentials either from a voter group or, in some states, a designation from a political party. Then challenge the challengers, the weird guys with BlackBerrys containing lists of "suspect" voters. Be firm, but no biting.

5. Join the Party

Any party. You can't influence them unless you're in them.

A lot of progressives think we need a third party in the USA. I'd settle for a *second* party. Instead of bellyaching about the Democratic Party, show up at those deadly dull local committee meetings, become a loudmouth activist, or run for committee person.

Same advice if you're a Republican: go to their meetings. Dress like Lincoln. Or his page.

6. Join the Insurgency

Don't rely on the parties. If you think the Democrats or Republicans will save your vote, forget it. In America, leaders are followers. They lead from behind. And that's how it *should* be in a democracy. We saw how Franklin Roosevelt only stamped his name on the New Deal *after* a million malcontents signed the insurgent "Share the Wealth" pledge. Paul Krugman told me, "We need to find a new Franklin Roosevelt." I disagree—if we create the movement, a Franklin Roosevelt will find *us*.

Start by hanging around with other democracy junkies. The list of groups to sign up with is a book in itself, but I'll begin with the spearheads of ballot reform: the Election Defense Alliance (www.Election DefenseAlliance.org), the Rainbow/PUSH Coalition, Network of Citizens (NetworkofCitizens.org), the Election Protection Coalition (via www.PFAW.org) that includes everyone from the Lawyers' Committee for Civil Rights under Law (www.LawyersComm.org), the Brennan Center for Justice, the ACLU, People for the American Way, the NAACP Voter Protection Fund, Democracy for America, Alliance for Democracy, ACORN, True Majority, Velvet Revolution, the state Voter Action Groups (can't list them all), the National Committee for Voting Integrity (via www.EPIC.org)—and others who will undoubtedly send me threatening letters for leaving them off this list (I love you all, but space is limited). Check www.ArmedMadhouse.com for more.

7. Occupy Ohio, Invade Nevada

If George Bush can drop democracy on Iraq from a B-52, why not occupy Ohio to insure the vote? The next election likely will be stolen in Nevada, so let's invade now.

However, I'd prefer to forestall the military option and invade states with poll workers.

The revolution will not be podcast. Let go of that mouse, get out of your PJs and take the resistance door to door—to register the vote, to canvass the voters, to get out the vote. Donate time to your union (if you're not in a union, why not?) or to the troublemakers I've already listed here and in the acknowledgments. This may seem a stupendously unoriginal suggestion, but I know of no other method more effective for confronting the armed and dangerous junta that has seized the White House.

8. Sue the Bastards

There aren't enough lawyers in America—at least not enough pushing back against the vote-fixing tide. But there are some. Shining examples include Bob Fitrakis and Cliff Arnebeck suing the state of Ohio to enjoin official "voter suppression tactics" and "vote tampering"; Lowell Findlay, who successfully took on the state of New Mexico's vote-destroying operations; People for the American Way, the NAACP Advancement Project, and the others in the Election Protection Coalition who maintain Election Day flying anti-suppression squads nationally; Bobby Kennedy Jr., Mike Papantonio, and Mike McCabe, who have aimed their lances at no-paper-trail voting, and . . . the list goes on.

You don't have to be an attorney to join the fight. These are political battles, in all cases supported by street-fighting activists who rouse the public behind the legal actions. Courtroom successes are rare. It's the exposure of shenanigans uncovered in documents churned up by the suits that has forced officials in New Mexico, Wisconsin, and elsewhere to clean up their act.

What is probably the most important legal battle hardly gets a line of newsprint: I've written about hundreds of thousands of vulnerable citizens who have wrongly lost their vote by being falsely identified as ex-cons. But what of those who, indeed, have a criminal record in their past? There are a breathtaking, election-changing 5.3 million citizens still barred from the polling stations because of some prior conviction. The Right to Vote campaign is fighting this Soviet-style loss of citizenship. Notably, lifetime loss of citizenship is imposed by only seven states of the Old Confederacy under laws originally created at the behest of the Ku Klux Klan.

9. Make the Democratic Demand: *No Vote Left Behind!*

For six years, I had this crazy fantasy in my head. In it, an election is stolen and the guy who's wrongly declared the loser stands up in front of the White House and says three magic words: *"Count the votes."*

In July 2006, my dream came true. Unfortunately, it was in Spanish—but I'll take what I can get. There was Andrés Manuel López Obrador, presidential challenger, standing in the "Zocalo," the square in front of Mexico's White House, telling the ruling clique inside, *"Count the votes!"*

Most important, his simple demand was echoed by half a million pissed-off, activated voters chanting with him, *"Voto por voto!"*—vote by vote.

In the Mexican election, 904,000 votes were "null"—four times the ruling party's alleged margin of victory. That is, nearly 1 million ballots were cast supposedly without a choice for president (which was the only race on the ballot). Here was the same undervote and spoilage game we saw in the USA in 2000 and 2004. It was *Florida con salsa*. But López Obrador, the un-Gore, demanded those empty ballots be opened in public and counted.

I'd like to tell you that López Obrador's courageous stand in Mexico in 2006 paid off as well. It will, but not yet. The ballots were never counted, and Mexico's ruling clique continues to rule to the cackling glee of the elite in Washington. However, the demand for democracy doesn't always fail. Mass demonstrations demanding a full vote count overturned election fraud in Ukraine (2004), Peru (2000), and Serbia (also in 2000).

In July 2004, candidate John Kerry told the NAACP that four years earlier, 1 million Black ballots weren't counted and, "I will not let that happen again." Then he let it happen again. Worse, actually. According to an insider, his campaign told the NAACP lawyers to back off from challenging the non-count in Ohio. Don't count on millionaires to count your vote.

You can have all the paper ballots in the world, but if you don't demand to *look* at them, publicly, in a recount, you might as well mark them with invisible ink.

Uncle Wiggily Goes to War

Traveling the USA, I'm asked again and again, after I explain the creepy details of how the last two presidential elections were fixed, stuffed, and shoplifted, *Why don't the Democrats scream bloody murder?*

It's not about a political party's electoral *cojones*; it's about a devotion to *democracy* deep in the bone. Weirdly, some candidates that call themselves "Democrats" seem kind of, well, *indifferent* to democracy. The reason is, elections are the radical weapon of the working class—the great leveler of the powerless against the too-powerful. But the candidates themselves, both Republican and Democrat, tend to come from the privileged and pampered class. Votes are just the surfboards on which their ambitions ride.

It's war out there—class war. If truth is the first casualty of war, your vote is second to be shot down. And now we are more vulnerable to attack than ever. Outside Baton Rouge at the Exxon refinery, I looked across the row on row of cheap mobile homes dumped in the middle of nowhere, near nothing save a Wal-Mart. Everyone in the grim encampment I spoke with had a job in New Orleans until the hurricane. The Bush men could have placed the mobile homes on these survivors' properties so they could be hired to rebuild their city. But the jobs in New Orleans are going to itinerant workers, most from Latin America. They don't vote and that's the way the Administration in Washington and the city's burghers like it.

Why let two hundred thousand displaced, angry, working-class and poor New Orleanians return home to vent their justified anger on the President and Mayor? We know why the President's men are happy to drown them in a Republican sea in Houston, isolate them in punishment camps until they give up and leave to join relatives in New York or Atlanta. The Diaspora is Democratic. But why does the Democratic Mayor of New Orleans fear their return?

To make sure they don't return, FEMA and the city have welded bars across the doors of some of the only dry, safe housing left in the city—the public housing complexes, beautiful townhouses much coveted by real estate developers. African-American leader Malik Rahim, who, in the face of official hostility, is leading New Orleanians to rebuild homes for themselves, said, "They just don't want them poor niggers back. And that's the bottom line." By "they," he meant the business elite surrounding Mayor Ray Nagin, a nominal Democrat, whose parents are African-American. The former corporate executive, like those in the Bush camp, foresees a New Orleans unburdened of its sweating port workers; a smaller, genteel city centered on the plantation-style homes of the Garden District and, for income, the Disney-fied Dixieland of the French Quarter for tourists. Call it Six Flags over New Orleans.

Before my encounter with the anti-terror gendarmes, I filmed, just by chance, a woman threatened with arrest when she tried to return to her apartment in the St. Bernard project. She had three kids with her and night was falling. She asked me, "Where'm I going now, mister? That's what I want to know? You tell me, where'm I going now?"

Not to America. Not to the America they're designing for us.

In New Orleans, I was witnessing the building of this New America, where the widening jaws of the income divide separate those who produce from those who profit.

As Christmas 2006 approached, the city began demolition of over four thousand units of housing though residents pleaded for their homes. The same week, 115 families who'd built new homes with Rahim's help received notice of eviction. Also that week, Goldman Sachs announced its investment banking executives would share $16.5 billion in Christmastime bonuses. Some would get over $100 million each.

It used to be that when Americans were under economic attack, whether from a hurricane or the threat of mass job losses, both parties raced to the rescue, competing for votes. In 1979, Congress unanimously signed off on $1 billion in loan guarantees to save Chrysler automotive jobs in Detroit. In 2004, FEMA poured $5.6 billion into the immediate rebuilding of the Florida coast after four hurricanes hit the state.

But today, new calculations are made. What are the electoral consequences of economic rescue? Whose voter do we pull from the flood? Four hundred thousand auto workers have lost their jobs under the bipartisan NAFTA regime. The average family income in Michigan has dropped by $9,914. Where's the life raft? It's safer to disperse and dispose of the losers of the economic wars where they cannot threaten the political courtesans of corporate plutocrats.

So what are you going to do about it?

Every Single Time

Are you discouraged? Well, we don't have time for that. Remember this: In every American generation, we've had to fight for the right to vote.

In 1776, Americans won taxation with representation—but only for white, male landowners. And we've battled to extend the franchise ever since. And, note, incidentally, that with every expansion of the right to vote came expansion of the economic rights of the working class.

It began when a crazy economic populist, Andrew Jackson, the Hugo Chávez of Tennessee, headed a movement that won the vote for the landless (1821 to 1844). Then came the vote for ex-slaves (1869, Fifteenth Amendment to the Constitution); then for women (1920, Nineteenth Amendment); then for the very poor (1964, Twenty-fourth Amendment, repealing the poll tax); then for those ex-slaves' great-grandchildren (1965, Voting Rights Act).

And do you know what each of these fights for the vote had in common? We won every time. When we fight, we win. Every single time.

INSURGENCY USA—JOIN TODAY!

So what can you do about it?

First thing is, sign up at *www.GregPalast.com* for video, audio and print updates of our team's investigations and reports on the Armed Madhouse.

Addicted to War ©Winston Smith 2002

ACKNOWLEDGMENTS, SOURCES, AND RESOURCES

I hold the pen, but this book is, ultimately, the work of dozens of fact-hunters and whistle-blowers more courageous and dedicated than I could ever be. Some cannot be acknowledged publicly. My gratitude and admiration to you all.

My unending thanks and devotion to those who pull the oars on the Greg Palast galley ship, the investigators, researchers, flak-catchers, webmasters, and producers who did the hard work for which I get the credit and they get the unpaid overtime. First and foremost among these, Matt *Give-Me-Slack-or-Give-Me-Death* Pascarella, next-wave 14-hour-a-day info-master, producer putting-it-all-together boy wonder—and the quadri-lingual Leni Badpenny von Eckardt, our undercover punk-a-licious investigatrix extraordinaire.

And to team members Oliver Shykles, researcher, "fairy, peace-nik, tree-hugging asshole," as one jealous reader called him and we love him for it; Duane Moonwalker Andrews, attorney-at-law and web wizard; Philippe Oui-Oui Borde; Rob iPunk Malchow; and deep-digging researchers Phil Tanfield, Marguerite Chandler, Gail Eilat, Lili Wilde and Adrianna Alty; video editor Jonathan Levin; and assistant producer/songstress Marylee Bussard; archivist Vickie Crawford; Charley Allan; and, in Venezuela, Delcy Rodriguez.

And to the nonpareil investigative journalist, my producer at BBC Television *Newsnight,* Meirion Jones, for getting our stories on the air and getting them right and for his reasoned advice ("No no no wrong wrong wrong you're fucking mad") and visionary Peter Barron.

And to all the jack-offs who send me death threats and thereby give me inspiration to live.

To Amy Goodman for *Democracy Now!* not later; for carrying my BBC reports across the electronic Berlin Wall, and to the *Democracy Now!* crew, especially Sharif Abdel-Kouddous and the incomparable Jeremy Scahill; and the lovely John Pilger.

To the radio broadcasters who first carried my samizdat reports: Randi Rhodes, who helped me wrestle the political alligators of the Florida swamps and to the other Air Americans, Janeane Garofalo and Sam Seder; the seditious Mark Riley and Marc Maron; the delicious Laura Flanders; Stacey Taylor, Thom Hartmann and Midnight Mike Malloy; and Al Truth-or-Consequences Franken and especially Wendy Wildes.

To the Pacifica Radio Network and its fearless voices, including Dennis Flash Bernstein, Rob Lorei, Christina Blosdale, Deepa Fernandez and Free Speech Radio, Eileen Sutton, Dred Scott Keyes, the courageous and astonishing Jerry Quickly, Verna Avery Brown; the Radio Free Georgia crew, Ron Pinchback, Sam Husseini (and Accuracy in Media), Renee Blake, Allison Cooper (and Lawyers Guild Radio), Bernard White, Marty Durlin from KGNU, and Alex Jones at the Genesis Radio Network.

To Alan Colmes for quiet intelligent discourse amidst screeching stupidity; to Alan Chartock of Northwest Public Radio; Carmen Jackson and Wisconsin Public Radio; reporter John Nichols and globalization know-it-alls Murray Dobbin, Ellen Gould, Mary Bottari, Lori Wallach, Global Trade Watch and Maude Barlow of Council of Canadians; and especially, Nancy Alexander and Sara Grusky's Citizens' Network on Essential Services, whose research everyone must read at servicesforall.org; the labor union consortium, Public Service International, and Kevin Danaher of Global Exchange and the other half of the dynamite duo, Medea Benjamin of Code Pink; Arun Gupta of Indymedia.

To Ed Asner, Alec Baldwin, Jello Biafra, Jim Hightower, Hon. Cynthia McKinney, Alexandra Paul, Shiva Rose, Brad Friedman and

Larry David for their time, encouragement and for volunteering their inestimable talents for translating my words into live voice. To my legal bodyguard, Bianca Jagger, and follow-the-money mavens Loretta Napoleoni and John Perkins.

To Internet guerrillas Commondreams.org, BartCop.org, Buzz Flash.com, AlterNet, GeorgeWBush.org, TomPaine.com, Salon.com, Truthout and Marc Ash, Scott Thill at Morphizm, and Shahram from MWC News.

To Noam Chomsky, who encourages when others discourage ("Greg, never underestimate the cowardice of intellectuals"), and Howard Zinn for memories of the civil rights movement. To the Reverend Jesse Jackson for the Gospel choir and arming us all for the battle ahead, and for coauthoring our article; and to his family, especially Santita and Congressman Jesse Jr.; and Butch Wing and John Mitchell. And thanks, Reverend, for taking the bagel away from Senator Edwards. And to Martin Luther King III for bringing me to Birmingham.

To Mark Swedlund and Deb Dobish for resuscitating the manuscript, and especially to Tom D'Adamo for begging me to remove the sentence "Tort reform has nothing to do with saving prostitutes from a life of sin."

To my provocative agent, Diana Finch; and Trena Keating, Jake Klisivitch, Susan Schwartz, Carla Bolte, Emily Haynes, Traci Maynigo, Alex Gigante, Clare Ferraro, Helen Conford in London, and the whole crew at Penguin; and Dan Simon, Lars Reilly, Ria Julian at Seven Stories, and Jessie, Maiko and Uli at Alternative Tentacles, Fat Mike at Fat Wreck Chords.

And to selfless activists especially Kat L'Estrange, who may singly prevent the theft of the next election: Hollis Jacobson, Ellen Thiessen, Warren Stewart, Lowell Findley, John Boyd, Linda Yardley and Voter Action New Mexico; People for the American Way; the visionary Greg Moore at the NAACP Voter Protection Fund; Lou Posner and Voter-March Patrick Bergy and Jay Crocker; Antonia Juhasz for the skinny on Iraq; Chris Hoofnagle, Lillie Coney and the better-than-anencyclopedia Wayne Madsen at the Electronic Privacy Information Center (EPIC.org); and for assistance from OpenSecrets.org., Christy Speicher, Charlene Johnstone at Democracy for America; and Howard Dean, who gets it; Roger Trilling, Liz Mescall, visionary Ed Rampell, Matt Blake; Daphne Wysham and the Institute for Policy Studies; Richard Luckett of AgitProperties, Michael Kieschnick and Lucy Radcliffe of Working Assets, Ronnie Dugger and Alliance for Democracy, Suzan Erem, Alex from Truth on Tees, Blase and Theresa Bonpane of Office of the Americas, and a big up to Tanja Winter and Martin Eder at Activist San Diego.

And to the dissenting voices of the web and air who've gotten the word out beginning with my guru, Danny Schechter the News Dissector (mediachannel.org), Sonali Sohatkar, Dave "Aloha" Rampell, Wilmer Leon, Scott Goodstein and Punk Voter, Chris Cook at CBC, Mike Webb, Chuck "This Is Hell" Mertz, Bev Smith, Eric Demby, Ruth Dreier, Mike Edison at Index, Greg Wilpert, John Grebe, the inventor of Internet radio reality Meria Heller, Nathan Fox and *Working for Change,* Bob McChesney, Mark Crispin Miller; and Jeff Cohen, Bobby Grossman and Phil Donahue (you courageous fools); Louie Free, Mike DeRosa, Pat Thurston, Nancy Skinner, Ski Andersen, Norman Stockwell, Joyce Riley and Power Hour maven Dave von-Kleist, Arianna Huffington, William Rivers Pitt, Free Speech TV, LINK TV, thoughtful Meera Cheriyan; investigator without compare Pratap Chatterjee and Corporate Watch; the ever-helpful Linda Starr; *Punk Planet; XLR8R;* Janine Jackson and Jim Naureckas at FAIR; Will Dana at *Rolling Stone;* Ruth Dreier, the marvelous Scott Harris of *Between the Lines;* Doug Henwood, the fair and balanced Scott Horton, Paul Krassner, Anthony Lappe and Ian Ianaba of GNN, Gary Null, Duke Skorich, Eleanor Smeal of *Ms.,* John Sugg of *Creative Loafing,* Hilary Wainwright of *Red Pepper,* Peter Werbe, Marc Ash, Mark Karlin, Scott Vogel, and Scott Beibin of *Hollywood Can Suck It*; and in the UK, Mark Thomas, Rob Newman, and Taikonaut Anna Chen.

To the Foundation for Taxpayer and Consumer Rights, Los Angeles (www.ConsumerWatchdog.org), for passing me the Ken Lay memos. And to the saviors of the Northwest Betty Snowden, Nancy Newell, KBOO, KAOS, Michael Papadapolous, Ed Mays and Michael McCormick at KEXP.

To Patt Morrison, E. J. Dionne, Paul Krugman, Bob Herbert, who snuck my words into their mainstream rags; and to Michael Moore, for introducing me and my work to the USA when the USA didn't want to hear it.

To those with the guts and lawyers to print this stuff, Rick MacArthur, Lewis Lapham, Roger Hodge and Bill Wasik at *Harper's*; Katrina Vanden Heuvel at *The Nation*; Larry Flynt and Bruce David at *Hustler*; Alan Rusbridger and Roger Alton at the *Guardian* and *Observer*; and *In These Times,* the *Utne Reader*, *The Progressive,* and Michael Albert at *Z Mag/ZNet* and Peter Phillips at Project Censored and the members of IndyMedia and the Independent Press Association, and in memorium, Bob Slattery.

And to the seditious Web sites Buzzflash, Common Dreams, Consortium News, Democrats.com, Democratic Underground, FAIR, Guerrilla News Network, IndyMedia, Online Journal, Truthout, Working For Change; and Scott Thill of Salon.com and Morphizm.com.

To the soul painters Winston Smith, Bob Grossman and Tom Tomorrow. To Boots Riley and the Coup, Moby, Daron Murphy, Anti-Flag, Farang and the other musicians who've carried our words on their pulse—and no one more than Jello Biafra who made the Dead rise.

To information and help from Jonathan Simon and Steven Freeman, Scott Young, Antonia Juhasz and IFG; Mark Weisbrot at the Center for Economic and Policy Research; Tom Fitton at Judicial Watch; Tony White; Joe Trento and National Security News Service; and my co-writers Dr. Ahamed Idris, the late Liz Idris-Soven, the beloved Anne Joelle Lonigro (*The World As a Company Town),* and the coauthors of *Democracy and Regulation,* Jerrold Oppenheim and Theo MacGregor.

To my lawyer Victor Kovner for making my attackers wish they were never born. To my helpmeets John Sloss, Ari Emanuel and Harris Tulchin. To Hunter Thompson, whom I never got to meet, for the sentence in this book I plagiarized from his gallant pen. (A free signed *Armed Madhouse* poster to the first ten readers who find it and notify us at www.GregPalast.com.)

And my gratitude to our sponsors, the two thousand readers who have supported the Palast Investigative Foundation, keeping us alive, independent and free from the obligation to thank corporate funders, of which we have none; and to the extra support for our research provided by Jeff Barden, the Friedell family, Lori Grace, Donna Litowitz, Sara McCay, Bill Perkins, Dr. Alice Tang, Norman Lear, Steven Bing and Working Assets.

Monster thanks to Code Pink street-fightin' women Gael Murphy and Jodie Evans (and sidekick Max Palevsky); brilliant attorney-radio hosts Mike Papantonio and Robert F. Kennedy Jr.; courageous filmmaker Ian Ianaba; and activists who inspire this book, among them Theron Horton in New Mexico, Malik Rahim in New Orleans, Shakoor Aljuwani in New York, Martin Eder in San Diego, Mary Ahrendt in Chicago and front line groups including Office of the Americas, Velvet Revolution, ACORN, the Service Employees International Union.

And to the media folk unafraid to put our investigations on the air: Scott Harris and Anna Manzo at Between the Lines; David Barsamian; Jeff Cohen; John Manzo, Randi Rhodes' visionary producer; Thom Hartmann, a reasonable voice in a mad world; Air Americans Cynthia Black, Bree Walker, Christiane Brown, Harrison of KTLK, Richard Greene, the Young Turks and Stephanie Miller; the astonishing Rob Newman; John Hamilton, Mike Castleman, Flip De-Fillipo and the whole Democracy Now crew; Deepa Fernandez; Link TV and RealNews and, in the belly of the mainstream, the extraordinary Gil Noble.

A big up to my back-up bands: Anti-Flag, Boots Riley and The Coup and Moby and his crew.

And to Larry David: fuck'm if they can't take a joke, eh?

And to new members of our investigations and operations team, Zach Roberts, Christie Speicher, Adam Chimienti, Ilene Proctor, Kim from LA, and the hands that rock the cameras and so rock the world,

Jacqui Soohen and Rick Rowley of Big Noise Films; and all our love and gratitude to The Kat, Ms. L'Estrange, for taking our show on the road as tour maven.

And to Linda Levy, leader of the pack and brainiac, the lightbulb above my head, my editor in chief and my comrade in facing down the bad guys for three decades.

INDEX

Page numbers followed by n indicate notes.

Winston Smith's wickedly satirical art has appeared on the albums of dozens of malcontents, including Dead Kennedys, D.O.A, Green Day, George Carlin, and Ben Harper. His works have also decorated the pages and covers of such distinguished rags as *Spin*, *Flipside*, *Details*, *Juxtapoz*, *The Progressive*, *Playboy*, and *The New Yorker*. Winston's latest book, *All Riot on the Western Front: The Montage Art of Winston Smith, Volume III*, is published by Last Gasp of San Francisco. Visit www.WinstonSmith.com to collect posters, T-shirts, fine art prints and original art.

For a full-size high-quality framable poster of Winston Smith's collage *Armed Madhouse*, go to www.GregPalast.com

The Joker's Wild. The tarot-sized four-color card-deck by Greg Palast and Robert Grossman. Grossman, whose brilliant caricatures are featured in *The New Yorker*, *The New York Times* and elsewhere, has outdone himself with 54 illustrations of Greg Palast's most cutting bios of the lives of the rich and shameless. There's also a suit of hearts—don't miss the Amy Goodman card. Available at your local bookstore or at www.GregPalast.com.

ILLUSTRATION CREDITS

Page 20: Patriot Act Poster © Citizens for an Informed Community, Bridgewater, MA. William D. Haff, Designer.

Page 127: Toy and catalog listing © MindWare, "Brainy toys for kids of all ages." mindwareonline.com. 1-800-999-0398.

Page 136: James Baker Caricature, excerpted from *The Joker's Wild: Dubya's Trick Deck* by Greg Palast, illustrated by Robert Grossman. © 2004 by Greg Palast. Published by Seven Stories Press. Reprinted by permission of the publisher. Illustrator's website: www.robertgrossman.com.

Page 192: Map by Mark J. Salling, PhD, Director, Northern Ohio Data and Information Service (NODIS), Levin Urban College, Cleveland State University.

Page 223: Data mapped by Prof. Sonja Klveck Elison and Walther Eric Elison. County map courtesy Bernalillo County, New Mexico.

Page 241: Photo of Moore and Greg © Matt Pascarella. Reprinted with permission of Matt Pascarella.

Page 317: Circus Coupon © Cole Brothers Circus

Page 327: U.S. Social Security Administration

THE ARMED MADHOUSE
SOUNDTRACK

Most important is getting the word out. Our team encourages sound and video response to our stories. Send us your tracks.

Moby's scoring of the BBC film *Bush Family Fortunes* can be obtained from www.GregPalast.com, and a sample video of our elections report can be obtained from PunkVoter.com, Fat Wreck Chords, and Vice Magazine.

If only to see Mr. Shady in a business suit, check out, at our site, Eminem's video *Mosh*, directed by Ian Inaba of Guerrilla News Network and inspired by our reports on disenfranchisement of minority voters. *New York* magazine called it "the most important piece of mainstream dissent since the 60s."

For audio and music samples from Greg Palast's reports, including Willie Steen's voice and story, listen to The Farangs' album *We Must Be Losing It* (Warner Bros.), AKIR's album *Politricks* (Fat Beats), White Noise's *Lynching by Laptop*, and Nadine MacKinnon (Et-Cetera) as well as Pacifica Radio Archives' "*Silence of the Media Lambs.*"

While reading Chapter 3: The Network, listen to the UK band Sell the Lexus, Burn the Olive Tree—named after my last book's chapter of the same title.

Also available: samples from the spoken-word CD, enhanced with documents "Weapon of Mass Instruction," produced by Jello Biafra and Matt Pascarella (Alternative Tentacles) and **the audio of Armed Madhouse** (Simon & Schuster, 2006); as well as the audio version of *The Best Democracy Money Can Buy* (Penguin), read by the author and friends including Ed Asner, Alec Baldwin, Jello Biafra, Al Franken, Janeane Garofalo, Amy Goodman, Jim Hightower, Hon. Cynthia Mckinney, Alexandra Paul and Shiva Rose.

All of our broadcast investigations for BBC Television Newsnight—from Venezuela, Texas, Washington and wherever—are available for viewing at www.GregPalast.com. For additional video expansions of these reports, see Danny Schechter's *Counting on Democracy;* Guerrilla News Network's *American Blackout;* Mike Bonanno and Andy Bichlbaum's film *The Yes Men;* Matt Pascarella and Dee Dee Halleck's *Channels of War;* Matt Kohn's *Call It Democracy;* Jeannie Ross and Bruce Yarock's *Florida Fights Back;* Penny Little's *Electile Dysfuntion;* Linda Byrket's *Video The Vote;* Michael Moore's *Fahrenheit 9-11* and Robert Greenwald's *Unprecedented.* Send your tracks to us at www.GregPalast.com.

Check out winners of our remix contest—the words of *Armed Madhouse* set to music—including "Mr. Beale, Meet Mr. Palast" by Funkspace, "Everything You Need to Know" by The Traveler, "Busted and Bloody" by Zen Rock Garden and more at GregPalast.com/remix/.

ABOUT THE AUTHOR

When Greg Palast, an investigator of corporate fraud and racketeering, turned his skills to journalism in 1997, he was quickly recognized as "the most important investigative reporter of our time" (*Tribune* magazine) in Britain, where his first reports appeared on BBC Television and in the *Guardian* newspapers.

Author of *The New York Times* bestseller *The Best Democracy Money Can Buy*, Palast is best known in his native USA as the journalist who broke the story of how Jeb Bush purged thousands of Black citizens from Florida's voter rolls before the 2000 election, thereby handing the White House to his brother George. Palast's reports on the theft of election 2004, the spike of the FBI investigations of the bin Ladens before September 11, the secret State Department documents planning the seizure of Iraq's oil fields and other exposés have won him a record six "Project Censored" prizes for reporting the news American media doesn't want you to hear. "The top investigative journalist in the United States is *persona non grata* in his own country's media" (*Asia Times*). In 2005, he returned to America to report for *Harper's* magazine.

Palast's Sam Spade–style television and print exposés about elections manipulations, War on Terror and globalization, have been seen and heard on BBC's *Newsnight* and Amy Goodman's *Democracy Now!*

Palast, who has led investigations for government on three continents, has an academic side: He is the author of *Democracy and Regulation,* a seminal treatise on energy corporations and government control commissioned by the United Nations based on his lectures at Cambridge University and the University of São Paulo.

Beginning in the 1970s, having earned his degree in finance studying under Milton Friedman and free-trade luminaries, Palast went on to challenge their vision of a New Global Order, working for the United Steelworkers of America, the Enron workers' coalition in Latin America and consumer and environmental groups worldwide. As an investigator for the Chugach Natives of Alaska, he uncovered the oil company frauds that led to the grounding of the Exxon Valdez. His racketeering probe of a nuclear plant operator led to one of the largest jury judgments in U.S. history.

In 1998, for Britain's *Observer*, Palast went undercover, worked his way inside the prime minister's inner circle and busted open Tony Blair's biggest scandal, "Lobbygate," chosen by Palast's press colleagues in the UK as "Story of the Year." As the *Chicago Tribune* said, he became a "fanatic about documents"—especially those marked "secret and confidential" from the locked file cabinets of the FBI, the World Bank, the U.S. State Department and other closed-door operations of government and industry—which regularly find their way into Palast's hands. The inside information he obtained on Rev. Pat Robertson won him a nomination as Britain's top business journalist.

Palast, Guerrilla News Network's Guerrilla of the Year, is Patron of the Trinity College Philosophical Society, an honor previously held by Jonathan Swift and Oscar Wilde. His writings have won the *Financial Times* David Thomas Prize—and inspired the Eminem video *Mosh*. "An American hero," said Martin Luther King III. In the BBC documentary *Bush Family Fortunes*, Palast exposed George Bush Jr.'s dodging the Vietnam War draft.

Greg Palast, says Noam Chomsky, "upsets all the right people."

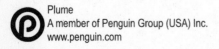